Goddess on the Rise

Goddess on the Rise

Pilgrimage and Popular Religion in Vietnam

Philip Taylor

University of Hawai'i Press
Honolulu

This publication has been supported in part by grants from the
Australian Academy of the Humanities and
the Australian National University.

Library of Congress Cataloging-in-Publication Data

Taylor, Philip

   Goddess on the rise : pilgrimage and popular religion in Vietnam / Philip Taylor.
    p. cm.
   Includes bibliographical references and index.
   ISBN 0-8248-2648-5 (alk. paper)—ISBN 0-8248-2801-1 (pbk. : alk. paper)
  1. Vietnam, Southern—Religious life and customs. I. Title.
BL2055.T39   2004
299.5'92—dc22   2003018419

Designed by University of Hawai'i Press Production Staff
Printed by The Maple-Vail Book Manufacturing Group

Contents

Preface

This work is an ethnographic account of pilgrimages and popular religion in Vietnam. It is about a goddess known as the Lady of the Realm, whose shrine near Vietnam's border with Cambodia attracts one of the biggest pilgrimages in the country. Part of a revival of religious activity in Vietnam, the pilgrimage to this goddess is an example of the phenomenal growth of interest in recent years in feminine spirits. Addressing aspects of this phenomenon in the southern parts of the country, this work opens a window onto the effervescence, creativity, social complexity, and interpretive ferment of popular religiosity in present-day Vietnam.

The research for this book was completed following *Fragments of the Present*, a work that explores shifting and contending notions about the cultural identity of southern Vietnam. Set in a postconflict cultural landscape of lingering enmities and new emerging inequalities, that work traces the history of reinventions, repudiations, and exclusions effected in the name of modernist ideals. Many of these attempts to remake Vietnamese society in the name of some universalistic vision of modernity failed to secure broad-based support because they attempted to enshrine as a national charter a partial experience of what it meant to be Vietnamese. The ideas and images addressed in that work are largely the products of an educated elite and, despite the influence of the political projects that have endorsed them, are somewhat removed from the ways that many others in Vietnam have experienced and made their history.

On completing the research for that book, I was motivated to explore other aspects of Vietnamese society that had wider appeal and deeper resonance. On consideration of the possibilities, I decided on my focus: the pilgrimage to the Lady of the Realm, a religious gathering that was big, spontaneous, variegated, and deeply absorbing to its many participants. I had dropped into the Ho Chi Minh City pilgrimage scene in 1995, when fascination with this goddess was at its peak among the people of that city and had attended the festival to the goddess on the sacred slopes of Sam Mountain. In 1998 I was drawn back to this site by its popularity, color, deep resonances, and the breadth of its attraction to different people. The pilgrimage appeared to be a significant social and cultural movement that was growing and transforming rapidly despite and perhaps also because of efforts of the government to regulate it and of my learned friends in Ho Chi Minh City and in Hanoi to impose a nationalistic or moralistic spin on the phenomenon.

As one who first visited Vietnam in 1991, when tourists who sought to travel domestically had to submit detailed itineraries to the police, I was fascinated by the quality of unrestricted movement and the apparent freedom of rites and interpretation that seemed to be in play not only at the biggest pilgrimage sites but at smaller temples as well. The circulation of ideas, bodies, and offerings in and out of these shrines very much cut against the grain of the world of bureaucratically mediated travel and scholarship to which I had been exposed while doing my Ph.D. research in the early 1990s. The single-minded dedication shown by some pilgrims, constant reporting on the powers manifested by this or that spirit, and animated airing of itineraries were as compelling to me as an observer of pilgrimages as they seemed to be to participants themselves. To track such practices would present a methodological challenge as well, requiring an approach that could address their evident complexity and diffuseness.

For six weeks I trooped around the south with busloads of pilgrims, milled around in the precincts of pilgrimage shrines, chatted with pilgrims at their homes, hung out in pagodas, and engaged Buddhist monks and nuns in debate. I spent all my time with religious travelers and their proximate observers: people who like myself were engrossed in an immense variety of ideas and practices. I frequented the market stalls and credit circles around Dakao, Tân Định, and Bà Chiểu markets, sat around in urban back alleys, street corners, noodle stalls, buses and boats, and all sorts of cool and tranquil interiors. I became acquainted with a rich symbolic world and came into repeated contact with a handful of goddesses around whom many people's lives revolved.

I had a marvelous time drinking endless sweetened coffees with pilgrims, smoking cigarettes, eating durians, and chatting endlessly about all manner of religious topics. Most of my fellow pilgrims were women. They included market traders, ferry operators, pilgrimage guides, nuns, hotel receptionists, cigarette vendors, photographic saleswomen, smugglers, landladies, farmers, credit dealers, gold traders, purveyors of religious wares, sex workers, retirees, teachers, Buddhist laywomen, hairdressers, students, and grandmothers. Among my principal male cultural guides on this trip, motorcycle and cyclo drivers, market vendors, porters, bus drivers, and conductors featured prominently, as well as a significant number of temple custodians, monks, and mediums. I am grateful to the many pilgrims, religious specialists, critics, and curbside observers of everyday religious practice whose engaging explanations brought the world of popular religion to life. I am especially indebted to my sisters Thuyết, Dung, Hai, Tư, Như, Hạnh, and my three sisters Nga; my two aunts Chín; my brothers Phong, Dũng, Bảy, and Mười. Their comments are cited in this text, but they are referred to using pseudonyms.

I visited the shrine to the Lady of the Realm in Vĩnh Tế village six times in all and spent two months over many trips in the village and in the river port of Châu Đốc. The members of the cult committee at the shrine in Vĩnh Tế were terribly busy on the occasions of the annual festival, yet generously shared their perspective with me and invited me to the ceremonies in 1995. Some of the most informed observers of the mobile religious world described in this book are people who make a living from the pilgrimage: bus drivers, café and restaurant proprietors, pilgrimage leaders, people who sell religious paraphernalia—those whose livelihood depends on their knowledge about trends in practice and belief. My thanks go to Nga, Chín, Mười, and Sơn for sharing with me their insights as well as to many other drivers, guides, and interlocutors whose names circumstances did not permit me to record. I learned a great deal from the many works by Vietnam-based scholars about these practices. In addition, my discussions with Huỳnh Ngọc Trảng, Đỗ Thái Đồng, and Lê Hồng Lý were particularly rewarding.

The anthropology and Asian studies departments at the University of Western Australia and the Department of Anthropology and Department of Political and Social Change at the Research School of Pacific and Asian Studies, Australian National University, each provided financial support and conducive environments in which to work on the manuscript. Many people read my drafts and made useful comments; among these I thank Keith Taylor, Do Thien, Edwin Zehner, Mandy Thomas, Pham Thu Thuy, David Marr, Kim Ninh, Alex Leonard, Catherine Earl, Alan Rumsey, Francesca Merlin, and Andrew Kipness. Chapter 2 draws in part on an article published in the journal *Asian Ethnicity* (P. Taylor 2002) and I thank the editor, Colin Mackerass, for permission to use this. Grant Evans' critical review encouraged me to improve this work, as did that of an anonymous reviewer for University of Hawai'i Press. The work evolved under the editorial guidance of Pamela

Kelley, Ann Ludeman, and Joanne Sandstrom of the University of Hawai'i Press.

The world and the memories this book evokes were part of my interior landscape for more than four years as I moved from place to place and job to job. Over time, aspects of my life, the life of the writer, began to seep into the work and color the phenomena I was describing. The experience of contract-based research work, the social wear and tear from many moves, a political environment of economic deregulation and reduced commitment to the public sector, the rise of entrepreneurialism in the academy, and the resurgence of exclusivist culturally essentialist identities in Australia influenced my image of the world I was describing and led me to emphasize certain themes. Given the somewhat parallel social and economic transformations under way in Vietnam these experiences if anything brought me closer to many of the concerns that have motivated the renewed emphasis on goddesses in that country.

Hence, the symbols and rites described in this book, while distinctive and spectacular, are not culturally otherworldly. Moreover, they are not so far from home. There are shopkeepers from Vietnam in my own suburb in Canberra who believe in the Lady of the Realm and speak her name with care lest they give offense. Members of my own family come from quite different religious traditions, yet they have been interested in my findings and have supported me in every turn of this work. While in Vietnam too I have found that my immersion in this topic has opened up fruitful channels of communication with a great many people and has allowed me to deepen my appreciation of that society. Others I hope will share my appreciation of the creativity and excitement of the world of religious practice that I have attempted, however imperfectly, to recount within these pages.

My thanks go to the families of Bảo Đạt, Ngô Thị Ngân Bình, Phan Ngọc Chiến, and Phúc Tiến as well as to Dung Hạnh, Phương and Thảo, who sustained me with their valuable friendship during the period of writing this work. I dedicate this book to my mother and two sisters and to my fellow pilgrims with whom I conversed and traveled during my six-week journey in 1998 through Her Ladyship's realm.

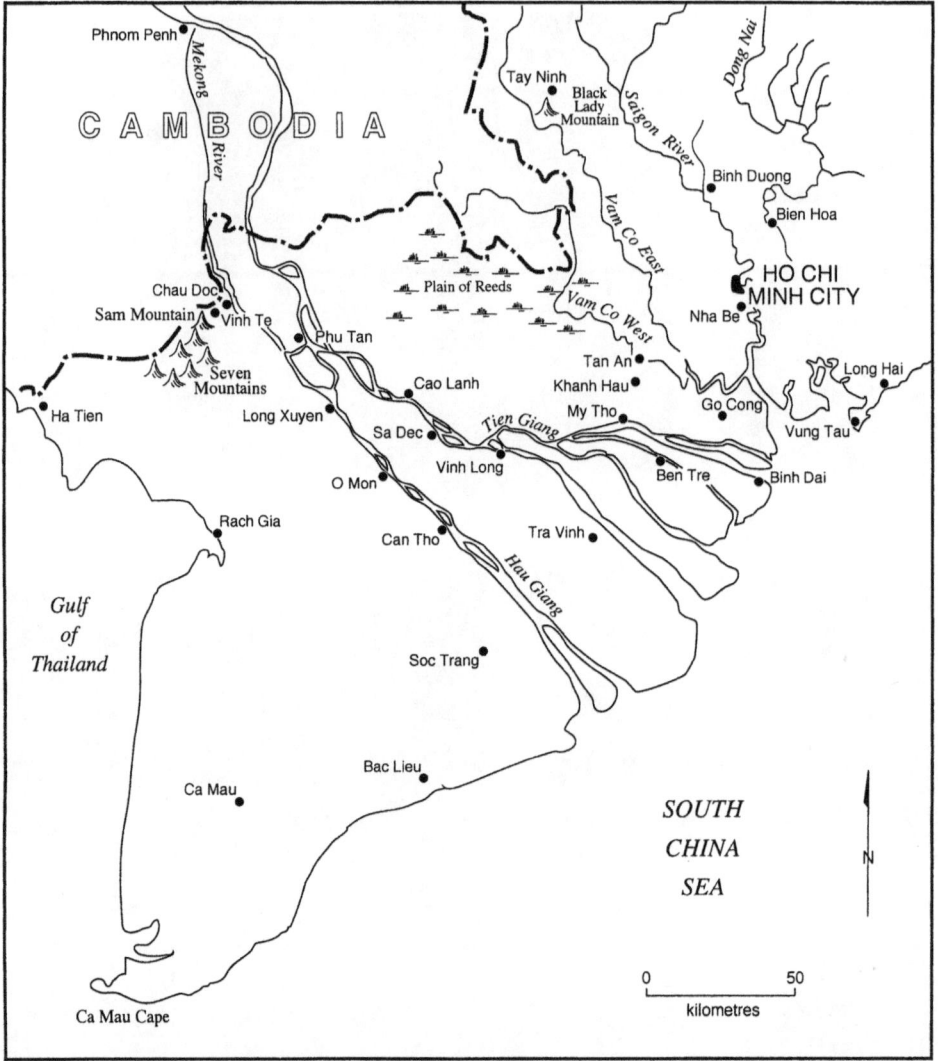

FIG. 1. Map of the southern Vietnamese plain

Introduction

An Outline of the Quest

At the base of a small mountain on Vietnam's border with Cambodia stands a shrine to a goddess known as Bà Chúa Xứ, the Lady of the Realm. This spirit is a feminine likeness in stone and rendered cement and is dressed in regal costume. Legends describe her as a local protector deity and relate her involvement in key events in local history. She is housed in a magnificent shrine flanked by large halls that display the offerings people have made to her. Every year at the start of the rainy season a round of ceremonies is held in her honor. The main events include an image-bathing and robe-changing ceremony performed by elderly women, a series of sacrifices performed by the shrine's cult committee, an invocation to the goddess for peace and protection, and a series of opera performances. These rites are conducted with great pomp and seriousness by representatives of the local community. Each year Vĩnh Tế village, the rural settlement that hosts these festivities, is transformed into an instant metropolis. Its canals are lined with passenger boats, the road into the village is choked with buses and mini-vans, and the road to the nearby township of Châu Đốc is as busy as a major urban thoroughfare. The area surrounding her shrine hums around the clock with entertainments as diverse as *cải lương* (southern Vietnamese opera), all-singing, all-dancing drag beauty queen contests, a sideshow alley, magic acts, a house of horrors, karaoke, gambling, restaurants, cafes, bars, and brothels. Inside the shrine pilgrims jostle, sardinelike, bodies superheating the air, incense tearing at their eyes, an endless stream of opulent gifts pouring toward the altar.

This activity is illustrative of the rich and burgeoning spiritual life of contemporary Vietnam. Most homes display a profusion of religious imagery and ritual altars. Temples and Buddhist pagodas are near to overflowing on the first and fifteenth of each lunar month, and are even more crowded at Tết, the Vietnamese New Year celebration. Altars are piled high with offerings; interiors are thick with incense. On the roads one can see devotees returning from offering prayers; they carry ornate rods of smoking incense, flowers, fruit, and other blessings from the gods who watch over their existence. Festivals to honor the spirits of the country's celebrated historical personages attract enormous crowds. Ceremonies honoring tutelary deities in village communal houses have undergone a revival after years of restrictions, and expenditure at religious festivals, fairs, and feasts is increasing dramatically. Vast amounts of time and money are being invested in the construction and restoration of religious edifices, from temples, Buddhist pagodas, and Catholic churches down to the lowly shrines to wandering ghosts. Sales of Taiwanese mass-produced images of Ông Địa (the earth god), Thần Tài (the god of wealth), and Quan Âm (the goddess of mercy), are booming, and all manner of entrepreneurs are selling religious goods and services from paper offerings to the dead to mediumistic and divinatory services.

Like every temple in Vietnam, the shrine to the Lady of the Realm has its prescribed rituals, supporting legends, customary officiants, and festive calendar. Yet as scholars of popular religion in China and elsewhere have noted, such sites of local cultural significance and collective relevance are often subject to a plurality of usages (Watson 1985; Weller 1987). In most shrines and temples in Vietnam, it is not rare to find several levels of activity going on simultaneously. Sometimes while a formal ceremony is being performed by the cult committee, one can see people scooting around the sides of the temple, making their way to auxiliary altars to make their own requests. These people enter with circumspection, seek out their preferred spirit, mumble unheard prayers, make their offerings, and depart, at times disregarding the rites taking place in the temple's central area. During the festival to the Lady of the Realm many supplicants do not even attempt to enter the shrine to observe the cycle of sacrifices, but instead go well before or after the ceremonies to conduct their own personal transactions with the goddess. Many of them come from far away, and when they have made their offerings they return home, having interacted only minimally with people from the local area. The gifts that these individuals make to the goddess are similar to those presented to her during the annual ceremony, and the rites they perform reflect similar assumptions about her spiritual potency. However, one cannot assume that they are directed toward similar ends or are informed by identical notions about her identity and powers.

To understand these projects one has to leave the vicinity of the shrine and retrace the itineraries of individual worshipers. The diverse pathways followed by the faithful begin in their homes in a flow of requests, gifts, and promises made before the altars to various spiritual figures enshrined there. They lead to the shrines to ghosts or to potent nature spirits in their neighborhood. Some paths lead to Buddhist pagodas, Christian churches, and temples to protector spirits, where a person might enter into dealings with one or several of the images found there. Ultimately they lead to distant sites, places whose reputed power draw pilgrims from far and wide. As they negotiate this complex symbolic world, adepts consult with any manner of astrologers, geomancers, physiognomists, fortune-tellers, mediums, monks, sorcerers, and temple custodians. Their itineraries are not predetermined by any religious order and are virtually impossible for the state to regulate. Rather, people's belief and practices are influenced by family, neighbors, colleagues, business clients, fellow worshipers, religious entrepreneurs, and popular publications. Believers exchange stories about the potency of different spirits, hearing of miraculous events and learning new solutions to their problems from those encountered along their way.

In this noninstitutionalized fund of advice, interpretation, and creative usage, novel interpretations are constantly being made; a syncretistic ferment is continually on the brew. A bad astrological reading, for example, can be rectified by adjusting one's karmic ledger; poor business fortunes might equally be addressed by doing good deeds, adjusting the geomantic directions of one's house, propitiating a pernicious spirit, or entering into a contract with a spiritually powerful god. Creativity is further evident in the identities attributed to the diverse deities venerated in the region of southern Vietnam. Sri Mariamam, a South Indian goddess, brought to Saigon by Chettiar moneylenders in early twentieth century, is regarded by some as Kuan Yin, the Chinese goddess of mercy, and by others as a Khmer goddess known as the Black Lady. Quan Công, a military hero in a popular Chinese novel, the *Romance of the Three Kingdoms*, is seen by some as an incarnation of Sakyamuni Buddha. Some even say that this third-century Chinese general was reincarnated in the personage of Ho Chi Minh. A nineteenth-century anticolonial martyr, Nguyễn Trung Trực, whose spirit is propitiated as the supernatural protector of a southern Vietnamese fishing town, is believed by many to be an incarnation of the whale god, Cá Ông, who in turn is an incarnation of the god of the South Seas.

Such fluid trajectories and creative interpretations are the context for the Lady of the Realm's recent rise as a prestigious spiritual protector. Since the early 1990s her shrine has become the most visited religious site in southern Vietnam, receiving more than a million visitors annually (figure 2).[1] Many southerners like to say she is the most efficacious spiritual personage in the

FIG. 2.   Crowds in the forecourt of the shrine to the Lady of the Realm, Vĩnh Tế village

entire country, pointing for evidence of this to the fact that pilgrims from as far afield as Hue and Hanoi have been known to come to make offerings to her. Her identity and reputed powers are a major topic of discussion in markets and on street corners in far-flung provinces and distant urban centers. These readings escape official categorization or interpretive policing, for they are forever being refashioned in the public realm. Mother, provider of children, benevolent creditor, healer, relationship adviser, business consultant— she is all things to all people. By some accounts an alien in drag, she has been painted and dressed up, created cosmetically from a statue of Shiva, appropriated from an earlier, Indianized civilization. Blinking Christmas tree lights and rotating neon swastikas create the colorful come-hither appeal usually associated with bars and entertainment venues. The fairground adjoining her shrine is a showcase of popular aesthetics, cross-dressing, flashing lights, blaring sound systems, magic shows, carnivalesque culture, and the grotesqueries of a sideshow alley. The tumultuous symbolism surrounding this figure makes it impossible to confine her to any particular interpretation, and indeed her resistance to being categorized may account for her broad appeal.

This spirit is one of a group of goddesses that has been on the ascendant in southern Vietnam since the mid 1980s as focal points of mass pilgrimages.[2] Each attracts up to a million pilgrims annually and in some cases more, eclipsing attendance at even the largest urban temples and Buddhist pagodas on the busiest of festivals. They are linked in an annual itinerary of pilgrimages, attracting a core of widely traveled pilgrims, most notably women who work in marketing and trade. Their attributes and biographies substantially overlap. Their most ardent supporters frequently collapse the distinctions maintained by cultural commentators and the local custodians who tend their shrines. Strands from various myths about their identity have been woven into each other. Their powers too are substantially similar. The principal quality attributed to such spirits is their responsiveness to prayers. In the parlance of their propitiants, they prove *(chứng)* themselves when requests are made of them. They are broadly efficacious, offering assistance for a range of matters, including business success, health, fertility, good fortune in love, domestic harmony, success at exams, and divination of the future. Pilgrims enter into bargains with them, and if they grant one's request, one has to return to repay them. It is known that their favorable disposition to one's pleas can be earned by pleasing them with offerings, dances, acrobatics, and theater. At the same time, they will punish those who show ingratitude toward them. These goddesses are considered powerful allies and contractual partners of outstanding efficacy and prestige. They are allies and independent arbiters of problems faced particularly by women. They are immanent beings with whom the needy can contract at any juncture in their lives. They are perpetually in popular consciousness as sources of support overseeing the activities of all who enter into relationships with them.

Dilemmas of Religious "Resurgence"

The intensification of activity in the shrines to these spirits takes place against a backdrop of major changes in Vietnamese society. The decline of a centralized socialist command economy, promulgation of liberal economic reforms, and increasing openness to new trade, investment, and aid relationships from the mid-1980s have transformed the country's social and cultural landscape. Vietnam has gone from a bureaucratically controlled society, whose external horizons opened onto the socialist world, to a society with increasingly intense and complex relations with the capitalist world. The commercialization of the economy, increase in trade, privatization of social services, and growth of industry, urbanization, infrastructure, and communications technology have touched all Vietnamese people's lives. Impressive declines in poverty and growth in household incomes have occurred alongside peoples' increasing subjection to the pitfalls of the market that they face with little to no assistance from the nominally socialist state. Indeed, as the ruling Communist Party has shrunk in relevance (Marr 1995) and the state has adopted a liberal governance stance (Nguyen Vo 1998), new social forces, interests, and agents have emerged as key to the political process (Abuza 2001), and new rifts and tensions have opened up between beneficiaries and losers in the reform process.

Recent studies link the upsurge in religious activity in Vietnam to these political, social, and cultural transformations. Although increased public participation in all manner of rituals flows from an easing in the state's policies, the government has long been involved in shaping the religious sphere and remains actively engaged in this area in order to promote its own normative agenda (De Tréglodé 2001; Endres 1999; Hue Tam Ho Tai 1995; Malarney 1996b; Marr 1986). Tensions continue to exist between state and society or between center and localities, although religious practice is very often the result of a process of dialogue and accommodation between these levels (Do Thien 1995; Endres 2001; Giebel 2001; Luong 1994; P. Taylor 2001a). Religious orientations in Vietnam can be understood as responses to existential concerns such as death, illness, and bereavement or as ways of articulating differences of status, gender, generation, or ethnicity, which persist despite or because of the government's programs of social restructuring (Malarney 2001, 2002; Nakamura 1999; Salemink 1997; Soucy 1999; P. Taylor 2002). The intensification of religious activity and reinvigoration of village rituals also reflect the emergence of new bases of wealth and the cultural influence of new economic agents (Kleinen 1999; Luong 1993). Contemporary Vietnamese religious sensibilities and practices are strikingly creative, although they equally address cultural anxieties unleashed by the reform process and rapid changes in the temporal and spatial coordinates of existence (Malarney 1996a; Lê Hồng Lý 2001).

In recent years a number of studies based in ethnographic fieldwork have tied the study of religion to emplaced communities, illustrating Vietnam's religious revival in terms of local factors. These include accounts of village-based religious practice by Malarney (2002), Luong (1993, 1994), Kleinen (1999), and Endres (1999, 2001); an ethnography of religion in an urban quarter by Soucy (1999); a study of a regional religion by Taylor (P. Taylor 2001a) and of religion in ethnic frontier areas by Nakamura (1999) and Taylor (P. Taylor 2002a). These works illuminate religious life in Vietnam as situated practice and collectively have helped advance understanding of ways in which the country's spatial diversity is mediated through symbolic and ritual forms. As contributions to the political economy and social history of Vietnam's colonial, socialist, and late-socialist eras, they describe the cultural transformations and accommodations of values that have been played out through ritual and symbolic practice and identify changes in policy, social relations, and cultural priorities that have been implicated in the refiguration of religious practice. Such accounts also reveal considerable societal complexity, suggesting that religion, far more than encoding an abstract realm of emergent "civil society," remains a significant terrain for the articulation of social difference as well as for the expression of social rifts and exclusions.

In contrast to this renewed interest in locality-based religious practice, few anthropological studies have paid attention to translocal cults of the kind that condense around the shrine to the Lady of the Realm, despite the size, effervescence, and dramatic nature of the latter (for an exception see Lê Hồng Lý 2001). Three reasons can be suggested for the lack of studies to date. The first is the methodological difficulty of describing such phenomena and the social and cultural processes that inform them. The religious journeys undertaken to these shrines involve large numbers of people who come from very different contexts. Each shrine is implicated in the diverse array of concerns that people bring with them from their respective homes. To grasp the spatial dimensions of this practice one needs to do research in these interlinked sites as well as follow people's passage between them. Furthermore, the religious activity at these shrines is forever changing in tandem with political, economic, ideological, and cultural transformations, not just in the local area but in the wider society as well. Researching the symbolic and ideational aspects of this practice is equally difficult. The people who flood the precincts of these shrines do not necessarily partake of the formal collective rituals. They often do not share ideas about the identity or powers of the spirit with each other, let alone with the local custodians; and their views are not codified, textualized, or systematized by a clergy. Although translocal cults of this kind do bring people together in one place and over a short time, it is not easy to dip into the flow of thousands of transient visitors to such sites and emerge with a reading of the collective experience of them or gauge the cumulative meaning of people's participation in such an encounter.[3]

The second reason for the lack of studies is that religious journeys and gatherings of the size, scope, and frequency one sees today are relatively recent phenomena. Although fairs, festivals, and religiously inspired travel were common during the precolonial and colonial periods, the scale of these was much smaller because the majority of the population lacked the wealth and means to engage in them and because transport infrastructure was poor. During the period 1954–1975, when the country was divided and at war, northern Vietnam was engaged in socialist reconstruction and national defense, and official restrictions were placed on movement and wasteful expenditure; such measures constrained those who would travel to the shrines of distant spirits. In the south during the war years, when much of the countryside was embroiled in warfare, religious journeys were difficult and were overshadowed by mass movements of refugees fleeing violence and by the maneuverings of armies involved in deadly combat. In the postwar period, Vietnam's people were again on the move; beset by economic crisis, many were forced to flee the country as refugees on perilously unstable boats. In consequence, gatherings of the magnitude and regularity of the festival to the Lady of the Realm are relatively recent phenomena. This is not to say that such conditions imposed insuperable obstacles to religious travel or that translocal religions are unprecedented in Vietnam; however, a satisfactory account of this history has yet to be written.

The third reason that such practices have not received scrutiny is a mind-set that marginalizes them. The massive movement of people to the shrines of powerful spirits challenges received images about the society in which they take place. One of these is the image of a nation whose people are irrevocably tied to their village or homeland *(quê hương)* (cf. Hardy 2003). Religion has been alternatively depicted as an indigenous or localist expression (Mus 1933)[4] or as a traveler—an imported or imposed doctrine. One of the key dramas in Vietnamese religious studies has thus been to account for the supposed tensions and accommodations played out between "local" and "extralocal" sites of religious articulation, all the while assuming an immobile or territorially contained population.[5] Scholars' difficulty in temporalizing Vietnamese society has also impeded their ability to account for such dynamic processes as a spirit who suddenly surges into notoriety. The study of religion in Vietnam has struggled to escape from Leopold Cadière's 1958 distinction between practice that is timeless, such as animism, and that which is an overlay, be it a world religion such as Buddhism or a political philosophy such as Marxism. As a result religious innovation has often been treated pathologically: as a substitute for a lost tradition, a compensatory reaction to crisis, a tool of oppression, or a form of cynical opportunism. Images of the society as collective, corporate, and hierarchical have also led to a focus on beliefs and rites that mirror such social structure and hence on religious practice that bespeaks community, continuity, coherence, and control, such as institutionalized religions, sutra-based practice, or movements that are led by charismatic leaders. Because Vietnam for a long while presented itself to scholars largely as a political conundrum and a military terrain, great interest has been shown in religions and doctrines that have promised or have challenged national integrative potential and those that have precipitated conflicts or expressed resistance.

From the perspective of Vietnamese elite or intellectual culture, popular religiosity has been marginalized or suppressed. In precolonial and colonial times, the court and Confucianized elite were often hostile to heterodoxy and localistic folk practice. Many modernist nationalists in the colonial period and the revolutionary socialist culture of postcolonial Vietnam thought that popular religion had little to offer in the country's modernization and liberation from colonialism. To many urban-based intellectuals, religion was geographically marked as the preoccupation of peasants or of ethnic minorities. By contrast, the cities were regarded as sites where science and reason, orientations that were themselves "foreign" in origin, were on their way to banishing belief in ignorant, delusional, and harmful "superstitions." Equally from this perspective, religion has been pinned to the past as temporally "backward" behavior destined to fade away with societal modernization. Critics of religion have also tended to regard it functionally as a form of mystification or weapon of oppressive feudal elites or domineering states. During much of the twentieth century there was no space, time, or conceivable social role accorded to the spirit world in the type of society that many Vietnamese aspired to create.

Since the promulgation of liberal reforms in the mid-1990s, there has been a rethinking of this position. The outpouring of popular religiosity has been closely followed by Vietnamese scholars. An extraordinary number of books and popular introductory works have appeared about folk beliefs and about religious philosophies, rites, customs, and festivals. The topic of goddesses has been particularly in vogue. Their worship has come to be regarded as an instance of local cultural survival, a view in part linked to a conservative reaction to the government's policies of "opening the door" to the capitalist world as well as fears about the intensification of exogenous cultural incursions. Such practices have also been taken as indications of the endurance or revival of an indigenous substratum or of the nation's traditional culture. This notion too can be seen in context of the rapid and often destabilizing changes unleashed by the economic and social reforms of the past two decades. Goddesses have also been seen functionally as psychological props to people in difficulty, underwriting the bonds of community and morality in circumstances of societal stress. This is how the Lady of the Realm is described in the pamphlets published about her in the local area (Tường Vân 1994; Châu Bích Thủy 1994; Mai Văn Tạo 1995) and the scholarly and comparative works that feature her cult (Nguyễn Minh San 1993; Thạch Phương and Lê Trung Vũ 1995; Thái Thị Bích Liên 1998). These works speak of the goddess' embodiment of cultural traditions, her meritorious protection of the local region, and her spiritual role of underpinning or sustaining its community. The rites held in her shrine are seen as links to the past, customary traditions, commemorative practices, or expressions of gratitude by the present generation to the ancestors. Her festival is attuned to the rhythms of wet-rice agriculture, addressing the difficulties of agricultural existence and helping sustain a cohesive and unified agricultural community.

The problem with this change in attitudes is that although now regarded with favor, such practices are still seen through a narrow lens: territorially marked as rural or local, temporally as pinned to the past and tradition, and functionally serving the current official dispensation. Contemporary accounts of the Lady of the Realm thereby miss much of significance about such a site. For instance, little attention is given to the fact that the majority of people who visit her shrine and those to her fellow goddesses come from well beyond the local area. Such works neither provide a sense of the creativity, social complexity, and cultural flux informing her worship nor explain the rapid growth in her following. No indication is given of the diversity of social projects in which the spirit is enmeshed or of her diverse meanings to various translocal propitiants. To the extent that such translocal, dynamic, and diffused processes are mentioned, they have been condemned as a form of ideological, moral, or social disintegration. In their diverse attentions, commentators exhibit a range of attitudes toward such practice from elite worries about aesthetic degradation, social disorder, cultural subversion, and heterodox, strange, or false beliefs to scientistic dismissiveness, moral condemnation, and modernist embarrassment. Stories about her magical efficacy are denounced as linked to such inappropriate, opportunistic, and allegedly superseded practices as mediumship, faith healing, and fortune-telling.

Reviewing the objections to such phenomena, one can identify three main processes about which Vietnamese critics are concerned. The first concern can be described as the fear of deterritorialization. As transport means and infrastructure have improved, the people who visit such shrines come from farther away. The communities of believers that coalesce around popular religious foci are characterized by increasing extension, mobility, and looseness. Books, pamphlets, and printed media have become more important in the reproduction of legends about her than the views of local authorities and ritual experts. The vitality of these sites now owes as much if not more to the flow of opinion and rumor in distant markets, bus stations, river ports, cities, and foreign contexts as it does to the messages projected by those based in the places of worship themselves. In response to such processes, scholars have voiced concerns about the loss of the distinctive local characteristics of such sites and the commercialization or urbanization of religious practice (Thạch Phương et al. 1992; Đặng Nghiêm Vạn 1998). Local custodians have worried about opportunistic copying and reproduction of images and exploitation of the site by mobile religious charlatans. The authorities have been worried about an upsurge in crime, disorderly conduct, political subversion, or exploitation of religion by hostile foreign forces.

The second concern is the loss of cultural roots *(mất gốc)*. Most of the people one encounters at the shrines to these goddesses are not overly concerned by a goddess' embodiment of tradition or typification of ancient essences. Instead, they seek her assistance with personal affairs and do so by forging an individualized compact with her. Most visitors to a goddess' shrine regard her as a responsive *(linh ứng)* spiritual being with a demonstrated history of fulfilling all manner of requests. This view of a particular goddess is largely dependent on personal observations and on tales and rumors that are passed between family and friends: views that circulate in marketplaces and residential neighborhoods or are exchanged among followers in the precincts of her shrine. Something of a celebrity in the region, the Lady of the Realm's reputation is a robe made of densely woven filaments of rumor. Her reputed efficacy is largely self-confirming. Followers cite as proof of her responsiveness the very fact that so many people visit her shrine. Conversely, a spirit not proving *(chứng)* or demonstrating its ability to respond to requests is often deemed not worthy of veneration: its shrine might be neglected or its image even beaten or discarded. Such actions have caused some observers to denounce practices such as these as based in mere fashion; they see in the extraordinary popularity of a goddess a sad reflection of the ignorance of credulous minds, a volatile cult of celebrity with no stability or connections to traditions or place, whose associated tales have no other reason than to generate profits for entrepreneurs.

The third concern is that this upsurge in extralocal, noninstitutional religious practice is somehow both an indication of and complicit in an outbreak of asocial and immoral practice. A common view is to regard the rise of certain powerful spirits as symptomatic of the ideological unmooring or cultural untethering of contemporary Vietnamese society, a sign of its postrevolutionary demoralization. This is kin to the argument made by some anthropologists that increased global interest in religious routes to rapid prosperity typify a moment of "millennial capitalism" (Comaroff and Comaroff 1999) that is particularly evident in postrevolutionary societies such as South Africa or Vietnam, assailed as they are by unpredictable and inexplicable economic forces, spatio-temporal disorientation, and unsanctioned, unbridgeable inequalities of wealth. In Vietnam such religious practices have been linked to corruption, illegitimate paths to prosperity, and the rise of individualized, asocial identities. Many people including educated professionals, local government officials, custodians of these shrines, and members of religious orders are concerned about the links between the rise of such spirits and growing amorality, societal disintegration, and disorder.

However, popular interest in such spirits could also be said to contradict these scenarios of the loss of culture, traditions, or moral integrity. It is significant that the heightened stature of these culturally distinctive shrines took place during a time when the country was going through major geopolitical and economic realignments and was host to increased transnational cultural flows. And yet, although the meaning of religious foci has been delocalized in such processes, it has also been relocalized, gaining significance and a following in distant and diverse political and social centers, urban neighborhoods, and marketplaces. The majority of propitiants to the Lady of the Realm are geographically identifiable, coming from a regional network of markets and urban settlements. They can be located socially as in large part being women involved in some way in petty entrepreneurial activity. One can also identify the cultural commentators, who pin specific place-based meanings to these spirits, in a similar way. They can be located with relative geo-social precision as urban-based, educated, white-collar professionals, the majority of them male.

The rise of these goddesses also contradicts Weber's classic argument that the growth of instrumental rationality might be expected to lead to a "disenchanted" world (Keyes, Kendall, and Hardacre 1994; Comaroff 1994; Jackson 1999a, b). Instead, momentous changes in the political system, the economy, and society have led to more, not less, ritual activity. Yet to treat such practices as the expression of a resurgent cultural substratum as many theorists in Vietnam are inclined to do equally fails to account for why some spirits have achieved superstar status while others have faded away or changed their identity. Such shifts have occurred in the context of transformations in social relations and cultural practices that have woven religious foci into new webs of meaning, transfiguring ritual practice and ineluctably altering the religious landscape. By the same token, practices of meaning making and the interpretation of religious phenomena must themselves be located within this social history, sometimes in reaction to or as attempts to impose meaning and direction on social change.

The emergence of a set of spirits with remarkably similar traits, location, and following also counters bleak scenarios of social or moral untethering. Those who would characterize these highly individualistic and noninstitutionalized aspects of Vietnam's religious resurgence as a descent into postrevolutionary disorder neglect the compelling patterns found in such religious practice. Important insights into aspects of Vietnamese society and history come from answers to such questions as why the spirits in whom people invest such faith are female, why their shrines are very often situated on borders, why there is so little agreement about their identities, and how these icons are able to front fundamentally different societal projects without provoking conflict. To answer them one has to pay close attention to social, political, and economic geography and the cultural histories by which power has been made intelligible. One has to understand the nature of symbolism as well as the locally salient spiritual technologies through which people engage the world. Thus one can see meaningful patterns and indeed continuity in this phenomenon rather than symptoms of moral and social disintegration.

Theorizing Pilgrimage

This study eschews assessments of such translocal, dynamic, and diffused religious practice as symptomatic of extralocal contamination, loss of roots, or moral disintegration for a more integrated view of such order of activity. The suggested alternative is to treat such practice as an example of pilgrimage, a variety of translocal religious action characteristic of societies that are geographically extensive and socially complex. Victor Turner, who did much to systematize the study of pilgrimage as an anthropological topic, described pilgrimages as the functional equivalent of rites of passage in smaller-scale societies. As in life-cycle ceremonies when ritual participants move through a period of liminality, pilgrimage entails the experience of "communitas," a transitory suspension of the structures of ordinary existence (Turner 1974). Turner described pilgrimages as journeys in nonordinary time and space that allow participants a release from quotidian roles and relationships, divisions and hierarchies. In his view, they entail the widening of horizons, out-of-the-ordinary experiences, and enjoyment of social relations of freedom or equality. As a result, they are often marked by social effervescence and heightened feeling. By participating in pilgrimages, people who lead compartmentalized or routinized existences can experience reintegration and revivification of social bonds. To Turner, the frequent location of pilgrimage sites on the periphery of polities and nation-states confirms their status as antistructural, liminal spaces. This view of pilgrimages as communitas also explains why the icons that attract pilgrims worldwide are often female, for as figures of maternal nurturance and solicitude, they are exemplary symbols of inclusion (Dubisch 1995, 247). Quite in contrast to those who might pose a divide between religion and modernity, this perspective accounts for the continuation of these collective practices into the present as societal solutions to the ills of social compartmentalization and alienation. To theorists inspired by Turner, this explains why pilgrimages are so popular among urban people, where the stresses of rule-governed lifestyles find a powerful and meaningful antidote in a transitory "escape from modernity" (Reader 1993b, 125).

Turner's portrait of pilgrimage is elegant and powerful, and it accounts for much of what one sees in contemporary Vietnam. Its main problem is that it posits pilgrimage as an escape from structure. This explanation has attracted criticism from a variety of observers who have pointed out that pilgrimages very often reflect and reproduce quotidian social relations and distinctions. Indeed, the findings from anthropology suggest that pilgrimages have been pivotal to the consolidation and reproduction of various political orders as well as of ethnic, regional, class-based, occupational, and gendered identities. Anthropologists have variously described how pilgrimage is profoundly implicated in the constitution of political authority (Perry and Echeverria 1988), ethnicity (Sallnow 1987), caste (Messerschmidt and Sharma 1981), class (Eickelman 1976), national identity (E. Wolf 1958; Dubisch 1995), cultural structures (Sangren 1987), and gender (Dubisch 1995). My own more general criticism of Turner's theory is that it situates this religious practice as somehow marginal or otherworldly, taking place outside ordinary space and time. As extraordinary, pilgrimage or religious travel does not fit within the proper business of modernity. A view of pilgrimage as a form of antistructure has the effect of displacing religion as a form of peripheral activity or as something that is exceptional: something one does in a sacred space, on a holy day, or in response to an extraordinary event or crisis.

That many pilgrimage shrines are indeed often in geographically marginal positions on borders, mountains, and other geographical features does not mean they are peripheral to the politico-economic formations or other salient collectivities that shape pilgrims' lives. Theorists of pilgrimage have explored the extent to which pilgrimage catchment areas, the area from where pilgrims are drawn, overlay or reflect other dimensions of spatially patterned social existence. One of the more interesting questions asked about pilgrimages is whether they are "expressions of economically determined religious identities" (Sangren 1987, 126). The answer appears to be inconclusive. Turner seems to have found some evidence in Mexico of a correspondence between pilgrimage catchment areas and political and economic regions (Turner 1974, 193), but Sangren was forced to conclude that ritual centrality in Taiwan does not correspond to economic or administrative centrality (Sangren 1987). Southern Vietnam's case is similar to both of these, for its main pilgrimage centers are found well away from the principal political and economic centers. The main pilgrimage sites lie in political and economic as well as cultural frontier areas. This fact does not weaken the hypothesis that there is a causal link between magical efficacy and political and economic power. Rather it encourages reconceptualization of the way power is often construed, precisely by those in political, economic, and cultural centers. Under certain circumstances and from certain perspectives, regions such as borders, hinterlands, or resource frontiers are seen as sources of power. This is particularly the case to those who are positioned to benefit most from their relationship to these margins—those who live in cities, capitals, and economic hubs, the places that are culturally, politically, or economically central to such borders, hinterlands, and resource frontiers.

One aspect of the relationship between the spatial patterns of social life and pilgrimage about which theorists are in agreement is that pilgrimages have major social and economic consequences. The religious landscapes of various pilgrimage sites are inscribed by the values and practices of distant and yet powerful social agents in cities, marketing and informational centers, and transport hubs. Pilgrimage centers are also shaped by processes of touristic consumption, cultural commodification, entrepreneurship, and mass culture. They are places where one can find remarkably developed catering, transport, lodging, and tourist services (Turner 1974, 210). As economic phenomena of considerable importance in their own right, pilgrimage centers can induce economic growth and regional development. Pilgrimages precipitate urban buildup, promote the development of transport facilities and infrastructure, and stimulate the growth of markets and of consumer and leisure industries. As pilgrimages become geographically more extensive, they serve to draw different locales into relationship with each other and can act as powerful forces of cultural transmission and standardization. They serve as nodes or cogs for the transfer of ideas and practices between centers of population and from centers to hinterlands.

Given these developments it is difficult to distinguish between pilgrimages and other forms of contemporary travel such as tourism. For some theorists of contemporary leisure culture, the journeys that tourists make can be regarded as pilgrimages in the Turnerian mold, for they are motivated by strivings for social transcendence (e.g., MacCannell 1976). Nevertheless, the state of effervescence, celebration, or affective or cultural disorientation experienced by pilgrim-tourists does not necessarily imply that they are experiencing antistructure, an inversion of or departure from quotidian social relations. Indeed, the enjoyment of mass cultural practices representative of consumerism, tourism, and leisure pursuits at pilgrimage sites today represents an extension of many of the qualities of urban culture to once remote rural shrines. Nor do such emphases imply the degradation of morality, bleaching of culture or evisceration of religious meaning but rather the restructuring of religious practice and subjectivities by an urbanized, commercialized moral order. The molding of practice by such processes in the pilgrimage sites of the world demonstrates this religious form's characteristic responsiveness to transformations in its social environment (Reader 1993a, 227).

Turner conceptualized the temporal character of pilgrimages in two ways. The first was to characterize them historically as typical of hierarchical, preindustrial, agrarian societies; this view led to his memorable observation that pilgrimage represents the "ordered antistructure of patrimonial feudal systems" (1974, 182). Second, he characterized the experience of pilgrimage (from the experiential standpoint of pilgrims) as temporally liminal, as in and out of time. Methodologically these observations run into the problem that pilgrimages have grown greatly in popularity in developed, urbanized, industrial postagricultural societies and among members of such societies who are among the most deeply enmeshed in nonagrarian lifestyles. In addition, pilgrimage sites are ever changing. Most contemporary pilgrimage sites are anything but liminal; instead, they address the economic, social, and cultural concerns of the places from which pilgrims are drawn. What characterizes such sites is their responsiveness to shifting cultural priorities rather than some property of structural liminality, and this very flexibility infuses these sites with cogency over time (Bowman 1993, 55; Dubisch 1995, 41). This responsiveness is due to the key quality of pilgrimage symbols, their multivalence, a property that Turner in an earlier work noted as a defining attribute of symbols (1967). The multivocality of their central symbols, their openness to multiple and changing perspectives, marks pilgrimages out as quintessentially contemporary phenomena. Their popularity in Vietnam at the present moment leads to the conclusion that pilgrimages are characteristic of societies in transition: marked by changing relationships to landscape, social structural dynamism, expanding cultural pluralism, and transitory forms of subjectivity.[6]

The "magnetic" attraction that pilgrimage shrines exert over pilgrims (Preston 1992, 33) cannot be understood negatively as due to the affective release from structures that they provide. Rather, as Sangren has argued for pilgrimage symbols in China, their power and facticity is constituted through their implication in the reproduction of social and cultural structures (Sangren 1987).[7] Pilgrimage sites derive their local salience from the specific historical, social, and cultural projects that imbue them with significance and power. As Morinis has argued, "The unique character of a place of pilgrimage emerges as the creation of the local forces of religion, history, economics, politics and geography" (Morinis 1984, 236). The culturally distinctive symbols at the heart of pilgrimage cults can be seen as a variety of folk historical consciousness that makes even profound social transformations locally intelligible (Sangren 1987).[8] As Ian Reader has argued, beyond their potentially universal dimensions, pilgrimages also act as important reflections of the cultures from which they emerge (Reader 1996, 268). These observations, which help account for differences between pilgrimage traditions, work best if leavened with the proviso that cultures are not static but are always changing. As societies and cultures change so too can we see these transformations through the changing of aspects of pilgrimage foci.

But how coherent are the cultures that pilgrimages encode? A number of theorists who have attempted to account for why feminine symbols are often found at the heart of pilgrimage cults have drawn attention to the counter-cultural qualities of such religious foci, which provide a form of release from or mediation of patriarchal cultural orders (E. Wolf 1958; Turner 1974; Sangren 1983). This approach, with its tendancy to emphasize male affect, values, and structural resolutions, is less helpful in pilgrimage traditions such as Vietnam's, whose dominant practitioners are women. In such contexts one needs to account for the power of feminine symbols in terms of women's experience, practices of self-making, and ritual negotiation of cultural norms. Pilgrimage practices in these circumstances are foremostly linked to women's self-portraiture and negotiation of their societal status; their distinctive affective character is a response to their own circumstances; and the rites are shaped by their own communicative practices. Nevertheless, even in situations where such symbolic foci have emerged most markedly in response to women's experience, they have commonly possessed the resonance and flexibility to enable them to serve as culturally coherent symbols of inclusion and demarcation as well as of societal reproduction, nurturance, and authority (Dubisch 1995, 246–249). Furthermore, the frequent status of such pilgrimage cults as society's largest and most dramatic rites makes them favored by theorists as symbols of cultural typicality or normative universality. On the other hand, as some feminist scholars have noted, one should be aware that the images of femininity venerated in many such cults are often incomplete or abject. As virgins, sexless mothers, or women who have died young or badly, they can be seen as a form of self-containment and an indication that the women who participate in such practices may have little option but to embrace a conditional status as a means to social integration and cultural validation (Warner 1976; Dubisch 1995).

The Social Contours of Popular Religion

Drawing upon these insights, this book provides an ethnographic account of pilgrimages in Vietnam. It uses as a case study the Lady of the Realm, whose large following illustrates the extraordinary popularity of feminine spirits in Vietnam in recent years. Shrines to goddesses are focal points for a diverse range of symbolic, ritual, and social projects. One of the intriguing qualities of such icons explored in this work is their ability to symbolize significantly different projects, divisions, and collective alignments without precipitating conflicts. Equally remarkable are the powers and effects attributed to them by social actors at the forefront of Vietnam's integration into global capitalist markets. Their implication in events of recent years has prompted me to explore these spirits' role in the encoding and negotiation of local histories, as a salient cultural framework that has received little scrutiny to date from either ethnographers or historians. Examination of the spatial dimensions of goddess worship in Vietnam reveals fascinating interdependencies between different locales and the dynamic inscription of religious space by processes of commercialism, urbanization, and technological change. Such religious practice is also socially located, and the power of spiritual beings such as the Lady of the Realm owes much to the relations that people, particularly women, entertain with them. However, one has to ask whether these goddesses, as consociates of the socially marginalized and partners in the acquittal of onerous burdens, should be seen simply as empowering allies or whether they thrive on vulnerabilities and even reproduce abjection.

Chapter 1 illustrates the centrality of such spirits in the symbolic constitution of political collectivity. Even though Vietnam's state is nominally socialist, the current government continues a long history of active state regulation of rites and cultivation of religious meanings. Indeed, the state's evolving response to the domain of popular religion is evidence of significant reliance on religion to underpin its vision for the country. The state's flexibility in this regard has undoubtedly given it significant purchase over popular practice. Nevertheless, the state has far from complete power to shape the religious landscape in contemporary Vietnam. For example, urban-based cultural nationalists, although they share much common ground with Party leaders; formulate their own views about goddess worship independently of Party dictates. Theirs is but one of many independent perspectives aired in this work that offer a corrective to a view of the state as all-encompassing or constitutive of social and cultural life in Vietnam or, conversely, as significant if only because of its critical loss of relevance.

A key dimension of the power ascribed to southern Vietnam's goddesses is their ethnicity. As chapter 2 makes clear, the ethnicity popularly attributed to the goddesses of the southern plain attests to the complex ethnohistory of the region and the importance of popular judgments about historically efficacious practices. Officially, the Lady of the Realm is regarded as a spiritual prop to the ethnic Vietnamese settlement and defense of the Mekong delta. However, many people attribute alternative identities to this goddess and associate her with histories quite at odds with the official narrative of resistance. The divergent tales told about the Lady of the Realm represent a fund of nonauthorized ideas about the historical contribution of different ethnic groups. Such goddesses serve to demarcate ethnic identities, naturalize difference, and reproduce borders. The ethnicity attributed to these goddesses not only highlights differences between ethnic groups but also conceptualizes distinctions between classes, status groups, genders, and generations, distinctions made salient and reproduced through ethnically marked symbols of this kind.

Chapter 3 demonstrates that this goddess is one of the ways in which the market economy in Vietnam is visualized and negotiated. The continuing appeal of goddesses such as the Lady of the Realm confounds the Weberian expectation that processes typically referred to as capitalist modernization are destined to lead to the decline of such religious practice. Instead, it is through symbols such as the goddess that credit, financial increase, capital, value, and market morality have been given expression. The elevation of feminine deities as the most powerful, multifunctional, and reliable beings of the southern Vietnamese religious landscape indicates the central role that female-dominated markets play in people's lives. The qualities of these deities—who are multiskilled, sometimes punitive, yet always responsive—embody widespread assessments of the social contribution of women. The gender of the most potent spirits and their siting along borders indicate the importance in the region of transnational flows of wealth and the critical role that women play in mediating them.

As chapter 4 relates, the location of major pilgrimage centers on borders and in rural areas indicates the importance of such sites not just to locals but also to people who live much farther afield. Contemporary attitudes about the Lady of the Realm illustrate the deep reinscription and reorientation of "local" religious practice by economic and cultural mediators who reside in urban centers, particularly Ho Chi Minh City. The magical properties of increase attributed to this goddess resonate strongly with the ideas that residents of urban areas have about the rural hinterland in which her shrine is located. The meaning of this goddess has been colonized by this city; the power to structure and reproduce her meaning has been exteriorized.

However, this view of the goddess is not unique or unopposed. Discussing the views of migrants from the Mekong delta to the city and the publications about the goddess that originate from her shrine in Châu Đốc, chapter 4 describes a creative synthesis of rural and urban, published and unpublished views about this goddess. It relates the ways those who live in the vicinity of the shrine have responded to the interpretations of those from farther afield and how locally negotiated understandings provide a model for other shrines dedicated to the goddess elsewhere in the Mekong delta.

Processes such as urbanization, consumerism, and marketing therefore have not undermined but have refigured goddess worship, altering the meaning of religious symbols, the nature of the rites, and the makeup of the body of propitiants. Chapter 5 shows how the pilgrimage to the Lady of the Realm is a prism through which important dimensions of urban experience are understood and enacted. Contemporary normative models explored in this chapter constitute pilgrimage either as an obligatory journey or, alternatively, as a way of intensifying conviviality between pilgrims. As the accounts of pilgrimage provided in chapter 5 illustrate, travel to her shrine, undertaken by groups of urban pilgrims, often conforms to these ideals. Whether they are journeys undertaken by individuals seeking to fulfill a promise or group experiences mediated by individuals from one's local area, pilgrimages entail the intensification of the familiar rather than an extraordinary moment of departure from conventional social practice. Pilgrims do not escape from the patterns of urban sociability as much as they reproduce them in the precincts of the goddess' shrine.

To some extent Turner's notion of communitas applies to temple festivals better than it does to pilgrimages, for in the former case one sees a higher degree of interaction and provisional association between people from different locales, as well as more frequent encounters with the new, the transient, and the unexpected. The ethnographic account of the annual festival to the Lady of the Realm provided in chapter 6 suggests that if one is to understand the true attraction of rural festivals such as this, one must incorporate into one's analysis activities taking place outside the walls of the shrine and events occurring before and after the formal ceremonies. These aspects, being diffuse, are hard to describe, but they ought not be seen as a sideshow or, even worse, as a corruption of the "central" meaning of the festival. People from the Mekong delta experience the annual festival to this goddess as a moment and a place of transient urbanism. Their dominant experience of this festival is one of consumption, of being a flaneur, a part of a crowd, washed by fleeting, hectic sensations and constantly shocked by the new. Nevertheless, one again sees in this festival the intensification of cultural values rather than the playing out of antistructure. The qualities of the festival that are most highly valued by its participants—its mass character and its opportunities for transient experience, spontaneous interactions, and communication with others—are characteristic of rather than structural inversions of the social structure and cultural environment of southern Vietnam.

An entrenched commodity economy—along with expanding market relations, trade, migration, urbanization, mass formation, and the rapid development of communications infrastructure—make for a region characterized by considerably diffused social relations and cultural volatility. Symbols that speak to different constituencies, different concerns, and changing priorities have thrived here as pilgrimage focal points while those that are more firmly tied to events, places, meanings, and publics have done less well. Chapter 7 makes the point that the key quality for pilgrimage symbols to thrive and be successful in such conditions is the quality of indeterminacy. This quality makes them adaptable to new circumstances and open to contradictory interpretations. I describe two sets of spiritual personages who are similarly valued for their magical responsiveness but who differ in terms of the fixedness of their identity. The reputed potency and translocal significance of the complex of goddesses featured in this work can be contrasted with the limited powers and local scope of an alternative class of deities glossed as military, literary, and official spirits, and this contrast is closely linked to the relative difference in the specificity of their identities. The indeterminacy of the former is conducive to diverse and shifting ideas about their magical potentiality while the social locatedness of the latter seriously restricts their meaning and relevance.

The rise of individualized and mass-mediated transactions between the spirits and propitiants from increasingly distant, disparate locales reflects a shift away from locally mediated, communal rites. However, it does not follow that these religious subjectivities are asocial or amoral. As chapter 8 discusses, spirits such as the Lady of the Realm are eminently social. They are attributed psychological qualities such as sensitivities, moods, and memories and are implicated in conversations, exchanges, and negotiations: the "transactive" and "interpersonal" relations that Ahern observed in Chinese popular religion (Ahern 1981, 4). Although such spirits are sometimes regarded instrumentally as an amoral source of power to be tapped, those who access that power are conditioned by mutual obligations. The spirits are partners with whom one transacts according to particular norms. This partnership challenges functionalist views of religious power as some autonomous force that can be accessed for use in social endeavors. On the contrary, the quality of responsiveness associated with these beings flows from the extension to the spirit world of assumptions and obligations of reciprocity. The efficacy attributed to the spirits arises from their susceptibility to indebtedness and their presumed desire for sociable inclusion, in return for which they are expected to provide assistance. Such relations of reciprocity are thought by many to apply as well to the Buddha, whose protection is extended and to whom veneration is given, on the condition that the needs of both parties to the exchange are met.

For some Vietnamese ethnologists, such symbols are considered resonant of societal and cultural freedom (Vũ Ngọc Khanh 2001, 150), with the veneration of goddesses indicating the high status of women in Vietnamese society. However, chapter 9 critically examines the proposition that goddesses symbolize or open areas of social autonomy for women. By describing four different perspectives, it finds that the high expectations invested in feminine spirits are not necessarily a positive indication of the social power of women. According to one perspective, the realm of popular religion, dominated as it is by women, represents merely a respite from oppressive patriarchal relations. Alternatively, it may be that goddesses do admit of a realm of relative feminine autonomy, although it may not be a domain that presents many alternatives to women. Indeed, it appears that some followers transact with these deities to seek relief from or acquittal of onerous and unfair burdens placed upon them. The abject stories told of the goddesses of truncated, violently terminated lives hardly sets them up as paragons of feminine self-empowerment, particularly where such tales resonate with extreme cases of their devotees' subordination to their own families. However, these readings are not obligatory, for some women do indeed draw upon versions of these tales creatively, using them as symbolic resources to chart genuinely new and liberating paths. This creative use again underscores that a key to the popularity of these deities is their amenability to a number of interpretations and implication in a variety of social processes, a theme that will be taken up again in the epilogue to this work.

1

Spiritualizing
the Borders

In a country ruled by a single party known for its tight social and ideological control, the public massing of people engaged in pilgrimages to the Lady of the Realm is a noteworthy phenomenon. The relatively unregulated flow of people to, from, and around the site provides many opportunities for pilgrims to associate freely with fellow believers. Tens of thousands of individual ritual acts, murmured prayers, swapped stories, and shared advice on how best to propitiate the goddess amount to a substantial outpouring of ritual and exegetical self-expression. The loosely organized nature of such practices appears to dramatically counter Vietnam's history of military authority, police surveillance, and bureaucratic restrictions on association and movement. This apparent freedom of practice is all the more intriguing given that many religions in Vietnam experienced very real constraints during the same period. The 1990s, a time of economic liberalization, was notable for ongoing tight state control over religious groups such as the Buddhists, Catholics, and Protestants. Several prominent figures from different institutional religions were arrested or put under house detention for their advocacy of greater religious freedoms. The ruling Communist Party made it clear that it would not tolerate the exploitation of religion to destabilize its rule.

One possible explanation for the flourishing of such religious dynamism under a strong state is that it takes place in areas where the state's presence is relatively weak. Shrines to spirits on the nation's borders are among the region's most effervescent religious and festive sites. The manifestation of popular religiosity in such locations suggests that being at the fringes of the polity they somehow lie beyond the reach of state power. The case of the Lady of the Realm, whose festival and pilgrimage are the biggest in the region, would appear to be a compelling example of this hypothesis. Her shrine is right on the border with Cambodia, on a former escape route from the country and beside an active smuggling route. It lies in the western region of the Mekong delta, a region often characterized as a frontier zone—Vietnam's Wild West —with a reputation for a diversity of grassroots or local religious expressions (Brocheux 1995; Hue Tam Ho Tai 1983). Being in the south of the country, it is remote from the political capital. In the days of old, this was Hue, the assimilationist Confucian court; in latter times, Hanoi, the capital of socialist bureaucratic centralism. The western delta's relatively low levels of educational participation (UNDP 2001), which are partly due to the region's unstable economic conditions and high degree of ethnic plurality, also make it harder for the state to influence the people there through the state school system than elsewhere. These geographical factors might support a view of such religious expressions as alternative, oppositional, or reflective of the ideological exhaustion of the regime (Marr 1995).

However, this hypothesis does not explain the state's strong contemporaneous interest in the activities of the Hòa Hảo Buddhists, whose following is concentrated along the same border, close by the shrine to the Lady of the Realm. The religion's various representatives both abroad and within Vietnam have bitterly complained about the imprisonment of their followers and the restriction of their rites, sacred text, and rights to associate (P. Taylor 2001a). One of their main contentions is that the state has inappropriately intervened in the faith, stacking the association of the faithful with Party loyalists, permitting only the selective publication of texts, restricting access to places of worship, and influencing the organization of ceremonies. Permission to commemorate the founding of the religion in the founder's birthplace was not given by the government until 1999, and even then certain texts by the founder of the faith could not be chanted or circulated, and the festive mood was dampened by an extremely heavy police presence. Nevertheless, this festival in this and subsequent years has been well attended. Some participants have favorably compared the size of such gatherings to the festival to the Lady of the Realm. And yet given the state's efforts in policing and managing this event, one cannot say this activity occurs independently, beyond the scope of or as a form of resistance to official culture.

In other words, the location of such religious gatherings in the political borderlands is far from compelling evidence of their cultural marginality. In the proliferation of rituals at the borders of the polity one can very often see the presence, not the absence, of the state. In the attempt to establish salient sanctions of authority in these regions, the state has devoted significant attention to the shaping of religious symbols and practice. The targets of this focus include the shrines to spirits such as the Lady of the Realm in whose cults a succession of states from precolonial times to the present has made substantial investments. This is not to say that such attention by the authorities has created the popular interest in such spirits, for this is due to a number of factors that are independent of state involvement. However, it is equally true that state attention has never entailed the blanket suppression of religious practice. Rather, the dominant approach pursued by different states in the search for effective bases of rule has been the selective cultivation for official use of particular symbolic foci and interpretations, along with the policing of rituals and criticism of popular practice.

What is most interesting in the authorities' dealing with these ritual foci is the ways they are used to delineate and manage the boundaries of political collectivity. This political boundary-marking function is suggested by the placement of many of the most prominent spirits in southern Vietnam along the margins of national territory. And yet the political boundaries to which such spirits give expression are more than territorial. They comprise the borders of idealized political community, the barricades that are imaginatively erected when concepts such as agency, culture, and collective identity are mobilized and invoked. These types of attentions have not necessarily disappeared with the emergence of "rational" political projects in the so-called modern era: projects that position themselves in various ways as secular, scientific, or postideological. In such circumstances interest in spirit worship by various political movements and projects has continued, motivated by a search for forms of cohesion, functional support, and markers of identity.

At the same time, this focus on goddesses as guarantors of collective identity has not been exclusive to state agents. Among societal elites writ large there has been no shortage of interest in the ways such figures might reinforce social and cultural solidarity. Particularly passionate investments in these deities exist even in the heart of cosmopolitan centers such as cities, paradoxically where one might expect to find a fading or blurring of traditional collective identifications. The concern to demarcate or reinforce the boundaries of cultural identity, particularly evident among urban people, has led to a renewed interest in border-dwelling spirits and the followings they attract. Even though this fascination reinforces the state's own message about the border-marking function of these spirits, this process is autonomously driven. Indeed, sometimes interest in such figures is motivated by concerns at odds with state policy and by people sometimes critical of the state's ideological direction.

The State and Its Spirits

One of the stories told about the Lady of the Realm credits her with extending protection to Thoại Ngọc Hầu (1761–1829), a mandarin representing the Vietnamese court who helped consolidate and defend the border with Cambodia in the early years of the Vietnamese court's occupation of southern Vietnam:

> On Sam Mountain, there was a shrine honoring Bà Chúa Xứ that was reputedly responsive to prayers. Mrs. Châu Thị Tế often went there to pray for her husband to defeat the enemy and bring peace and prosperity to the residents there. Her prayers became a reality and Thoại Ngọc Hầu defeated the Khmer troops. To show her gratitude toward Bà Chúa Xứ, Mrs. Châu Thị Tế rebuilt the shrine. On the occasion of finishing the rebuilding work, she held a big festival that lasted for three days. From that day on, villagers had the custom of celebrating those days as the anniversary of Bà Chúa Xứ (Vietnamese Women's Museum 1993, 29).

This story of the reconstruction of the Lady of the Realm's shrine and the founding of her festival by these agents of the Vietnamese court belongs to a particular genre of myth that can be situated in a longer history of Vietnamese statecraft. Keith Taylor has argued that from the earliest phase of the independent Vietnamese kingdom, kings honored such spirits as were believed to have protected the land against threats from outside, aided an orderly succession to the throne, or assisted the formation of a new royal lineage. A fourteenth-century register of such spirits, the *Việt Điện U Linh Tập* (Spirits of the Việt kingdom), is full of examples of such loyalty shown by diverse local deities. The leaders' ritual veneration of these spirits, Taylor argued, was part of a process of consolidating Vietnamese identity and centralizing state power (K. Taylor 1986, 45–46).

The Vietnamese case fits within a broader regional pattern of state intervention in religious practice. The standardization and reshaping of spirit worship have been major preoccupations of the bureaucratic polities that have emerged throughout the region. Local or kin-based religious phenomena such as spirit cults, gods of the soil, or ancestral spirits have been integral to various states' attempts to effect political centralization. The Devaraja cult in Cambodia initiated by Jayavarman II incorporated disparate local deities into a statewide cult, fusing Hindu deities such as Shiva with local deities, effecting political centralization through religious integration (Nidhi 1976, 133; Cohen 1993, 190). Spiro argued that the Burmese national cult of the Thirty-Seven Nats (spirits) was a creation of the eleventh-century Burmese throne, in which a court-imposed system deriving from Hindu and Buddhist cosmology replaced local guardian deities (Spiro 1967, 52).

The focus on the spiritual delineation of borders has been particularly evident. Much of the ethnography of northern Thailand bears out the proposition that the propitiation of ancestral spirits *(phi)* as religious foci on the borders of settlements, on behalf of a collective, is at core political (Davis 1984; Wijeyewardene 1986, 76; Maspero 1950). The relationship between tutelary deities and the borders of administrative territories also finds ample confirmation from China (Feuchtwang 2001, 63). In Vietnam this relationship is suggested by the practice of worshiping boundary stones, which Cadière noted were imbued with spiritual power (Cadière 1919, 40; 1958, 21). Drawing upon Cadière's ethnography, Paul Mus attributed to the "genie boundary" a magical virtue in relation to the territory it enclosed (Mus 1933, 16). Mus argued that in precolonial Indochina magical boundary stones and other spirits of the soil represented a contract between a group and its territory. According to Mus, the historical role of such spirits was juridical, effecting the stabilizing of rights over land (Mus 1933, 16). Both writers underlined the importance of ritual mediators in delineating the significance of spiritualized boundaries. For Mus, an indispensable part in this process was played by the chief or king, who acted as ritual intermediary between the divinity and the group.[1] Cadière noted that sorcerers played an interpretive role in the identification of a border stone as possessed and the elaboration of legends and stories about its miraculous qualities (Cadière 1958, 21).

The stories told about spirits on the borders of the Vietnamese polity frequently relate to their personal protection of a leader involved in danger on the frontiers of the polity. The story of the Lady of the Realm recalls those told of Bà Đen, the Black Lady, enshrined on a large mountain in Tây Ninh province, on Vietnam's border with Cambodia. One tale credits the Black Lady with providing refuge to Nguyễn Phúc Ánh, the founding king of the Nguyễn dynasty, when fleeing rebel troops in the late eighteenth century. In gratitude for this assistance he conferred upon her a decree of imperial recognition *(sắc phong)* as Holy Mother of the Sacred Mountain (Linh Sơn Thánh Mẫu).[2] The story is similar to that told of the Holy Mother of Mounts and Forests (Mẫu Thượng Ngàn), venerated in Lạng Sơn province, on the northern border with China. According to one legend, she was daughter of the mountain deity Tản Viên. She inherited as her fief the forests and mountains where she grew up, and the King of Heaven appointed her guardian of the forests of the south. She helped the Lý and Trần dynasties (eleventh–thirteenth centuries) to ward off foreign invaders, in return for which she received many certificates of honor. In the fifteenth century she appeared in a dream to warn the Vietnamese insurrectionist Lê Lợi, who was stationed in her domain, of the immanence of a counterattack by the occupying Chinese Ming troops. When he fled their attack she guided him and his adviser Nguyễn Trãi through the forest to safety. In return for her services she was titled the Holy Mother of Mounts and Forests. Many temples were erected in her name (Nguyễn Minh San 1999, 89–90). Regarded locally as the lady *(bà chúa)* of the forest regions, she has a prominent place in the pantheon of the cult of the Three Palaces (Tam Phủ).[3]

These tales are oral accounts *(huyền thoại)* collected by ethnographers and folklorists. One note of caution in using them for evidence of historical traditions of statecraft is that these stories cannot be dated. There is often no trace of them in court documents.[4] There are also many versions. For instance, another story about the Lady of the Realm relates that she was a Thai woman who, in the late eighteenth century, helped Nguyễn Phúc Ánh gain the throne. Some of these versions may be of relatively recent origin. Certainly the only written versions were recorded quite recently. However, the fact that these tales are not well documented does not mean they have not had long currency and local significance. Some of the events in these stories are also supported by the locations of shrines and the nature of rites. For example, residents of Vĩnh Tế village where the largest shrine to the Lady of the Realm is found recollected in discussions with me that the shrine was renovated at the end of the nineteenth century but that it had been built much earlier. The shrine is beside the temple to the mandarin Thoại Ngọc Hầu. The annual commemorative rites to the goddess do indeed reflect the tale of her protection of the mandarin, for they include *lễ thỉnh sắc,* the trooping into her shrine of the mandarin's imperial brevet, which remains there as a guest of the goddess during the three days of her festival. Similarly, the Black Lady enshrined on a mountain farther north along the border has been one of the most popular pilgrimage destinations in the southern region since at least the late nineteenth century (Baurac 1899, 270).

Furthermore, there is a certain consistency to these tales. These goddesses have similar biographies as local women or female spirits living among features such as mountains and forests, which form geographical limits to state power. Each is associated with providing shelter for or protection or guidance to the rulers or defenders of the kingdom, each of them male, individual figures of prowess. The dangerous military activities, travel in unfamiliar areas, exposure to hardships, and negotiation of strange environments that are reported in these tales are the kind of existential and gendered dilemmas that resonate with the historical realities of the Vietnamese state's expansion and the military defense of its frontiers. The endangered leader—

a rebel, fleeing ruler, or military occupier—becomes indebted to his bene-factress. The personal relationship between local frontier woman and male hero is rendered as one of mother to son. For their act of care each of these women was awarded the title Holy Mother (Thánh Mẫu). In time they were enshrined in palatial residences and ranked above all *(nương nương)* as ma-triarchs of the spirit world.

Keith Taylor refers to the Vietnamese spirit world as a "protective screen," firmly attached to the Vietnamese landscape and rooted in Viet-namese history (1986, 45). This interpretation is borne out in tales of these spirits' defense of the sovereign against incursions or dangers at the frontiers. Yet such interpretation casts such spirits in an overly defensive capacity, for the stories described here might equally be seen as means by which the state ritually projected itself into frontier spaces and legitimated its presence there. Tales of these goddesses' aid to the throne's representatives and founders of dynasties suggest that one of the ways the Vietnamese state insinuated itself into new frontiers was through tales of central debt to a local spirit. The as-similation of central power into the borderlands was effected through a met-aphor of kinship whereby kingly veneration is cast as performance of filial duties. The assistance rendered the leader by a local woman is of the life-and-death kind that engenders an existential debt in the leader's descendants, cementing between center of dynastic power and frontier region an enduring relationship of ritual obligation. Dynastic power is legitimated in frontier regions through ritual displays of filial gratitude.

Stories of the Lady of the Realm's and the Black Lady's aid to agents of the court are set in the late eighteenth and early nineteenth centuries when the Vietnamese state was asserting its authority over an area with an ethni-cally diverse population nominally under Cambodian control. Tales and rites that emphasized these spirits' preferential relationship with the Vietnamese center vied with or displaced other more localized identities and relationships to these spirits. This process recalls the case of the southern Chinese goddess Tien Hau, a local spirit whose imperial promotion formed a part of the Qing court's effort to consolidate its grip on the southern Chinese coastal region (Watson 1985, 307). The daughter of a fishing family, she foresaw danger to her male kin on the sea. After she died a virgin, her spirit continued to offer magical protection. When her deeds of protection extended to the court's mandarins traveling on the seas, she was promoted and eventually awarded the title Tien Hau (Empress of Heaven). The Chinese court's promotion of this female frontier deity did not confront or undermine local interpretations but indeed was a mechanism by which diverse local identities could be ritu-ally incorporated into a centralized cultural project (Watson 1985, 324).

Contemporary Vietnamese commentators take the fact that many of the gods venerated at the fringes of the Vietnamese polity are female as a sign of the weakened hold of Confucian patriarchy at Vietnam's cultural fringes. Yet their femininity suggests not the absence of the state but its very presence. These maternal symbols are less "security guards" defending borders, than sources of authority, agents of political transition, and means for the incorporation of new peoples. The promotion of Holy Mothers along the fringes of polity can be seen as a means by which frontiers could expand and be managed not as zones of competition between dynastic patrilineages but as sites of substitution of motherly attentions between siblings. The transition of regimes could thus be portrayed not a rupture but as the maintenance of continuity. Victor Turner speaks of a somewhat related tendency among the earth and fertility cults of West and Central Africa toward symbolizing inclusiveness and ritual bonds between groups, in contrast with what he describes as exclusionary and segmenting properties of "ancestral and political cults" (1974, 185). Because these Vietnamese spirits are associated with fertility and nurturing rain, with maternal reproductivity and nurturance, they are sometimes seen as originating in people's everyday needs and concerns, far from the preoccupations of the political realm. Yet such an interpretation does not exclude a political reading of such practices, for the state's recognition of its existential debt to these maternal spirits is consistent with their status as guarantors of the nurturance and well-being of the collectivity.

Such qualities have been particularly relevant at the southern fringes of the Vietnamese polity, where rulers have incorporated as spiritual protectors numerous deities endorsed by alternative ruling lineages, clans, and ethnically distinct groups. Nguyễn Thế Anh has documented the fascinating process by which the Cham goddess Po Nagar was appropriated by the court and Vietnamized in the north as Thánh Mẫu Liễu Hạnh and in the south as Thiên Y A Na (Nguyễn Thế Anh 1995). Completely absorbed, the Cham are now regarded by the majority ethnic Vietnamese as a "sibling nation" *(dân tộc anh em)*. Farther south, the Black Lady in contemporary Tây Ninh was Vietnamized as the Holy Mother of the Sacred Mountain (Linh Sơn Thánh Mẫu). The Lady of the Realm, herself an Indianized rendition of Shiva, was also Vietnamized, feminized, and conferred maternal status by the addition of a protruding cement stomach (Malleret 1959, 38). The Vietnamese state's veneration of these inclusive maternal figures, once propitiated by contiguous groups, was the means by which the absorption of such groups could be ritually managed. One can read these spirits as agents of continuity, enabling the incorporation of diversity by emphasis on common maternal origins.

Other kinship qualities attributed to these spirits suggest their equal value as symbols of exclusivity. Although venerated as mothers, the deities venerated on the fringes of the southern Vietnamese plain are described in tales as unmarried women. At least one tale is told about each of these figures whereby she repudiated marriage or resisted rape; in the case of Bà Đen there are several different versions. These tales relate the fidelity of daughters to their natal family writ large, a demonstration of loyalty to the clan or polity that suggests why they have been showered with the highest honors. The goddesses are also described as virgins. Even when sexually violated, they cast themselves to their deaths, ensuring no progeny issued from their union. Hence, no local lineage can claim actual descent from them. Such qualities have made these female figures amenable not only to the Vietnamese state's expanding claims over the frontier regions but to the articulation of differences between encompassed frontiers and encompassing dynastic center as well as to ongoing exclusivist claims made by different ethnic and other subcultures that are found in the vicinity of the shrines.[5]

The process of centralizing disparate local meanings has not gone unopposed. While such spirits have been used by the state for symbolic purposes, they have also been subject to counterreadings. In precolonial Vietnam, the Ministry of Rites was responsible for approving and certifying the deities to be venerated in the kingdom (Woodside 1971). Yet the court's functionaries perpetually had to contend with the innovations, the "false and strange beliefs," thrown up by village communities and wily local elites. Religious symbols such as tutelary spirits, although they were offered recognition by the court, were focal points of elite anxiety (Wolters 1988; Giebel 2001) and were sometimes caught up in the center-periphery struggle between the court and other actors over the authentication of cultural practice. These dynamics were particularly marked at the southern frontiers (Do Thien 1995; Cooke 1997). Đông Vĩnh notes that at the beginning of their dynasty in the nineteenth century, the Nguyễn kings

> regarded the cult of Holy Mothers with its mediums as a heretical magical practice. King Gia Long (reigned 1802–1820) formally forbade magical practices such as sorcery, prophecy, exorcism, curing of diseases with spells, etc. According to *Đại Nam thực lục chính biên* (Veracious chronicles of Vietnam), "Sorcerers, liturgical singers *(cung văn)* and mediums shall be punished with 100 whiplashes and 6 months of forced labor. Women-mediums, if caught red-handed, shall be subject to a 100-whiplash punishment and be condemned to pound rice for the state for 6 months" (*Đại Nam thực lục* 4:97). (Đông Vĩnh 1999, 77).

However, these rulings need not be regarded as Confucianist attacks on female spirits, as Đông Vĩnh has claimed. Rather, such policies aimed at consolidating the court's own reading of these spirits over those of rival practitioners. Indeed, a later representative of the Nguyễn dynasty, King Đồng
Khánh (reigned 1863–1888), learned about his enthronement dates from the
goddess Thiên Y A Na, for which he recognized her as a goddess of the first
category *(thượng đẳng thần)* (Đông Vĩnh 1999, 78).

Colonialism and the Problem of Inauthentic Spirits

The transition to the so-called modern era did not entail a reduction in these
types of attentions. Initial French colonial occupiers were exceedingly derogatory of local religious practice. In 1868 P. C. Richard, an artillery lieutenant,
observed, "The inhabitants of our provinces do not have religion properly
put. They lack this source of liberty, dignity, morale, consolation and hope
which is indeed the basis of the soul. One only finds among them a mix of
idolatry and native, gross superstitions" (Richard 1928, 246). However, from
the outset colonialists were thinking how local religious beliefs might be used
to help sustain their rule. In 1866 Du Hailly asserted that the Vietnamese
"profound indifference in religious matters" and what he alleged to be the
"vagueness" and "bizarre" confusion of doctrine was advantageous, as religion could therefore not form a basis for strong resistance to French rule
(Du Hailly 1866, 903). The local belief in spirits might even persuade the
indigenes of the permanence of the French occupation. For instance, he
speculated that the Minh Mạng emperor's profanation of the respected mandarin Lê Văn Duyệt's tomb provided locals with an intelligible explanation
about why the French had been able to take over Cochinchina (Du Hailly
1866, 905).

If the French entertained ideas of using spirit worship to consolidate
their rule, the spirits proved unwilling to cooperate. In 1882 the authorities
arrested a sorcerer who had announced to his followers that an army of spirits was about to descend from the Seven Mountains and would behead all
people who did not have one of his amulets (R. Smith 1972, 96). The French
worried about the relationship between much grassroots religious activity
and crime and feared the challenge to their political authority that resided in
figures such as Phan Xích Long, who, it was declared in 1913, would descend
from the sky as the new king (R. Smith 1972, 106). Colonial authorities were
preoccupied by the question of religious authenticity, what was indigenous
and what was external. Particularly troubling were the connections between
local secret societies and those in China. Sûreté agents from Coulet (1926)

to Savani (1955) paid detailed attention to the heterogeneous "cults" and "sects" in southern Vietnam. These investigations were undertaken with acute sensitivity to the political implications of such religion—in particular, their scope for subversion of the colonial body politic by external political agents. Later the regionally extensive Cao Đài and Hòa Hảo religions became the new focal points of colonial anxiety. Labeled in a derogatory manner as "feudal" or as led by madmen, they were repressed for fear of their exploitation by nationalists and by the Japanese. In 1940, at the end of their reign, the colonial authorities, in a sign that they had failed to bring the spirits into line, closed down the main Cao Đài temple and exiled its pope partly in response to the increasing incidence of spirit messages prophesying that the anticolonialist prince Cường Để would soon return from Japan (Hill 1971, 335).

In their pursuit of Durkheimian symbols of societal integration, French anthropologists struggled similarly with what they saw as inauthentic spiritual practices. Giran was inclined to read evolutionary tendencies into religious practice, seeing the cult to the historical hero Trần Hưng Đạo as a sign of a progression to a higher morality, while popular beliefs in his magical efficacy were a corruption of the spirit's true meaning. In effect Giran recycled the court's ambivalence toward nonprescribed religious practices, deeming "magical" rites at the temple to the deified general Trần Hưng Đạo in northern Vietnam as a diminution of the cult's true meaning (Giran 1912, 430). Such spirit cults were analyzed by the anthropologist Cadière as the true indigenous religion of the Viets, as opposed to what he claimed were weakly realized imports such as Buddhism (Cadière 1958, 6). Yet Cadière's disdain for sorcerers who "manufactured" tales about boundary stones and for the evanescent quality of the cults they promoted aligned him with the perspective of the central authorities: the court at Huế and the colonial regime (1958, 21). Another scholar, Paul Mus, saw underneath the Hinduized veneer of Indochinese spirit worship an enduring indigenous substratum (Mus 1933).[6] Mus' faith in Indochina's religious integrity resonated with ideas promoted in Vietnamese nationalist circles of the 1930s, of cultural endurance in the face of colonial suppression (Bayley 2000).[7] However, the classical scholar Mus was as troubled by the heterodox southern Vietnamese religious scene as the colonial authorities were. Unable to see in religion a vehicle for the creative fashioning of new identities, he saw the Cao Đài and Hòa Hảo not as "true" religions but as "substitutes" for an order that had been dismantled by the French (McAlister and Mus 1970). The anthropological study of such practices was thus impregnated with the concerns of the French colonial project, evidencing among such colonial elites competitive anxiety and paternalistic concern for the integrity and survival of the indigenous culture in the context of exogenous incursions and continuing local creativity.

Nationalist Displacements

Many of Vietnam's nationalist intellectuals had equally critical views about practices they viewed as historically outmoded. Early in the twentieth century, modernist intellectuals, endorsing a Social Darwinist evolutionist perspective, were critical of practices such as spirit worship. The scholar Phan Kế Bính, for example, thought belief in protection by spirits eroded people's confidence in their own abilities, citing Confucius, no less, for the inadvisability of relying on the spirit world. He considered it appropriate that people whose historical contribution was valued should be commemorated "in the European manner," with bronze statues, but that to demand favors and to believe in their miraculous posthumous deeds was "backward" and "harmful" (Phan Kế Bính 1972, 85). In the 1930s, urban intellectuals, influenced by European enlightenment critiques, distinguished religion *(tôn giáo)* from "superstition" *(mê tín dị đoan);* the latter, including the worship of a broad spectrum of spirits, was regarded as the domain of tricksters and immoral people, a fatalistic reaction to crisis, a self-defeating rejection of societal modernization *(Phụ Nữ Tân Văn* 1930a, 1). Some critics cordoned off belief in the spirits as unrepresentative of the "modern" *(văn minh)* age by identifying this embarrassing practice with specific social categories. Often described as a pursuit of old women *(bà già)* at the end of their days, stereotypes of religious practice as backward looking, otherworldly, escapist, or compensatory were strongly gendered. A series of articles appearing in the 1930s Saigonese magazine *Phụ Nữ Tân Văn* (Modern Woman) described superstition as a largely female problem and lamented the prevalence of practices such as spirit worship, fortune-telling, divination, and the calling of souls among women in the southern provinces (1930a, 1930b, 1933, 1934). Women's reliance on spirits was described as a function of their lack of self-belief and susceptibility to trickery. Spirit worship and feminine religiosity went hand in hand as practices that needed to be purged if the country was to advance into modernity. This set of views illustrates that in early-twentieth-century urban Vietnam, modernity was associated with notions of self-reliance and faith in one's own efforts *(sức mình).* In the early twentieth century the "self-strengthening" movement among the literati was an important vehicle for the introduction of ideas that it was thought would aid the modernizing of society (Jamieson 1993, 57). Science and the "new learning" encouraged people to believe in themselves rather than in the power of obscure forces. Presented as such, progress *(tiến bộ)* was a movement toward inclinations that were often gendered male in the Vietnamese cultural context.

Vietnamese modernist identities were also expressed in contrast to phenomena regarded as regional or rural. Articles in *Phụ Nữ Tân Văn* located the troublesome religious revival of the 1930s in the southern countryside. As the cities of Vietnam grew in stature as nodes of economic and political power and cultural prestige, the notion of superstition became strongly associated with nonurban identities. From the perspective of Saigon, Vietnam's largest urban center, a new picture emerged of the Mekong delta as a place of ignorance and darkness, a breeding ground for all manner of superstitions.[8] Through the colonial and postcolonial periods, the delta remained an area pervasively associated in Vietnamese thinking with grassroots prophets, peasant rebellions, and unorthodox religious movements (Sơn Nam 1992; Hue Tam Ho Tai 1983). According to urban-based intellectuals, this was due to the comparatively low level of education of its population. One university graduate, who studied in Saigon in the 1960s, explained to me that the practice of venerating spirits such as the Lady of the Realm was particularly strong in the Mekong delta, for it was a survival from the delta's pioneering era when its uneducated people misapprehended the forces of nature:

> The first Vietnamese settlers in the Mekong delta were only half-civilized. They lived in a dangerous and uncontrollable environment, subject to storms, dangerous animals and unfamiliar seasonal rhythms. Because they were not well educated they explained natural calamities in terms of the actions of spirits and other supernatural forces. (from field notes 1998)

Southern Vietnam's first postcolonial regime, the Republic of Vietnam (1955–1975), whose capital was in Saigon, exhibited this heavy urbanist bias. A centralist state, heavily dependent on foreign aid, the short-lived Republic foundered largely on its ineffectiveness in drawing rural people into the national community. According to the modernization discourse prevalent at the time, the nation, to survive, needed to achieve functional integration of disparate value systems (Geertz 1963). In practice, however, the Republic's authoritarian leadership attempted to achieve unity by suppressing ideological alternatives to its paternalistic rule. Attempts were made to assimilate the so-called montagnards or tribal upland people through Christian conversion, nationalistic education, and "sedentarization" (Salemink 1991). The indigenous religions of the Mekong delta, the Cao Đài and Hòa Hảo Buddhists, both of which had substantial rural followings, were attacked by the state,

their leaders variously discounted by critics as feudal, mad, obscurantist, du-
plicitous, ridiculous, or sinister. Buddhists, who comprised a large percentage
of the population, were also subject to unjust and chafing restrictions. In
1962 the Republic passed a law condemning spiritualism, occultism, and
other "superstitious" phenomena (Hill 1971, 346). These attacks were undertaken not only for political or security reasons but, as Anagnost noted was
the case in China, "to affirm the universal, homogenizing values of a modernizing state over the disparate inassimilable meanings of local cultures"
(cf. Anagnost 1994, 222). However, the effect of such attacks by the supposedly modern center on the recalcitrant periphery was the evisceration of the
diverse local identifications and symbols in which lay the state's only hope of
gaining local legitimacy. As observers at the time noted, the failure of President Ngô Đình Diệm and later Nguyễn Văn Thiệu to create local bases for
their legitimacy constituted a fatal weakness for the Republican regime (Hill
1971).

Some observers have argued that this modernist, urbanized state totally
broke with indigenous tradition (McAlister and Mus 1970; Fitzgerald 1972).
However, it is worthy of note that not all traditions were breached. During
the war-fed prosperity boom in the south, many pagodas, temples, and
shrines were rebuilt and refurbished. There was an upsurge in the veneration
of heroes whose historical contribution appealed to the southern regime's
view of its project as a nationalistic war against communism. During the Republic the temples to heroic ancestors such as Lê Văn Duyệt, the nineteenth-
century viceroy of Gia Định, and Trần Hưng Đạo, the thirteenth-century
general who defeated the Mongols, were well patronized by different levels of
the bureaucracy, various state organs, and high-profile politicians, including
the abdicated king Bảo Đại. In many respects this worship of ancestral spirits
was the undeclared state religion of the Republic. For a highly urbanized
state, it is relevant that the most potent of these temples were in the capital,
Saigon, or in rapidly swelling urban provincial centers such as Rạch Giá or
Cần Thơ. Urban areas in this time also witnessed a proliferation in practices
of divination and other ways to communicate with the souls of the departed
(Nguyễn Ngọc Huy and Young 1982; Toan Ánh 1997), a phenomenon surely
linked to the dislocations endured by millions of internally displaced people
and an increase in war-related mortalities and other varieties of "bad deaths"
(cf. Malarney 2001, 60). Pilgrimages to the shrines of goddesses on the borders of the nation also continued to be undertaken. In 1961 President Ngô
Đình Diệm led a large pilgrimage to La Vang, the site of an apparition of the
Virgin Mary. This shrine, only a few kilometers from the border with the
northern Communist state, was described as "a fortress of the free world

shielding itself against communism" (Templer 1999, 268). However, after a few years of relative peace, the Republic's land and sea borders were being systematically breached by newly arrived recruits to the Communist-led resistance and by clandestine supply lines. Over the decade of the 1960s, the Republican state's ability to guarantee its citizens safety of movement to the outlying shrines to many of these goddesses quickly eroded. For instance, the outbreak of war in the early 1960s saw a decline in the numbers of pilgrims visiting the Black Lady of Tây Ninh, as to get to her shrine one had to pass the guerrilla fortress of Củ Chi and traverse the insecure countryside of Tây Ninh province.[9]

Constituting Heroic Agency

On the face of it, the Republic's political adversaries appear even less likely to have been interested in cultivating the spirits as a basis for their rule. The Vietnamese Communist Party, founded in the 1920s, was heir to the high modernist concerns of early-twentieth-century urban modernism, ideological radicalism, and the global socialist movement (Hue Tam Ho Tai 1992). Vietnam's early Communist leadership had a violently rejectionist orientation to their cultural past, breaking with oppressive and hierarchical social relations and customs that were augmented by French colonialism (Ninh 2002). Drawing heavily on the ideas of Karl Marx and Friedrich Engels they associated religion with a "primitive" (nguyên thủy) misapprehension of natural forces and with attempts by ruling elites from precolonial to colonial times to mystify the masses and furnish supernatural underpinnings to worldly relations of inequality and exploitation (Trần Hữu Tiến 1977). On coming to power (in some regions of the country as early as the 1940s), they couched their attempts to eliminate or reform religious practice in the name of modernity, equality, economic sustainability, and national defense. The revolutionary government's modernist zeal led to the wholesale restriction of religious practices, the curtailing of rites, and the closure of religious buildings (Hunt 1982; Marr 1986; Luong 1993, 1994; Malarney 2002; Kleinen 1999).

Nevertheless, in the process of fighting French colonialism and later U.S. neocolonialism, the categories of tradition (truyền thống) and spirit (tinh thần) were serviceable tools for the forging of a national culture that met the needs of the present (Vasavakul 1994; Pelly 1995; Ninh 2002). Good (tốt đẹp) and wholesome (lành mạnh) traditions, of resistance (kháng chiến), industriousness (cần cù), and sacrifice (hy sinh), were to be fortified. The revolutionary struggle spirit (tinh thần đấu tranh cách mạng), heroism (chủ nghĩa anh *hùng*), and patriotism *(chủ nghĩa yêu nước)* were held up as timeless qualities of the Vietnamese people (Trần Văn Giàu 1992).

However, leaders sought to purge from the nation's spiritual culture all outdated, exploitative, and alien dimensions. The category of outmoded *(hủ tục)* or negative *(tiêu cực)* traditions represented indigenous practices associated with ignorance, waste, and exploitation, at variance with the regime's mobilizational and socialist reform project. Much popular religious activity, including communal house sacrifices and temple festivals, fell into this latter category (Malarney 2002). Practices such as spirit worship, sorcery, geomancy, physiognomy, and trance possession were frequently grouped under the pejorative category of superstition, which the revolutionary government aimed to eliminate (Kleinen 1999, 171). As scientific evolutionists, Vietnam's communist leaders saw the spirits worshiped in Vietnam as primitive survivals from an early stage of social evolution when people deified the forces of nature because they lacked the ability to control or overcome them (Trần Hữu Tiến 1977, 69). Belief in the power of spirits was illusory and rendered people impotent *(bất lực)* and fatalistic. It undermined people's confidence in their own agency and did not encourage them to believe they could solve their problems with their own minds and hands (Bùi Thị Kim Quý 1986). As social radicals the communists saw the spirits as tools of feudal elites, mystifications of relations of social exploitation. For example, titles awarded to Lady Liễu Hạnh by the feudal authorities showed her use as a tool by the feudal elite to validate their oppressive rule. Belief in her spiritual qualities was also considered an imported Daoist belief, a Sinicized accretion (Trường Chinh and Đặng Đức Siêu 1978, 122–142). Practices associated with spirit worship, such as mediumship and fortune-telling, were described as legacies of Chinese colonization. Indeed, the harshest critics considered all religions—Buddhism, Confucianism, Christianity—save ancestor worship suspect as imports. In Vietnam, according to one critique, they all became mixed, no longer a religion or beautiful philosophy but just superstition and "meaningless practice" *(tục lễ vô nghĩa)* (Trường Chinh and Đặng Đức Siêu 1978, 122–142).

These critiques had much in common with those mounted by urban nationalists. Yet Vietnam's socialist state came to power in a rural-based mass insurgency, controlling areas such as the countryside, mountains, and forests far better than did its colonial and nationalist rivals. A key to the Party's military victories was mobilizing peasant forces; and in essays and popular literary anthologies published in the north, the Vietnamese peasant world was depicted as traditionally disparaging of feudal elites, a pillar of the millennial struggle against nature and foreign invaders, and marked by collectivism and cooperation (see for instance Nguyễn Đổng Chi 1957). Rather than regard such a group as backward or marginal as urban modernists might be wont to do, the Party constructed the peasantry as the collective agent of history (Pelley 2002, 137). The peasant world was portrayed as the inner world of culture to be defended from attack by outsiders and upon which people could draw energy in their struggle to build socialism and expel the foreign enemy. Aspects of folk culture *(văn hóa dân gian),* peasant lifestyle, and peasant customs *(phong tục)* were depicted as a durable indigenous substratum, in contrast to the cultural detritus of foreign invaders and cultural imperialists (both ancient and more recent) and the suspect cultural tendencies of elites, court, and the cities (see for instance Nguyen Khac Vien 1974). In contrast to such deified female figures as Lady Liễu Hạnh, the government posed historical figures such as the two Trưng sisters and Lady Triệu, who were cited as examples of Vietnamese women's resistance to foreign incursions. The ethnic minorities *(dân tộc thiểu số)* were also deemed part of this tradition as compatriots *(đồng bào)* struggling against a common foreign enemy (Pelly 1995). This perception of their centrality owed much to the strategic placement of their homelands in the highlands and on the border with China, which were vital base areas for resistance activity.

Negotiating New Religious Frontiers

No sooner was the war against the U.S.-backed republican regime over than the Communist leadership faced the challenge of incorporating into the socialist polity the former South Vietnam, an ethnically diverse region shaped by capitalist social relations and influenced by consumerism and popular mass culture (Duiker 1989; P. Taylor 2001b). The integration of this region of Vietnam created a major problem for the Communist government, which was confronted by a plethora of religious sects, edifices, practices, and images that had been eliminated or controlled in the north and, somewhat selectively, in southern resistance zones (Hunt 1982). In addition were regionally specific religious forms that reflected strong influences from the ethnic Chinese, Cham, and Khmer peoples, as well as syncretic religions such as the Cao Đài and Hòa Hảo. To most of those who came from the northern Democratic Republic of Vietnam, these unfamiliar religious forms were indicators of South Vietnam's corruption and drift beyond the frontiers of the Vietnamese cultural world caused by the region's decades-long control by a foreign-backed government. In line with the attitude shown toward religion in the postcolonial state in northern Vietnam before 1975, such religions were considered, from the historically "advanced" perspective of Vietnamese

Marxism, as obsolete and feudal *(phong kiến)*, associated with the ruling elite's attempt to oppress the masses or with U.S. neocolonial attempts to distract the masses from their true revolutionary vocation (Bùi Thị Kim Quý 1986, 179). For a while, it appeared to southerners that virtually all their religion fell under the negative category of illegal superstition. Indigenous religions such as the Cao Đài and Hoà Hảo were severely treated and labeled as remnants of medieval sociopolitical relations or as the political tools of reactionaries and colonialists rather than as religious phenomena. Other religious groups such as the Catholics, Protestants, Buddhists, and Muslims were subject to close control, and in many cases their lands were confiscated and buildings appropriated.

In dramatic contrast with the cultural ideal of struggle-oriented peasants and self-sacrificing soldiers, the big, bloated southern cities encountered by the liberating troops at the end of the war seemed like an alien world. Far from being regarded as nodes of avant-garde culture and engines of growth, they were considered reservoirs of dangerous phenomena, construed as harmful to the regime's unifying and modernizing project. Particularly relevant in this phase was the Party's view of practices of fortune-telling, geomancy, divination, and spirit worship, which were deeply entrenched in the urban areas of the South. Such religions confirmed the regime's view of cities as purchase points for foreign subversion. With much urban religious activity considered as of Chinese origins, such backward practices were thought to have been deliberately encouraged by the Americans in the south of the country to neutralize the population's spirit of resistance (Hồ Sĩ Hiệp 1981). The development of religions in the southern cities was also linked to a purposeful attempt by the enemy to disorient people and induce fatalistic dispositions by bombing the countryside and driving peasants from their homes (Nguyen Khac Vien 1985, 40). The new regime was especially concerned about the obstacle that noninstitutionalized religion presented to government-led social renewal. Practices of making offerings to the ghosts *(cúng cô hồn)* or belief in spirits were particularly worrisome, for it was impossible to determine the interpretations people read from them. For example, the idea, which spread in 1976, that a statue of the Virgin Mary in Ho Chi Minh City was magically responsive was considered a wrong and wild belief, out of keeping with orderly (in this case, Catholic) practice and the values of a modern society. The spontaneous (i.e., uncontrollable) nature of such rumors was thought to make believers vulnerable to exploitation by antigovernment forces (All-Vietnam Catholic Liaison Committee 1976; Nguyễn Minh Vu 1976).

As a southern party leader, Trần Bạch Đằng, later reminisced, many

Party cadres in South Vietnam viewed religion as a site that enemies always sought to infiltrate in order to destroy the revolution, and this overly narrow perspective led them to restrict religious activities (2001, 37). Indeed, many religious buildings were closed down; were stripped of land, furnishings, and decorations; and were used by the authorities as schools, meeting halls, or storage facilities. However, attempts were made to restructure or reengineer the meaning of some religious foci, such as communal houses and select temples, to support the nation's militarist and collectivist orientation (Luong 1994; Giebel 2001). Many religious edifices were used as shrines to a militaristic view of history. With religious iconography removed and superstitious practices such as the shaking out of divination sticks banned, many temples and communal houses throughout the south were converted to museums, whose displays of images, weapons, and other material relics of the recently concluded war promoted an official view of a nation fighting collectively to overcome adversity and invasion. In some temples images of Ho Chi Minh or other heroic figures from the resistance wars were installed to promote an example to the younger generation of the requisite qualities needed to progress on the new front of the economy.

Tentative shifts away from a socialist planned economy and an increase in private trade in the early 1980s were accompanied by a resurgence in fortune-telling, palm reading, physiognomy, mediumship, the casting of divination sticks, the republishing of occult manuals, the printing and importation of votive money, and the practice of making offerings to spirits. The unwelcome revival of such practices was strongly associated with the resurgent power of the marketplace. The vivid journalistic accounts written in the early 1980s reveal that the government, although able to mobilize the sympathies of a wide range of critical commentators, was fighting a losing battle, as a diverse range of uncoordinated religious activities swept the country. Practitioners who peddled "superstition," such as mediums, palm readers, and astrologers, were lampooned in cartoons and roundly condemned in editorials as lazy people who shunned productive labor or as charlatans exploiting ignorant people, causing physical harm and wasting money.[10]

This resurgence of "backward" or "bad" traditions was particularly associated with the cities rather than with rural areas. Such practices were associated with smugglers, black marketeers, and other economic lawbreakers based in urban centers and at communications nodes such as ports and border crossings. This formulation continued to position urban lifestyles as culturally alien, and urban-based religious practices were singled out as phenomena to be controlled and regularized. Concerns were expressed that the religious practice of the resurgent urban entrepreneurial and trading class reopened an avenue for U.S. or Chinese schemes of subversion (Bùi Thị Kim Quý 1986). One article cited the port city of Hải Phòng as especially vulnerable to schemes by foreigners and the enemy to sabotage the government by importing superstitious works (Kim Khúc 1981). There, the state's attempts to regulate the meaning of religious institutions sometimes met with unexpected setbacks. For example, in Hải Phòng, it was reported that temples such as Nghè Temple, worshiping heroine Lê Chân, and Lương Xâm Temple, worshiping Ngô Quyền, had been "remodeled to become places for the remembrance of national heroes, with the statues of Buddha there being removed to pagodas." However, the same article reported that when the local cultural service rebuilt the temple of Ngô Quyền to turn it into a "center for the education of the antiaggression tradition," those allegedly taking advantage of superstition to carry out their political designs spread the news of a dream in which God announced the forthcoming arrival of war (Kim Khúc 1981).

During this time, pilgrimages to the shrines to goddesses were also on the rise. Because of their increasing popular appeal, goddesses were singled out as evidence of the probable use by the enemy and reactionaries to undermine the achievements of the state. The Lady of the Realm, Lady Liễu Hạnh, and several other goddesses were identified in an article in the *People's Army Daily* as among the most "nonsensical," "obscurantist," and "dangerous" instances of the revival of "superstition":

> The Phủ Giầy Festival in Hà Nam Ninh [commemorating the goddess Liễu Hạnh], a festival smacking of superstition, which was once abolished, has now been held again; and on certain days thousands of people came there to worship. Likewise the Princess Sư festival in An Giang is also a gathering of superstitious people, and it draws tens of thousands of worshipers every year. In Hải Phòng, there is the "Fairies" festival, and in Thái Bình there has emerged the Hóa Long–Di Lặc religious sect. In Hà Đông there is the tomb of an unknown harem girl under the Trịnh Mạc dynasty that draws thousands of worshipers on every first and fifteenth day of the lunar month. (*Quân Đội Nhân Dân* 1983)

With its title warning readers to "prevent the enemy from using superstition to bewitch the people and undermine us," this article also singled out the southern half of the country as a place where "the practice of superstitious rites and fortune-telling" was developing anew, where families were again setting up shrines and altars and rebuilding village temples in honor of local gods.

Spirits and Liberalism

During the 1980s a new viewpoint was articulated; it construed the worship of goddesses such as the Lady of the Realm as a product of deeper ecological, historical, and cultural conditions in the region in which such worship took place. Beginning early in the decade, studies of the southernmost part of the country attributed the rich and diverse religious life of this area to its status as a frontier zone, not subject to Confucianism or rigid court control and exposed to multiple ethnic and historical influences (Nguyễn Khánh Toàn et al. 1982). This approach gradually became more prevalent, and many locally distinctive beliefs and rites that were formerly considered primitive misunderstandings of nature (the worship of the earth, whale tiger, and goddesses), forms of feudal domination (sacrifices to the village tutelary deity), or superstitious practices (trance dancing, ritual singing, etc.), became reinterpreted as traditional folk beliefs *(tín ngưỡng dân gian truyền thống)*, folk culture *(văn hóa dân gian)*, and southern spiritual culture *(văn hóa tâm linh Nam Bộ)* (Huỳnh Ngọc Trang et al. 1993a; Nguyễn Phương Thảo 1997; Nguyễn Đăng Duy 1997). No longer regarded as culturally marginal, goddesses such as the Lady of the Realm were rehabilitated as symbols of southern Vietnamese rural folk culture. Less than a decade after her festival had been described as a "dangerous" and "obscurantist" gathering of superstitious people (*Quân Đội Nhân Dân* 1983), the practice was labeled with the resoundingly positive category of folk belief (Nguyễn Công Bình et al. 1990; Thạch Phương et al. 1992). This categorization was casting the "folk" net wide indeed, for increasing numbers of those who were behind this revival were coming from urban areas.

The regime's new policy of economic liberalism was accompanied by a broadening of official conceptions of identity, beyond the confines of peasant struggle or resistance traditions, a trend becoming something of an urgent quest when the effect of the open door investment policies began to kick in. Many communal houses *(đình)* once regarded as tools of the feudal elite or forms of superstitious activity were embraced as fine examples of the nation's arts, traditions, and culture (Thạch Phương and Lê Trung Vũ 1995; Hà Văn Tấn and Nguyễn Văn Kự 1998). After more than a decade of closure and neglect, temples and shrines were reopened, repaired, and used again to host sacrifices and festivities. By the early 1990s many such places had been registered by the Ministry of Culture and Information as historical and cultural vestiges *(di tích lịch sử văn hóa)*. Visits by leaders and articles in state publishing organs kept these sites and their associated festivities in the public eye. Considered beautiful, distinctive, and full of the national character, they were to be the touchstones by which Vietnamese could remember who they were in the chaos of economic liberalization and the perils of cultural exchange. As Vũ Quang, head of Vietnam's religious affairs committee told a journalist in 1993, folk festivals are valued as "bringing the country back to the roots of our traditional culture and customs" (Hiebert 1994, 89). Many of the places formerly used as museums to commemorate military traditions were deemed cultural heritage *(di sản văn hóa)* to be preserved and to aid in the defense against the perceived threat of foreign cultural inundation. Although Vietnam's military war with the United States was long over and economic hostilities ended with the lifting of the U.S. trade embargo, Vietnam remained at war; and in this cultural battle, such buildings and their associated rites and festivities were in the front line.

Recognizing the psychic value religious practice might have in helping people earn a living in the market economy and negotiate the complexities of contemporary existence, Vietnamese leaders in the 1990s were increasingly prone to take a functionalist approach to culture. Party and state leaders described the nation's cultural heritage as an aid to forging a cohesive society, slowing the presumed breakdown in moral values and generating societal energy for development.[11] The state's view was that ceremonial and festive practices provide cultural moorings, equilibrium, and spiritual solace to a country rapidly embarking on a process of cultural opening, rapid economic growth, and dramatic reforms. Đoàn Lâm applied this perspective to the cult of female deities in Vietnam, which he recognized as a pragmatic approach to solving this-worldly problems as well as a way of imagining a moral community in which good actions are rewarded and evil punished (Đoàn Lâm 1999, 15). No longer regarded as an outmoded practice, an alien accretion, or a tool of foreign intervention, the practice of making offerings to such spirits was accorded a place in the here and now, even if only as a useful adjunct to the real world of the economy. Even the Hòa Hảo religion could be rehabilitated under this formula, in terms of its contribution as a psychological support to the nation's premier rice-exporting farmers (Phạm Bích Hợp 1999, 161).

Indicative of the investments made by the leadership in defining and policing the category of religion, local authorities were enjoined to keep a close hand on these developments. Phạm Như Cương stressed that Political Bureau Resolution 24 (1990) spelled out that "religious morality has many features appropriate to the building of a new society." However, this recognition did not indicate that the government had abandoned its ambition to steer religion in the direction it saw appropriate. Cương noted that a resolution of the 1998 Fifth Central Conference on culture ruled that policies toward religion "should encourage thoughts of equality, love of humanity, and benevolence in religion" (Phạm Như Cương 2001, 66). Ho Chi Minh City–based Party stalwart Trần Bạch Đằng chastised his fellow Communist Party members for obstinately failing to recognize the many contributions made by Vietnam's religions in helping the needy and alleviating suffering (2001, 39). However, Đằng still mapped out the realm of "wholesome" *(lành mạnh)* religion from the domain of "superstition," which causes harm to society (2001, 38). These comments indicate that such leaders have been loath to relinquish their paternalistic role of determining which beliefs are acceptable and which are to be rejected as inappropriate to their society.

Well into the *đổi mới* (liberal reform) era, emphasis has been retained on refining and shaping what are seen as positive expressions of religious culture and expelling negative aspects. A large contingent of police has been posted at big pilgrimage sites such as the one to the Lady of the Realm to clamp down on thieves and political disturbances but also to deter mediums and fortune-tellers (figure 3). The site is today full of posters and billboards announcing that mediumship is a crime. In 2002 local authorities at the Perfume Pagoda in northern Vietnam went as far as to tear down the shrines built around the site by independent practitioners and religious entrepreneurs, who were accused of trying to profit from religious activities. Copies of a resolution passed in 1998 aimed at "realizing a civilized lifestyle in spiritual and religious activities" are posted in various places of worship. The resolution states that the duty of custodians of temples and shrines is to clearly understand the history and tales about the site they maintain, and it warns them and visitors to desist from a whole range of superstitious activities. It also underlines that religious and spiritual activities are not to take place in sites such as train stations, markets, flower gardens, places of study, and workplaces, but should be restricted to the proper places of worship. In some urban alleyways and residential concentrations, one sees announcements exhorting the building of a spiritual civilization and warning against participation in inappropriate superstitious practices.

Such interventions underline the role that the Vietnamese state plays in the constitution of the religious sphere and the regulation of religious practice. This role cautions one against setting up a dichotomy between religious practice and state power. Even large-scale practices such as pilgrimage occur within guidelines laid down by and enforced by the state. But the party's endorsement of the icons at the heart of such activities shows that it has come a long way from the days when such phenomena were to be excluded as obsolete vestiges from the past or alien cultural forms emanating from beyond the frontiers of the polity. What has occurred since the beginnings of reforms is

FIG. 3. Consulting a fortune-teller at the mausoleum of Lê Văn Duyệt

an act of domesticating, assimilating, and inducting these sometime unruly spirits into the service of the society, which is simultaneously reimagined as cosmopolitan, multicultural, and engaged in commerce as the ordinary business of the day. The Party's enthusiasm for goddesses who command a substantial following among southern marketeers and urban entrepreneurs points suggestively to the commercialization and urbanization of its own identity. Considered as the functional supports of Vietnam's urban-centric market economy and political system, these goddesses are now among the Party's key underwriters in sustaining its national project.

The Turn to Culture in an Era of Reform

The Party's embrace of the new creed of market economics and its embarkation on a program of drastic restructuring did have domestic critics, and the reforms were met with a kind of conservative backlash. A rising tide of cultural nationalism was noticeable in the early 1990s—in, for example, the neotraditionalist identifications espoused by some members of the urban population in the south around that time (P. Taylor 2001b). Ethnographers of other former socialist states have noted a similar upsurge in culturalist identifications that accompanied the dismantling of socialist structures and the introduction of economic reforms in such countries (e.g., Verdery 1996; Hann 1998; Bulag 1998). Far from leading to the effacement of cultural differences, the post–Cold War rise to global dominance of liberal market relations, a process known as globalization, has been accompanied by a new primordialism: a focus on ethnic, nationalist, religious, and indigenous identities that Friedman has attributed to the dissolution of the "encompassing structures" of imperialism of the colonial and Cold War variety (1994, 235). This somewhat unexpected turn toward cultural essences and identity politics has been equally evident in those countries, such as China, Cuba, and Vietnam, that have reinvented socialism, retaining socialist bureaucracies, state enterprises, and single-party rule while embarking on liberal economic reforms and expanded international relations. In the process they too have been confronted by a resurgence of cultural essentialism, including ethnonationalism (Gladney 1996), religious revival (Azicri 2000), and cultural nationalism (Barmé 1996).

By the 1990s the Vietnamese public sphere was given over to an urgently voiced and anxious preoccupation with cultural roots *(nguồn gốc văn hóa)* and national identity *(bản sắc dân tộc)*. Numerous books were published on the nature of Vietnamese identity, including dictionaries of Vietnamese culture, guides to traditional festivals and localities, and studies of folk beliefs, rites, and customs. A number of these were reprints of works that had been produced in periods of equivalent dynamism, cultural ferment, and escalating social tensions such as the colonial period and the era of the Republic. Perusing this literature, one is struck not only by the richness of Vietnam's religious culture and the cultural passions of its intellectuals but also by the fact that Vietnamese cultural anxieties were remarkably similar to those evident in other countries of Southeast Asia and further afield in the 1990s. Informing the endeavors of cultural researchers and commentators at the time was a sense of the dangers of cultural annihilation in the context of a surge in commercial activity, intensified transnational communications, and rapid urban development, which had all dramatically increased at the beginning of the decade. The open door *(mở cửa)* and liberal reform *(đổi mới)* policies were beginning to produce their anticipated effects of stimulating production and unleashing economic growth. The feeling that life was improving and possibilities expanding was widespread. Yet there was equally a sense of foreboding that such positive changes were accompanied by a downside: materialism, pragmatism, the cult of money, selfish individualism, social rifts, crime, corruption, and moral decline (P. Taylor 2001b). Even in such a place as Ho Chi Minh City, there was a strong feeling that Vietnam would need to fight to preserve its traditions, national essence, and distinctive psychology against the depredations of global culture.

This approach was particularly evident among those who worked in the city's cultural sector, whose role as culture brokers is in accordance with a strong vocational sense of being custodians of and instructors in the spiritual and cultural life of the collective. These included university-trained people, Party members, artists, craftspersons, teachers, and writers as well as many members of different religious orders and custodians of cultural sites such as museums and temples. It also included those working in the disciplines of folklore and ethnology. Vietnam's ethnologists have been described in the ethnographic record as agents of an assimilationist, progressivist state, involved in the dismantling of particularistic affiliations in the name of "the great unity" *(đại đoàn kết)*, a unified national culture (Evans 1985, 1992). However, in the early 1990s, one was just as likely to hear from them a critique of the harm done by former government policies to the nation's distinct culture. Southern-based intellectuals with whom I spoke in the early 1990s were concerned about the damage caused to the nation's indigenous religious culture by the postwar regime's flirtation with socialist policies. Making reference to the "Asian values" debates of the 1990s, some observed to me that the European roots of socialism made it incompatible with Vietnam's essentially Asian roots. Much of the work done by folklorists and ethnologists during this period was directed toward the cataloguing of ethnic and cultural diversity. The sentiment informing many such endeavors was the desire to preserve a traditional identity under threat. This was clearly evident in the meanings many invested in the popular worship of goddesses such as the Lady of the Realm.

Mothering the Nation

One of the most interesting aspects of the culturalist turn in the Vietnamese intellectual world in the *đổi mới* era has been the focus on female deities. The first substantive work devoted to this topic identified seventy-five goddesses venerated in the country (Đỗ Thị Hảo and Mai Thị Ngọc Chúc 1984). The phenomenon of goddess worship stimulated learned discussion among cultural commentators like few other subjects and gave rise to numerous theories. One of the most common hypotheses was that goddesses represented an anthropomorphization of natural forces of growth and reproduction (Do Lai Thuy 1996). Another interpretation connected the contemporary cult to ancient and culturally distinctive practices of wet-rice farming, representing the Vietnamese people's close links to the nation's land and waters (Ngô Đức Thịnh 1996, 12; Nguyễn Phương Thảo 1997, 181). True to their socialist heritage, many Vietnamese ethnologists and folklorists adhered to an evolutionary schema of development into which goddess worship was slotted as an enduring survival from what was claimed to be Vietnam's primitive or matriarchal period of history (Ngô Đức Thịnh 1996). Such analyses marked goddess worship as an indigenous belief, outlasting foreign and elite cultural accretions such as Confucianism. Among the beings venerated in this pantheon are female heroes of Vietnam's traditions of nation building and defense, and some commentators celebrated the role women have played in resistance to foreign incursions from the era of Chinese colonization to the recent past (Hà Hùng Tiến 1997; Nguyễn Minh San 1996). Many underlined the national typicality of such practices. Some ethnologists viewed goddess worship as the veneration of ancestors whose meritorious acts had served the country, a practice considered by some as a quintessentially Vietnamese custom (Đặng Nghiêm Vạn 1998). As an instance of the cult of spirits *(đạo thờ thần)*, goddess worship was considered by one author as an "authentically Vietnamese religion" *(một đạo thuần túy Việt Nam)* (Toan Ánh 1997, 109).[12] Studies of goddesses worshiped in the southern third of Vietnam (Nam Bộ) showed a growing appreciation for the regional complexity of the country. The culturally hybrid Lady of the Realm was regarded by some folklorists as typical of the multiethnic, constantly mutating cultural landscape of southern Vietnam, an original cultural accomplishment that enriched the storehouse of Vietnamese national culture.[13] Yet despite reflecting regional differences, Bà Đen, the Black Lady of Tây Ninh, was nevertheless described as a Vietnamese culture hero, and her veneration an instance of the beauty of Vietnam's traditional culture (Nguyễn Minh San 1996, 306). Studies that stressed the aesthetic dimension of goddess worship often gave this a patriotic slant. In going on pilgrimage, people sought to experience incomparable beauty or a moment of the sublime, or to celebrate the skill and creativity of the nation's traditional artisans (Thạch Phương and Lê Trung Vũ 1995). On socially functional grounds, the festivals to goddesses were seen as an elaboration of traditional harvest festivals or mating rituals, phenomena that had preceded and outlasted Chinese and court overlays (Do Lai Thuy 1996). On this theme could be heard frequent rhapsodies about the role of festivals as opportunities for boys and girls to meet and for the sanctioned breaking of taboos, thought by one writer to revitalize society (Đào Thế Hùng). Festivals were also viewed as integrative forces, uniting disparate sectors of society and preserving meaning though time (Trương Thìn 1990, 24). Similarly, they were described as cultural processes that reflected and reinforced a distinctly Vietnamese communalist spirit, particularly in rural areas (Hồ Hoàng Hoa 1998).

In short, although they have espoused a variety of explanations for this phenomenon, Vietnamese ethnologists and folklorists have found in the popularity of goddess worship clear signs of the endurance of the nation's traditions and of its cultural integrity. Questions of origins, survivals, identity, function, structure, and reproduction—all of them familiar concerns in the intellectual history of the anthropology of religion—have been turned consistently to the relationship between these religious symbols and the nation.

The selection of feminine images to carry the burden of representation is not unique to Vietnamese nationalism. As Yuval-Davis notes, the figure of a woman, be she Mother India or La Patrie, is frequently taken to symbolize the spirit of the national collectivity (1998, 29). The Vietnamese nation, like many others, is imagined as an enlarged version of the household, its cohesion symbolized through images drawn from the realm of kinship and familial politics.[14] The selection of feminine images to symbolize such qualities as regeneration, nurturance, purity, continuity, sacrifice, duty, and constancy, which are held to sustain the nation, draws on this familial metaphor reflecting the expectations placed upon women in Vietnam to reproduce and sustain families and embody their family's honor. The ethnogenetic female spirit Âu Cơ is described in school texts as the mother *(mẹ)* of the Vietnamese nation.[15] Other tales about these goddesses mention their resistance to rape or abduction, likening the nation's integrity to a woman's defense of her physical security or chastity. In times of cultural upheaval, the focus on femininity has been particularly acute, so that during wars of decolonization, resistance heroines such as the Trưng sisters and Lady Triệu featured prominently in nationalist discourse in both northern and southern regimes.[16]

In the 1990s, the renewed interest in such goddesses came at a time

FIG. 4. The shrine to Dinh Cô on the beach at Long Hải

when many in Vietnam were experiencing rapid change and conceptualizing it as a threat. This is similar to the way images of woman as mother symbols have become prominent in the culturally turbulent post-Soviet states of Eastern Europe, as rallying points for assertions of national and ethnic unity and survival (Marsh 1998). In Vietnam, during a time when fears were being voiced about the risks of social disintegration and cultural inundation resulting from the regime's "renovation" and "open door" policies (P. Taylor 2001b), goddesses such as the Lady of the Realm were taken as touchstones of cultural identity, and their well-attended annual festivals indicated in a reassuring way that Vietnam retained its traditional integrity. It is noteworthy in this context that many of the goddesses singled out by cultural commentators dwell on the fringes of the polity, like the Lady of the Realm and the Black Lady, enshrined on the border with Cambodia; Dinh Cô, venerated on the southern Vietnamese coast in Long Hải (figure 4); and Mẫu Thượng Ngàn, in the highlands of the northern border province of Lạng Sơn (Nguyễn Minh San 1999). In the compelling imagery of Nira Yuval-Davis (1997), such feminine symbols serve as "border guards" of the collectivity's identity.

While from one perspective a goddess such as the Lady of the Realm may be considered at the front line of the imaginatively threatened polity, her selection as a symbol of the nation's cultural identity also comes from her being as far from the political center as possible and thus remote from changes sweeping through the capital, elite political circles, marketplaces, and streets. Certainly in diagnosing the reasons for the loss of the country *(mất nước)* to foreign imperialists and the weaknesses in resistance to them, Vietnamese anticolonialist nationalists have in the past reserved their strongest criticisms for centers or nodes such as the court, markets, and cities, whose cultural orientation has been variously condemned as derivative, imported, weak, debilitating, depraved, hybridized, outmoded, or unrealistic. From this perspective, the countryside has been seen as a wellspring of undiluted, uncorrupted, or vital traditions.[17] Examples of rural *(thôn quê)* or folk beliefs such as the Lady of the Realm are thought to remain unscathed, out of reach, or are considered internal, the wellsprings, the roots, the origins, the uncorrupted, the still pure. What might be termed protective nationalism has sustained a fascination with folklore, customs, rural festivals, handicrafts, folk songs, neglected ritual practices, and the culture of regions, localities, and ethnic groups. Formulations such as "our peasants," "our minorities," or indeed "our women" reflect a proprietary attitude and a reassuring relationship to phenomena of the hinterland, the cultural interior, through accumulated knowledge of which cultural nationalists reproduce their assertions of social centrality.[18]

With a symbolically vital function of this kind, entities such as the Lady of the Realm have been considered vulnerable objects, whose meaning needs to be carefully tended and maintained. Commentators have placed emphasis on how to refine and shape what are seen as positive expressions of popular engagements with these icons and expel negative aspects that have persisted or grown up around them. Published commentaries on the Lady of the Realm's festival make critical references to superstitious practices such as fortune-telling or trance possession in the precincts of her shrine. These are regarded as unbefitting an important historical and cultural heritage site or "customary" practice. Nguyễn Phương Thảo attempted to detach the furtive acts of mediumship on Sam Mountain from the real meaning of the Lady of the Realm's festival, which he saw to be an agricultural rite (1997, 210).[19] Folklorist Nguyễn Chí Bền considered fortune-telling, divination, and the acquisition of amulets, still practiced in the shrine to the Lady of the Realm, as the work of opportunists exploiting the sanctity of a shrine to engage in an execrable "trade in spirits" *(buôn thần bán thánh)*. He described these as "parasitical" *(ký sinh)* activities, strictly outside the true structure of her folk festival (Nguyễn Chí Bền 2000, 188). Some commentators dwelt on the simple and wholesome quality of communal festivals as expressions of folk culture, reminding readers of their former appropriation by feudal elites who used festivals to prop up their power or compete in extravagant expenditure

(Thạch Phương et al. 1992, 86, 93). In a similar way many commentators lamented the cutthroat prices charged at the stalls around the shrine to the Lady of the Realm and the mindless commercialization of festivals. Observers of the festival to the goddess Dinh Cô on the coast at Long Hải decried "inappropriate" gaudy and faddish elements such as jeans, neon lights, and popular music as swamping or mingling haphazardly with its locally distinctive, elegant, and time-tested aesthetic practices (Thạch Phương et al. 1992, 89).

The scholars generating this critique are inheritors of Vietnam's rich, albeit diffuse, traditions of scholars and bureaucrats acting as cultural authorities, and their sometimes heavy-handed cultural policing is hardly novel. However, one can look to recent changes in their cultural and social environment for a new set of factors influencing their interpretation. In the 1990s as the political economy shifted to a decentralized commercial basis, people in such positions experienced a highly destabilizing loss of power. As intellectuals, they were witnesses to a society changing at a breakneck pace, moving in directions that often seemed very much out of control. Idealistic, romantic, and conservative, they consequently projected a static image of Vietnamese culture. Many were literal in their view of folk practices as ancient survivals. Their studies of folk religion were turned to the arrest of time.

One notable feature of ethnological discourse in Vietnam, as elsewhere, is the predominantly urban origins of its exponents. This origin reflects the overwhelmingly urban location of museums, research institutes, universities, and libraries—places sustaining ethnological work. Also home to the majority of the nation's newspapers, television stations, publishing houses, cultural associations, and theaters, urban areas are the centers for the reproduction of national public culture: they are where those who imagine the nation, and sustain it with their symbolic reproductive work, are situated. While globalization is sometimes portrayed as a challenge to borders and territoriality (Appadurai 1996), it is not at the territorial borders but in the cities where the imagined nation encounters its greatest challenges. This is particularly true in Ho Chi Minh City, Vietnam's commercial capital and center of technology, financial production, and support services. As such it has many of the characteristics of a global city, in which translocal economic forces have more weight than local policies in shaping urban economy, social structure, and cultural identity (Sassen 1991). Urban areas such as this are deluged by strong flows of peoples, goods, images, ideas, affectations, and orientations that know no borders, following paths opened through migration, trade, military occupation, and colonialism. Among the greatest contemporary cultural challenges to Vietnam's literate bureaucratic elite are the proliferation of video cassettes, tapes, and compact discs; the mushrooming of discos, karaoke saloons, and music cafes; the explosion of glossy magazines and advertising imagery; the rise of supermarkets and shopping malls; and the growth of cyber cafes. All of these phenomena are overwhelmingly concentrated in urban centers. For those who define the national orientation through the work of culture, these unfamiliar cultural codes and modes challenge their ability to reproduce messages of relevance to their national constituency. They have become tongue-tied and inept in the face of rapid cultural change. And few of their traditionally defined constituency are indeed listening, as Vietnam's youth are patched into more heady and highly accessible cultural offerings from MTV to Hello Kitty (Marr 1996). In many respects Ho Chi Minh City represents an "informational city" (Castells 1989) marked by rapid flows of information and proliferation of cultural signals. In such urban contexts, Setha Low has noted, there is a tendency for individuals to react by representing their values and interests through the reassertion of primary identities of self-identified communities; such reassertion results in the rejection of other communities, increasing racism and xenophobia (1996, 394).

Vietnam ethnologists' and folklorists' commentary on goddesses can be situated in this context, underlining the need to understand the discipline of anthropology not only as incorporating the study of cities (urban anthropology) but as a project that is conducted in the city. In a country such as Vietnam, where more than 70 percent of the population lives in rural areas, the urban cast of ethnology is significant. Putatively about a rural-based goddess, in many ways the experience to which the studies of Vietnamese ethnologists and folklorists give voice is the complexity of urban existence. A view of temples and festivals as bases of unchanged traditions reflects in a romantic (lãng mạn) manner urbanites' idealization of the countryside and longing for a stable point of purchase in their rapidly changing environment. Given its articulation from the ever-mutating world of Vietnam's cities, this preoccupation with cultural constancy is understandable. A view of folk festivals as simple and time-honored can be seen as an imaginative antidote to the complexity and unpredictability of urban life. The integrative function attributed to folk beliefs and practices reflects with some poignancy the perspective of the intellectual exponents of a formerly bureaucratic, military, and collectivist society confronting apparent social fragmentation, increasing individualism, and seeming cultural disorder. As the effects of International Monetary Fund– and World Bank–inspired reforms have taken the economic levers out of the hands of former societal leaders and shifted the center of gravity to the marketplace, there has been, if anything, a renewed emphasis on remembering past sacrifices, the value of the communal, the respect for old knowledge. A growing generation gap, migration to the cities, increased crime, and changing gender roles, particularly pronounced in the cities, have been seen by the society's teachers, scholars, and other moral preceptors as symptomatic of a cultural crisis, and this view too helps explain refocused attention on goddesses as exemplary icons of traditional morality. With Vietnam's cities the main nodes for foreign investors and new foreign cultural impacts, and home to the troubling feeling that cultural sovereignty is being lost, the search for viable forms of national inclusion is nowhere more urgent. If goddesses serve the function of patrolling the nation's imaginatively threatened boundaries, nowhere have these boundaries been more at risk than in the urban world.

Conclusion

The cultural nationalist approach to goddesses in Vietnam, which positions these symbols as ancient and nationally typical, reflects the key role played by members of the literate elite in using symbols to inculcate political affiliations in sections of the wider population (Gellner 1983; A. Smith 1986; Eriksen 1995). Such symbolic practices have been noted as characteristic of the Vietnamese Communist movement during the colonial period (Woodside 1976; Marr 1981). In the socialist era, which was marked by several significant policy shifts, Vietnamese social scientists continued to identify cultural elements that symbolically expressed the current national orientation, be it building socialism, striving for national unification, promulgating economic liberalism, or aiming for industrialization and modernization. Vietnamese ethnologists' and folklorists' systematic linkage of such symbols to the nation hence owes something to their role as representatives of the nation-state.[20] There is a much older history of this in Vietnam's bureaucratic polity, whose officially licensed interpreters have helped regulate and standardize local practices so that they emit messages appropriate to the state's concerns. Nowhere has this been more evident and urgent than at the margins of the polity. Over time these margins have shifted according to how the political center has been defined. Thus from the highland areas and southern frontier and physical margins one has seen the frontier shift inward to include cities, ethnic sojourners such as the Chinese, and market centers and also change its outward complexion in accordance with the redrawing of national lines, the changing of international alliances, and the redefinition of regionalist identities.

However, there is more to this story than one of paid, politically coerced or culturally like-minded intellectuals following the state's script. It is true that the views of this influential group of commentators are often aligned with those of the government. Yet one wonders if this convergence occurs mainly because intellectuals are paid by the state and share an affinity with the Party's traditions of paternalistic, bureaucratic, and culturally assimilationist rule. An alternative hypothesis is that the state in Vietnam has itself become increasingly urbanized, giving expression to powerful interests and its representatives sharing the cultural anxieties of those based in the economic strongholds and tumultuous cultural contact zones of the big cities. Clearly evident among intellectuals too is a response to recent reconfigurations of the social and cultural landscape they inhabit. Their anthropologies are a reaction to the pressures faced by a scholarly elite in the country's rapidly transforming urban centers. Rather than seeing in such religious symbols a popular realm beyond politics, perhaps one can appreciate how they figure in the articulation of social differences, including those that divide the state apparatus. Perhaps there are more subtle borders than those of national territory to which these goddesses give expression. Placing them in sociological context, one sees their interests in these goddesses as also giving voice to status, ethnicity, gender, and class-marking distinctions. Such considerations raise the possibility that the nonscripted views of urban-based scholarly commentators are not in fact the only views of such kind; indeed, given the complexity of cities, they are not even likely to be typical of the perspective of urban people.

2

The Ethnicity
of Efficacy

The Lady of the Realm is sometimes described as a spiritual patron of local Vietnamese resistance against foreign incursions. Such accounts situate her in a saga of antiforeign resistance, a view of the Vietnamese past common to Communist and nationalist perspectives, although one downplayed in recent times in an era of cooperation with foreign companies, governments, and transnational organizations. In the story most commonly cited in publications about the goddess, she is credited with extending support to the early-nineteenth-century hero Thoại Ngọc Hầu in his fight against enemy troops.[1] According to legend, the Lady of the Realm responded to the prayers of the mandarin's wife for the success of her husband's project; in gratitude, a shrine to the goddess was built.

A similar story, although less well known, was told to me by a Ho Chi Minh City businessman who regularly came to buy fish in the province where the goddess' shrine is. He said that the Lady of the Realm was the wife of a general who had defended Vietnam against the enemy. While her husband was away at war, she prayed for his safety and managed their home. Unfortunately, her husband was killed in battle. Even after his death, she remained faithful to him. The local people venerated her as a model of virtuous wifely conduct. This story emphasizes women's personal contribution to the defense of the nation, the goddess a symbol of fidelity in a long lineage of soldiers' wives whom scholars since the time of Nguyễn Trãi have eulogized.

Vietnam's history of resistance to foreign invasion can indeed be illustrated by many events in the southern region's history. It is a narrative related not only in museums, books, and popular stories but in the religious sphere as well, by the enshrinement of several national heroes *(anh hùng dân tộc)* and the state's memorials to revolutionary heroes and martyrs *(anh hùng liệt sĩ).* However, the formulation "antiforeign resistance" falls far short of encapsulating the entire history of the region. For instance, it fails to take into account Vietnam's colonization of formerly Cham and Cambodian lands; the alternative identities espoused by minority ethnic groups in the region; the various forms of collaboration with resident foreigners including occupying armies; intraethnic group hostilities and wars; and the importance in the region of foreign sources of wealth such as investment, remittances, and aid. If one looks to the types of religious symbols that are popular among residents of the southern plain, one sees that among those spirits and forces regarded as most efficacious in addressing the concerns of everyday life, the cultural legacy of groups that are not associated with Vietnamese resistance traditions is particularly evident. This is true of the Lady of the Realm, who reflects an extraordinary set of displacements and overlays. The multicultural dynamics of this symbol make us rethink narratives that enshrine resistance at the heart of Vietnamese culture and privilege the viewpoint of Vietnam's majority ethnic group, the Kinh or Việt.[2] Instead she exemplifies counter-readings of history as, among other things, the appropriation and positive evaluation of, the accomplishments of other ethnic groups.

Some Vietnamese folklorists note that southern Vietnamese goddesses such as the Lady of the Realm combine influences from a variety of regional and ethnic folk beliefs (Huỳnh Ngọc Trảng et al. 1993a; Nguyễn Đăng Duy 1997, 140). Distinctive features inflecting their worship such as ritual dancing *(múa bóng),* performances of *hát bội* (a quasi-religious operatic form), and use of the title *bà chúa* comprise evidence of cultural borrowings from the Khmer, Cham, and ethnic Chinese cultures (Huỳnh Ngọc Trảng 1993; Nguyễn Phương Thảo 1997; Đông Vĩnh 1999). This diversity is seen by such theorists as typical of the heterogeneous cultural makeup of southern Vietnam. In the late 1980s and early 1990s, there was a flowering of appreciation for the multiethnic, "constantly renovating," and hybridized cultural scene of southern Vietnam (e.g., Nguyễn Công Bình et al. 1990). Such renditions differ from those of the war years, when the accounts by Vietnamese nationalists and foreign social scientists portrayed the Mekong delta as a seat of ethnic Kinh culture and characterized issues such as colonialism and post-colonial wars as the confrontation between an indigenous Vietnamese culture and foreign cultures. This sensitivity to multiple sources of local cultural identity represents a step toward the conceptual decolonization of the Mekong delta.

Nevertheless, such inclusive ideas are often at odds with the kinds of partial investments that people make into symbols such as the Lady of the Realm. Flying in the face of the cosmopolitan identity with which some folklorists furnish her, people's engagements with her frequently proceed through ethnically compartmentalized identifications.[3] This chapter aims to show how piecemeal interpretations motivate believers and commentators alike and to draw attention to her role in the variously imagined ethnohistory of southern Vietnam. A fundamental aspect of her popularity is her ability to simultaneously support a significant divergence of views. The growth of her shrine as a translocal pilgrimage center has indeed led to a melding of belief and to people's exposure to different conceptions as to her identity. However, her increasing centrality to the spiritual life of the region has also drawn her into the articulation and reinforcement of ethnic distinctions.

The Ethnic Dynamics of a Found Object

A study by the French archaeologist Malleret concludes that the statue to the Lady of the Realm in Vĩnh Tế village, Châu Đốc, is rendered as a feminine likeness over the stone statue of the god Shiva, which was pre-Angkorean Khmer in origin (1943, 19).[4] This shrine on Sam Mountain was just one of a great many sites explored by this archaeologist in the latter years of the French colony of Cochinchina. Within the shrine, to the right of the goddess, there is a large stone lingam, covered in cloth. Other relatively anonymous stone linga are scattered around the mountain. These were taken as further evidence that the mountain had formed part of the religious geography of the Khmer world (Malleret 1959, 38). Mabbett and Chandler describe mountains as important sacred sites to the Khmer. Images of the Indian god Shiva, they argue, were indigenized in Cambodia as *nak ta*, or ancestral spirits of the neighborhood, and were venerated on hilltops. These authors note that the spirits' energies are most accessible on the summits of hills and indeed that "the shrines of spirit cults have been erected in high places throughout Khmer history." The form or ingredients of these shaivite images and Shiva linga might well have been imported from India; however, these authors see them as having been localized into a system of Khmer folk beliefs as protective deities (Mabbett and Chandler 1995, 110).

An elderly woman, a resident of the hillside village where the shrine is situated and who identified herself as ethnic Kinh, told me that the mountain at the base of which the shrine to the goddess stands had once been an island in the ocean off the coast. Her brow furrowing with concentration, she told me the following story:

> As the sea receded, people were able to reach it by foot and settle in the area. Long before the road leading up to the peak was built, local people

discovered Her Ladyship's image on the top of the mountain. She appeared to them in a dream, saying, "I am the Lady of the Realm, above all other goddesses." She told them she was sitting on top of the mountain and that she wanted to be brought down. That must have been about five hundred years ago.... She was a Miên sculpture. One arm was broken off; the other rested on one thigh. After being brought down, her face was repainted to make it more beautiful, and she was dressed in robes. (from fieldnotes 1998)

Although she extended the Vietnamese occupation of the Mekong delta by at least two centuries, this woman's story is one of the rare oral tales I have heard that refer to the statue of the Lady of the Realm as Khmer in origin.[5] The most popular accounts about its origins suggest no relationship between it and the Khmer occupants of the delta. Pilgrims at the goddess' shrine in Châu Đốc were not a little disturbed when I suggested the possibility that she was of Khmer origins. Many of the published accounts to which they had access give the statue a different origin. Some stories say the statue was brought "from afar," perhaps by an Indian prince or Indian missionaries (Lê Ngọc Bích 1994, 6). Such stories see her as a human product but discount any local community as involved in her creation.[6] Others speculate that the statue might have been on the mountaintop for many thousands of years, it being unclear how she got there.[7] Far more popular were the oral stories I heard that gave her no human origin: she just emerged as the water level dropped; or, composed of "living stone," she and the mountain on which she was perched "grew" out of the sea. As naturally emerging from the sea, the statue came with no strings attached. Alternatively, she grew from a small rock, an example of the phenomenon of growing stones mentioned by Mus (Mus 1933, 10). Popular mythology surrounding the goddess thus differs significantly from foreign scholars' histories of the much-venerated figure as an achievement of local Khmer culture. The distant, ancient, or supposedly natural origins of the goddess finesse such questions as whose property she might have been, or even who might have been responsible for her creation.

The reported discovery of the goddess lonely and abandoned on the peak of an island or mountain makes no reference to the presence of indigenous people in the region. "I've read her biography," said Son, an underemployed motorcycle taxi driver in Ho Chi Minh City. "In the distant past, the whole region was covered by seawater. It was only when the waters started to recede that people came across her image, seated on the top of an island. When the waters went down further, the island became a hill and people built a pagoda and started to worship her." This recurrent image evokes the emergence of

the delta lands from the ocean as a result of alluvial sedimentation and oceanic dynamics, a process that commenced about five thousand years ago (Lê
Bá Thảo 1997, 526). It also recalls the periodic draining of the inland sea that
covers the Mekong plain during the annual floods, a cycle that continues to
this day. However, the image of new land emerging pristine from the sea
equally reprises the fiction employed by agents of the Vietnamese state with
respect to the Mekong lands annexed from Cambodia, as unpeopled wilderness *(đất hoang vu)*.[8] A recent textbook on Vietnam's geographical regions
still describes the Mekong delta as a "deserted region," which, within three
hundred years of Vietnamese settlement, "has been turned into a rich and
prosperous agricultural region" (Lê Bá Thảo 1997, 530). This ideological displacement of Khmer and other people from the lower Mekong delta has resonances in other popular religious imagery as well. The commemoration in
various temples in the Mekong delta of the Vietnamese general Nguyễn Hữu
Cảnh (1650–1700), who "pacified" *(dẹp yên)* Cambodia in the late eighteenth century, as a "pioneer opening up new lands" *(anh hùng khai phá)*,[9]
and the cult of the tiger as powerful protector symbolizing nature tamed are
examples of the way the most cogent challenge to the new settlers in the delta
has been imaginatively grasped as a confrontation with nature rather than
with other cultures. While there is no doubt that they reflect people's historical experiences of a sparsely populated region, images of the pioneering
general and the tamed tiger are also cultural lenses through which those who
identify as Kinh people have continued to imagine their settlement of the
delta as a dramatic confrontation with unpeopled nature.

Stories describing the miraculous way the statue of the Lady of the Realm
was supposedly brought into the sphere of Vietnamese religious practice are
supportive of a version of Vietnamese manifest destiny in the Mekong delta.
Most pilgrims, locals, and published commentators are able to relate the tale
of how the goddess' statue came to be discovered. A local girl was possessed
by a spirit who announced her identity as the Lady of the Realm. The spirit
made known her location and her desire to be venerated. Following this,
the statue, in the form of a woman, was discovered on the summit of Sam
Mountain. Efforts by forty strong men to lift it failed. The goddess re-
appeared, saying that only nine virgin girls could carry her down the mountain. When they reached the base of the hill, where the shrine currently
stands, she became magically heavy again, indicating her decision to stay in
this place, and thus they were obliged to deposit her there. The goddess' reputed possession of a local village girl through whom she revealed herself
and issued instructions for worship is a myth that legitimates newly arrived,

Vietnamese-court-sponsored settlers as the elected beneficiaries of the local goddess. In another commonly told story the goddess displays miraculous force to resist being taken from the mountain by foreign troops. This account attributes the statue's one broken arm to early-nineteenth-century Siamese raiders, who supposedly damaged the statue while trying unsuccessfully to remove her; the foreign perpetrators were killed on the spot by the injured goddess. Such stories lend supernatural sanctions to Vietnamese claims to the Mekong delta, the goddess nominating this group for her sponsorship in preference to the other contenders.

The ultimate instance of the Vietnamese assimilation of this found object are the stories about the statue that recruit it into the pantheon of spirits abetting the defense of the nation. The most striking example is the tale attributing the goddess with protecting Thoại Ngọc Hầu; this tale mobilizes the statue against none other than the Khmer themselves (e.g., Vietnamese Women's Museum 1993, 29) and places the Khmer among the ranks of foreign aggressors, when the Vietnamese court's push into the delta and domination of Cambodian politics makes the reverse case a more compelling interpretation. The shrine and the festivities in honor of the goddess are roped into an epic of cultural and military resistance that unites the Vietnamese people, north to south. This is an example of appropriating other cultures' symbols the better to dominate them. Ideas of the goddess as a patron of resistance against the Khmer, repeated in officially sanctioned publications, do little to diminish the climate of ethnic tension in parts of the Mekong delta in Vietnam, where sentiments expressing fear and disparagement of both Cambodia and the local Khmer are common among the Kinh population. This image of the goddess feeds the bellicose association many locals still make between the ethnic Khmer and the Khmer Rouge; the latter group are remembered for their cross-border incursions and genocidal violence in Cambodia in the late 1970s.[10]

Appropriating Khmer Beliefs

While often regarded with fear or disdain by local members of Vietnam's ethnic majority, the ethnic Khmer are widely considered to be holders of valued occult knowledge and powers. The inverse of the stereotypes that Kinh people sometimes espouse of the Khmer as lazy or unintelligent are their expressions of esteem for the religiosity of Khmer monks, as well as Khmer knowledge of magic and sorcery and esoteric knowledge of medicinal plants. Many Khmer pagodas function as dispensaries of medicinal cures, and Khmer monks are approached for amulets and other forms of magical protection. Khmer children, who frequent the streets of Ho Chi Minh City as beggars, are said to have a mysterious power in their stare to force those from whom they beseech money to part with it, however unwillingly (Christophe Robert, pers. comm.). The powers attributed to the Khmer are associated with beliefs that accord their lands a mysterious and conditional potency. For example, ethnic Kinh people sometimes say that it is easy to make money in Cambodia or in places formerly belonging to Cambodia such as Phú Quốc Island but that it is impossible to repatriate the wealth made in such places. Similarly one can have children there but never bring them home.

Ethnic Kinh migrants who settled in the flat southern plain and occasional limestone mountain of the lower Mekong delta have also taken on many of the beliefs of those whom they live among and have displaced. The use of protective amulets, tattoos, medicines, and charms that are deemed to be Khmer in origin is still widespread and is integrated with other practices. For example, in the coastal province of Bạc Liêu, home to a significant minority of Khmer people, I met an ethnic Kinh man who had been orphaned at an early age. He had been taken in by a Khmer monk and grew up in a pagoda surrounded by Khmer magic practices. A devout Buddhist, he displayed inscribed Khmer amulets in a prominent place between his domestic ancestral altar and altar to a Mahayana-tradition Buddha image. He said he prayed to the inscriptions for success whenever he went to deal with government officials. Similarly, many ethnic Kinh fish raisers in the Mekong River display bamboo altars to the Khmer protector spirit Ông Tà on the front porch of their raft houses. These altars are made of a piece of bamboo, the top section of which is split into slivers, which are bent into a goblet shape and sharpened like a multipronged fish spear. The prongs are joined together by a loop of knotted red thread. The spirit is worshiped by these river dwellers to protect their families and ensure their livelihood.

Nevertheless, the ethnic majority's engagements with the religious practices of the Khmer have not always served to bolster recognition of the latter group's claims to indigenous status in the Mekong delta. The ethnic Kinh seldom visit the Therevada Buddhist monasteries of the delta's Khmer inhabitants. Instead, they go to pagodas in the Buddhist Mahayana tradition, which are less remote. Even in those few provinces of Vietnam where Khmer culture remains a vital tradition, most of the Khmer monasteries are situated well away from the center of rural settlements, where the port, market, and administrative buildings are found and where the temples patronized by ethnic Vietnamese and Chinese cluster. Khmer monasteries are usually in poor, marginal lands, and the poverty of the communities that support them often accounts for their dilapidated condition. Some ethnic Khmer also accuse the Kinh majority of actively marginalizing their unique religious culture, of appropriating monastery lands for political or economic reasons. However, the appropriation of Khmer religious sites can have the reverse effect. Sometimes a Khmer monastery achieves a degree of recognition among other groups as in some way possessing special or magical properties. One such monastery is Wat Mahatup, otherwise known as Bat Pagoda (Chùa Dơi) in Sóc Trăng province. The monastery owes its name to its large colony of fruit bats, which sleep in the canopy of the monastery's mulberry tree grove during the daylight hours. When I visited it in the late 1990s, two chartered pilgrimage tour buses were parked in the shade beside the monastery. At the entrance to the monastery was a collection of cafés, restaurants, and kiosks, and across the road was a karaoke bar. Unlike a great many Khmer monasteries, this one was in good condition, freshly painted and brightly decorated. One of the reasons for this was that it had acquired a reputation among people from far and wide, in particular those from other ethnic groups, as a place of magical power.

Beside the main worship hall was a smaller shrine to a spirit whom the resident monks told me was Bà Đen, the Black Lady. According to them, she was a Khmer goddess, the self-same spirit enshrined on a large hill near the Cambodian border, to the northwest of Ho Chi Minh City. The shrine to this goddess in the grounds of their monastery was known for curing all kinds of diseases, protecting people from physical harm, and sponsoring them in their works. Recently, this particular statue of the goddess had acquired a reputation throughout the region as being able to prevent traffic accidents. As the numbers of deaths and injuries increased on Vietnam's busy roads, many people were inclined to see the cause of such misfortune in the malign spirits residing in the vehicle, be it a motorbike or bus. The services of the monastery's resident monks were contracted to purify vehicles that had been involved in an accident by sprinkling them with consecrated water taken from the goddess' altar and by planting incense offerings in joints in the vehicles' plastic and metal molding.

The popular attention accorded to this spirit would appear to heighten the profile of a symbol that the ethnic Khmer residents of the monastery identify with their own indigenous culture. However, when I asked the ethnic Vietnamese and Chinese visitors queuing to have their vehicle blessed about the identity of the goddess, I was told that she was not in fact the Black Lady, but the Lady of the Realm. In their view the figure venerated in this shrine was a different and more powerful goddess, whom they did not consider to be Khmer in identity. Although the celebrity of this goddess ensured that the monastery was kept on the map and maintained in good condition, the story of this substitution illustrates the danger of one's religion being appreciated by others in this way: that one may risk losing one's identity altogether.

The Localization of Cham Beliefs

When Hạnh, an English teacher from a Mekong delta provincial capital, found out that I was interested in Vietnamese culture, she was bemused by my focus on the Lady of the Realm. Why did I consider this an example of Vietnamese culture? She asked me if anyone had ever informed me of the real identity of the so-called goddess: "People give her the title Bà Chúa Xứ—the Lady of the Realm, but it should really be spelled Bà Chúa Sứ, which is a borrowing from Chinese, meaning wife of the king, or queen. As for her proper name, it is actually Thiên Y A Na. It is not a Vietnamese but a Cham name." Hạnh then recounted the legend:

> Thiên Y A Na was a queen of the Cham people, who lived in the fourteenth century, when the kingdom of Champa located in what is now Central Vietnam still existed. Her husband, the king of the Chams, was killed in a Vietnamese invasion. Rather than suffer the indignity of being captured by the Vietnamese, she threw herself off a precipice, intending to do away with her life. However, she was rescued by a Chinese prince from Hainan Island, who was passing near the coast. He was struck by her beautiful dark complexion, legacy of the Indian influence on the kingdom of Champa. He resolved to marry her, and she went along with his plans, more out of gratitude than love.
>
> The wedding was arranged, to be held on the prince's boat. On the day of the ceremony, she decided she could not go ahead with the marriage and threw herself off the boat. She perished in the ocean waves. Her body washed onto a log of perfumed sandalwood, which drifted all the way back to the land of Champa. She was discovered by her countrymen, washed up onto a beach. Although she was dead, her complexion was fresh and beautiful, as if she were only sleeping. Her subjects erected a shrine to her, which is still there. After her enshrinement, traders, sailors, and others who made a living from the seas reported that during violent storms, Thiên Y A Na had appeared, had calmed the waves and saved them from certain death.
>
> After taking over the kingdom of Champa, the Vietnamese came to share the Chams' belief in her as a protector deity. In their ongoing migration, they brought the worship of Thiên Y A Na southward. When they arrived down in An Giang province, in the Mekong delta on the border with Cambodia, the settlers erected an altar to Thiên Y A Na on Sam Mountain, believing in her as a protector deity. But the main shrine to Thiên Y A Na is still to be found near Phan Thiết, where the Chams continue to venerate her.

Hạnh concluded, "I doubt that anyone else would have told you this tale. Probably only one out of every hundred people who go to visit the so-called Lady of the Realm knows that she is actually Thiên Y A Na from Champa."

Hạnh was right in saying that very few of those who go on pilgrimage to Châu Đốc share her view of the ethnic origins of this symbol. Yet her account of Cham influence on Vietnamese folk beliefs is supported by authors such as Tạ Chí Đại Trường (1989), Do Thien (1995), and Nguyễn Thế Anh (1995), who describe how the Cham goddess Po Nagar, a Cham religious figure and symbol of the Cham state, was appropriated by the Vietnamese, who overran and absorbed this kingdom. Lady Liễu Hạnh and Bà Chúa Ngọc are among the Vietnamese goddesses whose identity has been attributed to influences from this Cham spirit (see also Huỳnh Ngọc Trảng et al. 1993a). Huỳnh Ngọc Trảng notes that Cham influences on Bà Đen date from the eighteenth century, when Cham migrants settled near her shrine in Tây Ninh beside the Cambodia frontier (Huỳnh Ngọc Trảng, pers. com.).

Despite the careful scholarly work that informs such analyses, profound discontinuities often exist between the views of erudite commentators who attribute a specific ethnic origin to such religious symbols and people who themselves identify with that ethnicity. For example, many of the Cham who now live on the border with Cambodia emphatically reject the practice of venerating such spirits, saying it is a form of idolatry inconsistent with their ethnic identity as Sunni Muslims. For Hạnh, too, such figures were most emphatically not goddesses. When I asked her why so many people in southern Vietnam believed in goddesses, she restated her view that the Lady of the Realm was a Cham queen, a historical figure. When I said I was sure that there were plenty of other examples of goddesses to choose from, she disagreed and asked me to furnish evidence. I mentioned Bà Đen, the Black Lady, whose mountain shrine in Tây Ninh province drew hundreds of thousands of pilgrims annually. Hạnh replied, "Bà Đen is not a goddess either but an actual historical personage. Her name was Nguyễn Thị Đen, and she was a Khmer guerrilla soldier." She looked at me questioningly:

> Have you heard of the female guerrilla soldiers in the war against the French? They fought the return of France with methods such as the use of bamboo stakes concealed in pits in the ground that could pierce a man's foot. Well, Nguyễn Thị Đen was of such ilk. She lived in the eighteenth century and was loyal to the Vietnamese Tây Sơn general Nguyễn Huệ in his numerous battles with Gia Long, the eventual victor and founder of the Nguyễn dynasty. Gia Long, when he was still known as Nguyễn Ánh gave, the French a foothold in Vietnam by requesting their assistance in fighting Nguyễn Huệ. Once, on a raid-

ing expedition, Nguyễn Ánh's forces encountered Nguyễn Thị Đen on the slopes of her mountain abode in Tây Ninh. Capturing her, they were preparing to rape her when she escaped dishonor by leaping to her death off a precipice. A small shrine was erected to her, and soon tales of her honorable act of self-immolation reached the ears of the now-victorious Gia Long emperor. Despite the fact that it was his own troops who had precipitated her early death, Gia Long resolved to award her recognition as one of the meritorious historical personages of the Vietnamese people.

I asked her if Dinh Cô, venerated annually by hundreds of thousands of pilgrims in her beachside shrine in Long Hải to the east of Ho Chi Minh City, was not another example of Vietnamese belief in goddesses. "No," she said. "Dinh Cô too was a historical figure. 'Dinh Cô' means damsel. The person worshiped there was a girl who died a virgin." Hạnh couldn't re-member the exact circumstances: "She possibly threw herself off a boat as well." She said the story of Dinh Cô seemed to be the result of people mixing up the story of Thiên Y A Na with that of another local woman. Both had perished at sea. The difference, as she saw it, was that Thiên Y A Na was a queen, while Dinh Cô was still a young virginal girl when she died.

For Hạnh, these feminine symbols were foremost the bearers of ethnic or national identity, and she strove to maintain distinctions between the cultural identities of these different figures. Explanations such as hers drew a clear line between culturally appropriate activity and religion. I was more than once told that it was misguided to consider ritual activity around the shrines of these feminine icons as religious *(thuộc về tôn giáo)*. Rather, such activ-ity belonged to the category of culturally distinctive customs and practices *(phong tục tập quán)*. Some intellectuals with whom I spoke were at pains to assure me that in making offerings to such figures, people were not worship-ping *(thờ)* them but merely paying respect *(kính trọng)* to them as culturally meritorious figures. Hạnh assured me this was the attitude characteristically adopted by those from the locales of such shrines: "The people in the local area only make offerings to her out of respect for her heroic and noble deeds. I myself know her story but have never gone to her shrine. I don't believe *(tin tưởng)* in her. I just respect her."

Hạnh was disinclined to view these symbols as sources of religious power, a view she regarded as extrinsic to Vietnamese culture. A teacher and university-educated member of provincial society, whose work was the trans-mission and centralization of cultural standards, Hạnh's line on the Lady of the Realm as a customary rather than religious practice was set against what she deemed culturally illiterate views. Like the views of other influential culture brokers, Hạnh's view was a ruling on what were culturally authentic and what were inappropriate or bastardized readings. Such assertions can be seen as attempts to establish control over these symbols and rites as emblems of ethnic identity and to expunge from them readings regarded as inconsistent with their true cultural identity.

Sinophobia/Sinophilia

In defending my case to Hạnh, I argued that many people who went and made offerings in the shrines of the Lady of the Realm and the Black Lady considered them magically responsive *(linh thiêng)*, which was why they deserved the title goddesses *(thần nữ)*. She conceded that this perception was common but explained, "That is only due to the influence of the ethnic Chinese *(người Hoa)*. Those gentlemen *(mấy ổng)* chiefly make their living out of business. The Chinese here as in China believe deeply in superstitious religions *(tôn giáo mê tín dị đoan)*. They believe in the Black Lady's magical assistance and go there to make requests."

The first significant group of Chinese settlers in the Mekong delta arrived by sea as refugees from Qing China in the late seventeenth century. Many made their living from oceanic trade. Economic life was centered on the river ports of the Mekong delta, which were hubs for commerce, for the collection of rice and the provision of credit, goods, and services for the expanding agrarian capitalist economy. In the multicultural society of the Mekong delta, the Chinese are usually to be found at the heart of these riverside settlements. The ethnic Chinese or Hoa remained the most significant business force in southern Vietnam until their mass exodus beginning in 1978. In the *đổi mới* era they gained a renewed role as mediators and local agents for diverse economic interests in the era of globalization as Chinese from Taiwan, the PRC, Hong Kong, and Singapore as well as from other nations became some of the leading traders and investors in Vietnam.

The temples and pagodas built by the ethnic Chinese wherever they settled are among the Mekong delta's most architecturally impressive institutions. These immigrants' loyalty to their imported gods Tien Hau, Quan Công, and Ông Bổn, as well as to the Buddha, is a byword in the region. So too is the religiosity noted in the frequency of their attendance at temples, the size of their offerings, practices such as borrowing banknotes from the gods, and a range of beliefs in magical causality. Many of these practices bear the imprint of the regionally distinct seaboard culture of southern China, where the gods have long been implicated in a petty capitalist mode of production, involved in people's trading activities and propitiated through cash transactions (Gates 1996). These practices have often attracted elite scorn in China, particularly from the perspective of the bureaucrats and scholarly class that historically dominated its agrarian-oriented central state apparatus.

Elite denigration of popular religiosity and attribution of it to the influence of the ethnic Chinese has a significant history in Vietnam. In the 1930s journalists writing for the Saigonese magazine *Phữ Nữ Tân Văn* attributed what they saw as a lamentable upsurge in religious movements in the Mekong delta in part to the arrival of religious charlatans among the Chinese migrants fleeing from the Nationalists' crackdown on "feudal superstitions" (*Phụ Nữ Tân Văn* 1930a). In an era of official mistrust of the ethnic Chinese influences in postwar southern Vietnam, imported religious practices from China were regarded as having been key to the U.S. effort to weaken people's revolutionary resolve (Hồ Sĩ Hiệp 1981, 22). Buddhist nuns and monks with whom I spoke in the late 1990s attributed "erroneous" beliefs in the Buddha's material potency to their country's former colonization by the "superstitious" Chinese. One way or another the Chinese religious influence has been seen as weakening Vietnamese culture.

Although to some cultural elites the intense religiosity of the ethnic Chinese is a negative trait, from the perspective of pilgrims in the shrine to the goddess, this characteristic is wholly praiseworthy. From the late 1980s, a model of religious veneration considered to be of Chinese origin became particularly influential in southern Vietnamese society. The spirits propitiated by the ethnic Chinese were considered to have the greatest spiritual efficacy, and close attention was paid to the rites they engaged in. Positive estimation of the religious practices of the ethnic Chinese is particularly noticeable among petty traders and entrepreneurs. As the private commercial activities formerly dominated by the ethnic Chinese in this part of Vietnam replaced socialist bureaucratic planning, many people in business sought to cultivate the powerful forces they associated with this group's economic success. In the process, spirits and modes of propitiating them, whose identity was nominally ethnically distinct, have been charged with a renewed significance as "Chinese." This ethnically marked approach to the spirit world forms the template for much contemporary popular religious activity in a region of Vietnam in full flight from socialist economic institutions.

Phát, who identified himself as of Kinh ethnicity, worked in a small curbside stall in Ho Chi Minh City where he and his wife sold boiled pig intestines and other choice organs. He explained that the current popularity of the Lady of the Realm owed much to Chinese businesspeople's devotion to her: "The ethnic Chinese are the best business people in Vietnam. In the past, very few Viet people did business. More than ten years ago, the liberation forced the ethnic Chinese to close their businesses and leave the country. After that, more and more Viet people started doing business, and consequently more and more they started going to make offerings to the Lady of the Realm." Nevertheless, Phát said the ethnic Chinese remained the most prominent pilgrims to the shrine: "Although now most of the pilgrims are Viet people, proportionately speaking, more Chinese than Vietnamese go to worship her. Ten out of ten Chinese go and make offerings to her compared with only two-thirds of the Viet people. Also, most of the Viet people going to the Lady of Châu Đốc are women, while for the Chinese, both men and women go."

His wife, whose father was born in the Chinese mainland province of Guandong, agreed that Kinh people's belief in these gods was influenced by their perception of ethnic Chinese success at business. She told me that these days most of those praying to the Lady of the Realm were businesspeople requesting lucky purchases and fast sales *(mua may bán đắc)*. Many of the people who participate in the pilgrimage to the Châu Đốc deity see it as a Chinese practice either in terms of origins or the intensity of their involvement. The shrine is inscribed throughout with Chinese characters, undecipherable to the majority of pilgrims but recognized by them as Chinese. Most of the gold plaques and donated robes displayed in endless cases in her Châu Đốc shrine have Chinese characters affixed to them, and the envelopes that contain gifts from the goddess' altar such as rice, salt, and money, are printed with these characters.[11] The offering of robes, headdresses, and roast pigs is also considered typically Chinese. It is common for people to contrast the manner in which the ethnic Chinese and the Kinh worship. The latter, it is said, do not believe in Her Ladyship as deeply nor offer as lavish gifts as the former.

In the markets and back alleys of southern Vietnam's urban areas, it is not rare to come across praise for things Chinese to a degree that unsettles a view of Vietnamese identity as formed in resistance to such perceived cultural outsiders. This is not necessarily a new development. For as many as three centuries, urban-based merchants of Chinese origin represented the epitome of cultivation and of prosperous high living for many residents of the southern Vietnamese plain (see Hyùnh Ngọc Trảng 1992). They were people associated with built-up centers of population, literate in some Chinese characters, ethnically linked to the prestigious culture of the great power to the north of Vietnam, inheritors of an immigrant's work ethic, and considered to have a good head for business. As the most successful entrepreneurial group in society, their prestige is high among marketers, urban workers and rural traders, and transport workers. I was frequently told by ethnic Kinh in these occupations that the ethnic Chinese were good at making a living because they were hardworking, evenhanded, and trustworthy. The ethnic Chinese reputedly played as hard as they worked, but they did not squander their money on continuous pleasures as some said was the case with the ethnic Kinh.

To share with me his appreciation of Chinese culture, Phát took me on a tour of the temples of Bình Dương, thirty kilometers northwest of Ho Chi Minh City, a place famous for its lacquerware and pottery industry. Built by Bình Dương's formerly large ethnic Chinese community, the temples to the goddess Tien Hau and the male god Quan Công were richly decorated and crowded even on a weekday. His wife told me that during Tết the temple of Tien Hau in Bình Dương was particularly popular among ethnic Kinh businesspeople. Although there were several temples to this goddess in the ethnic-Chinese dominated urban area of Cho Lon, the one in Bình Dương was where the goddess was allegedly the most responsive to prayers: "That is where people from Saigon go during Tết." After visiting Tien Hau's temple, we spent some time at Quan Công's temple, which Phát said he knew more about. He told me something of the spirit it housed: "Quan Công was a Chinese warrior. He is considered the most skilled in martial arts and at the same time the most morally upright: you can't bribe him. Quan Công can be very fierce, but only when he is in the right. He is frank but easily angered. This quality is evident by his red face. Worshiped in a household altar, he prevents disturbances occurring in the home."

Phát told me that all I needed to know about Quan Công could be found in *Quan Công,* the Hong Kong film about him. He said that the righteousness *(chính nghĩa)* of Quan Công is clearly demonstrated by the fact that the Hong Kong Police Department reveres him as their patron. In the temple, the fierce-faced general, flanked by two scowling companions, was seated, hand contemplatively stroking a full black beard. The approach to the main altar was lined with props or accessories of rule that indicated the general's qualities: a spear, a pike, a staff, a book, and a hand holding a pen. To the left of Quan Công's altar was an auxiliary altar on which were displayed a plaster bust and a framed picture of Ho Chi Minh, with a dish full of smoking incense set before them. Forming the backdrop to the altar was a framed poster with images of Vietnam's "modern resistance heroes," such as Phan Châu Trinh, Phan Bội Châu, Lê Hồng Phong, and Nguyễn An Ninh, all of them male, leaning against the wall (figure 5). I saw no like altar in the nearby temple to the goddess Tien Hau. These two gods were both immigrants, introduced by settlers from southern China. They were cosmopolitans, not revolutionaries, patrons foremost of business and of the region's influential

FIG. 5. A framed
poster of Viet-
namese resistance
heroes in the temple
to Quan Công in
Bình Dương

ethnic Chinese community. Was it because of her gender that the goddess
was not considered an enemy or rival? Certainly the Vietnamese state has a
predilection for representing the country's ethnic minorities through images
of female members of such groups.[12] On the other hand, Quan Công, a general, a literatus, and foreign mandarin, was a presence warranting supervision
by Vietnam's male resistance lineage, to underscore the dominance of Vietnamese patriarchs. Was the installation of their images an act of aggressive
mirroring, triggered by the Chinese general's fierce red visage?

Phát told me that before 1975 many ethnic Chinese lived in Bình Dương:
"Now they have all gone overseas." We were relaxing in the spacious house
built by his wife's father, who had migrated from Guandong in the 1930s.

Phát said this dwelling was much finer than his own. His wife had been raised in this house. His two daughters were being brought up by their aunt in their grandfather's house. Phát and I were visiting alone; his wife was back in Ho Chi Minh City, tending to their business. We had just finished a meal prepared for us by his wife's sister. Phát's youngest daughter offered me a sapodilla fruit. "The Chinese are very hospitable *(hiếu khách),*" he said, a trait often regarded as characteristic of southern Vietnamese regional culture. He showed me a picture of the former master of the house, who he said had been "excellent at martial arts." Phát was full of admiration for things Chinese; he considered the Chinese as a standard to be emulated. We were speaking of *cải lương* opera, a theatrical form generally considered indigenous to southern Vietnam, synthesized in the 1920s and incorporating Vietnamese, Chinese, and European forms. Phát emphasized its Chinese lineage: "If you want to learn the correct *cải lương* opera gestures, study with the most proficient teachers and adopt the standard forms, you would have to go to China to study." His daughter pulled him up. She said *cải lương* was a mixture of all sorts of things. She said many, although not all, of the stories were based on the Chinese feudal era, but actors wore costumes that followed their fancy, rather than historical accuracy. His daughter said, "Anyway, now many people shun *cải lương* as rustic." Phát continued with his homage to Chinese culture: "The majority of Vietnamese follow the religion of ancestor worship. It is a person-making religion *(đạo làm người).* Just like that of the Chinese. Have you had the chance to read the works of Confucius yet? He raised some very interesting ideas. If you want to know anything about Vietnam you should read his books. Few can master all of the ideas."

Phát's tribute to China as a classical source was delivered as he sat facing the well-kept ancestral altar in the house of his accomplished Chinese-born father-in-law. While perhaps he was more effusive than many, his admiration of things Chinese is not uncommon among those who, like him, identify as Viet or Kinh people. In the 1990s, many of his peers were entranced by various Chinese cultural forms, attending kung fu classes and mandarin language lessons, listening to Cantonese music, and watching serialized romances, mysteries, and adventure stories based on Chinese feudal history and the world of the supernatural.

A history of resistance to Chinese incursions has been foundational to characterizations of the Vietnamese as resistors against foreign domination. Yet in many cases Vietnamese identity has been imagined through models borrowed from such colonizers (Woodside 1971). In the early twentieth century the uncompromising rejection by Vietnam's modernists of an inherited past led to self-deprecating comparisons with European or Japanese models. Attacking French colonialism and American imperialism, Vietnam's Communist Party was deeply influenced by the revolutionary path pioneered by the Chinese Communist Party (Bui Tin 1995). In certain cases unwelcome foreign influences were attacked through an ideological framework borrowed from the same cultural source. For example, in the late 1970s the ethnic Chinese business class, whose loyalty was considered suspect, was expelled from a postwar Vietnamese polity that was officially imagined through images heavily borrowed from revolutionary culture derived from the People's Republic of China. The postwar regime brought to the classrooms of the postwar south a view of history as Party-led resistance to foreign aggression, yet did so through Soviet and East European symbols of identity that many people in urban and rural settings considered more foreign than cultural imagery of American, French, or southern Chinese provenance. Such contradictions eroded the Party's capability to capture popular sympathy, particularly in southern Vietnam, whose inhabitants' historical engagements with the non-Vietnamese world differed significantly from that of those in the north of the country, home to the political capital. In recent years, there has been a widening in conceptions of Vietnamese identity and a more inclusive appreciation for the multiethnic character of the Vietnamese nation. This attitude has included renewed acceptance of the value and beauty of ethnic Chinese religious practices as a contribution to southern Vietnamese regional culture (e.g., Phan An 1990; Mạc Đường 1994). Many folklorists see Chinese cultural influences as key ingredients of local identity (e.g., Huỳnh Ngọc Trắng 1992). This view represents not just an objective reevaluation of distinctive local traditions, but the major impact in the region of investment and trade with the East Asian world and particularly with the diverse societies of greater China.

The Goddess in the Eyes of the Ethnic Chinese

An appreciation of the multiethnic character of the nation's religious culture is not necessarily shared by all Vietnamese, who, as we have seen, often associate religious practice with a particular ethnicity. Some, like Hạnh, may impose a restrictive reading on the ethnicity of a symbol such as the Lady of the Realm while others, like Phát, may consider the practice of propitiating her as largely borrowed. One finds this process of boundary delineation among other ethnic groups as well. Among many ethnic Chinese, for instance, there is a conception that the Lady of the Realm is a Chinese goddess and that the practice of venerating such spirits is similarly Chinese. This view is particularly noticeable in Chợ Lớn, a large and economically powerful ethnic Chinese enclave sometimes criticized by Vietnamese nationalists for its chauvinism and isolation.

In one of the shops selling religious items owned by ethnic Chinese merchants in Nguyễn Chí Thanh Street in the heart of Chợ Lớn, I asked to be shown a statue of the Lady of the Realm. I was shown a statue of the goddess Tien Hau, which the saleswoman told me was made in Guandong province, China. I asked her how the Chinese knew how to make a Vietnamese goddess. She said the people of China also worship the Lady of the Realm but call her Tien Hau. At a neighboring shop I again asked to see the Lady of the Realm who was worshiped in Châu Đốc and was shown a statue that had "Holy Mother Tien Hau" in Chinese characters on its base. Also for sale in these shops owned by ethnic Chinese were pictures of the same goddess painted on mirrors or framed and fitted out with radiating halo lights.

The goddess Tien Hau is considered by many of Vietnam's ethnic Chinese as the spiritual protector overseeing their presence in the region. Temples to her are found in almost every settlement in the region where concentrations of people of Chinese descent are to be found. Rich iconography and decorations featuring boats adorn her temples, attesting to people's view of her as the spirit who oversees departures and arrivals and protects people during water passages. The cult to this goddess, already prolific in southern China, grew in an era of movement, expanding trade, and migration. She oversaw one of the most dramatic and successful migrations in the world's history: that of the Chinese expansion into Southeast Asia. Aside from these functions, Tien Hau is regarded as a patron of commerce, from whom money can be borrowed; such money has the magical property of augmenting one's own capital, providing one regularly repays the interest. The goddess is also regarded as a guarantor of fertility. Often the goddess of birth (Mẹ Sanh) accompanies her on a side altar, and the images of various mythological animals playing with their progeny adorn the walls of her temples.

To many ethnic Chinese, the Lady of the Realm in Châu Đốc has identical functions of overseeing travel, commerce, fertility, and health. One elderly man from Chợ Lớn told me his parents were from the southern Chinese province of Guandong. He said that he had been going to visit the Lady of the Realm in Châu Đốc annually for thirty years. He first went in 1970 to cure an outbreak of cankers on his hands. The goddess answered his prayers and cured him. He also obtained an amulet from her that helped him travel safely through the war-torn countryside. He said that in those days the shrine was much smaller. Few people went there, and they had to sleep in the street or in a pagoda. The shrine was rebuilt to its present size in 1972, entirely with

Chinese money. At that time, he said, the only people who went there were the ethnic Chinese. The Kinh people came much later, in the 1980s. He thought that even the local people only started coming to her shrine as a result of Hoa people's interest. He pointed out that all of the characters in the shrine are in Chinese, which for him was proof of the Chinese origins of this belief.

It would be a mistake to regard this ethnic Chinese chauvinism as exclusively limited to Chợ Lớn. One sometimes finds it in ethnic Chinese concentrations in the Mekong delta as well. In Long Sơn village, which is on the Mekong River about seventeen kilometers from Sam Mountain, are quite a number of Chinese temples, including one to Ông Bổn (patron of many Southeast Asia's Chinese migrants) and one to the Lady of the Realm. The latter shrine's front courtyard was tiled and decorated with ornamental shrubs. Sitting on an altar at its rear, the goddess had an open line of sight to a *hát bội* theater stage beside the the river. On the wall to her left was an altar to Tien Hau. On her right was an altar to Địa Mẫu, the earth mother goddess, whose figure was standing on a flattened depiction of the globe, seas, and continents painted in bright glossy colors.

In the shrine was a seventy-three-year-old man, his face puckered, tanned, and wrinkled but his eyes shining bright and his movements lithe and purposive. His grandfather had come from southern China in the late nineteenth century when there had already been up to three generations of Chinese people living on the island. The shrine was one hundred years old. Neighboring villages also had a shrine to the goddess, but he thought none were as fine as this one, save the much larger Châu Đốc shrine. He said groups from "the city" (Ho Chi Minh City) stopped by frequently. They donated robes and the brightly embroidered banners that hung from the shrine's rafters. "This is a Chinese belief," he told me. "Vietnamese don't have these goddesses," he said, pointing to Tien Hau and Địa Mẫu. Both these statues came from Chợ Lớn, where they were made by skilled craftsmen. The statue to the Lady of the Realm was made by local Chinese, who he said were responsible for the veneration of the goddess in Châu Đốc as well.[13] The robes and embroidered banners were gifts from the Chinese. He said the goddess had become very popular among Vietnamese "because they don't believe in themselves *(không tin vào mình)*. We Chinese have a self-belief *(tự tin vào mình)*. The Vietnamese have watched and followed what we do. The customary new year and midyear celebrations were also taken *(lấy)* from us Chinese," he said.

Chinese ethnocentrism is so pronounced in some areas of southern Vietnam that the region itself is sometimes seen by members of that group as having been formerly part of China, until taken from them by the Vietnamese. In some renditions, the ethnic origin of the Vietnamese is in the north of the country, while the south was originally a Chinese domain. In 1975, those who held this view were to get a rude shock when the Vietnamese state attempted to break the trading monopoly of the ethnic Chinese in Chợ Lớn and elsewhere, and many of them were forced to leave the country. Some philosophically inclined members of this group have said their departure at that time represented no real rupture with their history, for they had come to the region to make a living, and when this became too difficult, it was time to move on to other places.

In their seaborne exodus, many ethnic Chinese again turned to the spirits for patronage of the next chapter in their migration. At the seaside temple to Dinh Cô in Long Hải, I was told that the most opulent gifts were from overseas Chinese propitiants. Worship of the goddess picked up dramatically in the late 1980s and early 1990s, when former residents of Vietnam of Chinese descent began to return and make sumptuous offerings to her and fund the renovation of her temple in gratitude for her patronizing their successful escapes from the country. The similarities between the stories told of Dinh Cô's patronage of risky voyages and those told about Tien Hau, also regarded as a patroness of seaborne ventures, are marked. It is difficult to unpick whether the local goddess Dinh Cô received such attention from the ethnic Chinese because of this resemblance or whether, in the wake of the veneration demonstrated by the ethnic Chinese, elements of her biography closely resembling those of Tien Hau were to receive greater prominence.[14]

The Consolidation of Indigenous Spirits

The attribution of Chinese identities to the spirits of the region is not the sole effect of the ethnic Chinese people's engagement with these spirits. One of the practices for which the ethnic Chinese are known is making offerings to the local spirits who are considered to watch over existence in a particular area. The Chinese propitiation of locality based deities has accompanied ventures as diverse as settling in the region, establishing good relations with others, doing business, and preserving one's life and livelihood intact. The attention paid to the spirit of the early-nineteenth-century viceroy Lê Văn Duyệt, whose mausoleum is on the fringes of Bà Chiểu market in Ho Chi Minh City, is an example of this process. Viceroy Lê Văn Duyệt, a renowned soldier and eunuch, was the most powerful figure in the southern region of Vietnam before it came under centralized Vietnamese control in the first half of the nineteenth century. Born in the Mekong delta in 1763, Lê Văn Duyệt was the trusted lieutenant of Gia Long (reigned 1802–1820), the founding monarch of the Nguyễn dynasty, whom he had helped attain power over a unified kingdom by making available the resources of his southern power base (Choi Byung Wook 1999). His tomb, known universally as His Lordship's Mausoleum (Lăng Ông), was built after his death in 1832. Many people consider the mausoleum and surrounding area the most auspicious site in the city, and indeed many fortune-tellers congregate in the vicinity, benefiting from the viceroy's reputed ability to divine the future.

The viceroy, although generally regarded as of Việt or Kinh ethnicity, has long been popular among the city's ethnic Chinese. A female café owner in a lane near my residence in Ho Chi Minh City's Dakao market told me that ethnic Chinese, herself included, regularly went to his mausoleum to make offerings to him for protecting their business interests. The propitiation of such figures underlines the continuing investment by members of the ethnic Chinese community in an ethnic division of labor. The world of politics in Vietnam is sometimes described by the region's ethnic Chinese residents as a preserve of the Kinh and exemplified by the historical role of figures such as the viceroy. Some people who identify as ethnic Chinese refer to themselves as guests *(khách)* of the Kinh people and hence as well advised to stay outside the realm of politics. Although a host of counterexamples attesting to the historical involvement of people of ethnic Chinese descent in the administration of the region and in other noncommercial activities can be found— including Mạc Thiên Tích (1706–1780), administrator of Hà Tiên and poet, and Trịnh Hoài Đức (1765–1825), a scholar and diplomat—one still encounters a perception among all ethnic groups that the ethnic Chinese are a specialist business class. One of the ways these occupationally based ethnic distinctions are reproduced is through the veneration of spirits and attribution to them of ethnically specific functions.

The custodian who attended the altar to the viceroy told me that during Lê Văn Duyệt's reign in the first decades of the nineteenth century, the ethnic Chinese had thrived as a specialized trading group, and they had made the region into an important regional entrepôt thanks to him. He said that successive Chinese migrants to the southern Vietnamese metropolis believed that the viceroy's spirit continued to support their enterprises and that throughout the colonial and postcolonial period his mausoleum had been considered one of the most spiritually potent sites in the region. The custodian's explanation ceased abruptly as a small group of women came and knelt before the main altar and started shaking out numbered divination sticks, each corresponding to a distinct fortune. As they mumbled their requests, the attendant struck the bell three times and used the opportunity to inhale a few times on his cigarette. When the tone faded, he said, "In the past, ethnic Chinese people came to pray here, to seek His Lordship's continued protection. Now, they have all fled the country. These days it is mainly people of Viet ethnicity who come here. It has become their custom." He said, "At Tết, the whole of the Gia Định area comes here to worship. His Lordship's death anniversary is also well attended."

Here was striking attribution from a temple custodian, no less, of the ethnic Chinese contribution to the cult to this Vietnamese culture hero. While the viceroy is regarded as a historically acclaimed member of the Kinh group, many in the city are unaware that the ethnic Chinese have helped construct his mausoleum to its present magnificence. As the intricacies of regional history are not always well known, perhaps only a minority are aware of the role this figure has played in the life of the local Chinese Vietnamese community. This is particularly true of those living in the city who are themselves recent immigrants from central and northern Vietnam. They are likely, when pressed, to assume that the outlines of a Kinh ethnonationalist version of history, according to which Vietnamese have spent much of their time resisting foreign aggressors, particularly the Chinese, who colonized the country for more than a thousand years, apply equally well in all quarters of their homeland. Once, I discussed the identity of the viceroy with a cyclo driver who had just arrived in the city from central Vietnam to make his fortune and the Catholic woman outside my residence from whom I usually bought cigarettes. The cyclo driver told me that Lê Văn Duyệt was venerated by the citizens of the city largely because he had been excellent at martial arts (võ thuật).

I asked them whom he had fought.

"The Chinese," they said.

"Was he not allies with them?" I asked.

"Of course not. He was a local, born in Gia Định. People here erected a shrine to him, out of gratitude for defeating the Chinese invaders."

"When did this happen?"

"Don't you know? The Chinese have tried to invade Vietnam continuously."

I asked if he was responsive to people's prayers.

"No," they chorused.

I asked if people ever made requests to him.

"No [emphatically]. That's no fitting way to treat a national hero."

To add another layer to this picture, some of the ethnic Chinese living in the Mekong delta regard the Lady of the Realm in a similar manner as a historical contributor to the Vietnamese state's settlement and defense of the region. This is the case with the ethnic Chinese farmer from Long Sơn village, An Giang province, who thought the practice of venerating this spirit was a Chinese custom, borrowed by the Vietnamese. Nevertheless, when I asked him about the identity of the Lady of the Realm, he said the goddess was a local historical personage to whom people erected a shrine in gratitude for her posthumous acts of patronage. He said she was a Thai woman who had assisted the Nguyễn emperor Gia Long defeat the Tây Sơn rebels who had overthrown Nguyễn rule in the late eighteenth century. She had come to this part of the country on the king's behest, along with her husband. She had died here and was buried on the island of Phú Quốc. Strictly speaking, he observed, that is the appropriate place to venerate her, but people had taken a stick of incense from her grave site on the island to this temple and the big shrine in Châu Đốc in order to establish a cult in her honor. She ensured well-being for individuals (granting health, wealth, and success in business and relationships) and for families (maintaining domestic harmony, the health and education of children, and the safety of family members who traveled far from home).

A different tale told to me by an ethnic Chinese man from another predominantly ethnic Chinese village in the same province related that the Lady of the Realm was Vietnamese in identity. This man, whose parents were from Guandong, had been born close to the Châu Đốc shrine. He said that during the 1960s his mother used to take him there. The shrine had been full of Việt people, and he had never considered the veneration of the goddess as anything other than a Vietnamese practice. He said there were several other female spirits venerated in the region. When I asked him why so many goddesses were worshiped in the south, he said he believed the whole southern region had been settled thanks to a Vietnamese woman, and for this reason people venerated them to express a debt of gratitude to her:

> There is a shrine to a woman somewhere in Saigon as well. I can't remember her name. She was in fact the Việt wife of the king of Champa. Several hundred years ago, the Vietnamese Nguyễn lords, who were based in the central region of the country, allied with the kingdom of Champa through this marriage in order to fight the Trịnh lords in what is now northern Vietnam. The Chams were powerful—they had a large navy. However, the Cham king died and, to avoid a Trịnh invasion, his queen moved farther south, bringing her people with her. Her strategy was to wait until her sons grew up and could lead a defense against the Trịnh. In the meantime, she professed to want to lead a peaceful, obscure existence, building pagodas. During her reign in the south, people

flourished. Generals such as Lê Văn Duyệt rose through the ranks. Others came south. When she died, people erected a shrine to honor her.[15]

His account, which collapsed many hundred years of history into the lifetime of this one personage, attributed great credit to a woman for the acquisition, settlement, defense, and prosperity of the southern parts of the country, giving her rank over male culture heroes such as Lê Văn Duyệt. These were, furthermore, the acts of a widow of a Cham king, who settled here to defend the territory from Vietnamese challengers, the Trịnh. An obscure and some may say inaccurate historical account, with the characteristic potency of a myth to summarize the experience of a people over time, his explanation represented an ethnic Chinese view of the circumstances they faced in settling in the southern region of the country. The story alludes to a history of male migrants establishing themselves in the region by marriage to local women, who provided them descendants, entrepreneurial tenure, legal rights through relations of affinity and descent, and a network of local contacts. As a maternal figure, nurturing the sons of a non-Kinh father in a new land, she condensed the proper wifely virtues in the mind of this ethnic Chinese man. Similarly, the qualities of virginity, fertility, patronage of business, and ability to increase prosperity, often associated with the goddesses of the region, are feminine attributes idealized by these mostly male sojourners.

Conclusion

For many members of Vietnam's dominant ethnic group, the Lady of the Realm and her fellow goddesses perform a boundary-marking function (Yuval-Davis 1997), patrolling the ethnically charged borders of a polity with which they identify as its original *(chính gốc)* inhabitants. Like the shrines to the Black Lady and the Palace Damsel, her shrine in Châu Đốc is situated on a border that is widely deemed to have ethnic as well as political valence. Other temples to goddesses are found in enclaves formerly dominated by migrant minorities, sometimes considered points of vulnerability by nationalist politicians and commentators.[16] These female figures feature in the narratives told by members of the dominant ethnic group, about resistance, cultural survival, regional specificity, or cultural syncretism. On the other hand, these figures are just as liable to be attached to a specific non-Kinh ethnicity, either through identification of their distinct attributes or appreciation of their role toward a particular community. Alternatively, their ethnicity might become a topic of debate, for example in reference to ritual practices regarded as exogenous, which are seen to violate authentic traditions.

However, as powerful spirits, the goddesses of the southern Vietnamese plain encode interpretations of the past with which orthodox cultural commentators have not been entirely comfortable, as they burst the bounds of ethnonationalism, giving efficacy a very different ethnicity, not always congruent with conventional Vietnamese myths of self. The popular attribution of magical efficacy to the multiethnic protector deities of the southern plain stands in contrast to views of Vietnamese history in which resistance directed at perceived outsiders and the defense of cultural integrity are the benchmarks of national success. These goddesses reflect a vision of history in which the accomplishments of different ethnic groups are accorded prestige or potency. These are beliefs that point to parallel historical ventures: of appropriation rather than resistance, of nonmartial solutions, of making do rather than victoriously overcoming, of flight versus fighting, of accommodations forged across cultures, and of emulating other ethnic groups.

Goddesses such as the Black Lady, the Lady of the Realm, the Palace Damsel, Tien Hau, and Sri Mariamam are legacies of the Khmer, Kinh, Cham, Chinese, Indian, and other groups' historical presence in the region. Each of these groups brought specific stories, beliefs, and ritual practices to their veneration of these spirits that, over time, were to influence each other. The presence of these ethnically diverse deities graphically illustrates that this is a region whose ethnic Kinh settlers cohabit with other Vietnamese people, sharing significantly different cultural worldviews. It is a place of intense cultural exchange and assimilation, home to multiple and overlapping colonialist projects. Yet as one might expect in such a culturally complex region, beliefs are not just borrowed but can be used to shore up the boundaries between ethnic groups and to reinforce exclusionary identities. In this it is important to note that use of such symbols to delimit one's ethnicity is not just the preserve of the numerically dominant Kinh. These goddesses are equally significant reference points against which ethnic distinctions are asserted by other groups in the region. To add to this complex tableau, local ethnic groups are not necessarily united through these symbols. There are differences in opinion within such groups according to social factors of class, occupation, geography, and gender. Sometimes, too, the interpretations asserted by members of one group unexpectedly reinforce the beliefs of members of another. Such dynamics are to be expected in a region that is diverse not just in terms of ethnicity but many other societal factors as well.

3

Embodying Market Relations

An upsurge in fortune-telling, mediumship, spirit worship, and pilgrimages occurred in Vietnam as government policies were pushing the country into unprecedented integration with the capitalist world and as market relations were transforming the face of the society. In many respects this religious efflorescence poses a conundrum, contradicting expected scenarios of the disenchantment of the world or the waning of religious worldviews. According to modernization theorists, such examples of religious sensibility, which were associated with traditional societies, would fade away with the rise of allegedly more rational systems of belief and motivation such as capitalism (cf. Keyes, Kendall, and Hardacre 1994, 4; Jackson 1999a). The Vietnamese case is not unique in forcing a rethinking of a social scientific hypothesis in vogue since the time of Max Weber. Throughout the region the resurgence of capitalist market relations has been accompanied by increase in "new forms of religiosity" (Roberts 1995, 2). Observers have noted that the global spread of capitalism in the 1990s was attended by a dramatic intensification of appeals to enchantment, evidenced in the growth of witchcraft accusations, prosperity cults, the trade in icons and amulets, deals with powerful spirits, and pacts with the devil (Comaroff and Comaroff 1999).

In the Comaroffs' view, religious practices such as zombie conjuring or prosperity cults are linked to the nature of capitalism itself. They situate what they refer to as examples of "occult economies" in a postrevolutionary moment marked by social, spatial, and temporal disorientation, disappointment, and despair. The global upsurge they detect in deployments of magic for material ends reflects variously the allure of accruing wealth from nothing, the insecurities of life in a capricious market (where greed and luck appear as effective as work and rational choice), and a situation in which the majority of the world's population is boxed out of an anticipated share in global prosperity (Comaroff 1994, 310; Comaroff and Comaroff 2000). From this perspective the current penchant for magic is no archaic survival but diagnoses the postsocialist moment, addressing the unpredictable and iniquitous social relations attending the abandonment of the socialist economic alternative. Closer to Vietnam, Taylor (J. Taylor 1999) and Jackson (1999a) saw the popularity of magical monks and other prosperity religions in Thailand as examples of the post modernization of Thai religion: the attempt "to impose meaningfulness upon the disorienting dynamism of economic, political and social life during the disruptions of the boom years, spiritualizing the market and symbolically taming the unruly power of globalising capitalism" (Jackson 1999a).

The value of such studies is that they aim to "de-exoticize" phenomena such as witchcraft and spirit worship by demonstrating the place of such beliefs in the now, specifically, as people's symbolic rendition of contemporary social processes. In Vietnam's case, the emergence of new goddesses such as the Lady of the Storehouse (Bà Chúa Kho) and the expansion of pilgrimages to the shrines of spirits such as the Lady of the Realm were very much tied up in the deepening and extension of market relations in the country. These goddesses can be seen as a lens through which those inhabiting the marketplaces and residential neighborhoods of Vietnam contemplated and negotiated processes of rapid commercialization and global integration in the late 1980s and 90s. As such, these symbolic practices can be compared to other religious responses to the global spread of market relations. Yet we are still far from accounting for the diversity of ways in which such relations have been variably symbolized and negotiated around the world. Why in southern Vietnam has a sorority of goddesses situated on political and ethnic borders emerged as prime underwriter of newfound wealth instead of an epidemic of witches and body snatchers as is the case in southern Africa, pacts with the devil as in parts of South America (Taussig 1980), or "prosperity monks" as in Thailand (Jackson 1999a)? While all such phenomena represent spiritualized dimensions of the new social relations of the market, differences in their content and form indicate that practices of domesticating these geographically extensive economic processes are culturally localized.

The diversity of ways in which the economy is imagined bears the imprint of culture, social structure, and history. The personalistic spiritual beings through whom Vietnamese people's encounter with market relations has been mediated can be understood in this way. Transacting with spirits for existential needs is a culturally familiar practice in Vietnam. Relations of biological reproduction, kinship, and membership of a political community have long been comprehended and negotiated in such a manner and have lent the spirit world a distinct social identity. Such practices have been flexible enough to be adapted to the symbolization of capitalist relations. The identity of the spiritual agents with whom people transact for economic benefit is further influenced by the social structure and gender of the market economy in Vietnam. The preference for female spirits draws upon and affirms notions of female efficacy in commercial pursuits. As beings with whom those involved in commerce have long transacted, female spirits also have a reputation as historical agents in their own right. These spirits' rise to prominence in the mid-1980s reflects the heightened status given to the type of economic practice they have long overseen but have until recently been relatively marginalized. As beings on the borders of the nation-state, these spirits also reflect understandings of new transnational sources of economic value and socialized practices of tapping such flows of wealth. Hence, while indeed typical of a contemporary moment of global religiosity and implicated in new paths to prosperity, these spiritual embodiments of the market do not represent a complete disjuncture. Rather they are continuous with local economic history, which is at the same time a cultural and social history of conceptualizing value and obtaining well-being in partnership with the spirit world.

Embodying Market Relations

Motorcycle taxi drivers in the downtown area of Ho Chi Minh City told me that one can obtain from the shrine to the Lady of the Realm a set of blessed gifts or *lộc* from the goddess sufficient to cover all one's basic needs. A package of salt and rice will ensure that one has enough to eat throughout the year. Squares of paper, painted gold and silver, bring one money, "enough to spend" *(đủ xài)*, for a year. A leaf of gold foil represents capital *(vốn)*, and a pair of candles allows the light *(đuốc)* of Her Ladyship to fill one's house. This set of gifts demonstrates the expectation invested in the goddess for assistance in making a living *(làm ăn)*. These views are voiced by a group of people occupying a precarious niche in their city's commercialized economy. At best, they live from day to day; fares are scarce, and their motorbikes are often repossessed by creditors who lend money at usurious rates. Given the difficulties of their job, the hopes that they invest in the goddess, for subsistence, spending money, and some investment capital, although modest, are relatively ambitious.

Many of these workers consider their physical well-being to be a blessing conferred upon them by the goddess. When I asked Sơn, one of the drivers, if he had ever gone to the shrine to the goddess in Châu Đốc, he said just once, which gave him the chance to make a request for good health.[1] When I asked if his request had been granted he assented, saying that his health was now good enough. He told me that by accessing the image of the goddess, by physically stroking or tapping her, one can transfer her powers to protect one's own body. People seek to obtain an item that has been in contact with the goddess such as a piece of one of her robes, with which they wipe themselves over. The cloths that are used to bathe the goddess at her annual bathing rite *(lễ tắm bà)* are sometimes distributed to worshipers after the ceremony for the same purpose.[2] People also seek the run-off water from her ritual bath and use it to wash their faces and bodies. It provides a protective film, defending the integrity of the body against disease, injury, and the operation of curses. Such practices implicate the goddess in the maintenance of physical vitality and well-being, the very basis on which the livelihood of these workers depends. To be sick might mean defaulting on a loan repayment and courting ruinous loss of capital. If a family member is sick the cost of treatment might require that a driver sell his motorbike, plunging the family into desperate poverty.

Throughout southern Vietnam, the region from which most of the goddess' propitiants are drawn, economic activity is profoundly shaped by market relations. Farming families sell their agricultural crops, livestock, and even land on the market, and their members routinely work for wages or migrate to the city for cash jobs. Many of the necessities of existence from cooking oil to electricity and housing must be purchased, although the definition of "need" in recent years has stretched to encompass a television set or a new Chinese motorcycle. Primary producers have to spend to produce, buying pesticide, fertilizer, or feed for livestock; renting machinery; purchasing a vehicle on credit; employing workers for big jobs such as converting a rice field into a fruit orchard or digging a fishpond. Most families strive to acquire some capital so that they can open a small business such as renting out a threshing machine, running a home dressmaking business, operating a ferry service, or managing a market stall. In the highly commercialized society of the region even the health and education sectors are deeply privatized, regarded by those who provide these services as a way of earning money and by the clients of such services as unavoidable costs. Ritual occasions and life-cycle commemorations also require expensive outlays, for gifts, feasting foods, and alcohol, as well as such exceptional expenses as getting a wedding ceremony videotaped or hiring a vehicle to transport guests.

Life in the region's commoditized economy is fraught with uncertainty, double binds, and risks. The revitalization and normalization of the private commercial sphere and the growth of foreign investment and trade have given the whole region and indeed country a major boost. According to the UNDP, the country's per capita income doubled over the 1990s to U.S.$400, and between 1993 and 1998 poverty decreased to 37 percent from 55 percent (Haughton 2001). Yet the path to greater prosperity has been complex and unpredictable: fortunes have been made and just as inexplicably lost, impeccable-looking investments have gone bad, commodity prices have soared and slumped. In a rapidly changing domestic cultural, political, and legal environment, people have had to deal with poor information, fuzzy laws, erratic implementation, and variable regulation. Added to this has been the instability of the macroeconomic environment. Most economies in the Asian region went from economic boom to bust during the 1990s. People have learned that many things can go wrong in a market economy that can seriously effect an individual and family's well-being. The weather could turn bad, floods could wipe out a crop, a family member could get sick, prices could fall through the floor, business could dry up, a factory could shut down. People frequently have to sell off major assets, uproot to make a living elsewhere, or venture into an unknown sector.

The intensification of market relations in the region since the mid-1980s has given rise to religious subjectivities that relate to the assertion of personal agency, the quest for predictability, and the management of anxiety. Exposure to the market has transformed their lives, causing dislocations, a sense of powerlessness, and a feeling of being controlled by invisible, remote, and powerful forces. People have turned for assistance to a cast of powerful spirits that concretize and give familiar form to that which is ineffable and apparently uncontrollable. Transacting with them has become one of the key means through which the path to success and avoidance of disaster have been imagined. When people propitiate the Lady of the Realm, they address the concerns that arise from their enmeshment in such uncertain and unstable social relations.

People's interactions with the Lady of the Realm reflect their economic circumstances in both the style of the transaction and the nature of their requests. Although the motorcycle taxi drivers describe themselves as laborers *(người lao động)*, their success depends on the vagaries of the market in small-scale mechanized transport services. Their reliance on the goddess as a guarantor of physical integrity speaks to the importance attaching to their corporeal power and the vulnerabilities attending its sale on the market. Such a perspective is shared by those who are involved in small-scale

entrepreneurial activity though ownership or rental of a small capital base
(cơ sở). These include mobile vendors, small food-stall operators, and home-
based clothing makers, to name a few representative trades. They also include
those who work for a fee or tip (bò), with or without a retainer, as drinks
hostesses (tiếp viên) and prostitutes (gái điếm), whose capital outlays include
rental accommodation and transport as well as investments in fancy clothing,
cosmetic modifications, and beauty treatments. What unites such people is
the low value of the capital they own and the high labor component and
relatively low returns they enjoy. They are also prone to the "windfall syn-
drome," on occasion getting a large fare, order, or tip, after which they may
go for days earning little or nothing, a process that can reinforce a sense of
life as a lottery. As their economic conditions are unstable, their veneration
of the goddess is sporadic, and sometimes such intermittent attendance is
used to confirm their variable fortunes.

Another group of people who propitiate the goddess on a more regular
basis are those who work in petty trade (buôn bán nhỏ), who own or rent a
small stall in the market (chợ) or outlet on the ground floor or in front of
their house, keeping it provisioned with goods and spending most of their
waking hours attending it. The request one most commonly hears being
made to the goddess—lucky purchases and quick sales is the petty trader's
mantra. Every trader wants to be able to buy at favorable prices and sell
quickly, thus ensuing capital is not tied up. For many in this sector the Lady
of the Realm is a being from whom permission must be asked to conduct
business and to whom credit must be given for their economic fortunes. The
individualized and transactional relationships that such people entertain with
spirits such as the Lady of the Realm reflect the social relations of their economic practice. The practices of cultivating the spirits, building goodwill,
seeking advance benefits, and making promised repayments are modeled on
the long-term, personalistic, and negotiational approach they take to their
business dealings with clients, suppliers, creditors, and debtors.

One of the most common requests put to the goddess is for assistance in
making one's financial capital grow. Like the goddess Bà Chúa Kho, whose
shrine is just north of Hanoi,[3] the Châu Đốc goddess has come to be seen as
a spirit of financial increase. In a folk religious practice similar to that which
Harrell (1987) and Gates (1996) have studied in China and Jackson in Thailand (1999b), people "borrow" money from her, which is imbued with the
power to magically augment one's own financial reserves. The money is represented in a variety of forms, including various kinds of colored paper,
stamped notes, U.S.-dollar-style "hell" banknotes, gold sheets, and bills of
Vietnamese legal tender. Although one requests (xin) this money from the

goddess, it consists of the money already presented to her either by oneself or by earlier supplicants. After lying on the altar for a while the bills become infused with her powers of reproduction and growth. These bills are kept and never spent, for they are thought capable of reproducing more money and making one's capital grow. Nga, a seamstress outworker and dedicated Châu Ðốc pilgrim, told me that the main reason people went to Her Ladyship's shrine in Châu Ðốc was to borrow money: "The money is wrapped up in red paper envelopes *(bao)* in trays on the altar. There also is replica money, stamped gold sheets, gold and silver foil, and colored paper. There is no shortage of it. You bring it home and place it on the altar to the god of wealth in your house. It will make your money grow, no fear."

Belief in the power of money to reproduce itself reflects the often-voiced conviction among all manner of traders in Vietnam that one needs money to make money. The goddess, whose magical money self-reproduces, offers a circuit breaker to those who lack the capital required to beget more capital. It is not entirely clear for how long she has played this role of spiritual banker. Early accounts of her pilgrimage do not mention this practice (Lam Minh 1942; Malleret 1959). While the ethnic Chinese may have regarded the Lady of the Realm in this light for quite some time, in line with their tradition of borrowing money from the spirits, it would appear that her reputation as a spirit of financial increase spread to the wider population only relatively recently, during the expansion of the finance sector in the late 1980s and early 1990s.

The use of credit is now regarded as normal business practice throughout much of Vietnam, and nowhere is this more true than in southern Vietnam, where much economic activity is dependent on obtaining it though informal channels. Such practices as playing credit circles *(chơi hụi)* and borrowing from private lenders have become preferred means of obtaining credit in a country where institutional banking is not well established.[4] The provision of credit is a favored investment strategy for those who have capital to invest. The demand for credit is great, and the returns are higher than most other sectors provide. People who manage several credit circles at once can live comfortably off the interest. However, keeping track of one's debtors is mentally and psychologically demanding. This is especially true of those people who are immersed in simultaneous relationships of credit and debt as is the case for a large proportion of those who deal in credit (Haughton 2001, 27). People who sell in the market routinely extend purchasing credits to customers while at the same time participating in one or more *hụi*s and sometimes also borrowing for their own needs from private moneylenders. The provision of credit is also relatively risky. One is constantly exposed to default and is constantly forced to reschedule repayments. There are no legal sanctions available to back one up if an informal loan goes bad.

The practice of transacting with the goddess is particularly entrenched among those who are involved in providing commercial credit. It is these people who make the offerings of pigs, gold, and costumes to her and who propitiate her most faithfully. The stories they tell about the goddess at one level symbolize these credit relations, as an idealized "model of and for" such social practices (Geertz 1973). People describe how one can freely borrow from the goddess, provided one repays as promised and does so on time. To fail to keep one's word to her is to attract serious retribution from her. The goddess can reportedly stop the flow of clients to your stall, fill your nights with bad dreams, inflict headaches, and, in certain circumstances, even kill, using the preferred method of wringing one's neck. This is a fable that highlights the responsibilities and sanctions attending the use of credit, propagating a credit ethic of responsible and timely repayment. Furthermore, the goddess plays an active role as a partner in these relationships. Many of those who lend money for interest or who manage *hụi* seek her assistance in securing outstanding repayments. Here the goddess is something of a psychological ally to whom one might turn for solace and self-confirmation when the exposure to risk seems intolerable or when the circle of trust is ruptured when a debtor absconds.

Creditors are not the only ones exposed to risk in such relationships. So too are the people who borrow money. Major capital start-ups in sectors that have promised miracle returns such as longans, catfish, tiger shrimp, or coffee have been lavishly financed with credit. Credit is widely used by young people to finance leisure pursuits and status-oriented consumer purchases. Other uses include education, health needs, land acquisition, and house building. Migrant laborers and would-be petty entrepreneurs who have flocked into the city from the countryside have borrowed money for rent, business capital, and assistance for family needs back home. In the precarious circumstances of establishing themselves in the city, they have experienced with particular intensity the volatile and contradictory emotions associated with credit: a sense of freedom and opportunity, indeed, but also dependence and vulnerability. Transacting with informal creditors in an economically unstable and unpredictable economic environment is a risky business, and many people have experienced the social relations of credit as demanding, threatening, and pitiless. For such people, this goddess, with her punitive rages, her reputed capacity to trouble people in their sleep, to choke off sales and inflict violent death, is the very face of the finance markets.

Coming to Terms with Market Spirits

Vietnam in many ways is like South Africa—a postrevolutionary society that is embarked on a course of rapid and disorienting cultural, social, and economic transformation—and it makes sense that one might encounter critiques of the concomitant rapid rise in goddess worship similar to those voiced by the Comaroffs in depicting the "occult economies" of "millennial capitalism" (1999, 2000). Given depictions of the goddess as a punitive or threatening being, one might well ask whether one is hearing in her a folk critique of the effect in Vietnam of global capitalist relations. Examples of this latter orientation include the "spirits of resistance" to capitalist labor discipline Aihwa Ong (1987) found in Malaysian factories or the pacts undertaken between South American peasants and the devil, described by Taussig (1980) as a critical folk conceptualization of the capitalist commodity form. Can one consider her cult a counterhegemonic discourse on capitalist-oriented development after the manner of the widow ghosts that Mills (1995) encountered in northeast Thailand? Indeed, some people I have spoken with note the monopolistic and jealous nature of the goddess and do fear her powerful sanctions. However, although she is no placid font of benevolence, the goddess is seen by most of those who propitiate her as a positive and potent accomplice. The tales of her tantrums and punitive episodes are taken as cautionary tales: useful guides to transacting with her. Believers sometimes tell such tales to emphasize that all who honor their promises to her and treat her with respect have nothing to fear. Tales about her conditional assistance and tough sense of justice appear to act as a mechanism to inculcate marketing discipline and propagate ideals of fair dealing. Propitiation of the Lady of the Realm, a figure associated with business success, is based on acceptance rather than on a critique of the economic practices she patronizes.

Some Vietnamese friends with whom I have shared stories about the magnificent gifts offered to the goddess have questioned the value that could inhere in worshiping such an acquisitive and demanding being. Her purported episodes of violence, especially if one does not keep one's promises to repay her, cause some critics to question her benevolent disposition. Some Buddhists say that the conditional nature of the assistance offered by such spirits indicates their low moral value and aver that only the Buddha, who demands no such favors, offers accessible and lasting aid to those who suffer. Nevertheless, many people accept the type of conditional aid they receive from the goddess as the only or most reliable form of assistance they know. They do not distinguish this deal-based assistance from the type of help that

Buddhism offers, for many identify the goddess as Lady Buddha (Phật Bà). Interactions with her are based on an expectation of reciprocity as well as beliefs in this-worldly karmic desserts. The notion that what goes around come around (and in this lifetime, too) is a common way of interpreting the doctrine of Karma in the marketplaces where most of her followers work.

There are those in Vietnamese society who regard the practice of making offerings to spirits like her as symptomatic of societal marginality, much as the way "asocial" ghost cults in Taiwan have been represented (Weller 1994a). Writing as early as the 1930s, critical commentators in Saigon opined that those who made offerings to powerful spirits did so to seek exculpation for their misdeeds and then, once they felt they had obtained supernatural assent for their ill-gotten gains, returned to their nefarious practices with re-newed confidence (*Phụ Nữ Tân Văn* 1930a). One hears criticisms by some lay Buddhists and even members of Vietnam's Buddhist clergy (e.g., Thích Quảng Độ 2000) who associate the practice of making offerings to the spirits with those engaging in immoral or cruel (*ác*) practices such as selling fake medicines, stealing, or cheating. Nevertheless, while those who deal with the Lady of the Realm are often criticized for aspiring to a shortcut to easy wealth, her propitiants do not regard their transactions with her, let alone their economic practices, as marginal or abnormal. Transactions with her conform to norms of communication and negotiation and notions of in-debtedness common in families and in the marketplaces where most of her propitiants work. Prescriptions for dealing with her reinforce normative ideas about everyday social exchange. Just as she is expected to fulfill requests on pain of being shunned, so too her debtors make their promised repayments on pain of all manner of misfortunes. Communications with her are reflec-tive of the most intimate of social relationships, taking place at her altar through whispered confidences, strokes, and gentle taps. A pilgrimage to her shrine is seen by those who undertake such a journey as an indication of their moral uprightness. Even her most devout followers criticize the immoral in-tentions that impel some to resort to the spirits for assistance in evil or illicit acts. However, her followers are quick to assert that the goddess herself is not to blame for these, that she is good (*hiền lành*) and only wants to do well by people.

Many of those who associate the practice of making offerings to the Lady of the Realm with get-rich-quick schemes or alternatively the nefarious get-out-of-jail ploys of corrupt individuals work in relatively stable occupations as intellectuals, professionals, or salaried employees. Many people in waged jobs, even though they work in close vicinity to or in the same workplace as her more passionate devotees, are unaware of the existence of this goddess.

Such criticisms or lack of awareness reflect her fairly restricted relevance to a particular occupational sector, one that is defined by its instability. She is particularly well known and has her largest following among the petty traders, small entrepreneurs, money traders, and financiers who work in nonsalaried, entrepreneurial employment.[5] For them, low income is not so much a constant preoccupation as are absence of income stability and juggling of exposure to risk. A common perception among traders is that even though their incomes are high, as nonsalaried workers they lack the financial stability and safety net that those on a wage enjoy. Thus the goddess has been described by her followers, who work in such trades, as their only form of insurance *(bảo hiểm xã hội)* or even as a personalistic mafia-style "fixer" *(bảo kê)*, who helps them out of the tight spots they invariably get into with clients, creditors, and debtors, as well as with the law and other representatives of the state. One also finds among the goddess' petitioners businesspeople *(nhà kinh doanh)*, commercial traders *(nhà thương nghiệp)* associated with more stable flows, and owners *(chủ)* of enterprises such as hotels and restaurants with a more substantial capital base. I know of instances of people in this category who have disassociated themselves from the goddess, risking her retribution, as their business has become more consolidated, although I am equally familiar with cases of people whose involvement with the goddess has only increased as their capital and exposure to risk have grown.

The criticism this business-oriented goddess attracts from educated professionals can also be attributed to their investment in an occupational status system. Financially or commercially based paths to social standing are not overly prestigious according to the Confucian and Communist scales of values that have had a historical presence in Vietnam and whose similarities have often been noted (e.g., Woodside 1976; Luong 1992). These cultural projects place scholarship, farming, clerical work, or even soldiering higher on the occupational hierarchy than finance or commerce. Such perspectives were critical to the attempt to restrict market practice in the north in the 1950s and in southern Vietnam after 1975. Although the society has since switched to a market-based economy and private commercial relations have become officially espoused as a norm, one still encounters views from societal elites that are critical of market-based cultural practice. Practices of divination or of making offerings to spirits in return for favors have been described variously as ignorance, misunderstanding, a waste, an absurdity, a mark of backwardness, or a sign of underdevelopment (Templer 1999, 261; Soucy 1999, 135; Lê Hồng Lý 2001, 31). While one is tempted to say that this is a northern Vietnamese perspective perhaps reflecting what Malarney has described as the "stigmatization of commerce" in the Red River delta

(Malarney 1998), such views are commonly voiced by members of southern Vietnam's educated, professional elite. This attitude reflects an attitude of superiority toward market-oriented, nonliterate, nonbureaucratic culture. Denigration of the religious practices of traders and marketers is one means by which some cultural commentators maintain social distinctions in a world where their own power is being undermined by such relations.

Nevertheless, with the rise of the market and the expansion of market-based cultural practices, some observers have begun to view the worship of spirits as integral to the fundamental transition in which their society is embroiled. For example, in a recent paper on the Lady of the Storehouse cult, one Hanoi-based folklorist argued that the explosive rise of such spirits of financial increase reflected people's sense of bewilderment at the pace of change: "This espousal of the market economy is a reasonable adaptation to objective social trends, but it represents a transition to a totally different world, and the Vietnamese people, however adaptable, cannot help being puzzled and dazed by the new system" (Lê Hồng Lý 2001, 33).[6]

Although many Vietnamese intellectuals may continue to denigrate such religious practice, they have been forced to acknowledge its ubiquity and indeed growth. Some have gone further, relating it to the everyday emotional and psychological needs of people involved in difficult circumstances. As the society has switched to a more commercial footing, many of those who formerly worked in the state sector have moved into more commercial-based practice and have themselves been exposed, often for the first time, to the vagaries of the market. Many who were formerly ignorant about the existence of spirits overseeing market practice have gained an appreciation for the assistance they can provide. For example, one Ho Chi Minh City–based schoolteacher told me that she was aware that most people went to Châu Đốc seeking assistance with business or other practical matters. She told me dismissively, "They think that they can succeed in life by drawing on the magical powers of this or that spirit." Nevertheless, although she herself did not believe in the goddess she said she could understand the logic of their practice: "Many of those who go to propitiate her are poor and endure precarious economic circumstances. One of the most common practices is to borrow a small amount of money from her. This has no real economic benefit; however, it encourages people to think that they have procured the patronage of a powerful being. Belief in her responsiveness to their prayers increases people's own self-confidence. It helps them endure uncertainty and economic misfortune. As a consequence, it is true people's fortunes frequently improve noticeably after visiting her shrine, and they return a year later to repay her for helping them advance economically."

FIG. 6. The earth god (Ông Địa) and the god of wealth (Thần Tài) on a curbside stall

This person grew up in a family of intellectuals and had trained in the state school system for a career in education. Influenced by Vietnam's Confucianist bureaucratic culture, and sharing many intellectuals' preoccupations with progress, scientific rationality, and modernist occupational distinctions, she had not always been so appreciative of such beliefs. Without a doubt one of the factors that caused her to be better-disposed toward the practice of goddess worship was her own experience, during the centralist-socialist period 1975–1986, of having to abandon teaching and work in a market stall in order to make a living. There she came to appreciate if not share the strategies and beliefs of her fellow marketers (figure 6).

Spirits and the Socialized Contours of Existence

This vein of opinion accepts that religious practice such as goddess worship is implicated in contemporary social realities. Such a view is fundamentally distinct from perspectives that consign spirit worship to the past, either as a venerable cultural survival or alternatively as a form of benighted ignorance, incompatible with modernity. Rather, appeals to spirits such as the Lady of the Realm are seen as a way of achieving some kind of equilibrium in the difficult and unprecedented circumstances of a market economy. The practice builds upon a model of conceptualizing power that has had long tenure in Vietnamese society.[7] And yet the spiritual agents to whom people turn in such circumstances draw inspiration from and affirm the social relations in which their petitioners' lives are enmeshed.

The custom of making offerings to the Lady of the Realm is based on the view that people share the world with powerful spiritual beings—ancestors, ghosts, gods, and other spirits—many of whom they rely upon for their existential well-being (Cadière 1958, 6; Hue Tam Ho Tai 1985, 23). According to this conception, the forces that affect human existence are given human form. For example, the five constitutive elements of existence *(ngũ hành)*— earth *(thổ)*, water *(thủy)*, fire *(hỏa)*, wood *(mộc)*, and metal *(kim)*—are humanized as the Five Mothers (Năm Mẹ) (figure 7). These qualities are not thought to reside in a distinct domain called nature but in a socialized realm, where they have a social identity, status, and rank. Imagined in personalistic terms as having individual qualities and existential needs, they are also

FIG. 7. The five elements *(ngũ hành)* depicted as the Five Mothers

amenable to negotiation or control. The necessities of human existence are not resources to be extracted from the domain of nature but rather are obtained through interaction with the anthropomorphized inhabitants of the spiritual realm.

Kin categories such as *ông* (grandfather), *bà* (grandmother), *cô* (paternal aunt), and *cậu* (maternal uncle) are used to refer to a wide range of spiritualized principles and entities including the sky, earth, water, forests, plants, and animals, as well as spirits of human provenance. These naming practices attest to the role of kinship in people's apprehension of and interaction with the world. Depictions of the five constitutive elements of existence as mothers reflect the socialized relations of human reproduction, which, in Vietnam, accord primacy to mothers as givers and sustainers of life. The capability attributed to such spirits to provide health, prosperity, and progeny is modeled on perceptions of female powers to bear and nurture life. Deities who are described with affection as "mother" *(mẹ)* encode the positive sentiments and debt of gratitude extended to mothers, who gave birth to *(đẻ)*, nurtured *(nuôi)*, cared for *(chăm sóc)*, educated *(dạy)*, shared confidences with *(tâm sự)*, and empathized with *(thông cảm)* one. The high rank such spirits are often assigned relates to the substantial powers wielded at home by mothers, who are sometimes accorded the title general of the interior *(nội tướng)* by their husbands. The substantial punitive sanctions with which maternal spirits are equipped draw on people's experience of their mothers as the household's prime educators and disciplinarians and their role as managers of daughters-in-law and supervisors of childhood conduct. They are less intercessors to a male patriarch than ultimate authorities over children and residential in-laws. The term "Lady" or "Her Ladyship" used for these spirits encodes the stature and authority that is wielded by this most influential member of the Vietnamese household.

The powers of financial increase acorded to some spirits are also linked to their identity as mothers. As examples of "sympathetic magic" or analogous reasoning, such symbols of increase draw inspiration from cultural ideas about reproductive powers. Hill Gates speaks of the association in Chinese folk thinking between financial increase and feminine gender that is also evident in Vietnamese religious thinking: "Women reproduce. So, in the appropriate political-economic context, does money" (1996, 196). This association accounts for the imagery one sees on the walls of the shrines to goddesses such as Tien Hau who are known for their powers of financial increase: depictions of mother tigresses with their cubs and dragonesses proudly eyeing their writhing little dragonlets.

One of the qualities associated with spirits such as the Lady of the Realm is their responsiveness *(linh ứng)*. A number of believers have described this as an innate feminine characteristic, explaining that this accounts for the preference for female spirits in Vietnam. One example sometimes given is the high profile enjoyed by the Bodhisattva Kuan Yin, under the Vietnamized name Quan Âm. A ubiquitous figure in Vietnamese households, her image is displayed in homes more commonly than those of male incarnations of the Buddha. An image of this beloved figure is usually found in the forecourt or front room of Mahayana Buddhist pagodas, while smaller versions of her are also found on the altars within. One also finds her statue displayed on top of people's houses, on external verandas that overlook streets, or at intersections. As the Hearer of the World's Cries she is considered more responsive and compassionate than male incarnations of the Buddha. Her femininity is sometimes described as a feature of her magical responsiveness. A formerly male god, Avalokitésvara, she incarnated as a female in China and Vietnam to better respond to people's needs. People say she is like their mother, who is easier to influence and more ready to forgive misdeeds than their more distant father. As Kuan Yin of the South Seas she is considered a savior of the lost and hopeless. Portrayals of her with a thousand eyes and a thousand hands show her to be infinitely compassionate toward human suffering.

The multitalented nature of many of the goddesses venerated in Vietnam can be related to the gendered structure of the household. The Lady of the Realm's diverse powers relate to areas that are deemed to fall within the conventionally defined sphere of responsibilities of female household members. The goddess will help ensure marital fidelity and guarantee domestic peace, harmony, and family health. She brings the desired number and sex of progeny, and healthy and obedient children. She delivers success in children's study, as well as in their attempts to find work and a spouse. Goddesses such as the Lady of the Realm are put upon for assistance in all questions of the household economy, entreated to help with sales of household produce and purchases of all sorts of household needs. This constellation of skills reflects the multitude of roles that female members of Vietnamese households assume as mothers, grandmothers, aunts, sisters, wives, daughters, and daughters-in-law. The potency attributed to such feminine spirits is a function of the diverse and heavy responsibilities that women assume in the household division of labor.

Such spirits also derive authority from modeling generational authority, and the forms of propitiating them draw upon Vietnamese notions of transgenerational reciprocity. In Vietnamese thinking, children are indebted to their parents. The birth of a child is more than a natural or biological event.

It is the opening transaction in a life-long relationship of reciprocity, during which one must display the proper gratitude and fully discharge oneself of his or her existential debt. This debt is often felt most directly to one's mother, who went through the pain of childbirth. One contracts further debts by being nurtured, principally by one's mother. Into adulthood one must return the debt to one's parents *(trả nợ)*; and when the parents are aged and infirm, the relationship is reversed and one must nurture his or her parents and, after their death, continue to feed and house their spirits. As one mother with many children explained to me, "Children are our debts. When they grow we become theirs." These assumptions are the reason it seems normal to enter into transactions with a feminine spiritual being for one's most basic life needs. Although deities such as the Lady of the Realm are held to underwrite the very conditions for one's existence, one is not beholden to them absolutely, for like one's parents, they too have their needs and expectations of the relationship—to be fed, housed, cleaned, clothed, and catered to socially.

As Eric Wolf notes of the Virgin of Guadaloupe in Mexico, in such complex societies the family is but one relay in the circuit within which such symbols are generated (E. Wolf 1958, 36). In many respects the spirits also model the Vietnamese political order, with its historically eclectic mix of merit-based mandarins, members of noble lineages, scheming courtiers, corruptly appointed officials, and charismatic individuals. People's interactions with spirits is based on experience with their leaders, to whom a person might best put his or her case through the use of an intermediary, such as a member of the official's family, and whose assent can be purchased and will softened through presentation of a suitable gift. People access the powers of the spirit world in a similar way, through sacrificial offerings and presenting the deity with a written petition for peace *(cầu bình an)*. Individuals rely on someone experienced in such matters to draft messages to the spirits in Chinese characters, recite their wishes in formulaic chants, and give guidance in ritual protocols; or they employ a practitioner such as a medium *(ông đồng/bà đồng)* to learn the spirit's will. The spirits speak through the body of the mediums, who dramatize their persona, voice, acts, and wishes though dance, costume, and gesture. These figures act as channels to the world of the spirits, enabling and energizing the relationship between gods and a wider body of devotees.

In southern Vietnam the use of mediums and other ritual intermediaries is not as common or elaborate as in the north of the country. Southern Vietnamese people approach their spirits more directly, preferring oral to written communication, muttering their own introductions, stating their own requests, presenting their own gifts, casting divination sticks and woodblocks in preference to using mediums, collecting their own benefits *(hái lộc)* directly from the altar, and stroking *(vuốt)* the deity to tap its spiritual power.[8] Many people visit the spirits as the need arises. The shrines to these spirits are frequently crowded outside the times of formal propitiation ceremonies conducted by a cult committee. To some extent such visits attest to the less formal and hierarchical nature of southern society. Being a frontier land only recently settled by the Vietnamese, it is a place where more individualistic, egalitarian, and spontaneous social relations pertain, a place many of whose leaders and founding figures have been personalistic, unpolished, and egalitarian. When the feudal court system was annulled in the French colonial period, these individualistic, informal social tendencies were further accentuated. These social conditions have influenced the way people relate to the spirits and have shaped a cast of spirits who are multifunctional, can-do, personable, and easy to gain access to.

Modeling Economic Power

The identity of deities such as the Lady of the Realm who are valued for their ability to provide economic assistance is also influenced by the social contours of the marketplace, which is one of the most markedly gendered institutions in Vietnamese society. As the main actors in the exchange of commodities, women in Vietnam are key to what Gates (1996) calls the "petty capitalist mode of production." Women are highly visible in the marketplaces and domestic trade routes, operating wholesale and retail outlets, engaging in trade, and supplying goods and credit in remote rural areas. As the main providers of commodities and consumer goods to the household and to others, they are the principal channel through which people obtain the necessities and desirable commodities of life (Hoskins 1976; O'Harrow 1995, 164). As the principal sellers of home-grown produce and purchasers of a household's subsistence needs, women are the key mediators between house and market and are the household's representatives at the marketplace.

The stature of women as economic agents feeds into the metaphoric construction of powerful deities such as the Lady of the Realm. Recourse to such a deity for a diverse range of economic ends relates to the embeddedness of women in the economy. Her can-do responsiveness reflects widespread appreciation for the everyday social meaning of femininity as economically competent, efficacious, and reliable. The economic potency assigned to her is a function of the power female traders obtain in the economy and their association with the benefits of production, exchange, and consumption.

Her punitive aspects relate to the influence of such economically powerful social actors. Her high public profile reflects the central position that female-dominated markets occupy in local society. Her role as indispensable mediator in important economic and financial transactions relates to the familiar intermediary role women play as representatives of their households and families in the wider economic world.

The gender of financial increase deities such as the Lady of the Realm also draws upon popular perceptions that women are, in general, better at handling money than men (cf. Gates 1996, 196). In Vietnam there is a strong perception that women are financially more skillful than men: shrewder financial managers, harder bargainers, more patient at building customer goodwill, less likely to be angered in negotiations, and less spendthrift.[9] This perception reflects the central role Vietnamese women play in the household's financial and other economic transactions. As the main handlers, managers, and keepers of a household's finances, women are intimately associated with money (O'Harrow 1995, 165). Women also take the lead in the running of *huis*. It is said that women's extended social relations, negotiation skills, flexibility, social orientation, and knowledge of people's diverse circumstances strengthen a creditor's hand in managing an informal credit network, especially in an environment where legal or capital guarantees are lacking. As the Vietnamese economy has commercialized and as credit has become increasingly central to the reproduction of wealth, their informal service has assumed a critical importance for all those who make a living as petty entrepreneurs. Most of the creditors to whom male motorcycle taxi drivers in Ho Chi Minh City are in debt are women from their local neighborhood. Little wonder then that to those who work in financial and commercial circles, the spiritual figure they most widely associate with financial increase and healthy sales assumes a feminine form.

I was told that if I wanted to learn about the goddess, I should talk to Hoa, the owner of a gold shop that was outside the main market building in a bustling downtown urban quarter of Ho Chi Minh City. Many in her neighborhood considered Hoa an astute businesswoman and believed that her religious piety was exemplary and the key to her business success. Hoa steadfastly observed calendrical ceremonies such as the midyear festival and twice-monthly ritual days at the local Buddhist pagoda and was well known for her generous offerings. She transacted with a great variety of spiritual entities, be they ghosts *(ma)*, the god of finance (Thần Tài), the earth god (Ông Địa), the Buddha (Phật), local deities, or those figures such as the Lady of the Realm known to embody certain exemplary traits useful in business. As her neighborhood's most often cited economic success story, Hoa's actions and deeds in matters religious and other areas were watched by others for guidance as to how to prosper in life.

Hoa's shop is a local landmark. Its walls are lined with religious iconography such as paired fish and horses and shrines to spirits of all hues: Sakyamuni Buddha, Kuan Yin, the Laughing Buddha, the Taoist Immortals, the Earth God, the God of Wealth, the Money Toad, the Mother of Birth, and the Jade Princess. When I visited, its halogen lights were blazing, and its banks of glass cabinets, their gold and jewels displayed on red velvet, fragmented the light into millions of gleaming points. A cube of dazzling light spilled from the shop onto the road and illuminated a section of the pavement with the unmistakable aura of prosperity. The shop was full of people. A pair of customers inspected a sample from a trayful of gold Buddha pendants. Others waited in line, their hands clenching foreign currency of unfamiliar hues. In front of the counter, a young shop assistant was taking and counting their money, while behind it, Hoa, a plump, smiling woman with pale skin, was calmly wielding a calculator. For each large-denomination U.S. note she took from her assistant, she handed back several bricks of Vietnamese notes of even larger denomination.

Hoa told me that the gold plaques *(khánh vàng)*, stamped images, and festive congratulations in Vietnamese and Chinese that were hanging on the wall of her shop were gifts to present at weddings, birthdays, and the like. "At this time of year a lot of people buy them to present as gifts to the Lady of the Realm." When I asked who the goddess was Hoa replied, "Her Ladyship is the one who supports *(phù hộ)* us. She assists in everything. She is responsive to prayers. That is to say she responds to whatever you request." I asked Hoa if the goddess would grant any wish at all. Hoa assented. "Providing you have the right orientation, you ask properly, and you do the right thing by Heaven, Her Ladyship will grant whatever you wish. But be careful if you promise her anything in return," she added. "If you break your promise, you will be punished." I asked Hoa, "What do you request?" She replied, "I always request lucky purchases and quick sales." I queried further: "So did she grant your requests?" Hoa smiled and nodded in response. She and her sister had just been down to Châu Đốc. Her sister had requested Her Ladyship's help in collecting repayment of a loan of several thousand dollars. The debtor had come good with the outstanding money. A gift of gratitude to Her Ladyship was in order, and they had offered the goddess an entire roast pig (figure 8).

For Hoa the expensive gold plaques and display cabinets full of expensively embroidered robes and headpieces that she had seen at the goddess'

FIG. 8. A roast pig offering to the Lady of the Realm

shrine, plus the sheer number of pigs on offer before her altar, proved beyond doubt the goddess' efficacy. Conversely, those in the shrine in Châu Đốc observe that the biggest of these gifts come from urban businesspeople such as Hoa. To the ever-attentive community of believers, the goddess is the being to whom such successful businesspeople and financiers return, without fail, to thank each year. Both the goddess and the businesswoman have thrived off each other's successes. Both have been integral to local people's involvement in the market economy. In many respects the goddess could herself said to be modeled on Hoa. She is a pale skinned and bejeweled woman, surrounded by golden offerings and religious iconography. She has recently become very wealthy, and her shrine displays the signs of this prosperity in the most resplendent manner. Like Hoa, a woman of considerable girth, she is said to have physically grown in size in tandem with her reputed growth in powers. She is surrounded each day by a cluster of people, mostly women, who offer bills and gold and receive from her gold and bills that are used to augment their business.

The Gender of Authority

The nexus between female commercial prowess and commerce-oriented goddesses that is illustrated by the relationship between the gold trader Hoa and the Lady of the Realm undoubtedly has a long history in Vietnam. Observations by early foreign visitors such as Barrow offer evidence that for centuries women in Vietnam have been centrally involved in marketing and in trade (1975, 303). Visiting northern Vietnam in the seventeenth century, the English traveler Dampier noted that women were deeply involved in finance and money changing (Luong 1998, 301). When John White went to the region of southern Vietnam in the early nineteenth century on a trade mission, he was approached by Vietnamese female merchants offering to sell goods such as sugar, cotton, and silk (White 1972, 208). The significance of the trade flows and marketing activity in southern Vietnam created opportunities for women to achieve considerable societal status. This could be one reason for the noted prevalence of female deities at the time. One local observer described the high social stature of women in Gia Định society in the early nineteenth century in the same breath as mentioning the large number of goddesses worshiped in this area (Trịnh Hoài Đức 1972). It is quite possible, given the importance of commercial routes to social standing at this time, that these deities' prominence reflected the successes obtained by women in the commercial field.

Goddesses were implicated in the fortunes of female traders more recently, during an era in which both spirit worship and commerce were circumscribed realms of activity. This was the period 1976–1990, following the collapse of the South Vietnamese Republic and before the new regime's economic reform policies started to deliver substantive results. During this period the state's breakup of the ethnic Chinese trading monopoly in the south and its failure to establish an effective alternative distributive network significantly heightened the demands placed on the female-dominated commercial sector. In a time of transition and crisis in economic leadership, women's informal trading practices assumed a significance and scope that was neither intended nor acknowledged by the state's explicit program of reform. Nevertheless, residents of the region recollected women's prominent involvement in these informal economic activities in their conversations with me in the late 1990s.

In the late 1970s and early 1980s, women were the main organizers of the thriving black economy, informal credit providers, and liaison points for smuggling. Many women coordinated black-market dealings from home. In Ho Chi Minh City in the early postwar years the black market in agricultural commodities often had no actual location. People would go to the houses of family, colleagues, and acquaintances to make their purchases and sales. Such outlets enabled those without residence permits in the city (e.g., reeducation camp returnees or fugitives from new economic zones) access to a supply of food, and it gave farmers a point of sale in the cities. Throughout the postwar years, although markets were supposed to be replaced by state-managed distribution cooperatives, the small stalls set up in front of people's houses, often manned by small children or the elderly, remained one of the most pervasive features of the southern landscape. Women also took the lead in coordinating larger, illegal open-air market stalls. Men with very little else to do with their time would sell from the pavement or street corners, but acquaintances who were involved in the informal markets of the late 1970s commonly noted that their female relatives frequently ran the business behind the scenes.

In the postwar years women played a key role in internal smuggling. To some extent they could draw on their relations to rural kin. As there were obstacles to movement, and restrictions on trade, much rural-urban smuggling took place under the pretext of claiming to visit relatives. One woman told me that in the late 1970s, she used to frequently smuggle produce from her relatives' village for resale in the city. By making weekly or more frequent visits, one could smuggle in a great deal of produce. For bona fide visits, a maximum of ten kilograms of rice could be brought back to the city. Many people would notify relatives of their next trip so the relatives could buy up rice in advance. People would also commonly strap sacks of grain and pieces of meat to their bodies, underneath their clothes, for the return trip. During the late 1970s and the 1980s, a time when private trade was banned, a number of people said that female traders had an advantage, for with the majority of law enforcement officials being men, it was easier for women to talk their way through checkpoints. In the early 1980s, the police set up a series of blockades at various points along the main transport routes in the south. Anyone who wanted to trade had to negotiate with the police. It was very often women who were sent to do this, according to Nguyệt, a woman in the capital of a Mekong delta province: "In the mid-eighties, women from Ho Chi Minh City would regularly travel to our market with smuggled goods for sale. They would pay a fee to the bus driver to conceal goods throughout the bus. Certain bus drivers were known to have cultivated relations with the police at the various customs points *(trạm kiểm soát)* along the route. They would give packets of cigarettes and monetary bribes to the police, to evade a comprehensive check of the vehicle. On their arrival in rural towns, these women would be treated like royalty. People would vie to offer them food and lodging in hope of a purchasing their precious commodities for a favorable price."

Nguyệt, who was studying in Ho Chi Minh City in the early 1980s, recounted that her placement in the city enabled her to help her mother, who ran a small cosmetics stall at the local market back home. Cosmetics were available, but prices had been driven high through the monopoly of the "smuggling queens." "Because we disliked their arrogance, people like my mother were forced to arrange their own smuggling system, relying on their own connections to people in the city. My mother entrusted me with several hundred dollars worth of gold to buy up supplies at the market in Chợ Lớn and bring them back for resale. She sent me enough to make several trips, so that if I got caught, I wouldn't lose everything. In those days, there were police stationed along the main roads leading away from Chợ Lớn market to try to catch smugglers. But I didn't have much time, so I bought everything at once, loaded it onto a cyclo and tried to conceal it, to make it past the police. I was lucky and didn't get caught. When the pile of goods in my dormitory room had grown, I divided them into small packages for the bus trip home, paying the bus driver to place them where, according to agreement, the police would not search."

Despite the illegality of such practices, there were incentives in state agents not being overly punitive in exercising their responsibilities. Against the gains to be made on the black market, official salaries represented a pittance, hardly enough to purchase a cup of coffee in the mornings. Rationing, shortages of goods, inflation, and currency changes added further frustrations to the task of supporting one's family on the income from official salary. Indeed, over time, local police came to use small business owners in their precinct to deal for them on the black market. Lan, now a successful Saigonese boutique owner who formerly operated a small *bánh cuốn* stall in front of her house, was known by the police to have extensive black-market dealings. The police would frequently approach her and ask her to purchase goods on the black market, for to do so themselves would be too risky. In turn, she cultivated relations with them for her own ends. To maintain her business, she had to provide them with free meals. At one stage, she estimated that she was providing breakfasts to thirty local cadres. Not only did this allow her to maintain her business and her position as a nerve center for local black-market wheelings and dealings, but she could secure travel documents that allowed members of her family to make arrangements to escape from Vietnam from her powerful beneficiaries.

Today the altar in Lan's house, like the altars of those of most of her fellow petty traders in Vietnam, is crowded with deities and offerings. Most prominent are female deities such as Kuan Yin and the Jade Princess (Bà Chúa Ngọc), whom Lan calls her personal guardian mother *(mẹ độ mạng)*. Also present are bills obtained from the shrine to the Lady of the Realm to which Lan has been making pilgrimages since the late 1980s. These spirits accompanied Lan in the days when her commercial activities were proscribed as they continue to assist her today. Goddesses such as the Lady of the Realm provided succor to women like Lan during some of the most difficult times in popular memory. The stature today of these commerce-oriented goddesses is bound up in the societal contributions made by women who, during the postwar years, were involved in a vast but informal economic movement that defied and perhaps helped transform from within the patriarchal political economic orders dominated by the state. The goddesses are thus collaborators in and agents of an unrecorded history. They represent a popular reworking and telling of history, where women's activity is considered socially central, where commercial prowess is highly valued, where smugglers are the epitome of efficacy, and where flight from the country is granted to the virtuous and is rewarded by prosperity. They celebrate informal social and economic initiatives that the government has labeled criminal, negative, and treacherous or has habitually overlooked.[10] But they point to widely held notions of success and prestige. Those values have attained a central place in contemporary public culture, ways substantially opened up by women.

Gendering Transnational Value

Spirits such as the Lady of the Realm are also ways of conceptualizing sources of value that originate beyond the boundaries of the nation-state. Many of those who propitiate the goddess associate her with fortunes enjoyed beyond the country's borders and wealth flowing back across them. Her reputed patronage of refugees' risky gambles and of ongoing possibilities for migration have given the goddess considerable prestige in the outwardly and upwardly mobile society of the postwar era. I asked Phượng, a resident of Ho Chi Minh City and frequent visitor to Châu Đốc, why she thought the goddess was so popular. She replied, "In the past, many people who wanted to flee the country *(vượt biên)* went to request assistance from Her Ladyship, and she helped them escape. Afterwards, they returned and made gifts to thank her. As a result of this she is well known for granting any requests."

In this account, the goddess features as a hidden player in the "boat people" exodus of the late 1970s and early 1980s. By virtue of such exceptional assistance, not only did many people leapfrog outside the frame of postwar Vietnam's dire social and economic woes, but the remittances from her overseas beneficiaries, which began to flow back across Vietnam's borders, have been key to the postwar reconstruction of society (Dang Phong and Beresford 1998).[11] This is particularly true of southern Vietnam, from which the majority of the diaspora are drawn. During a time when it was difficult to stay afloat in the region's postwar economic doldrums, assistance from overseas relatives proved critical to people's survival. A great many people's access to cash or capital start-up was through an overseas relative rather than a bank or government scheme. A relatively small cash injection—by American, Canadian, or Australian standards—was enough to get a local business going. The effect of this assistance is highly visible in those parts of the country (such as the coastal regions, from which many refugees were drawn) that have suffered from relatively little economic investment. Wherever one travels in such regions one is pointed to successful enterprises, substantial capital holdings, and opulent houses and possessions as due to the financial support from an overseas relative.

Much of the newfound wealth in southern Vietnam thus has a profoundly human face, based as it is on economic transfers across borders but within families. Motivated by sentiments such as loyalty, duty, guilt, compassion, patriotism, and revenge, these flows have incidentally given the economy a vital stimulus. While the rhetoric of economic laws and globalization have been used by Vietnamese policy makers to account for GDP growth of about 10 percent in urban areas of Vietnam, a substantial degree of this economic growth results from the playing out of familial ties of sentiment and indebtedness and expectations of assistance across national borders. Such powerful emotions have been given enduring expression in the massive construction of residences, shops, boats, and agricultural infrastructure and in the proliferation of vehicles and goods of all kinds, transforming the landscape of Vietnam. The personal dimension of this transfer of wealth helps explain why economic success stories in the 1990s were popularly attributed to very human-looking spiritual agents rather than to the operation of abstract economic laws. The emergence of a group of prosperity-bringing goddesses along southern Vietnam's international borders is a compelling indication of the economic importance in the region of transnational sources of wealth. Nowhere is this more evident than in Ho Chi Minh City, provider of the bulk of the region's refugee population, recipient of large amounts of remittances, and also national stage for the most lavish displays of newfound prosperity by those who have struck it lucky abroad. These dramatic displays are repeated in the shrines to goddesses such as the Lady of the Realm and Dinh Co, where the most opulent of gifts, or so it is said, come from overseas Vietnamese. The debt owed to these goddesses is recorded in the size and caliber of their gifts, and such largesse has led many people to consider these goddesses to be key to successfully dealing with the forces at play beyond the nation's borders.

The gender of these spirits reflects the central role that women have played in the development of these new transnational linkages. A great deal of the wealth that has been generated locally as a result of the country's increased economic integration has been mediated by women. Several sources of this wealth can be identified. In the 1980s, as remitted income began to arrive from abroad in the form of a quantity of gold, foreign cash, or medicines, it was often made locally accessible by a Vietnam-based female relative operating a domestic credit service or used to fund a business or engage in land speculation. Also beginning in the late 1980s, many young women began to find a path of upward mobility in marriages to overseas-based men and in other modes of sponsored migration. Based in diverse overseas contexts, Vietnamese women have played a leading role in supporting families back home in Vietnam (Thomas 1999). Commercialized sexual relations, both within and beyond Vietnam's borders, have been another source of foreign wealth mediated by local women. Income from foreign investment and trade earned both formally and informally by government officials has been parlayed into lasting and more respectable capital assets by female family members. Increased economic activity and rising incomes boosted consumption and marketing activities, raising the profile of market women and other entrepreneurs and service-sector providers.

Future Feminine?

Among the players who have been key to the processes of commercial re-engagement under way in the cities and marketplaces of southern Vietnam, the Lady of the Realm figures as the engine driving economic growth. As an existential creditor, spiritual banker, and reliable partner, the Lady of the Realm is central to the way economic value is comprehended and obtained by those who have been at the forefront of Vietnam's transition to a market-based economy. Both the extraordinary responsiveness and the hierarchical and punitive qualities attributed to this personalistic spirit represent a socialized theory of value, an understanding of power and how to get it or engage it. This framework, sometimes described as animism, has been readily applied to the new economic forces and powers that have transfigured people's lives. For those who make offerings to her she is not an archaic symbol but a figure in the present, the key means through which the power to reproduce human life, to maintain households, and to consolidate financial and commercial power has been imagined and accessed.

The Lady of the Realm emerged as a religious superstar during the 1980s and 1990s, an indigenous creation more than able to hold her own against whatever globalization had to offer. However, seeds of societal change were sown in that era that might lead to a lessening or change in the goddess' public appeal. The reforms of the 1980s, which normalized the arrangements of the informal economy, came clothed in the appearance of reason, science, and progress, images that in Vietnamese modernist culture have been associated with male capacities. Thus the reforms gave male prestige a great fillip, bringing practices in which women had been involved in an unrecognized way since the end of the war in 1975 into the legal realm, incorporating them under government control, and making them the focus of the science of economics and the domain of reason.

In the 1990s, much foreign investment went into male hands as local authorities became the principal partners in foreign joint ventures. Development aid activity favored male officials, managers, and workers, despite the gender equity imperative in many official aid programs. Deregulation saw male-dominated state enterprises calve off into the private sphere and cadres transform into company directors. Success lay in negotiating the wide band of gray that was the state/private divide, using connections, sharing information, and collaborating with government insiders, but dealing flexibly with clients and private partners to tap social flows of wealth. The Vietnamese middle class moved rapidly toward professionalization and higher training. The same period saw an increase in the number of female school dropouts and a decline in women's access to capital and formal business training (Lê Thi 1996). In the early to mid-1990s, large-scale corporations such as Unilever, Proctor and Gamble, and Coke began to centralize and systematize distribution networks, employing young mostly male economics graduates to rationalize distribution, develop marketing strategies, and plan human resources. This might translate into secularization whereby "increase deities" such as the Lady of the Realm attract progressively fewer adherents and have less work to do as the male-dominated commercial and professional sectors eat further into the sphere of female petty entrepreneurs. It may lead to a masculinization of the religious sphere, and certainly recent years have seen a renewed emphasis on venerating Confucius, in a spate of published appreciations, in shrine refurbishments, and in rituals. Or it may be that female spirits are drawn into the imagination and affirmation of new gendered alignments in the economy. Given changes in the Lady of the Realm's own ethnic and gender status and in the array of occupational responsibilities attributed to her, such transformations in the religious landscape would not be unprecedented.

4

Reinscribing
Rural Religion

Vietnamese ethnologists have described the worship of the Lady of the
Realm as a spiritual practice originating out of the concerns of local
agricultural communities (Thạch Phương et al. 1992, 91). This goddess is
widely venerated in the Mekong delta, most of whose population of fifteen
million are engaged in farming. The delta is renowned for its agriculture,
producing the nation's highest yields of rice and diverse other products including fruit, livestock, and fish (Vo Tong Xuan and Matsui 1998). Considered a fertility symbol representing the generative power of Mother Earth,
goddesses such as the Lady of the Realm are said to be prominent in all
societies that practice cultivation (Do Lai Thuy 1996, 29). Her stature in the
Mekong delta has been attributed to her symbolization of its distinctive environmental factors, the fertile lands and plentiful waters that sustain its human life (Nguyễn Đăng Duy 1997, 142). Each year alluvium-rich floodwaters
cover western parts of the delta to a depth of several meters flushing out
buildups of acid and salt. When the waters recede they leave behind a coating
of rich topsoil. During the rest of the year, water from the main river is dispersed throughout the plain by a dense network of canals and streams, providing year-round irrigation and drainage. Such conditions enable the delta
to sustain population densities of four hundred per square kilometer.

According to Nguyễn Phương Thảo, the cult of mother goddesses *(tục
thờ mẫu)* in southern Vietnam addresses the age-old spiritual needs of the
Vietnamese farmer living according to the seasonal cycles of wet-rice farming
(1997, 181). The rites surrounding the Lady of the Realm, as others have
noted, are finely attuned to local seasonal rhythms. Nguyễn Minh San (1993,
33) describes the annual *xây chầu* rite conducted at her shrine in Vĩnh Tế
village near Châu Đốc as a rain-invoking ceremony *(lễ cầu mưa)* linking the

rites to a new cycle of the local agricultural year. Nguyễn Đăng Duy accords similar significance to the rite of bathing the goddess *(lễ tắm bà)* that takes place on the previous day. That these rites are conducted in the fourth lunar month shows how finely calibrated the festival is to local environmental conditions, for the rains in this area begin each year in the fourth month (Nguyễn Đăng Duy 1997, 162).[1] The bathing of the statue and changing of its robes are rites that inaugurate the beginning of a calendrical cycle of local relevance, whose purpose is to see out the old, welcome in the new, and seek a year of prosperous living (Nguyễn Đăng Duy 1997, 162).[2]

Such studies also indicate that this goddess addresses locationally specific concerns: "The people settling in Châu Đốc made a living by farming. As a result they put their trust in the earth, in Mother Earth, for a bounteous season and to be well off" (Thái Thị Bích Liên 1998, 35). Some tie her specifically to rice farming as a "goddess of rice fields" (Huỳnh Ngọc Trảng and Trương Ngọc Tường 1997, 144). By contrast, in the U Minh mangrove forest the woodcutters and honey gatherers make offerings to the goddess to request health and avoid malaria and to protect against other specific risks their work entails (Nguyễn Công Bình et al. 1990, 377). In the coastal regions there are numerous shrines to the goddess that attest to her overseeing of a local fishing economy. Such rites also serve to demarcate space. "In southern Vietnam every house has a shrine to the Lady of the Realm, placed at the corner of the house or orchard" (Nguyễn Công Bình et al. 1990, 377). In Bình Phú village, Tiền Giang province, shrines to the goddess, resembling a small house of wood or leaves, are placed at the corner of people's orchards. The goddess is venerated only on the side of National Highway One where the village's rice fields are found (Lương Hồng Quang 1997, 186). Shrines to her are often erected at the ecological limits of human habitation. Huỳnh Ngọc Trảng considers that the shrine to the goddess at Sam Mountain could have been built in this location because it was hilly and the area was difficult to exploit and thus lay on the fringe of local settlement (Huỳnh Ngọc Trảng, pers. com.). Many other examples of these can be found along the coastal fringes of the Mekong delta. A small and beautiful shrine dedicated to her is on the seaward side of Bạc Liêu town. Nguyễn Phương Thảo mentions that most villages in coastal Bình Đại district of Bến Tre province have a shrine to the Lady of the Realm (1997, 185).

Accounts of the ceremonies surrounding the goddess tie her veneration to the concerns of discrete social groupings. In Bình Phú village, offerings of incense to the goddess to request peace in the family are made each time households celebrate a calendrical and life-cycle ceremony (Lương Hồng Quang 1997, 186). Larger shrines to the goddess, found throughout the region, are a focus for community festivals *(lễ hội)*. According to ethnologists, such festivals are "the spiritual products of an agricultural people" (Thạch Phương 1993, 21) and serve to reflect and reinforce bonds of rural community (Hồ Hoàng Hoa 1998). The festival to the Lady of the Realm in Vĩnh Tế is said to have originated as a village festival *(hội làng)* (Thạch Phương et al. 1992, 91), whose function was to bring together all strata of village society (Thạch Phương et al. 1992, 83). As such, the societal cohesion she provided was inherently limited. Phan Dai Doan notes that the efficacy of such guardian spirits is confined to the village that venerates them (1995, 185). For these reasons, the rural festivals of the southern Vietnamese region were traditionally isolated affairs, manifesting a harmony among nature, cosmos, and people (Thạch Phương et al. 1992, 89), although recently, "infiltration" by urban, consumerist, and commercial culture has regrettably caused them to lose their "innocent and pure rustic character" (Thạch Phương et al. 1992, 77).

In brief, the veneration of the Lady of the Realm is seen by these writers as an expression of the Mekong delta's rural culture. Hers is an agricultural cult addressing the temporal and spatial patterns of its inhabitants' lives. She symbolizes the elements that underpin local livelihoods and evokes the delta's ecological diversity, underlining the profound but variable ties between its people and environment. Her festival encodes environmental rhythms that inflect a whole way of life and consolidates bonds between members of rural communities. Situated on the margins of settlements, her shrines mark the limited horizons of the rural world. Her worship is hence depicted as integral to the ritual "production of locality" according to which logic "space and time are themselves socialised and localised through complex practices of performance and representation and action" (Appadurai 1996, 180).

Despite the compelling picture this literature offers of this goddess' spiritual relationship to place, such a perspective cannot deal with various translocal manifestations of her worship. An account of the festival to the Lady of the Realm held on Sam Mountain near Châu Đốc in June 1942 noted that her fete attracted six to seven thousand people drawn from all corners of Cochinchina (Lam Minh 1942). The scope of this gathering indicates a very different kind of relationship between the goddess and petitioners. A report about the Black Lady of Tây Ninh in the late nineteenth century noted similarly,

> The deity of Tây Ninh is one of the most well known gods in Cochinchina. Pilgrims from all the corners of the region flock to Đền Bà Đen pagoda every year to invoke this powerful divinity of the mountain and present votive

offerings. These pilgrimages are made every year, on the 15th day of the 1st, 9th and 10th lunar months. Rich pilgrims bring with them votive bars of gold and silver. The less affluent offer to the famous pagoda the fruits of their land and production, which they have reaped after many days and even months. Likewise, the Chinese also make the divinity of the mountain their cult (Jammes in Baurac 1899, 270).

These accounts caution against seeing worship of these goddesses as the spiritual product of isolated, ecologically autarchic, or remote rural communities. They alert us to these spirits' evident investment with powers that transcend the limits of their local areas. The scope of their followings is suggestive of significant relationships between such sites and the distant locales from which the propitiants are drawn. That certain shrines should attract such a following is perhaps to be expected in a region well-served internally by a vast network of waterways and whose human settlements have been transformed by their incorporation into increasingly extensive relationships. It is unlikely that these goddesses and their imputed powers would not bear the traces of the complex interdependencies and dynamic relationships that inflect life in the region. Such religious practice entails relationships between people and places of considerable complexity, extension, and dynamism.

What follows is a history of connections between a number of significant sites that have helped shape the worship of the Lady of the Realm in the Mekong delta. Focusing on a single shrine to this goddess in Vĩnh Tế village, An Giang province, the history explores the shrine's significance to pilgrims from farther afield. Noting the importance of the shrine to pilgrims from Ho Chi Minh City, it examines how the potency assigned to the goddess encodes a specific historical relationship between this city and the Mekong delta. It shows the way both urban and rural understandings of the goddess are modified in encounters between different people and places. The hybridized understandings that ensue feed back to diverse rural areas forming the basis for new local understandings of the Lady of the Realm.

Connecting to the City

In the first few months of each year, the shrine to the Lady of the Realm is a favorite destination of pilgrims from Ho Chi Minh City. During this time, the well-paved streets of the hillside village of Vĩnh Tế are full of cars, minibuses, motorcycles, and coaches from that city, giving it an urban feel, almost as if an entire urban quarter has been transported over the rice fields and branches of the delta and deposited in this new location. In counterpoint to this immense influx of humanity, the old-timers in the village evoke the days when their village was an isolated settlement in the delta. Indeed it was an island surrounded by Mekong floodwaters for several months of each year.

Local memories of venerating the goddess extend back to the 1890s when, according to some elderly residents, the shrine was refurbished by a wealthy landowning family. An elderly woman, the owner of a café in Vĩnh Tế village, recalled that in the decades before the Second World War the festival had lasted ten days and mainly involved the people who lived in the immediate vicinity of the shrine. In those days, for the majority of people living in the western Mekong, mobility was relatively restricted. Her elderly male neigbor attributed this to technological deficiencies: the western delta was "not yet civilized" *(chưa được văn minh)*. People frequently walked wherever they wanted to go. In his youth, a trip by foot of fifteen to twenty kilometers was not unusual. The unsealed roads built along the banks of canals were rough and narrow, and the numerous river crossings became impassable during the rainy season. The only means of mass land transport were pony-drawn carts, each carrying four to six passengers, yet they were more common near the provincial centers than out in the countryside.[3] A rickshaw on rubber wheels called a *xe kéo*, the precursor of the bicycle-pulled cart *(xe lôi)*, a cheap form of transport, was used in the towns. They were banned in 1939 for being "too slavelike." Rowboats *(xuồng)* were common and, during the floods, the only means of transport. He thought most families had owned one. Sometimes very poor families would fashion a raft out of five or six banana-tree trunks. People rowed their boats everywhere, even to Long Xuyên, about eighty kilometers distant. The 267-kilometer trip from Châu Đốc to Saigon took fifteen to seventeen days. Travelers rowed with the river flow and with the tides, stopping for the duration of the opposing tide, then continuing when it turned. Boats of various sizes plied this route, with various numbers of rowers. Motor-powered passenger boats *(tàu)* connected Châu Đốc to other provinces but did not service the smaller water routes.

Economic constraints also restricted mobility. Early in the century bicycles made an appearance albeit used with difficulty on footpaths of silt. These were conveyances of the very wealthy or those who had worked for France in the highest positions of the village administration. In the 1930s one local man estimated there had only been one bicycle per hundred people. By midcentury, bicycles were still rare in most of the southern rural region.[4] As late as 1950, in some villages, there was not even a single one. Those were very poor and wretched times, he said. Only in the late 1960s did bicycles become prevalent. Cars were only used by the French and those Vietnamese who worked for them. There were a variety of makes of motorbike, mostly

French-built, but again these were restricted to wealthy people. In those days there were few privately owned motorized boats. Only wealthy people could afford their own motors. People had to go to Saigon to buy one. Such conditions had the effect of restricting the numbers of people who could attend the festival to the goddess.

This was to change dramatically during these locals' lifetimes. The motorization of watercraft in the 1960s brought increasing numbers of pilgrims from distant provinces.[5] Improvements in the roads and the introduction of cheap forms of mechanized mass transport during that period led to an increase in the numbers of pilgrims from farther afield. Among the new influx of pilgrims to the shrine, those from Saigon and Chợ Lớn were particularly noticeable. In the late 1960s, the café owner recalled, increasing numbers of Saigonese began to arrive in her village by bus, car, and motorized *xe lôi*. Black and chrome-colored Honda motorbikes were first seen in the village in 1967 or 1968.[6] They were intimations of the consumer culture that was rapidly transforming urban areas.

However, with the escalating war and the deteriorating security situation in the countryside, the newfound mobility these forms of transport provided to urbanites was quickly attenuated. This impact was most evident in the rural areas subject to the heaviest fighting. For example, bus drivers who regularly ply the pilgrimage route between Ho Chi Minh City and Châu Đốc told me that during the war pilgrims from Saigon, who used to visit the mountain shrine to the Black Lady in Tây Ninh province, found the way impassable because of heavy fighting all along the road to Tây Ninh. By contrast, the area around Châu Đốc, although farther from Saigon, was relatively secure because of the presence of the Hòa Hảo forces, whose historical grievances with the Communists created an environment unfavorable to insurgency and severely limited the latter's guerrilla activities in the middle delta and An Giang area. As a result of this relative difference in safety of access, the Lady of the Realm began to receive visits from those urban pilgrims who had formerly made offerings to the Black Lady, whose shrine had become inaccessible. Today, a statue of the Lady of the Realm shares the main altar alongside the Black Lady in the latter's Tây Ninh shrine, which some say is a marker of this historical substitution (figure 9).

The shrine to the Lady of the Realm in Vĩnh Tế village was again renovated dramatically in 1972, late in the war. The elderly café owner attributed funding for the upgrades to money from the urban areas of Saigon and Chợ Lớn. She said many of these people came to visit the shrine outside the dates of the fourth-month festival. However, the numbers were comparatively small, and the festival itself remained a largely province-based affair. After the

FIG. 9. The Lady of the Realm and the Black Lady enshrined on
Black Lady Mountain

war ended, this continued to be the case; and in 1978, during the Khmer
Rouge attacks across the border, when shells hit some of the religious structures on the mountainside, the flow of pilgrims temporarily dried up. Numbers started to build up discernibly in the mid-1980s. Huge crowds began
coming in 1992, and about the same time the number of people coming before the festival season increased significantly. In the peak years of the mid-
1990s, she estimated there had been at least a million pilgrims in the fourth
month alone, the same again for the rest of the year. Saigonese made up
about 40 percent of the annual visitors, she figured. Numbers came right
down in 1998 and 1999, coinciding with a sharp contraction in economic

growth. Still, in the first four months of each lunar year, the period during which most of the visitors from the big city preferred to come to the site, her café was open twenty-four hours a day. This was equally true of dozens of neighboring establishments. Such levels of activity are exceptional for a rural village of about ten thousand people in the remote stretches of the delta.

Seeing the Goddess through Urban Eyes

It seems curious that a goddess in such a remote location should so galvanize the residents of an outward-looking city awash with foreign visitors and fascinating new cultural foci, consumer items, fashions, and lifestyles. Ho Chi Minh City's feel is forward-looking, its urban landscape transformed by the massive construction of private and public buildings and by street widening, slum clearance, bridge building, drainage, electrification, and other ventures. As Vietnam's largest city; the national leader in economic growth, investment, industrialization, and trade; and the home of the reform and open-door policies, Ho Chi Minh City is one of the main engines of Vietnam's integration with the wider capitalist world. One might have expected those who lived in this city to move further away in cultural terms from such a folk icon. However, as the city's fortunes have grown, so too has the degree of interest shown in this goddess.

According to some locals with whom I discussed these questions, the reasons for this lie in the expense of conducting pilgrimages. Until recently few could afford the cost of transport, accommodation, and gifts. For a long time these expenses served to limit pilgrimages to the wealthy, who were concentrated in urban areas. The presence of so many pilgrims from the area of Saigon and Chợ Lớn reflected the concentration of wealth in those quarters. Rural areas, despite being closer, have lagged behind because their inhabitants lacked the means to pay for such pilgrimages.

Yet this explanation fails to account for what motivates people to make these pilgrimages. Because the reasons for undertaking journeys to her shrine are diverse, I will restrict this question to the group of pilgrims who are renowned as the most devout followers of the goddess: the traders and entrepreneurs of Ho Chi Minh City. As mentioned in the previous chapter, pilgrims in this category travel annually to Châu Đốc to request the goddess' assistance in business, considering her the surest guarantor of wealth they know. To them the Lady of the Realm is a powerful being, an existential guarantor, a reliable source of wealth and a partner in business who will guarantee profits to those who propitiate her. Of all the pilgrims making their way to Her Ladyship's shrine, the business class of the big southern metropolis visit her shrine most regularly and make the largest offerings. Why, for such people, does the path to business success lead through the Mekong delta? Why do they attribute their wealth to a figure in a region that they, like most urbanites, consider deep *(sâu)* in the countryside?

One way to make sense of the value these pilgrims attribute to this goddess is to understand the relationship that exists between the region where her shrine is located and the nation's largest city. The Lady of the Realm's meaning to her Ho Chi Minh City–based followers as a font of wealth draws its inspiration from the economic relationship that obtains between this urban center and the Mekong delta. One way of conceptualizing the Mekong delta's relationship to this city is as a resource frontier or hinterland. The Mekong delta is a primary commodity-producing area, rich in resources and a major exporter of rice and other agricultural and aquacultural commodities as well as of labor. The delta has lacked the capital concentrations, processing and service industries, transport infrastructure, differentiation of labor, and technical and intellectual resources to add value to most of what is produced locally. For this it has been dependent on Ho Chi Minh City, which is the nearest major industrial, processing, trading, marketing, finance, service, and educational center. A great deal of the Mekong delta's primary produce is consumed in Ho Chi Minh City, channeled through its port, marketed in its service industries, or processed in its factories. Much of the venture capital for economic intensification as well as the equipment and material needed for agricultural and infrastructural development are imported to the Mekong delta from or through the city. A substantial proportion of the business sector in this city is involved in trade of some kind with the delta, and many who work in the city live off and profit from this unequal and extractive economic relationship.

A similar situation pertains in the regions that are home to the shrines to the other major goddesses venerated in the southern Vietnamese plain. The southern Vietnamese economic system can be likened to a bicycle wheel. Ho Chi Minh City lies at its hub, the region's most significant marketing, finance, processing, manufacturing, service, trading, educational, and communications center. The main areas of commodity production, resource extraction, and cross-border trade are situated at its rim, where the shrines to these goddesses are also found. To the south and east of the city lie the rich fisheries and trade routes of the South China Sea and the port of Vũng Tàu. To the north and northwest lie the richly forested uplands, the Đồng Nai basin and red earth rubber-producing lands. To the west and southwest lie the Mekong delta plain, the Mekong River, and Cambodia. The roads and waterways that radiate between the city and the hinterlands like spokes funnel in trade goods, commodities, and labor from the hinterlands and channel out pilgrims to the shrines of goddesses.

It is significant that the goddesses who are considered to be the region's most potent sources of wealth dwell in these outlying resource-rich and commodity-producing hinterlands. Equally intriguing is that the city is the single biggest provider of pilgrims to their shrines. The journeys made by urban residents to these shrines connect them to the regions upon which a substantial degree of this city's wealth is based. Perceptions of these goddesses as underwriters of urban fortunes cast into relief the economic geography of the region and offer an insight into the significance of these hinterland areas to those who live in the city.

Constructions of the Lady of the Realm as a responsive magical agent reflect and draw meaning from the processes of articulating the Mekong's deltaic region into broader political and economic structures. Since the early days of Vietnamese settlement, when it began to emerge as a site of agricultural trade production, the Mekong delta countryside has been made over by commodity relations and fashioned in a dependent relationship to far-away centers of economic power. One of the Lady of the Realm's earliest purported manifestations of power was her benevolent protection of the mandarin in charge of overseeing the construction of the Vĩnh Tế Canal in the early nineteenth century. Major waterworks of this kind were key to the Vietnamese occupation of the delta. Drainage canals were dug that emptied the deltaic swamps, helped flush out acidic water, and channeled away floodwaters. These works not only facilitated an increase in agricultural production but provided living space (along their banks) and a ready route for transporting produce out of the delta. The most significant phase of canal development took place in the late nineteenth and early twentieth centuries, when vast tracts of land were opened for migration and exploitation using mechanized dredges, with the assistance of French civil engineers (Robequain 1944). A large proportion of the reclaimed land was allocated in concessions to those with good connections to the colonial government (Osborne 1969; Brocheux 1995). Many smallholders migrated westward to exploit the lands, yet the unequal and risky nature of the rice monoculture economy further polarized class relations (Brocheux 1995). The delta's rural tracts became home to increasing numbers of tenant farmers, poverty-stricken smallholders, and landless laborers. By the end of the colonial period, the majority of the land was concentrated into remarkably few large estates, farmed by tenant farmers and owned by a class of absentee landlords who resided in urban centers and sent their children to study even farther away.

Brocheux (1995) describes the paternalistic relationship that existed between the delta's large landlords and their tenants. The former even extended credit to the latter. However, during this time an even more important horizontal system of differentiation was emerging in the form of an urban-rural divide. Settlements such as Mỹ Tho, Vĩnh Long, and Sa Đéc that lay at the intersection of important canals, rivers, and roads were some of the delta's earliest urban centers thanks to their role as the region's transport and communications hubs, strategic headquarters, and market centers. In the colonial era, new towns such as Cần Thơ sprang up to service the needs of the rapidly expanding western delta. Such towns swelled with an assortment of small traders, craftspeople, transport workers, tradespeople, teachers, students, petty clerks, and colonial functionaries, as well as those who lived off the income of their estates. Such sites became many-headed hydras drawing commodities, rents, taxes, debt payments, and intellectual resources out of the countryside. Above all of these loomed the Saigon/Chợ Lớn area, which in the colonial era held a virtual monopoly over the milling of Mekong delta rice. In addition to being the political capital of the region, it was the principal communications, commercial, financial, service, and educational center for the delta.

Embodying urban views of the region in which she is housed, the Lady of the Realm is frequently conceptualized in narrow terms as a source of wealth and a font of economic potential. Although cheap agricultural commodities and a low-paid rural workforce as well as high-yield investments in the delta underwrite many urban fortunes, many people who benefit from these advantages attribute their prosperity to the goddess. Such beliefs are echoed in stories about the Lady of the Realm as springing up naturally from the ocean, made of naturally growing stone, or as having power one can tap with infallible results. These religious ideas accord with ecological conceptions that hold the Mekong delta to be an inexhaustible resource and place of natural wealth, where relatively little work is needed to prosper. A frequently uttered observation about the Mekong delta's exuberant fertility is that you can just stick something in the ground there and it will grow. This observation was still current in the 1990s, despite the serious overpopulation and environmental exhaustion of the delta.[7] These ideas occlude the social history by which the delta was and is exploited through the work of human hands. Such stories reflect an urban perspective: that of creditors, process factory owners, and tax agents who benefit from the agricultural wealth of the delta without having to undertake the manual labor or suffer the loss of livelihood and well-being in the economically and environmentally unstable conditions of agricultural commodity production. The wealth of the land is imagined not as a human product for which a substantial debt of gratitude might be owed, but as a natural blessing to the Vietnamese people, a view reflected in the myths woven around the goddess as a living, accessible, and fecund source of power.

The wealth of the delta is becoming tapped in new ways: Ho Chi Minh City–based real estate speculators now invest huge sums in housing construction in the provincial capitals, capital-intensive aquaculture operations, and large timber plantations. One of the major industries through which urbanites exploit the resources of the delta is tourism. Domestic tourists visit the Mekong's rural areas to experience what they call traditional ways of life. Postcards depicting various rustic scenes from the delta show that even the past can be recycled into a commercial proposition. People go on boat rides along the waterways and pay to catch its fish and eat its fruit, variously consuming the Mekong delta as a place of "nature." Ideas about the delta's largely unpeopled stretches and abundant fertility continue to attract labor migrants from elsewhere in the country, many of whom consider the delta as a place of still unrealized potential. All these travelers brush shoulders with a substantial flow of urban pilgrims into the delta who go to the shrine of the Lady of the Realm in Châu Đốc with the intention of making and giving thanks for their fortunes.

The Effect of Migration: Transmission and Synthesis

While the Mekong attracts streams of labor migrants, tourists, and pilgrims, one cannot overlook the significant counterflow of people away from the Mekong delta. Today, as the place of the strongest economic growth in Vietnam, Ho Chi Minh City, and its surrounding satellite industrial processing zones, exerts in its own right a powerful attraction for those living elsewhere in the country (Forbes 1996).[8] Many of its newest residents have come from the Mekong delta, seeking to escape poverty and repay debts and work in the city's booming service, construction, trade, and industrial sectors. The exodus of migrants to the city from the rural areas of the Mekong has quite a long history and reflects the politically and economically unequal and structurally unstable relationship between the Saigon/Chợ Lớn metropolis and the Mekong hinterland. In times of war, or economic cycles of boom and bust, the people who live and work in the delta as its primary producers have been subject to impossible burdens and have had to up and leave. The knowledge migrants from the Mekong delta have brought with them to Saigon has added another layer to the reinscription of its religious landscape by the residents of the urban world. This confirms Hansen's insights, in her study of popular religion in medieval China, that the catchment area of pilgrimage cults were linked to migration flows (1990).

Cẩm, a migrant to Ho Chi Minh City from a Mekong delta province, shared with me the first tale she had been told about the goddess: "I remember as a child in Gò Công my mother warning us children that if we did not behave, the Lady of the Realm would break our necks." She grimaced, making the motion of wringing a chicken's neck. In her mind the goddess was a stern accomplice of her mother's rule of the familial domain. She also remembered being told the goddess was like Buddha: helping local people to live in peace, rewarding the good, punishing the bad. She recalled an aphorism: The honest always meet with fortune: their work makes them rich. Tyrants always fear being punished *(Những người lương thiện luôn gặp điều may mắn, làm ăn phát đạt. Kẻ ác lúc nào cũng lo sợ bị trừng phạt)*. Cẩm's memory of the goddess was as a keeper of social order, a guardian of morality. However, when asked whether the goddess was worshiped in any particular location in her house or village, she thought this was not so. Rather, she saw her as an omniscient figure of authority whose presence would quickly become manifest in the event of an episode of childish disorderly conduct.

In the late 1960s following the bombing of her home during the American military escalation, Cẩm was forced to leave Gò Công province and migrate to Saigon. For a long while following her move to the city, she said she heard nothing more of the Lady of the Realm. In the early 1990s she began to sell fruit from the Mekong delta in a Ho Chi Minh City market. It was there in the market that she began to hear people talking about a goddess they called the Lady of Châu Đốc. Whenever they realized a profit her fellow sellers would make a trip to Vĩnh Tế village, just outside Châu Đốc, to offer thanks to her. She said she had never before heard mention of any Lady of Châu Đốc. Nevertheless, assured by her fellow saleswomen of the efficacious power of that deity, Cẩm undertook her first trip with them to the large shrine just outside this border town. She made offerings to the goddess, requested assistance with her fruit business, and also borrowed some money from the goddess' altar.

This trip was significant for Cẩm, for during it she made an important discovery: "It was when making my pilgrimage to Châu Đốc that I finally learned who the Lady of the Realm was." She related the tale she had been told while visiting the site on that occasion:

> A long time ago, Thoại Ngọc Hầu, who was then the king, came to the area around Châu Đốc.[9] When he came to the very place where her shrine now

stands, he encountered Her Ladyship and he said to her, "You must yield to me. I am your king." Her Ladyship would not stand for this. She replied, "I am the Lady of this realm of Châu Đốc *(Tao là Bà Chúa của xứ Châu Đốc này)*. It is *you* who must yield to me." And so an altar was constructed and the king worshiped Her Ladyship.

On hearing this, Cẩm said she realized that the goddess worshiped in Châu Đốc was none other than the Lady of the Realm of childhood memory. This she said was a revelation, for although Gò Công was much closer to Châu Đốc than her current home in Ho Chi Minh City, she had not heard in Gò Công references to Châu Đốc as the seat of the Lady of the Realm. Yet neither had she made this connection in the city, for her fellow saleswomen seldom referred to the goddess by the generic title the Lady of the Realm but instead as the Lady of Châu Đốc. Few of them were aware that the self-same goddess was venerated elsewhere. When the existence of other shrines to the Lady of the Realm is brought to their attention, they often dismiss them as opportunistic copies of the Châu Đốc shrine.

In her extended round trip, from the Mekong delta to the city as a migrant and back to the delta as a pilgrim, Cẩm pieced together stories from her childhood and her adult life and from rural and urban locations to furnish a new image of the Lady of the Realm's identity as the Lady of Châu Đốc. Cẩm's picture of the goddess represents a synthesis of influences and views to which she had been exposed in three different locations. Her mental image of the hierarchically inclined goddess closely resembles the spiritual figure her mother had invoked to establish parental authority. Still very much the authority figure of childhood memory, the goddess was identified as the overseer of a defined domain to whom all who entered must defer. Cẩm's attribution of the seat of the goddess' territorial jurisdiction exclusively to Châu Đốc also indicates the influence on her thinking of the Ho Chi Minh City marketplace where she worked, as well as a healthy dose of Châu Đốc parochialism encountered at the pilgrimage site. The influence of the transactional culture of the market is also evident in the negotiational identity she accorded the goddess, as a partner whose veneration was earned on the condition that she help Cẩm with her business.

Cẩm's neighbor, Phượng, similarly first learned of the goddess when she began to sell fruit in the same market. She had been born in Hanoi in 1954 and was carried in her parents' arms when they fled south later that year. Her parents, who had been Buddhist landlords, were fearful of being persecuted for their class background when the Communists took power in the North. Phượng had worked as a poorly paid elementary teacher in a Ho Chi Minh

City school until she reached her midtwenties in the early 1980s. After her first child was born she resigned from teaching and switched to what was then becoming a more lucrative profession, selling fruit in her local market. It was in the fruit market that she had first heard about the goddess.

As far as Phượng knew, none of her former colleagues at school had ever heard about the shrine in Châu Đốc. Indeed, she thought that before 1975, hardly anybody knew about Her Ladyship: "Only after liberation did her repute spread and pilgrimages begin." She told me that Her Ladyship was an actual person who lived in Châu Đốc: "However, she was far more than just a farmer. She was a woman who was excellent at her studies. After she died, people erected a shrine to honor her memory as the Lady of the Châu Đốc Realm." I asked her what she knew about the goddess' powers. "She is responsive. She grants whatever requests people make of her. If a child misbehaves, she will break its arm. If a person tries to steal from the shrine, she will wring their neck." The attributes she accorded the Lady of the Realm in some respects reflected Phượng's educational and family background. She attributed to the goddess what she saw as desirable human qualities such as excellence in studies, discipline, and the respect for others' property. Belief in the potency of a stone statue was shunned by most of her fellow schoolteachers as the product of ignorant minds. However, it was only when Phượng had started going to the Châu Đốc shrine, along with members of her new profession, that her fortunes had indeed improved.

Peter Jackson (1999b) and Jim Taylor (1999) have pointed out that many urban adepts of new urbanized forms of popular religion in Thailand have themselves recently come from rural backgrounds. A characteristically rural way of thinking remains with them, even after they have moved to the city. These religions are products of rapid urbanization, projections of folk conceptual registers onto urban experiences, hybrids of a rural and urban worldview. These are referred to as "postmodern religions," giving expression to new experiences and reconfiguring and recombining traditional elements. However, people's thinking is not entirely transfigured in the intellectual blender of urban capitalism. These two examples from Ho Chi Minh City show that there is a degree of continuity in the moral identity and scope of responsibilities attributed to the goddess. Cẩm saw the Châu Đốc deity as a moral guardian; Phượng considered her as an exemplary feminine ideal. Yet these views are more than a simple survival of traditional viewpoints, for if these two women had not migrated to the city, they might never have heard of the Châu Đốc goddess nor ever felt compelled to visit her shrine. Their views, while inflected by their upbringings, also reflect the preoccupations of their new urban home.

Local Reaction

Although rural Vietnam is a favorite screen upon which urban imaginations work to configure for themselves new tales of the city, it is by no means a blank slate upon which they can write at will. While the Lady of the Realm's presence in institutionalized cults, stories, and memories is attested to by folklorists and others as an authentic expression of the Mekong delta's local culture, there are many people living in the adjacent area who reject such a view. For example, many Hòa Hảo Buddhists in the vicinity of the large shrine in Vĩnh Tế village say that the goddess is a sham and her shrine a cult promoted by charlatans. They quote the preachings of their prophet Huỳnh Phú Sổ, who, in the late colonial period, during similar conditions of economic instability and growth in spirit worship, denounced such practices as irrational superstition. Followers of this reformist Buddhist movement say that one is mistaken to invest one's hopes in the spirits and that one's own efforts and contributions to the community are the only guaranteed paths to advancement. Many members of the sizable Cham Islamic community, who have lived across the main river from the shrine for centuries, also reject her cultural heritage, condemning belief in such spirits as false and misguided. Some local Catholics think of her not as an indigenous Vietnamese tradition, but as a Buddhist import. Many of the ethnic Khmer, who live not far from the mountain shrine, consider the annual pilgrimage and festival a largely ethnic Vietnamese affair. Some Khmer monks disassociate such practices from the religion of Theravada Buddhism, which they consider the more valid religion of the indigenous people of the Mekong. People living just to the south of Sam Mountain do venerate the Lady of the Realm in a small shrine, which they say was built early in the nineteenth century by the Buddha Master of Western Peace (Phật Thầy Tây An); they refer to her as Lady Buddha and consider her a moral overseer of their community. These local people observed critically that the shrine to the goddess in Vĩnh Tế is less relevant to locals than their own for it draws the majority of its visitors from far away. Rather than seeing veneration of the figure at the Vĩnh Tế shrine as continuous with local traditions, they regard her as externally oriented, a goddess of foreign affairs *(thần ngoại giao),* and her festival a practice that now signifies nothing but money.

Some of the ideas about the goddess that visitors bring with them to her shrine in Vĩnh Tế cause concerns even among locals who do accept her role as a local protector deity. The influx of pilgrims has led many of those who live in the local area to deemphasize those beliefs and practices deemed imported or illegitimate. In the vicinity of the shrine one can obtain booklets that relate different tales about the origins of the goddess and describe the rites at her annual festival (Tường Vân 1994; Mai Văn Tạo 1995; Thái Thị Bích Liên 1998). Most of these booklets make negative reference to a variety of activities associated with a reading of the goddess as magically responsive (*linh thiêng*), such as the borrowing of money from Her Ladyship, healing by drinking her bathwater, possession, and divination. According to these publications these superstitious activities were formerly practiced by preliberation elements whose business was the sale of spirits. A small book published by the Culture and Arts Association of Châu Đốc in 1995 relates a fictional forty-eight-hour tour around the pilgrimage site by a small group from Saigon. The Saigonese visitors engage in conversation with a local guide from Châu Đốc, who assures them that preliberation superstitious practices such as borrowing money from the goddess (as well as seeking amulets and drinking her bathwater) have been reformed and no longer take place (Trịnh Bửu Hoài 1995, 9).[10] Such booklets have been published and endlessly printed to respond to the demand from visitors for information about the goddess. They are sold in the precincts of the shrine with the approval of the local committee and are vetted by local authorities, who too wish to prescribe a line on her identity and proper worship. Scarce in details of the types of individualized rites one sees practiced in the goddess' shrine on any given day of the year, they focus almost exclusively on the rites conducted by the shrine's management committee, on behalf of the community and in conformity with the nation's "beautiful" cultural traditions.

Tribute to the importance placed on the goddess in sustaining the local community is the thicket of regulations that have sprouted about and hedged the activities around her shrine, precluding the infiltration of "extraneous," "inappropriate" elements. Divination rites, still practiced in other shrines in the region, are banned in the main shrine in Vĩnh Tế. Local people say that the bans on the shaking out of divination sticks began in the mid-1980s, coinciding with the increase in crowds of pilgrims to the site. Photography is banned in the shrine, unlike in most other shrines, pagodas, and cultural sites in Vietnam. As for mediumship, one of the most consistently criticized of the popular practices surrounding the goddess, prominently displayed signs at the Vĩnh Tế pilgrimage site declare it a forbidden superstitious activity. Along with the secular police who enforce the ban, the Vĩnh Tế temple committee is formally responsible for barring mediums from the shrine, and publications sold at the shrine include mediumship in their lists of untoward activity. Nevertheless, the local committee is far from draconian in enforcing these proscriptions. The practice of shaking out divination sticks has continued but is done discretely and is especially evident in the quieter months. People still cast wood blocks quite openly to divine the goddess' response to their requests. While taking photographs of the goddess and mediumship are more difficult, both too are possible, providing one gives an attendant a suitable inducement.

Given the state's surveillance of all manner of religious activities in Vietnam, one might be inclined to see these restrictions on ritual practice as reflecting the long arm of the state in imposing a politically orthodox line on local cults. Certainly the state does have a bearing on the content of the publications sold at the site as the authorities have the means to censor unacceptable viewpoints and confiscate illicit publications. Uniformed police agents are installed permanently in a front room of the shrine. Alternatively, given the local origins of the pamphlets that denounce inappropriate behavior and ideas, and the state's recent turn toward the promotion of distinctively local cultural practice, one might be inclined to see these restrictive measures as attempts to maintain the integrity of a local religious practice in the face of its potential inundation by outside forces. Certainly there is an element of truth in each of these hypotheses. Yet it might be more useful to see these reactions as produced out of the tension between local and translocal perspectives. For example, it would appear that the ban on photographing the goddess' image is motivated by a desire to channel the benefits of increased interest shown in her by distant visitors. Officials tell curious visitors that the ban is aimed at preventing reproductions being used in the sale of religion *(buôn thần bán thánh)*, although there is nothing to distinguish this from the local government's own benefits from the massive donations to the shrine. Visitors are told by attendants that the goddess will not actually permit her image to be photographically registered, although all of the booklets of the goddess display copies of her photographic likeness. One should avoid seeing these perceptions as examples of either the official line or of local conservatism but as attempts by locals to maintain a degree of control over the significant translocal interest shown in their shrine. One might even say that they are promoting the shrine in Vĩnh Tế to that following as the unique location for the legitimate worship of the Lady of the Realm. It is easy to understand local custodians' unease with the appropriation and mass reproduction of their symbol when one sees rival shrines that display large photographs of the Vĩnh Tế goddess such as Châu Đốc Hai (Châu Đốc Two), a shrine in Nhà Bè in the suburbs of Ho Chi Minh City, set up in 1993 to deliberately tap the huge Saigonese interest in the Lady of the Realm.

While the Vĩnh Tế shrine committee joins its efforts with the authors of local guide books to discourage mediumship and other acts of fortune-telling and faith healing in the shrine precincts, one aspect of the goddess' miraculous powers they do endorse is her alleged power to punish theft and wrong-doing in the shrine. As the number of costly offerings on display in her shrine and adjacent display halls has continued to mount, as the crowds of pilgrims have grown and people have come from farther afield, notions of the goddess as a guardian of security, particularly the security of the shrine, have increased in currency and relevance.[11] Most of the locally available booklets relate stories of the goddess' punishment of those who would steal from her shrine. The most common tale relates how an extremely ingenious robber managed to steal the necklace from around her neck by entering the shrine walking on his hands. The robber knew that if he walked in on his feet, she would instantly wring his neck. So he went in upside down. He approached Her Ladyship, grabbed her necklace, and made off with it, still walking on his hands. However, his stratagem was to no avail. As soon as he returned home and stood up, he died on the spot. Although pertaining to the realm of superstition, this is a myth that those involved with maintaining security in the shrine to the goddess have been happy to see circulate freely. This concession to the supernatural realm enlists the goddess herself in policing the huge and potentially unruly crowds flowing through the shrine.

Interpretation as Alchemy

The publications that are produced and sold in the vicinity of the shrine in Vĩnh Tế are one of the most important ways in which local views seep into urban consciousness. Nevertheless, the intentions of local actors to advance a preferred line through such means have been only partly successful. Their locally authorized views, readily available to pilgrims from far away, have influenced and partially standardized people's thinking. Yet these interpretations have overlapped and sometimes are contested by stories about the goddess that circulate through other channels in the public sphere. Stories are transformed in an alchemical process that reveals interdependencies between local and more-distant urban-based practice.

Many people in Ho Chi Minh City told me that I could learn all about the Lady of the Realm from the publications available at her shrine. My landlady, a prominent Ho Chi Minh City businesswoman, was able to procure for me a number of battered copies of the booklets she had purchased in Châu Đốc. For information on her powers, I myself could check the books, which, she averred, confirm that the goddess is magically responsive and that she assists all who pray to her (see, e.g., Lê Ngọc Bích 1994; Châu Bích Thủy 1994; Hạnh Nguyễn 1993, 1995). These booklets speculate on the origins of the statue, when her shrine might have been built, and when her commemorative festival had commenced. Adopting a scientistic tone, they refer to the proliferation of stories about the mysterious origins and discovery of the goddess and her supposed powers. Such tales are discounted as superstitious myths, propagated by those who wished to profit from the belief in the spirit's powers. And yet despite this typically brief disclaimer, these booklets do relate such stories in some detail. For example, most publications relate the miraculous story in which the goddess possesses a young woman and reveals the location of her statue. After forty strong men fail to move the statue, it is successfully carried to its present location by nine virgin girls (see chapter 2).

Although these booklets relate this story to reject the premises on which supposedly superstitious activity at the pilgrimage site is based, frequent repetition has made it and associated versions the most popular explanation of the origins of the cult to the goddess. The fact of being printed in these publications has confirmed for many who have visited the site that the goddess is indeed possessed of mysterious powers. The story serves as a core around which people have spun tales about her statue's magical efficacy and responsiveness. Bảy, a frequent visitor to the site, proved a case in point. He told me that when the statue had first been discovered, it had been small. He demonstrated by tracing an orange-sized outline of the statue in front of him: "Over many years, it has grown to reach its present size. When it became necessary to move the statue, forty grown men could not lift it! And it has continued to grow."

Stories of the goddess' punitive nature had also come to Bảy's attention in a similar way. He swore to me that the goddess was extremely powerful, illustrating with the tale about the goddess' killing of the thief, which he had read in a booklet sold at the shrine. Passionate believer that he was, Bảy added a detail not to be found in such publications: "You must have heard that when the revolution came down to the South, they tried to demolish the shrine to Her Ladyship. Her Ladyship responded by killing many of those who had tried to evict her. Even those who didn't believe in her were killed! That is how powerful she is." For this reason he said, people didn't dare break their promises to her. Such people would experience bad luck in everything they ventured: "They won't be able to sell a thing. That is why people return every year to give to Her Ladyship whatever they promised her."

The sheaf of available publications with their host of carefully debunked stories, which aim to restore a view of the goddess as a local protector deity, a symbol of resistance, an ancient cultural treasure, or a venerable rural folk belief, can do little to undermine this ferment of self-confirming popularity, and indeed, have just added fuel to the flames. Perhaps for this reason, most publications that refer to the Châu Đốc figure do not otherwise discuss in detail the various rites and practices they associate with a reading of her as magically powerful *(linh thiêng)*. In fact, most publications deny that these still occur, advancing the line that since 1975, with the incorporation of this part of the country under a socialist regime, such unwholesome *(không lành mạnh)* activities are no longer practiced. Faced by the immense creativity of interpretations at the pilgrimage site, all that can be practically done by local authorities and commentators to quell this is to tactfully avert their eyes.

Refigurations of Rural Practice

Urban areas and marketplaces of southern Vietnam have been particularly influential in the transformation and transmission of ideas about the goddess vis-à-vis the wider society. Conceptions of the goddess enshrined in Vĩnh Tế village as a responsive and reliable business partner have filtered from person to person throughout the entire mesh of markets in the Mekong delta and beyond. The pilgrimage site in Vĩnh Tế has similarly served as such a relay point. Today people from an extensive catchment area journey to that shrine and take home with them a remarkably unified conception of the goddess' identity, powers, and appropriate mode of veneration.

One effect of the increasing centrality of the Vĩnh Tế shrine throughout the region is that various shrines to local goddesses have come to be regarded as branches *(chi nhánh)* of that shrine (popular thinking locates this in Châu Đốc). For instance the Lady of Châu Đốc is now the main spirit worshiped in Châu Đốc Two in Nhà Bè district. Before 1993, the Five Mothers were the sole ritual focus at this place. Other shrines dedicated to the Lady of the Realm are often described by locals as shrines to the Lady of Châu Đốc. The shrine to the Lady of the Realm situated to the east of Bạc Liêu town is referred to in this way. Women selling in the Trà Vinh market make regular offerings to a goddess on the outskirts of that town to whom they refer as the Lady of Châu Đốc. After traveling at least once to Vĩnh Tế village to request assistance of the goddess, many people in such locations decide to make their offerings of thanks to her at a local neighborhood shrine because, as they say, the expense of going all the way to Vĩnh Tế is too great. Hence, the regional importance of the deity enshrined in Vĩnh Tế and her centrality to a host of individualized transactions is not immediately evident to those who look for evidence of this at her shrine in Vĩnh Tế, for many transactions with her take place elsewhere in shrines that have been reconfigured as its branches.

Although the costs of traveling explain why some of this goddess' strongest devotees do not put in regular appearances at her shrine in Vĩnh Tế, it is surprising that many residents of the nearby town of Châu Đốc, after which the goddess is so famously named, do not pay much attention to her either. The townspeople of Châu Đốc benefit enormously from the region-wide interest in the pilgrimage and festival. However, many of them display pronounced detachment toward the goddess. Despite the fact that she is a magnet to people from the larger cities as well as from overseas, many locals are spectacularly unfazed by the hype. Most residents of Châu Đốc see out the entire festival in their places of work without once taking the short ride to Vĩnh Tế village. Although some go to the site during the festival for entertainment or because their work takes them there, they are less likely than those from farther afield to step into the shrine to the goddess. Many do go up to the mountainside shrine at Tết to make requests for the New Year, offer a stick of incense, and learn their fortunes for the forthcoming year. However, one does not detect among Châu Đốc townsfolk the degree of commitment and fervid belief in her powers that people from farther afield display.

In some cases townspeople's lack of engagement in the festivities reflects their principled rejection of this goddess as a magical ally. Sometimes, however, their belief in her powers is just not obvious. Thủy, who lived in Châu Đốc town, said she had never once been to Her Ladyship's shrine in Vĩnh Tế village, although she had been born and lived her whole life only five kilometers away. Thủy made her living as a long-distance cigarette smuggler, buying cigarettes each day at the Cambodian border and selling them in the Chợ Lớn bus station. She was forty-one, single, and had been doing the trip seven days a week for several years. On her travels, she had seen the number of pilgrims traveling to Châu Đốc from Ho Chi Minh City peak in the mid-1990s and then ebb toward the end of the decade. Nevertheless, despite never going to the shrine, she did believe in the goddess, whom she regarded as a partner in her trade. Thủy said she prayed to Her Ladyship at home: "That is just as effective," she shrugged.

Another reason that Châu Đốc townsfolk rarely visit the shrine at the height of the pilgrimage and festival season is that they are too busy profiting from the crowds that pass through their town, which is the main gateway to the shrine. I asked the manager of a bustling Chinese restaurant near the main market in Châu Đốc if she planned to make offerings to the goddess during her annual festival. Like most local businesspeople in town, she said her family was too busy to make it up to the hillside shrine during this time. The amount of custom their restaurant got during the festival easily explained their lack of involvement, yet it also confirmed for them the value of the event. Over the years it had helped them make their fortune. Hence they did make visits to the shrine to the goddess for thanks outside of the festival season, although without spending as lavishly on offerings as people from places such as Chợ Lớn and Saigon. Instead, rather like those self-same pilgrims, her family dedicated more energy to taking their own trips farther afield. Much of their fortune was spent on trips to distant locales. The manager said a package tour to China was "cheap"—only a thousand U.S. dollars. Thailand was even cheaper—eight hundred U.S. dollars for eight days. Their newly renovated restaurant was lined with tourist maps, photographs, and souvenirs that commemorated the household patriarch's many visits overseas. Six or seven trips in total were commemorated on the walls of the restaurant, all of them her grandfather's, and the pictures, brochures, and maps advertised his descendants' filial piety as much as their wealth.

Another reason the manager didn't go to the shrine during the festival was that this event, with its reputation for attracting locals, had little appeal to this rapidly rising provincial sophisticate. She laughed at the idea of visiting during the festival: "The only ones visiting now are the hicks *(hai lúa)* from the surrounding rural areas. There are so many of them it is impossible to get in and make an offering. They like going to the festival market, watching *hát bội* opera, and staring at the transvestites." Her sister also laughed and told me that most of those coming during the festival were too poor for the likes of their restaurant. "They eat vegetarian only," she joked, a reference to the food that is provided by Buddhist pagodas free of charge to visitors. The expensive journeys to distant locales, commemorated on the walls of their restaurant, helped further underline distinctions she asserted between herself and the "rustic" festivalgoers from surrounding rural areas. However, these images also indicated that the opportunities for religious travel among members of this family were not equally shared but were apportioned by generation and gender.

Despite these marks of sophistication and her looking down on those attending the festival as ignorant peasants, this restaurateur herself did believe strongly in the local deity's powers. She told me the Lady of the Realm had to be respected. For example, the bathing ceremony, which took place each year on the twenty-third day of the fourth lunar month, had to take place at the stroke of midnight: "Her Ladyship demands it. On one occasion, a person entered to bathe Her Ladyship five minutes too early. She was killed on the spot! Her Ladyship has also killed robbers who came into the shrine to steal her possessions. She wants people to be good. She gives good people help in earning a living, raising children, and curing diseases. But she has killed people for not respecting their parents, for gambling, drinking, and other bad behavior."

This view of the goddess as a stickler for ritual, protector of property, and generalized defender of morality was common among local townsfolk. However, rather than see in this the unbroken survival of older communal traditions, to adequately contextualize such views of the goddess, one must be mindful of her relevance in a border town where trade, smuggling, corruption, and human trafficking find fertile ground. Indeed, her pilgrimage is just one element of a booming local economy based on the movement of people and goods. Views of the goddess as a local authority can be seen very much as a contemporary response to the challenges to moral community in this major human thoroughfare, meeting place, and economic and cultural frontier. They are a dynamic reaction to other conceptions about the goddess that are generated in different circumstances and locales.

5

Familiar Journeys

The study of pilgrimage is replete with the idea that such sacred journeys transcend the here and now, whether as voyages "somewhere beyond the known world" (Morinis 1992, 1) or as prompted by the "simple wish to step outside the normal flow of life" (Reader 1993a, 220). According to Victor Turner (1974) and Victor and Edith Turner (1978), pilgrimage is an exceptional experience: representing an inversion of the everyday, the falling away of barriers between people, or a form of liberation from commonplace constraints and social roles. Equally prevalent are propositions to the effect that pilgrims move in non-ordinary space and time. Pilgrimage destinations are liminal, both spatially peripheral and "in and out of time" (Turner 1974, 197). Evidence abounds in the concepts and practices of sacred journeys around the world that lends weight to such constructions of pilgrimage as socially and culturally exceptional. In Vietnam, for instance, one finds considerable support for the idea that pilgrimages *(cuộc hành hương)* are experiences beyond the everyday flow of life, journeys to another place and time. The pilgrimage to the Perfume Pagoda (Chùa Hương) in northern Vietnam is construed by many pilgrims as a journey to a remote, otherworldly place. Pilgrims travel far through the countryside, along idyllic waterways, past awe-inspiring limestone formations, and into the interior recesses of a great mountain cavern. This culturally paradigmatic pilgrimage is interiorized in paintings, reminiscences, songs, stories, and proverbs as a dreamscape, a place accessed through nostalgia, a Vietnamese spiritual homeland.

Notwithstanding the merits of regarding pilgrimages as "journeys out of the ordinary" (Reader 1993a, 222), there are methodological and empirical problems with this approach. It places such practices off center, constructing them as somehow alternate or salvational in relation to an order of reality that is construed as more central, everyday, and properly this-worldly. As Holsten notes, one distinction sometimes asserted between "modernity" and religious practice is to regard the latter in subordinate relationship to the former as compensatory or escapist (Holston 1999, 613). More sympathetic approaches such as functionalism still understand religion as a solace, a safety valve, or, in more desperate times, a radical alternative to a strife-torn secular order. Applied in relation to phenomena as disparate as so-called animist practice and millenarian movements, such an approach fails to give credit to the pervasive normalcy of religious worldviews, the persistence and indeed growth of religious projects at the very heart of contemporary societies and cultures. Any argument for reserving such an "exceptionalist" perspective for the study of pilgrimages, presumably because they take people beyond the "known world" or "across the boundaries of their familiar territory" (Morinis 1992, 1), is rapidly diminishing, given the increasing normalcy of travel, movement, and spatial dislocation.

On empirical grounds the exceptionalist perspective fails to account for the everyday or ordinary tenor of pilgrimage in Vietnam as elsewhere, which theorists since Victor Turner (1974) have noted is becoming increasingly indistinguishable from such concerns as tourism, business, shopping, or holidays. An example of this issue is found in Asakusa, a thriving Buddhist pilgrimage site in the heart of Tokyo, easily accessed by subway and complete with market, refreshment outlets, entertainments, and red-light district. Pilgrims' experience of this site can be hard to distinguish and disentangle from their other mundane activities in the metropolis. Are we to accept that this "normalization" of religion represents a diminution of its essence? Some have argued to the contrary, that supposedly secular phenomena such as tourism, sight-seeing, and migration themselves encode the types of sacred concerns and experience of transcendence that the Turners and other theorists have found in pilgrimage (MacCannell 1976; Graburn 1978; Eickelman and Piscatori 1990).[1] A different approach, and one attempted in this chapter, is to emphasize the quotidian and normative dimensions of pilgrimage itself, to downplay the exceptionality of these journeys. Pilgrims to the Perfume Pagoda from Hanoi have their journeys arranged by tour companies, travel in convenience on good roads, and use an efficient boat service. Their path up the mountain is lined by guest houses, cafés, restaurants, stalls, markets, and vendors. Similarly, commentators who write about the festival to the Lady of the Realm in Vĩnh Tế village invariably mention commercialism and high prices, showing the ubiquity of experiencing the place through the role of consumer. The Châu Đốc pilgrimage is impossible to disentangle from people's pursuits in the city, and in many ways it is an extension of them. To ignore these dimensions or to seek out examples of behavior that can be contrasted with everyday life in the places from which pilgrims come means that one misses much of what goes on at these sites.

Urbanization is transfiguring the pilgrimage site to the Lady of the Realm: altering the physical layout of the village in which she is enshrined, the scope of the goddess' powers, the social composition of her visitors, and the nature of their rituals. And yet pilgrimage sites have always been shaped by the preoccupations of the places from which pilgrims have come and by the processes that have transformed them. The rapid growth of Vietnamese pilgrimage activity in tandem with the proliferation at these sacred sites of everyday modes of urban culture leads us toward a view of pilgrimage as a process in which one finds the values of a culture exemplified and celebrated, rather than in some respects transcended or evaded. Particularly useful in this respect is Alan Morinis' minimalist definition of pilgrimage as "a journey undertaken by a person in quest of a place or a state that he or she believes to embody a valued ideal" (Morinis 1992, 2). This definition has the added merit of allowing one to see how pilgrimage sites change over time and still retain their relevance to pilgrims. Pilgrims inscribe onto the landscape of the pilgrimage site their contemporary values, infusing them with the cultural qualities that keep them relevant. Yet conversely, just as such sites are fashioned anew by each wave of pilgrims, those who access that site become subject to its meanings. This iterative inscription and reading of the religious landscape by pilgrims is a key quality of pilgrimage practice and what makes it such a dynamic and enduring process in social life.

One can take this a step further to conceptualize pilgrimage as a focusing or intensification of the familiar rather than the mere extension onto sacred geography of the world of everyday experience. Alan Morinis, from whom I borrow these terms, speaks of the significance of such sacred centers as

> developing and projecting an image which is a magnification of some accepted ideals of the culture. They represent a higher or purer or more ideal version of what the potential pilgrim already values and seeks by dint of membership in a culture. Cultural intensification of this sort is the central force in the creation, maintenance, and success of pilgrimage shrines. A center that ceases to embody an intensified version of cultural values goes into decline. (Morinis 1992, 18)

One needn't interpret culture as a set of values inherited from the past. Urban pilgrimages to the shrine to the Lady of the Realm in Châu Đốc for instance embody and celebrate the values of urban culture. Pilgrims bring with them the baggage of everyday relationships; in their travels they accentuate familiar kinds of sociability and at their destination find, in often intensified form, known relations and sensations. Although their journeys take them far from their urban home, pilgrims are often unlikely to escape urban reference points that pervade all aspects of the pilgrimage experience.

Of Voluntarism and Hardship

To learn about how pilgrims from Ho Chi Minh City traveled to Châu Đốc, I was advised by my neighbors to talk with Hoa in my local gold shop. People thought she could give me better advice than most, as she visited the site annually. Hoa had undertaken the pilgrimage even in the days when police checkpoints, bad roads, and long delays at the cross-river ferry terminals meant that the six-hundred-kilometer round trip lasted sixteen to twenty hours and had to be undertaken at night. Considering she had more than enough business to attend to in her busy marketside shop, such journeys on the face of it appear strikingly voluntaristic. Certainly her reasons for undertaking the trip would appear to contrast with the motives of her driver, who was obliged to travel to earn his living. Her undertaking of such long and seemingly arduous journeys would also appear to fly in the face of the comparatively easy life she could otherwise afford.

These two dimensions of her journey, voluntarism and hardship, are often associated with pilgrimage. Victor Turner says that pilgrimages in all historic, large-scale religions rest initially on voluntarism (1974, 198). As instances of communitas, they are a means of release or "salvation" from roles that embroil and bind the individual (1974, 203). This stance reflects his view of pilgrimage as originating in the "ordered antistructure of feudal patrimonial systems" (1974, 182). Other theorists have applied this perspective to the contemporary context, analyzing the various ways in which pilgrimages variously provide participants a way out of the rule-governed, compartmentalized, or routinized existences of modern life. For instance, writing about the Shikoku pilgrimage, Ian Reader suggests that many older Japanese find the pilgrimage a good means to escape from the pressures of contemporary urban society by entering into the idealized cultural world of the pilgrimage (Reader 1993b, 125).

Such voluntaristic motivations are abundantly at play in Vietnam, where one finds many people who travel to pilgrimage sites to lift their spirits, widen their horizons, and meet new people. Nevertheless, there is a problem applying this perspective to that core group of Châu Đốc pilgrims such as Hoa who are mostly female urban residents, involved in commerce, many of them ethnic Chinese. Many undertake such journeys not as volunteers, but in acquittal of relations of obligation to the goddess based on long-term relations of reciprocation and backed up by a sanction of punishment. Having been granted a request by the goddess, so some accounts go, one is constrained to return to thank her annually for the rest of one's life. The penalties for not going, meted out by the goddess, are diverse and unpleasant. Although Hoa conceptualized her relationship with the goddess less as a fearful obligation than a beneficial compact, it was nevertheless a binding one. Far from achieving liberation, her journeys were motivated by obligations of reciprocity.[2] This quality of involuntarism is also evident among many residents of Hanoi who undertake the Perfume Pagoda pilgrimage. Despite its reputation as a supposedly Buddhist site, many sellers in the capital city's markets are fearful of saying they will go on this pilgrimage, in case it transpires that they cannot go. Construed as a promise, the consequences of breaching one's word include not being able to sell and never attracting customers. Once one does go, one is constrained to return repeatedly. This is why fewer men than women go on this pilgrimage, for after receiving a benefit, it is said that men are obliged to return consecutively for the next nine years whereas the requirement for women is only seven years. According to one small trader in Hanoi, this is why one rarely meets small traders on the pilgrimage, for to go just once commits one to go seven or nine times, and who but the large traders can afford that?

Another factor shaping the mode of Hoa's journey was the need to get back to her business as quickly as possible. Like most successful saleswomen, she had little free time. Many in this predicament traveled to Châu Đốc by minibus—not an overly safe means of transport, but a rapid one. Như, the busy proprietor of a funeral wares stall, told me she was organizing an air-conditioned minibus to leave Ho Chi Minh City at 3 A.M., arriving home before midnight on the same day. Each year she organized a trip of this kind and, with the fees levied, just covered costs. Như confirmed that the goddess was most popular among businesspeople and traders such as herself. She said for people like her the annual pilgrimage to Châu Đốc had become a customary practice: "If you go once, you must return to offer gratitude. In effect, people have to seek Her Ladyship's permission *(xin phép)* to do business." This approach to the pilgrimage suited the lives of busy urbanites, whose thriving businesses, like that of Như, were a sign that they owed a visit to the goddess but who, for that same reason, had little time to make the lengthy round-trip.

Despite the convenience provided by new forms of transport, these trips had their share of difficulty and danger, such that one might even ask whether these factors actually motivated such journeys. Pilgrimage has often been construed in the theoretical literature as an ordeal or austere quest. Redemption, transcendence, communitas—some of the moral states associated with pilgrimage—are attained by undergoing some physical challenge, overcoming a difficult obstacle, propelling the body into an extreme state, and traveling to another place "hundreds of difficult miles away" (Morinis 1992, 28; Preston 1992, 36; Reader 1993a, 224; Dubisch 1995, 76).[3] Whether the Marian pilgrimage undertaken in penance, the arduous journeys conducted by Hindus and Buddhists into the Himalayas, or the moral trials related by Paul Bunyan, pilgrimages are considered almost by definition physically and morally challenging. In Vietnam, although pilgrimage is not well theorized in scholarly circles, one sometimes encounters the perspective that pilgrimages are valuable manifestations of one's religious commitment, the difficult climb up to a mountain shrine showing evidence of the pains taken for one's faith. Consequently, the focus on the pleasures to be had at pilgrimage sites tend to be seen as a degradation of their original meaning. James Preston argues that difficulty of access is one of the key attributes that infuse pilgrimage sites with their quality of "spiritual magnetism." According to Preston and the Indian priests and pilgrims he interviewed, "modern tourism [with its urban comforts] erodes the penitential dimension of pilgrimages" (1992, 36) and may have led to a decline in the spiritual magnetism of pilgrimage sites. Hence in this age of transport convenience, he speculated, the voluntary assumption of various penitential acts at some pilgrimage sites may help keep such sites charged with spiritual potentiality (1992, 37).

Hoa's own comments could be construed to confirm that she valued the austerity of these trips. When I asked her if she found her regular visits to the shrine fun *(vui)*, she reacted strongly, saying my question was "strange." When I then asked her if she would ever like to undertake a pilgrimage on a bus with a video or karaoke machine, she was scandalized: "What do you want karaoke and video for? That is mere leisure *(giải trí)*, like going to Dalat![4] Going on a pilgrimage is altogether different." Hoa articulated a view common among those who transact steadfastly with the goddess: that pilgrimage is not to be confused with travel for pleasure. She was concerned that I was approaching the pilgrimage with the wrong attitude. She worried that my impious questions about video coaches and videos might faze the other members of my own forthcoming trip to the site. She said most of the people going on pilgrimages were older people who were very pious: "You will have to speak properly with them. You cannot be insolent."

Nevertheless, closer examination of Hoa's motivations show that her project was not designed to accentuate hardship, but was simply predicated on the concern to acquit herself of her reciprocal duties. Certainly her notion of pilgrimage was not inconsistent, for instance, with traveling to the site by air-conditioned car, the most comfortable means available to her. Such convenience did not impugn her high level of devotion. Conversely, it was important to undertake the journey as quickly and effectively as possible, for it was a given that she would go each year. The car was necessary because she went to the site and back in a day. Similarly, Như, who was also concerned to get back to her business as quickly as possible, thought that whatever helped make the trip more bearable was acceptable. When I asked her if she thought that going in an air-conditioned video coach and drinking beer on the way to the shrine was consistent with a pilgrimage, she shrugged: "Why shouldn't one do whatever one can to make oneself comfortable on a long trip? If you like it, drinking a can or two of beer is good for relaxation provided you don't overdo it. One should not drink beer in Her Ladyship's shrine; however, there are plenty of bars selling beer all around it."

These women approached their trips to Châu Đốc as largely instrumental affairs, providing the opportunity to repay the spiritual patron to whom they attributed credit for their business. Although Hoa's trips to Châu Đốc were shaped around the expectation of practical benefit *(lợi thức dụng)*, her neighbors regarded her as particularly devout. Hoa's journeys exemplify the expectations many in Vietnam place on their deities to respond to a range of pragmatic concerns, be they health, educational success, fertility, marital happiness, migration, or consumer purchases. This orientation to this-worldly benefits, which Reader and Tanabe have identified as the common religion in Japan (Reader and Tanabe 1998), is widespread in East Asian popular religions (e.g., Gates 1996; Weller 1994a) and is a dimension of Southeast Asian religious practice that is receiving increasing attention as well (e.g., Jackson 1999a, 1999b). Hoa's pious journeys very much approximated her own and her neighbors' daily invocations to gods, ghosts, and spirits in and near home, her pilgrimage a magnified version of these everyday this-worldly religious acts. Her trips to Châu Đốc were considered exemplary for their scale, something her neighbors too would do if they had the means.

Indicative of the focus characterizing her journeys to Châu Đốc, Hoa dismissed the notion that she take in supplementary leisure activities on the way as simply extraneous. According to her, one went to Châu Đốc to make offerings. When that was done one should leave the shrine and return. Vivid confirmation of the narrowness of her focus was her erroneous perception that there was very little else to do in the whole of Vĩnh Tế village or on Sam Mountain but to make offerings in the shrine. The seriousness with which Hoa approached her quest was also reflected in her no-nonsense approach to the goddess. She said the goddess would help one with anything one asked, from business success to leaving the country. However, one should restrict oneself to making just one request. And one should not weigh the goddess down with frivolous requests like buying a house or a motorbike. Because such religious journeys are not crafted around austerity or penitence but on accessing the goddess, the increasing ease of travel to the shrine resulting from technological improvements has not led to a process of secularization. Indeed, judging by the level of interest shown in her by residents of Ho Chi Minh City throughout the 1990s, the magnetic pull of the Châu Đốc shrine rose in tandem with improvements in the roads and new forms of mass transport.[5]

Such pilgrims impugn the idea of leisure largely because these dimensions detract from the pragmatic and obligatory considerations that drive their engagement with the goddess. Similarly, Turneresque communitas, or voluntaristic participation in the mingling of humanity, is not an important factor driving this style of pilgrimage. According to many residents of Ho Chi Minh City, traveling to the shrine during the customary annual festival to the goddess was inconsistent with what they sought to gain from their encounter with the goddess. In their comments people cited the threat of pickpockets but also the aggravations of smoke, heat, and jostling—in short, the overwhelming intensity of the festival as a mass religious experience. The rationale given by Hoa was typical: "During the festival itself it is too crowded—it is impossible to get into the shrine. Last year I wanted to see the main rite, her Ladyship's bath, which is performed at midnight, but I couldn't get in. There were too many people. The incense really stung my eyes. It wasn't at all comfortable. This year I went just after New Year to avoid the crush and it was already getting crowded! Also at this time of year, the journey down to Châu Đốc can take seven or eight hours." For similar reasons, some urban pilgrims traveled to Châu Đốc after the annual ceremonies ended. This was an alternative means of avoiding the large crowds.

This attitude in large measure evidenced the wish to tap the goddess' powers and acquit oneself of one's debt to her. One person who organized trips from Ho Chi Minh City to the site told me that it was impossible to observe the appropriate rites during the festival. She said it was more efficacious to stand directly in front of the altar when making a request of Her Ladyship. This could only be done outside the festival season, when the crowds abated: "The goddess is responsive all through the year." With fewer people in the pagoda I could also wipe Her Ladyship's image with a cloth soaked in perfumed water. For a small fee, she could arrange to get this done for me thanks to an agreement she had with shrine attendants. Or I could arrange to have the goddess' robes changed if I so desired. Indeed, there was nothing the annual festival had that her own later tour could not offer.

This disinterest in the festival cannot, for this reason, be regarded as an instance of secularization or cultural loss. Rather, such arrangements under-line the importance people place on individual compacts with the goddess, reflecting the individualized, pragmatic, and quasi-contractual ritual rela-tionship many urbanites entertain with her. Economic motivations in these pilgrimages are no indicator of reduced religiosity. Rather, economic and re-ligious modes of behavior are closely associated and overlapping projects. City residents' decisions to stay away from the festival to the goddess have not led to the waning of this icon of religious culture. On the contrary, their interaction with the goddess, comprising as it does an unbroken stream of hundreds of thousands of individual transactions, has prolonged the festival season, which half a century ago lasted less than two weeks. As a result of the interest shown in the goddess by people from the city, at its peak in the mid-1990s, the pilgrimage season *(mùa hành hương)* lasted more than five months, from the Western New Year until well after the fourth-lunar-month festival. Such is vivid evidence of the reshaping of this religious event by the distinctive preoccupations of urban culture.

Pilgrimage as Intensification of Conviviality

A large and perhaps increasing component of pilgrims who travel to Châu Đốc is only partially focused upon the acquittal of their reciprocal obligations to the goddess. For many pilgrims, other motivations loom large as the ra-tionale and organizing principle of their journeys. As in Japan (Reader 1996b, 136), pilgrimages in Vietnam often have a ludic dimension, which overlaps other modes of behavior. While some pilgrims' emphasis on the practical benefits to be derived from their religious journeys discounts playful or leisurely components from their conception of such practice, the ludic dimension is abundantly evident in other accounts. As one moves away from strictly pragmatic motivations such as Hoa's, with their emphasis on vertical compacts made between pilgrims and the goddess, to trips framed to a greater degree around ludic pursuits, one finds increased emphasis in accounts and espoused ideals of pilgrimage on horizontal relations between pilgrims. Much of the time this ludic element is expressed through the improved opportunities for conviviality or intensification of bonds between participants that pilgrimages present.

Nevertheless, even in pilgrimages organized around such ends, one

detects limits to conviviality and the maintenance in the practice of traveling of pronounced spatio-temporal divisions, evidenced in urban pilgrims'
aversion to visiting the shrine in Châu Đốc during the annual festival,
a time many urbanites associate with crowds of people from the provinces.
Although their journeys take them into a rural area, which they would characterize as remote, urban pilgrims usually travel with acquaintances, be they
neighbors, family members, colleagues, or clients. Surrounding themselves
with trappings of the familiar, they rarely leave each other's company and
rarely, if ever, come into close proximity with residents of the local area.

One regular pilgrimage group who traveled in this manner was made up
of the family of durian sellers outside my residence. When I passed them, I
had to be careful not to impale myself on a mound of their spiky merchan-
dise. The durians' bristling armor and olive color and the formidable ram-
parts into which they were piled suggested that the street was under siege.
Over time, the family had expanded into other fruit: rambutans, dragon fruit,
lychees, jackfruit, and Thai tamarinds. They sold every year from the same
place to build customer awareness and had spread to several locations on the
street to maximize sales flow. They sold all day and all night. They remained
in place for the duration of the fruit season, which began in April and lasted
until September. "By that time we really need a break." On occasion, the face
of the senior male in the group looked frighteningly haggard, worry lines
etched deep in the slanting light of the early morning: "We can only manage
because we share responsibilities within the extended family," he said.

Just as the family occupied space so distinctively, surrounded by their
piles of fortified fruit, and worked punishing hours that were governed by the
cycles of the fruit season, so too were their religious journeys also distinctive;
they visited the shrine to the goddess together as a group, according to their
own timing and with their own reasons. The whole family went off on a pilgrimage to Sam Mountain at the end of each fruit-selling season. This trip
usually lasted five days. According to the senior male family member, there
were obligations to discharge on this trip: "As soon as all the fruit is sold, we
go to Châu Đốc to make thanksgiving offerings to Her Ladyship for a good
season. We also get salt and rice packets from Her Ladyship to ensure we will
have enough to eat throughout the rest of year and a strip of gold that
will help us make money." While it coincided with the end of their half-year
selling cycle, September also had the important advantage of being one of
the quietest months to visit the shrine: "At other times you cannot find the
elbowroom to make your offerings," he said.

The family's end-of-season trip to Châu Đốc was the second they made
each year. Their first, undertaken in the first month of the lunar year, was

designed to garner the goddess' support for the forthcoming selling season: "Every year we pack up and go on pilgrimage for the entire month of January. Thirty of us rent a bus for the month and travel around, visiting pagodas and temples throughout all of southern Vietnam." One of the accents in this trip was on comprehensive devotions: "It takes a month to visit all the sites in the vicinity of Sam Mountain alone," the oldest saleswoman said. "We usually go there via my uncle's place in Long Xuyên—he has a large pagoda, where we stay—then on to Sam Mountain and Forbidden Mountain to visit Big Buddha Pagoda." The durian sellers also regularly went north to Phan Thiết, to visit the forty-nine-meter reclining Buddha ("it's even bigger than the one in Vũng Tàu") and the temple to Kuan Yin on Trà Cổ Mountain in Long Thành. An equally forceful emphasis was on restful socializing and recreation, at a good price: "Apart from the bus hire, we don't usually spend much money." Wherever they went, they stayed in pagodas and cheap guest houses at a cost of only 3,000–4,000 dong per person per night. Food was available free in the pagodas or was cooked in kitchens in guest houses. They knew people all over the south and had close friendships with the monks in some pagodas. For example, at Sam Mountain they always stayed in the pagoda of the Buddha of Western Peace. Although it was always crowded, they weren't afraid of theft. They always had their own room, and the monks took care of them, bringing them coffee and snacks at no charge. These ludic goals also shaped the timing of this journey: "We try to stay away from temples during the period of their main festival. It is expensive and arduous. Crowds, beggars, and pickpockets make the experience unpleasant and tiring."

While to maximize comfort many people designed their journeys around avoiding the crowds at the festival, for most people the pilgrimage presented an unrivaled chance to socialize. One elderly pilgrim went on the Châu Đốc pilgrimage each year with her fellow Buddhist laywomen and a nun from their local pagoda. There were benefits to going on pilgrimage with a group of like-minded people. "Traveling together with a group of acquaintances is definitely the best way to go. Because you hire a bus as part of a group, you can visit any pagoda you like, such as the pagodas offering free meals to Châu Đốc pilgrims. You can talk with friends, sit anywhere you like, and change seats as often as you please. It is a lot more enjoyable than buying a ticket in a bus where no one knows each other and each has their own seat number. Down at the pilgrimage site, you can also rent a room together, to save on costs. If you sleep together overnight, you have better fun!" she said, laughing. Although the goal was certainly not to undergo trials in the name of religion, the popularity of the trip and the crush on the roads made some hardship inevitable: "The buses have to leave very early in the morning to avoid the traffic. Leading up to the main festival days, the journey starts to become very slow. There are long traffic jams at the ferry crossings, in Vĩnh Long, Cần Thơ, Cao Lãnh, and Long Xuyên. By this stage, in Châu Đốc, it is extremely crowded. You'll find it hard to get into Her Ladyship's shrine. The smoke from incense is extremely thick and painful to the eyes. It is so hot and crowded that people don't sleep—they go from dusk to dawn without sleeping."

In pursuit of value for money, convenience, and ease, some people make the journey entirely by night to save on accommodation, maximize the time spent at the site, and avoid traffic. An underemployed motorcycle taxi driver in the city enthused about the forthcoming travel arrangements of his neighbors, who were planning a trip to Châu Đốc. Their bus would be air-conditioned and equipped with a karaoke machine. It would leave at 9 P.M. and arrive in Châu Đốc at 6 A.M. the following day. It would then leave Châu Đốc at 3 P.M. that afternoon and return home by midnight. By driving nights and staying for just one day, they could prolong the trip but avoid the expense of accommodation. "You should go," he said. "It will be good value and great fun." I listened to his pitch, which, with its emphasis on nocturnal travel and air-conditioned mobile comfort, I found quite alluring. In his view a trip to the goddess was as a nonstop road party from departure to return. The participants would surely not sleep a wink during the entire journey.

The rhythms of this approach are not inconsistent with the lifestyle of a city of shift workers, round-the-clock markets, and active nightlife and with a reputation for never sleeping. Such approaches challenge the conception of pilgrimage as characteristically taking place in nonordinary space and time. On the contrary, the notion of damning the scenery and blinkering off the rural backdrop to the journey by doing it almost entirely at night suggests that for these participants, pilgrimage is a continuation or rather intensification of their urban existence. These pilgrims would leave the city and arrive at dawn at a remote village, which was transformed for the duration of the pilgrimage season into a sprawling and bustling urban center. The transport arrangements promised to accentuate this impression. The image of being encased in a metal and glass bubble of cabin-lit comfort and air-conditioned luxury, indulging in the musical pleasures of karaoke, and never for a moment leaving the company of urban neighbors conspired to create a general impression of remove from the traditional rural landscape through which the bus would travel.

For this motorcycle taxi driver, however, the alluring delights of such a pilgrimage were an unrealizable dream, an experience to which he only had access vicariously, through the plans of his wealthier neighbors. In contrast, pilgrimages are a constant topic of pleasurable planning and reminiscences for those who have the means to travel. An acquaintance, Thúy, had a stall selling toiletries and beauty products at Tân Định market. Since the early 1990s, she had been a regular pilgrim to the shrine of the Lady of the Realm, traveling to Châu Đốc in a bus full of saleswomen from her market to request the goddess' assistance in business. Thúy told me that now, thanks to higher sales, she had the means to travel several times a year. As her youngest daughter had joined her at work, she could now leave her business in capable hands for extended periods. These days whenever she traveled she tended to go with her husband.

She spoke dreamily: "This year I went to Châu Đốc alone with my husband. We took our new Honda Dream 100 cc motorbike. Traveling this way allows us a lot more flexibility than in a tour group." She spoke fondly about the food, the sights, the destinations, giving an exhaustive account of the costs, the dates, the times, and the accommodation arrangements. After several customers had made their purchases, she continued to reminisce about other trips she had taken: "Last year, I went to the city of Huế on a seven-day tour. I went to the mausoleums of emperors Minh Mạng and Tứ Đức and ate on a floating restaurant on the Perfume River. That trip was great fun." She spoke softly and smiled wistfully: "Huế was so beautiful." More customers made purchases and Thúy moved on to news of other travel, this time plans for her forthcoming trips. "I'll be going to Buôn Mê Thuột to visit the pagodas, and go sightseeing. It will be my first time there. We will also be going with a bus group back to Châu Đốc and down to Hà Tiên for four days of sight-seeing after Her Ladyship's festival winds up. I plan to go to Thailand next but haven't yet saved enough money." Her account of these projected journeys dwelt again on the travel arrangements, the mode of transport, the cost of the tickets, and the promise of extended days of leisure.

Thúy's reminiscences and plans for further journeys emphasized the sensual intensification afforded through travel and dwelt on the highlights of her itinerary. These emphases can be contrasted with her earlier approach to the Châu Đốc pilgrimage, pragmatically shaped around the search for results and the moral obligation of repayment. Over ten years her pilgrimage activities have changed focus, from being a way to acquire wealth to a mode of enjoyably and meaningfully spending it.

In a country whose urban areas have experienced an explosion of consumer affluence, the experience of pilgrimage has increasingly been shaped by such sensual and ludic considerations. One way of interpreting this is advanced by Reader, who sees that the emphasis on leisure and having a good time in pilgrimages reflects the changing priorities of the cultures from which pilgrims are drawn (Reader 1993a, 227). If pilgrimage is understood as an intensification of the highest values of a culture, the Châu Đốc pilgrimage gives an insight into the value placed on leisure, comfort, and consumption in the lives of those who undertake it. Such themes were evident in one pilgrimage that I undertook to Châu Đốc in 1998 with a group of pilgrims from a market quarter in Ho Chi Minh City. While not presented as typical, it does illustrate the importance of ludic and sensuous considerations in the shaping of this pilgrimage.

Urban Pilgrims in Progress

At 3:30 A.M., half an hour before the scheduled departure, I drank a morning cup of coffee at the pickup point with my motorcycle taxi driver. Lady Chiểu market was alive with people in the cool predawn air. "It never closes," observed the driver. Many of the people we could see in the marketplace had themselves already undertaken the pilgrimage. Such early departure times were no disruption of the routine of market vendors, stall owners, and transport workers. Aunt Six, the pilgrimage leader, arrived next. With her own coffee stall in this market, she was used to early starts, making deliveries of coffee and tea to fellow marketers in the market as early as 3 A.M. When she was on pilgrimage, which was most of the time, her business was run by her two daughters.

The pilgrimage leader ordered iced black coffees, and as we waited for the pilgrims to assemble, she spoke about the trips she had made, her raspy voice constantly breaking into throaty chuckles. She had just returned from a three-week bus trip to Hanoi and across the border into southern China, and she had been to Châu Đốc on pilgrimage already more than twenty times in the first three months of that year. As people arrived, she invited them over for a coffee. Our bus arrived next, a gleaming import from Korea, with widely spaced reclining seats. As more passengers descended from motorcycles, Aunt Six invited each to come and have a coffee. Some entered the vehicle to sleep. Others dispersed along the string of cafés in front of the theater for a morning bowl of noodles. When most were present, Aunt Six consulted the passenger list and dispatched her son to wake up and collect the remaining few. Aunt Six said she knew most of the people, that they went with her each year.

We pulled out through Ho Chi Minh City's outer suburbs before dawn broke. It was first light when we reached the rural zone. The driver switched off the cabin lights, and the bus dissolved back into half night. Heads lolled, arms stretched back over the tops of seats as passengers sought maximum reach and comfort. In the back a twenty-two-year-old youth with bright eyes and close-cropped hair entertained Aunt Six with an extended, animated tale. His was the only audible voice. Lolling luxuriously across two seats, a young woman in bright red silk pajamas irritably complained that if he really loved his young pregnant wife he should go back to the front of the bus and sit with her. He returned, chastened, and all those around me dozed for a while. The sun rose, briefly awakening some passengers, who pulled curtains shut before resuming their interrupted sleep. The Mekong delta provinces of Long An and Tiền Giang slipped by, observed by few.

The bus lurched to a halt at a roadside restaurant just before the Mekong River. Aunt Six opened her eyes, appraised the situation, and invited her "senior aunts and uncles" to descend and eat breakfast. Lines of men and women filed out to the toilets at the rear of the café, men pissing at ease in the long trough provided for their comfort, women queuing in discomfort in front of the two small cubicles available to them. Several passengers dozed on in the bus. Inside the restaurant, we pilgrims settled around the tables. Noodle soups were ordered all around and, at our table, another round of coffees. Aunt Six, being the group leader, ate for free as did the bus driver and his assistant.

We filed back onto the bus, which rolled on up to the banks of the Mekong River's northern branch. As the bus pulled into the Mỹ Thuận ferry terminal, Aunt Six requested that passengers get off the bus for the ferry crossing. She bought a wad of ferry tickets and distributed them to us as we filed out of the bus. We negotiated ranks of snack stalls and boarded the ferry, commenting on how cool it was on the river. Once all were back on board on the other side, the bus continued its journey across the narrow strip of rice fields and fruit orchards between the two main branches of the Mekong delta. Another ferry crossing was negotiated, followed by more hours of rolling through the Mekong delta plain. The assistant bus driver slipped a *cải lương* opera cassette into the video player: *Bao Cung Marries.* Passengers ripped open packets of chewing gum, gnawed on dried fruit and sheets of milk toffee, and slurped cold drinks while appraising the opening stanzas of the opera. One or two heads poked out of windows to watch the early morning activities of the countryside. The brief exercising of limbs, the cool river breeze, and the chemical infusion of sugar and preservatives stimulated passengers into brief consciousness. Most, however, seduced by the twangy strains of the *vọng cổ* melody, were soon reclaimed by sleep.

We pilgrims who remained awake sat with heads tilted backward, eyes raised and gazes absorbed in the splendid vision on the TV screen at the front of the bus. A few were riveted by the story of the heavenly prince Bao Cung, condemned to descend to earth for committing the impropriety of falling in love with a fairy. The video was true to the *cải lương* genre, depicting a romantic world where men are tender to their wives, effeminate, respectful of their parents, guiless to a fault, and observant of debts to the spirit world. *Cải lương*'s men are like credulous children. The genre incorporates an unpredictable mixture of musical styles as accompaniment to the shouting, pouting, sudden shifts of emotional tone, burlesques, rowdiness, boasting, and rural accents of its unpolished, simple characters. It is set in a moral universe of benevolent feudal rulers, ingenuous heroes, innocent maidens, faithful companions, and minor despots. Its political universe is based on the family —its harmony, its tensions, and the small-time ruses by which people negotiate their existence within it. Politics is interpreted as an art of emotional manipulation, transparent scheming, mildly despotic stratagems. The family world is projected fancifully/wishfully onto the level of the kingdom, the celestial court itself riven by all-too-familiar domestic tensions. The feminine realm of the marketplace and the cafés and food and market stalls presided over by women seem to be another model for the world of *cải lương*. It is a world that conforms to the logic of the heart, where cruelty and unfaithfulness are punished, innocence is rewarded, and devotion repaid.

The *cải lương* video was followed by a program featuring a kindly old woman telling cautionary tales to children that illustrated the negative consequences of greed, vanity, and theft. Each of her tales took viewers into a dreamworld where fabulous and magical creatures interacted with simple and childlike adults. The viewers slipped more comfortably into childlike states of passivity, occasionally sipping on sweetened drinks. The rest of the group slept on.

Just outside the town of Long Xuyên, the bus stopped for lunch. Aunt Six again invited her senior aunts and uncles to descend. A lone voice rose, questioning why we needed to stop to eat when we were less than an hour from our destination. Aunt Six responded that we needed "to eat and refresh ourselves." When we arrived at the guest house we could then rest "for our health" and after that go to worship. Fewer than half the passengers descended. Some continued snoozing; others opened snacks purchased during the ferry crossing. A trickle of guests headed for the toilets, the remainder for the dining area. Rice, pork chops, and roast chicken were on the menu. Before I could order, Aunt Six, the driver, and the driver's assistant, who had installed themselves in the restaurant next door, invited me over to partake of the generous repast arranged before them. Steamed pork, roast pork, sweet and sour fish soup, candied prawns, and cucumber and tomato salad defied the appetites of the pilgrimage group's nonpaying guests, one of them a vegetarian. We left an enormous quantity uneaten when we reboarded the bus.

Aunt Six tried to get the bus to stop again at the market in Châu Đốc so she could buy some trade goods for resale back in the city, but she was again challenged by the forceful passenger who said if Aunt Six wanted to go shopping she should do it herself rather than divert the entire bus to the marketplace for her own personal needs. We eventually entered the mountainside village of Vĩnh Tế and proceeded directly to our guest house, situated about a hundred meters from Her Ladyship's shrine. Aunt Six greeted the owner and shepherded us through the downstairs café and upstairs into a large room, which would serve as our communal sleeping area. Three fans beat the hot air, making the room into a convection oven. Aunt Six invited us to rest, and we pilgrims heeded our group leader like dutiful children. Each of us pulled a thin straw mat off the balustrade and sought a sleeping space as close to a fan as possible. A few considered the merits of sleeping on the veranda and were warned by a veteran pilgrim that at night they would be eaten alive by mosquitoes. Moments later, the entire group was asleep.

Our guided journey to the site had taken us not so much out of time, into a nonordinary temporal state, as backward in time, recalling in us more passive, childlike states. Rather than taking us into unfamiliar territory, the journey brought to the fore memories of infancy—a time of confinement, feeding, and constant sleeping. Although this process of deferral to the pilgrimage leader and progressive abandonment of duties can seem like the shucking off of everyday roles, close to what Turner means when he says that pilgrims are liberated from the obligatory everyday constraints of status and role (1974, 207), it is not quite accurate to convey this as an escape from structure. Rather, it entailed a return to or rehabitation of a familiar childhood status. The social process of our pilgrimage was closer to infantilization than liberation. The pilgrimage also reinforced and sanctioned our status as consumers, for whom the sharpest dilemma revolved around which purchase to make. In our purchase-filled peregrination through the plethora of consumerist opportunities available at the site, we were a band of wandering players acting out a familiar script.

On the Sensual Mountain

One of the most common components of a pilgrimage to the Lady of the Realm is the ascent of Sam Mountain, whose peak towers some two hundred meters above the shrine (figure 10). An arrangement was made among some

FIG. 10. The main street of Vĩnh Tế village on the slopes of Sam Mountain

members of our group to regroup at the end of the afternoon to make our own ascent. Various motives were evident in this suggestion. For some, climbing the mountain was a must. To stroll through a picturesque landscape dotted with rocks and religious architecture and to take in one of the few panoramic views available of the Mekong plain was an indispensable part of any trip to the shrine. It also had religious connotations, providing an opportunity to accrue some merit and pay obeisance to local spirits on a mountain whose slopes were dotted by hundreds of shrines and pagodas. Some undertook the climb in a physical reaction to the prolonged inactivity of the trip thus far and in response to excessive eating. To climb the mountain was also to participate in the conquest of geography by urban leisure culture. This project was particularly true of our own group's climb, whose trajectory scarcely grazed the flanks of the mountain.

At about 5 P.M., when the air had cooled, we pierced the cordon of porridge sellers that had encircled our overflowing guest house and flowed into the main street of the hillside village. The street was lined with rest houses, restaurants, cafés, souvenir stands, and photo-developing kiosks. Relatively focused and unified, but scarcely insensate to their appeals, we moved past them all in the wake of our charismatic leader, Aunt Six. Trishaw and motorcycle taxi drivers could not tempt any of us to abandon the planned conquest of the mountain by foot for mechanized comfort up the winding road to the peak. Neither did the infectious rhythm of Cantonese pop music, the musical strains from a battery of karaoke machines, or the flickering of video screens in the cafés that lined the road cause anyone from our group to break stride. We were subjected to the constant prompting of saliva glands, which responded to the smells of roast pork, candy, and fistfuls of ripe fruit thrust questioningly before us by walking vendors. However, perhaps thanks to the cigarettes consumed by the male members of the group and the sweets and chewing gum that many of the female pilgrims had armed themselves with at the outset, the passage of the group along the first hundred meters of Vĩnh Tế's main street was not interrupted by a single mundane purchase.

We reached the foot of the trail up the mountain. Raising one's eyes one could make out the outline of the route by the unbroken line of pagodas and cafés that stretched to the peak of the mountain. Our ascent commenced with a visit to the temple of the mandarin Thoại Ngọc Hầu, which was on the path, several steps up from the street. We filed in, purchasing incense and proffering prayers to the spirit of the historical personage, whom a biography installed by the Department of Culture and Information credited with defending this patch of the fatherland against the military incursions of Siamese "pirates." One of our group, a cyclo driver, perused the large framed document studiously. An older woman stroked the rugged bronze features of her heroic ancestor in a hesitating gesture of aesthetic appreciation that in midexecution appeared to be overtaken by a religious imperative. Her hand paused uncertainly, then swiftly rose to stroke her own head—transferring the potency of the spirit to her body. For others in the group, the lighting of incense and conventional three bobs of the head had fulfilled their dues to the spirit, and they waited in a huddle on the front steps.

"Let's go," said Aunt Six imperatively as soon as our last group member emerged from the temple. We moved on to the next stage of the ascent, a short climb of ten steps up to an image of Kuan Yin, the bodhisattva of compassion, whose tender smile urged us upward. One member of the party exclaimed at the heat. Kuan Yin smiled compassionately, perched coolly under a wide umbrella. The first to scale the run of steps were a pair of young couples impelled by the wish to be photographed in front of the goddess considered the efficacious guarantor of children and conjugal happiness. A sheen of sweat was dabbed off brows, and instant cameras unsheathed from cases. Each of the women was photographed by her husband, after which each in turn photographed her husband. Then one of the hovering professional photographers photographed each couple.

As their commemorative moment was drawing to a close, the full complement of pilgrims had made it to the feet of the statue, and the next leg of our journey was being contemplated. It consisted of a short traverse across the slope to a pagoda beside the path. Although the way was horizontal and well paved, the chance of successfully negotiating the passage was lessened by the placement of a beckoning café alongside the path right at the halfway mark. With resolve, Aunt Six set off. The charm of the thatched café and cool promise of clinking ice worked on our senses as we negotiated the first half of the traverse. Ignoring murmurs of invitation from the proprietor, a number of people made it all the way across to the pagoda. Others who succumbed purchased take-away bags of iced lemonade to succor them en route. Slowly we regrouped at the corner of the pagoda. New arrivals were rewarded by a guarantee of good fortune made by the weather-beaten incumbent of the stool on the veranda of the pagoda—one of Sam Mountain's legion of state lottery ticket sellers. The encounter with this figure was considered auspicious by a number of the pilgrims. They leafed through his paper offerings and purchased eagerly. Aunt Six checked his list of winning numbers from the previous day. Undaunted by not having selected a winner, she sowed her useless tickets across the slope in front of the pagoda and purchased a handful more.

Meanwhile the resident monk of the pagoda emerged, roused by the sounds of the pilgrims accumulating at the entrance to his refuge. Buttoning up his tunic, he surveyed the scene before him, then refocused his look upon me, the sole member of the group showing interest in his place of abode. He greeted me formally in English: "Hello Sir. Welcome to Sam Mountain! Please come inside." I explained to him that I was just waiting there for the others: "I think my group is about to leave." Glancing over my shoulder, I saw that the group had completed their fling with the state lottery and were starting to move on. "Permit me to depart," I said, as his gaze shifted to another group of approaching pilgrims.

Rejoining my group, I learned that some were talking about visiting the famed "historical and cultural vestige" of "Cave Pagoda," written up in all the guidebooks about Sam Mountain. It would be by our standards a relatively arduous, half-kilometer climb to this site, high on the side of the mountain, but some thought one well worth the effort. Before we had reached consensus, some people set off to tackle the next stage. This entailed climbing another short set of steps and making another traverse, passing several more cafés, scenic rest points, and small shrines. Our rate of progress was not increasing. Frequent breaks, small purchases, photographic opportunities, and occasional acts of religious veneration made this thirty-meter leg into the longest thus far on the climb. Our group was dispersed, strung out along the mountainside, its unity dissolved by numerous competing demands on its members' attention.

Slowly, however, we regrouped behind Sister Two, a former school-teacher and present durian seller, who was transfixed by the miraculous sight of a tree flowering out of season: "Look at this—a Mai flower tree blooming in April. Normally it only flowers in January." As the group bottlenecked behind the place where she stood, awestruck on the path, the significance of the unseasonable crop of yellow flowers was explained in turn to each arrival. "So late in the year," "so many flowers," "so fresh" sounded the responses as explanations flowed down the logjam of pilgrims. "Coming through! Coming through!" came the voice of the garrulous twenty-two-year-old, dragging his pregnant newlywed wife riskily along the rock-strewn outer edge of the mountain path. "Make way. Let us get a photograph." Those standing in their path breathed in to accommodate the couple's unstoppable overtaking maneuver. Their camera was thrust into someone's hands. The young pair positioned themselves. A few rounds were pressed off until someone observed that the mechanism on the newly acquired Taiwanese import had failed to deliver a convincing click.

"Film's finished," opined one of the group. "No, the batteries have gone," proclaimed another, peering at the dial on the top of the camera. "Can't be. See? The light is still on," came another expert opinion. "Open it; you'll probably find that the film hasn't even begun to wind onto the spool." Everyone had an explanation, but the device was passed over for the expert advice of Aunt Six, who authoritatively ruled in favor of the latter hypothesis. The back was popped open to reveal that the first suggestion had been right; the film had finished and, unnoticed by its owner, the camera had automatically rewound the film. "What luck!" exclaimed one of our group. "At the bottom of the hill there are any number of places to develop the film. You'll have the pictures in less than an hour."

The group now stood at a crossroads. We could continue what would be a long ascent to Cave Pagoda or fork off to cross a picturesque suspension bridge that stretched attractively across a smallish gulch on a path that would lead us back down the mountain. Due consideration of aesthetics and heeding of the prompting issuing from tired legs made the latter option the unanimous choice. Bouncing unsteadily across the bridge, we arrived in a small clearing surrounded by religious symbolism. Above us loomed a brightly painted statue of an emaciated Buddha fasting under the protective canopy of a garish, green, multiheaded snake. "How horrid!" exclaimed one of the group. Aunt Six explained that this was Lord Buddha, depicted before he renounced excessive austerity as a means of attaining enlightenment and expounded the characteristic salvational approach of Buddhism known as the Middle Way. We gazed for a while at this image. The modified aims and downward inclination of our course suggested that we too had mutually renounced excessive exertion as the key to our pilgrimage.

Behind the pained-looking ascetic towered the summit of Sam Mountain. Suddenly, Sister Two exclaimed, "Look at the people climbing the mountain; they look just like ants!" Here and there along the string of cafés, kiosks, and pagodas that line the pilgrimage trail up the mountain could be seen a multicolored, slowly moving trickle of figures. Their insectlike appearance suggested their industry to be the manifestation of a lowlier incarnation of being. Turning away from this exemplary demonstration of the truth of the Middle Way, we strolled across the clearing to where another Buddha image sat beneath a protective rock overhang. "Look, it's Cave Pagoda after all," one of our group said happily about the edifice, which was, plausibly, a pagoda in a cave. The last loaded camera left in the group was pressed into recording this unexpected attainment of the goal of our quest. Aunt Six read out the mantra embossed on the pedestal beneath the figure: Homage to Amida. According to the practice of Pure Land Buddhism, of which the bodhisattva Amida was the central figure, the pronouncement of these words infused one with karmic merit. These were familiar words to Buddhists in Vietnam, who pronounce them each time they chant the sutras. However, Aunt Six's reading of the words was hesitant, and the rest of us looked at the stone figure of the bodhisattva in silence. We soon poured out of the clearing toward a small pagoda with a glorious view of the plain and a refreshment stall operated by its nuns.

On the way, we passed another cave, where a bright pink–turbaned figure with well-defined breasts and swollen belly was installed. The hand-painted title, Mr. Earth, was scrawled on a nearby rock. "Look," I said. "It's Mr. Earth!" The rough-hewn, effeminate character hardly approximated the sleek, mass-produced earth god installed back in the homes of each and every pilgrim among us. "That's not Mr. Earth; it's Maitreya Buddha," chorused a few voices. "No, he's right. Look, it says 'Mr. Earth,'" said another. People looked doubtfully at the dribbling painted caption. "Maybe it's a Cambodian Mr. Earth," one of the group suggested. This remark produced a number of dissenting murmurs. Sensibilities slightly shaken, the pilgrims moved on to the more reliable prospect of sweet liquid refreshments waiting ahead of us. A young woman was the last to file past the figure. She accorded the suspect rendition of the god its due veneration by diffidently flicking the dregs of her drink bag into the precincts of the shrine, where it plopped wetly on the rock. She moved on for a refill to where, after a cursory inspection of the pagoda, we had slumped into the pagoda's café seats to be shouted lemonades by Aunt Six.

From our vantage point of some thirty meters above the plain, we surveyed the rice fields and canals of the Mekong delta. "An outstandingly beautiful view," ruled Sister Two. A slight breeze stirred the air as the last rays of the sun slipped away. "Feel the breeze," said her son. "But we're in the mountains now," said another, as if retorting to a debating point. Talk turned to other trips taken by some among us. "Have you ever been to Dalat?" asked one of my companions, referring to the old French hill station and romantic holiday destination of many middle-class Vietnamese. "Dalat has lots of beautiful scenery." Another replied, "Aunt Ten here has just been to Hà Tiên, isn't that right? Hà Tiên is just as beautiful as Dalat, isn't it?" "Yes," Aunt Ten replied; "I went for four days and three nights. We went to all the pagodas, climbed the mountain, swam and went out to the islands. Very beautiful." We slurped on our lemonades. Aunt Six self-effacingly shared the last inch of lemonade from a bottle into four of her fellow pilgrims' glasses. While we were in the thrall of our small debt to her, she seized the opportunity to refer casually to a couple of forthcoming pilgrimages to the pagodas and beach resorts of Nha Trang and Vũng Tàu that she was organizing later in the month. "We'll be going in the same bus, so it will be comfortable. Quite a few have already booked, but there are a few seats left. It promises to be great fun," she advertised not so subtly.

Retreating light started to soften the contours of the hillside. As ice cubes began to hit bottom, someone put into words the sentiments of the group: "Ready to go yet?" Aunt Six added, laughing, "Hungry yet?" We pulled ourselves out of the luxurious poses shaped for us by the angle of the reclining chairs and staged a retreat off the mountain. Charting a direct path down stone steps, one of our group muttered, "I didn't realize we had climbed up so far." As the main road of the village came within view she was encouraged by another: "We're almost there." The tributary of pilgrims fed into the thronging multitudes extruded from countless guest houses by the first cool breezes of early dusk. Our peregrination came to a close with a renewed burst of consumption. The young newlyweds made a beeline for the nearest photo-development shop. Others peeled off into small roadside restaurants. The remainder returned to eat at our guest house, shower, and change clothes. Now that dusk was upon us, at last it was time to encounter the Lady of the Realm.

Accessing the Power of the Goddess

Morinis argues that the shrine to which the pilgrim comes is an "extraordinary place" (1992, 17), a "rupture in the ordinary domain, through which heaven peeks" (1992, 5). The shrine at the heart of the Châu Đốc pilgrimage site exemplifies this in some measure: it houses a being whom many consider the most efficacious deity in Vietnam, one able to grant all manner of wishes and around whom marvelous tales are woven. Yet even when faced by such a focal point our experience of this place was mediated by processes that, familiarized and normalized its sacred geography and personalized its meaning. Here once more our journey demonstrated the ways in which pilgrimage domesticates space, drawing out and dramatizing what is most intimate and familiar, passing over what is alien and most extraordinary.

Aunt Six played a leading role in guiding our group of pilgrims through the unfamiliar geography of the mountainside pilgrimage site. Its features were mediated for us by this figure from the familiar urban world, and we largely deferred to her itinerary. Once we entered the shrine, however, Aunt Six was replaced in her role as facilitator of the experience by another member of the pilgrimage group, a thirty-five-year-old man called Nine, who, it transpired, was a medium. Drawing his fellow pilgrims into communication with the goddess, Nine provided a channel for us to access and tap her powers. By acting as a vessel for her voice, he allowed the imposing religious icon to be refigured into a flesh-and-blood human agent. The ritual encounter touched upon the extraordinary but did so through the intensification of the familiar. On entering the space of the shrine, our new mediator assumed the persona of a mother figure. Through his assumption of this persona, we neither confronted the goddess as extraordinary nor slipped out of our childlike roles.

Nine had escaped previous notice. He had slept on the back seat of the bus for the duration of our outbound journey and had shunned afternoon activities and the ascent of the mountain to rest in the cool of his private room. He emerged in the evening, casually clad in pajamas, fingernails painted bright pink and gold sparkles affixed to his cheeks. With hair freshly slicked down from a shower he sat at the table and complained bitterly about the heat. He fanned himself with elaborate gestures of discomfort. He unbuttoned his pajama top and fanned his chest then pulled his collar away from his neck and fanned there too. As the sweat beaded and grew on his face and neck, he gave up the struggle and set to fanning the rest of the group with energetic if ineffective sweeps of the fan. Aunt Six introduced him to the rest of us as her nephew. She had finished her fifth or sixth iced coffee of the day and took his appearance as a cue to announce that she was ready to go to the shrine and pray. With members of the group in tow, Nine led the way.

At 10 P.M. the shrine was still full of people. Presiding over the eddying sea of heads was the goddess; her pale face, her glassy eyes, and the tense set of her mouth made her look like a dignitary strained by the demands of her office. Her embroidered robes were resplendent, and her headpiece was set off by a neon halo. With squarish facial features, no neck, and a thick torso, the goddess was no classical willowy beauty; but it was clear that the crowd, the great majority of them women, were there for results as much as aesthetic contemplation. Lined before the altar were several women kneeling and concentrating intently on a pair of wood blocks they clasped between their hands. Aunt Six explained to me what the people were doing when they tossed the wood blocks: "You ask whether a specific aim will be realized and she answers yes or no. You divine her answer by casting a pair of coins or carved wood blocks. If both faces land the same way up her answer is no. One up, one down means yes. If you like, you can get a more detailed answer by shaking out a numbered baton from a container holding one hundred batons. Each number corresponds to a different fortune, which you can learn by consulting a book or a temple assistant. Each of the one hundred fortunes is broken down into the categories of wealth, health, family, et cetera."

A number of written requests were affixed to the sides of and below the altar that supported the goddess. One of these, with the name and address of the intercessor and the place and date of the request formally affixed, asked the goddess to make her husband drink less, go out less with his friends, stop going to brothels, be less angry, shout less, spend more time with the kids, and bring home more of his wages. "Wow, what a stirrer that guy must be!" said a member of our group, who was looking over my shoulder to read the unfortunate woman's desperate plea. On either side of us, women were leaning languidly against the base of the altar, bent into poses of great intimacy, pressed close to the plinth, arms shielding their faces, lips centimeters away from the cold stone, they were entering into confidential pacts with the goddess. As they whispered their conspiracies, they alternatively stroked the smooth surface in a tactile caress of encouragement or tapped it lightly to rouse the goddess and keep her attention fixed on their prayers. I was transfixed by the passionate and highly physical nature of their communications, which reminded me of moments of swoonlike bonding that occur between mother and child, to the exclusion of all the world.

After several minutes of milling, I made my way to the front, where a particularly dense concentration of worshipers had gathered to one side of Her Ladyship's altar. Sister Two's head poked out of the anonymous gaggle, and she beckoned me to come closer. As I entered the huddle, whose inner ring was made up of members of the Ho Chi Minh City pilgrimage group, I realized that the center of attention was none other than Nine himself. He held all those at the front of the shrine spellbound with an evenly paced, mesmerizing chant of devotion to Her Ladyship, his voice rising and falling melodically as he moved through each sentence. He stood to her left, where the goddess' robe flowed over the altar. His hands were held out in front of him, fist in palm, and he gazed raptly upward at her. Calling himself a "child," he requested her assistance.

"Wow, Nine prays beautifully," said one of our group, staring at Nine wonderingly. His prayer complete, Nine turned to the nearest awestruck spectator and, in unctuous parental tones, asked her softly, "What is your name, child?" She told him. Without asking anything more about her, he turned and spoke in her name, requesting the goddess' help with her market stall. For the next half hour, he mediated likewise for the scores of people who surrounded him beside the altar. He only asked each person's name, sometimes just the name of their family. He chanted a series of requests on their behalf, sometimes for help coming to terms with the death of a relative, sometimes for good health, the easing of melancholy, cessation of worries, success with studies and love.

He pulled some of the pilgrims close toward the altar and brushed away the perspiration on their foreheads with the fringes of the goddess' robe. With others, he stroked her robe or buried his arm beneath her garments and rubbed her torso vigorously before stroking their heads and shoulders, transferring her potency onto them. He made others stroke her robe themselves or place their hands beneath her robe to stroke her enormous rough stone hand, to access her power directly. All around him, as if released by his mediation, people were invading the altar area, caressing the goddess' robe or the altar and reaching within her petticoats to tap the power of her blunt body. Some burrowed beneath the table that, placed against the front of her altar, formed a dark tunnel, and made direct contact with the base of the altar or affixed pieces of paper recording their names and requests onto the altar and the underside of the table.

Suddenly it was over. There was no one left beside Nine requiring his intercession. Someone tapped me on the shoulder, whispering that it was time to go, releasing me from a spell. We filed out of the altar area, and an attendant closed and locked the gate we had come through. A pilgrim sought Nine out and pressed a 10,000-dong note into his hand. He looked at it in puzzlement, realized what it was, and hurried over to stuff it in a temple attendant's pocket. On the way back, I told the male medium that fellow pilgrims had praised his style of worship as beautiful. He replied that he personally wasn't capable of beautiful speech at all. Only in the presence of Her Ladyship did the words come forth. Aunt Six spoke of him in the third person. "He has religion. He can see people's future," she said, referring to the illegal activity of divination softly. "He is telepathic. He knows what people's requests are without their even needing to speak, and he can speak on their behalf to Her Ladyship. He is possessed by the spirits. They speak through him." Whenever a trip was being organized, she said, she tried to bring him along, to tell fortunes for people.

Later that night, back in the guest house, the young men in the group played a game of cards in the center of our room that lasted into the early dawn hours. Gambling with cards is a common leisurely pursuit among petty entrepreneurs and businesspeople. Through it they mark time between customers and hone the occupationally important disciplines of counting, calculation, risk taking, and defying the odds. Here, close to the shrine of the goddess, the outcome of the game was charged with portent and winnings potentially magnified manyfold. Older women tried with difficulty to get some sleep despite the increasing noise of the card game, the heat and the flickering of the fluorescent light tubes. A stream of people moved between the room and the showers. One by one, the younger women in the bus group came to see the forty-year-old medium, who was presiding in a corner of the guest house with a pack of cards, which he used to tell fortunes. He sat cross-legged with paunch slightly protruding. Two fingernails on each hand were lacquered fluorescent pink, and the golden sparkles still adhered to his deeply tanned face. He softly held forth on people's fortunes, calling each in turn "child." For the duration of his divination they were his children and he, serving as her medium, the goddess. He prefixed his predictions with a comment to each supplicant that they were "here in your Lady's realm." The women, most of them mothers themselves, asked questions concerning money, business, family, and their children's studies. He added unsolicited observations about relationships with husbands. Each woman gave him a 10,000-dong note, which he accumulated between his big toe and its neighbor.

At 2 A.M. as the card game petered out and the trickle of women seeking Nine's advice dried up, I had a moment to reflect upon the path we had been traveling on our journey. We had enjoyed the pleasures of the pilgrimage site and had experienced with heightened intensity the reality of the goddess thanks to the authoritative mediation of our two charismatic intercessors. Yet in what manner had this journey been transformative or liberating? Ian Reader argues that the experience of pilgrimage can transform the participant into a hero, citing Vincent Crapanzano's depiction of Tuhami, whose ability to cite legends and magical stories at the shrines he visited made him into a hero (1993a, 236). Certainly this observation captures what happened to Aunt Six and Nine, who emerged as the true focal points of our pilgrimage. By bringing us into contact with the pilgrimage site and the spiritual under pinnings of the world of kinship, commerce, and consumption, their authority as existential mediators was established. However, for most of us the result was somewhat opposite as the process confirmed our status as childlike followers and cosmic dependents. Such an outcome suggests that the pilgrimage be viewed less as an experience of transcendence than as a process in which the familiar is discovered, the routine reinvested, and the everyday sacralized in the guise of the extraordinary.

Return

Every pilgrimage has as one of its components a return, even those in which the distance traveled brings one nearer to, not farther from, the known world. It was still dark as we assembled for departure in the foyer of the guest house, drinking hot black coffees sweetened with sugar and thickened to the consistency of syrup. All along the street were groups of people huddled against the cold: drinkers, card players, hawkers, masseurs, healers, prostitutes, fortune-tellers, and insomniacs. People moved along the road between the shrine and their guest houses on unknown missions. Outside our bus idled, sending acrid clouds wafting through the cool morning air, communicating to the laggards the driver's impatience to leave. Pulling out through the activity in the street, the driver observed that the site remained active twenty-four hours a day for at least four months of a year—paralleling the ever-active urban world of Ho Chi Minh City. As the sun rose, I reflected on the hyper-real dimension of our pilgrimage. Speeding through the countryside, we were watching a *Paris by Night* music video, produced by the Vietnamese community abroad and expressing their nostalgia for a land left behind—that very same land that was flashing past closed curtains. Transfixed by heart-piercing renditions of folk songs and exquisitely choreographed traditional dances, not one of the city folk in the bus paid the slightest attention to the earthy and mundane details of rural existence, which passed us by unobserved.

The bus stopped for a midmorning meal at a roadside restaurant with which Aunt Six had an arrangement. As on the outbound trip, the rest stops were episodes of consumption. By the end of the trip Nine had gravitated to the dining table, groaning with food, where the bus driver, assistant, tour group leader, and I sat and ate for free. Nine's inclusion caused some trepidation to the restaurant owner, who said that the medium ate enough for two people. Previously, there had been a pile of leftovers when we left the table. "Before, I was as thin as him," Nine said, indicating the wiry cyclo driver who was economizing by sharing a bowl of noodle soup with his daughter. "Only when I put my trust in Her Ladyship did I begin to put on weight and fill out. Now, some years I come on pilgrimage as often as twenty times." He was dressed eccentrically in pajamas of rough linen, buttoned up in hilltribes style. Some on the bus called him familiarly by his first name, Nine. Despite peoples' respect for him, some joked at his girth. On one of the ferry crossings, the twenty-two-year-old youth told me, "Lucky there is a ferry. If we had to swim, Nine wouldn't make it five meters before sinking."

We took a last break in a café in Bến Lức village, just outside Ho Chi Minh City's urban perimeter. The vegetarian driver's assistant snatched a snack of noodles to top up his flagging energy for the last and most chaotic hour of the drive home. The cyclo driver and his daughter sat up properly in chairs. Sister Two bought two pineapples and explained to me that the north and the south had different terms for them. A black puppy wandered in, and I was quizzed on the special word for "black" used in reference to dogs. Everyone else stretched out luxuriously in hammocks. Nine looked utterly comfortable. He reclined regally, his only expenditure of energy being to focus his numerological skills on a sheaf of lottery tickets peddled about the group by a young boy who had come running in from the fields when our bus lurched to a stop in his territory. Aunt Six held forth in a loud voice about a forthcoming trip she was organizing to visit the pagodas of Long Hải in Bà Rịa–Vũng Tàu. Few responded. We were all sapped by the heat. The plump arm of a newly married marketer draped limply over the rim of a hammock. It clutched a half-gnawed pineapple slice, the apparent choice being whether to surrender the already half-consumed delicacy to gravity or to expend the effort to retract it within the hammock to complete the meal. The rest of her body was lost to view. Another hammock sprouted two arms, which defied the heat to coerce a glass containing water, ice, and coffee into the drinkable solution of an iced coffee by jabbing it weakly with a spoon.

Many bulges in the bottoms of hammocks showed no sign of life. Before the unscheduled rest stop threatened to become a semipermanent encampment, the bus driver stood up and requested that we pay our tabs. We trickled back onto the bus. Nine and the hyperactive twenty-two-year-old leapt up and down trying to strip berries from an ornamental vine shading the café, but their miscalculated acrobatics only succeeded in harvesting it of a good number of its leaves.

We stopped to pay a toll for the privilege of using the potholed strip of laterite—called wishfully Saigon Parkway South—cutting through recently reclaimed swampland. Then suddenly, we were in the city. Members of our group began to descend, on street corners and outside bus stations. Finally we were back at the market where we had begun our journey on the previous day. As the group broke apart and dissolved into the ferment of the great southern metropolis, I felt a brief pang. Was it regret at the unexpected cessation of this short moment of Turnerian solidarity? Or was it a register of my shock at the abrupt termination of our moveable feast of consumption, comfort, and sensual stimulation? Like many of my fellow pilgrims, however, I was quickly reengaged by the compelling demands of the city, joining other provisional groupings and being swept up into the tumultuous broil of experiences that constituted its daily life. After all, our provisional mobile community had not traveled so far away from our everyday lives, our pilgrimage representing at the same time a microcosm of urban society, an expression of its tastes, preoccupations, and values and an episode in it.

6

The Experience
of Festival

The annual festival to the Lady of the Realm taking place in Vĩnh Tế village in the fourth lunar month is largely avoided by pilgrims from the region's biggest cities because of the difficulties they have during that time in realizing their ritual, economic, and ludic pursuits. On the other hand, the festival is the near-exclusive preoccupation of the cultural commentators who write about the Lady of the Realm, who devote almost no attention to the ritual interactions with her that transpire at other times of the year. In these accounts the festival is an illustration of time-honored rural traditions, a repository of local culture, or an exemplary event in which Vietnam's cultural essence finds expression. Both sets of views illustrate the way the countryside *(nông thôn)* itself is constructed by many of Vietnam's middle-class city dwellers, as temporally anterior, a place that is "backward" or, alternatively, a site of unscathed tradition, a spiritual home *(quê hương)* to which one might return to take part in New Year rites of temporal regeneration (P. Taylor 2001b). Most people's experience of the Châu Đốc festival, however, is as far as one can get from such stereotypes about the timeless patterns of rural life. My observations of the goddess' annual festival have led me to different set of conclusions about its temporal significance. First, to understand the appeal of such major events one has to grasp the quality of simultaneity that informs and lends value to mass religious experience. Second, people who do take part in the festival very often experience it as a period of transience, during which fleeting sensations, fortuitous events, provisional associations, and consumption of novelty are the rule. Those who visit at this time are enfolded in a stream of new, hectic, and seemingly open-ended experiences, barraged by sounds, images, smells, tastes, and tactile sensations that they continuously encounter and consume. Such dimensions of the festival are not extraneous or inauthentic but central to rural people's experience of festivals of this kind and are key to their recent growth.

Some of the ritual aspects of the festival, particularly the formal ceremonies coordinated by the local shrine committee, who serve as intermediaries between community members and the goddess, are well described by folklorists and in the popular publications sold locally (see Hạnh Nguyên 1995; Tường Vân 1994; Mai Văn Tạo 1995; Thái Thị Bích Liên 1998; Thạch Phương et al. 1992; Nguyễn Minh San 1996; Nguyễn Phương Thảo 1997; Nguyễn Đăng Duy 1997). These accounts identify the heart of the festival in these rituals, whose elegance, pomp, and elaborate choreography confirm the richness of Vietnam's highly localized religious culture. Nevertheless, the very popularity of the goddess' festival makes it difficult or impossible for the majority of those who attend it to witness these rites. Most festival participants come into more significant contact with the goddess before or after these ceremonial events. In these encounters, mediators assigned by the cult committee facilitate the circulation of offerings and gifts between petitioners and the altar and keep order among the masses of people who fill the shrine. Hence, a more complete or representative ethnographic account of the festival as experienced has to take as its focus this dimension of ritual as mass mediation. Although somewhat mechanical and superficially devoid of aesthetic elegance, respectful reverence, or charismatic connectivity, the police-like ministrations that most petitioners experience at the hands of shrine attendants do not leach their encounters of spiritual significance but indeed reinforce views of the goddess' outstanding power.

Accounts that describe the annual festival also privilege events inside the shrine over those taking place in the fairground and in the cafés and guest houses in its precincts or farther away and in the homes of those who come on pilgrimage. However, despite being the overwhelming focus of domestic ethnographic literature, the shrine is by no means the still circle or privileged vessel of meaning of the festival. People's visits to the shrine, although a mandatory part of their itineraries, are not the only or the most transformative moments for them in their extended, eventful peregrinations about the site. While the interlocking gaze of religious practitioners, the state, ethnographers, and pilgrims upon the high-stakes ritual events unfolding inside the shrine has led to the expunging of some key religious practices such as mediumship and transvestitism, these forms appear in aestheticized or banalized but clearly recognizable form in the fairgrounds. Outside in such environs, where festival participants themselves prefer to spend most of their time, one is able to connect with the wellsprings of the mass experience of the festival.

These experiential dimensions of festivals are hard to capture, and observers have sometimes capitulated before the task, falling back on terms that defuse their analytical demoralization such as "disorder" and "chaos." Often, big festivals like that of the Lady of the Realm are described as plagued by the same problems as Vietnam's cities: overcrowding, theft, begging, social evils, and gambling (Hồ Hoàng Hoa 1998, 168). Another set of criticisms sees the commercialist dimension of such festivals as inauthentic overlays that dilute and dissipate their unique significance (Thạch Phường et al. 1992). Yet meaning can be found in such dimensions of festive activity even if acknowledging this fact bursts the cloistered parameters for the study of festival set up in ethnographic works and local guidebooks. The festival site is a place for social alchemy. Social projects, itineraries, and meetings that occur there are highly fluid; yet despite the exciting feeling of open possibilities that pervade them, they are intelligibly patterned. They are neither traditional nor disintegrative social forms but conform to complex dynamics. For their part, the consumerist and leisure activities occurring in the Châu Đốc pilgrimage site are far from superficial accretions and are one reason for the rapid growth of the festival. My ethnographic depiction of such aspects of the festival takes up the corrective task that Michael Gilsenan (2000, 606) calls for in recognizing the incongruous, the ludic, and the instances of seemingly banal commercialism of Islamic pilgrimages as critical dimensions of the religious experience that have been unjustifiably left out of anthropological accounts (figure 11).

Mediums for the Masses

In 1998 when I spent a week participating in the Lady of the Realm's festival, the road from Châu Đốc to the hillside village of Vĩnh Tế was clogged with traffic. Each day I had to get off my motorbike on the outskirts of the settlement and walk through the crowds that choked the village thoroughfares. It took some milling at the entrance to the shrine before I could make it inside. Needless to say, the interior was also packed with people. As I entered the shrine I noticed that Her Ladyship's face had changed dramatically since I had last seen it, only a month earlier, while visiting with a group of urban pilgrims. It was freshly painted and noticeably darker in complexion, like that of a woman who had worked a good many years in the fields. Furthermore, she no longer glared but now returned an unambiguously sweet smile to her propitiants. This somewhat mysterious transformation seemed fitting in a festival where, by all accounts, the majority of participants were from rural areas. I asked a pilgrim standing beside me if she had noticed that the

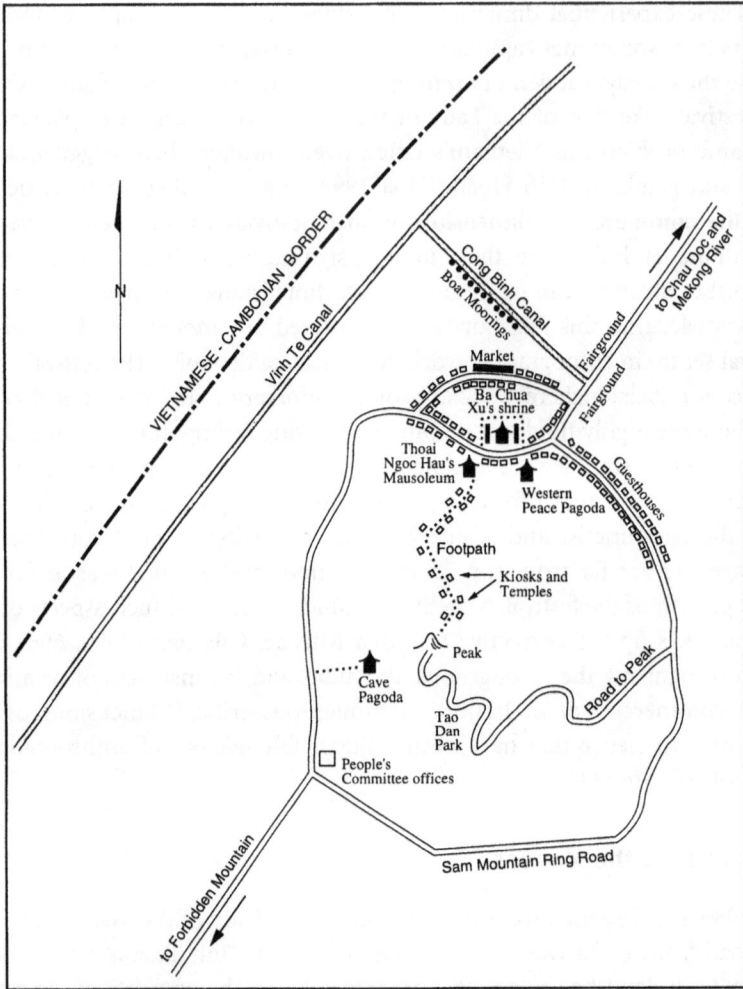

FIG. 11. Map of Sam Mountain pilgrimage site

goddess' face had changed its expression. Her eyes widened in amazement: "How could you possibly know that?" she asked. I told her that I had been there several weeks before the festival and at that time the face of the deity had been paler and her countenance more frightening. I asked her if the face had been repainted. "No," she said. "Her face changes of its own accord. Not just this once, but constantly." The goddess' constantly changing appearance was a dimension of her magical powers and confirmed her responsiveness to those who came before her. "How can you be sure she has these powers?" I asked my neighbor. She dismissed my skepticism with a question: "Do you see all the people out there. Look at them! Would they be here if it were not true?"

The shrine's organizing committee, with responsibilities for conducting the annual rites to the goddess, very much shared this notion of her efficacy. The centerpiece of their elaborate devotions was a ceremonial request to the goddess for peace *(cầu an)*. Each year they did this formally, with much pomp and splendor, interceding on behalf of the local community. The cluster of rites opened at midnight on the twenty-third of the fourth lunar month with the bathing rite, which was conducted by a select group of women.[1] Few people were able to observe the rite, however, not only because only a small fraction of those attending the festival could possibly fit into the shrine itself but because the bathing and robe changing were done behind drawn curtains. This rite was followed, the next day, by a ceremony to invite the spirit of the mandarin Thoại Ngọc Hầu into the shrine of the goddess *(lễ thỉnh sắc)*. He was enshrined in a nearby temple, and the colorful, noisy procession to the goddess' shrine, which took place in the afternoon, was observed by large numbers of pilgrims. The main ceremony, called *lễ túc yết*, commenced at midnight on the following day. It was performed by the cult committee and was attended only by invited guests. On the year I attended, the proceedings were being filmed by a local television station, the blazing arc lights blinding many of the guests and banishing the subtle colors and play of shadows from the shrine. The rites consisted of the dramatic offering of a gigantic white pig carcass, a sequence of formal offerings to the goddess (of water, incense, fruit, flowers, and lighted candles), and the chanted reading of a request to the goddess on behalf of the village for peace. This rite was followed immediately by *lễ xây chầu*, a ritual that set the stage for a performance of *hát bội* opera on behalf of the goddess. At this point in the proceedings, the formal atmosphere suddenly collapsed, and noninvited guests who had been swelling outside in anticipation suddenly poured into the shrine to secure the best ringside position for the performance, which would continue until dawn.

While the ceremonies staged by the local committee would be considered by most people in attendence at the festival as an integral part of the event, in practical terms these proceedings were tangential to most people's experience of the festival. Pilgrims took these periods of inaccessibility into account and adjusted their itineraries accordingly. As soon as people arrived at the pilgrimage site they hurried inside the shrine to present their individual offerings to the goddess. They spent some time in whispered communion, making offerings to the goddess and silently divining her intent and then left the shrine with items from her altar considered to be charged with her power. Their encounter with the goddess was undertaken directly, not formally mediated by any ritual specialist. At best, people's transactions were aided by a few words of advice or a small gesture of assistance by one of the many attendants appointed by the shrine committee. With so many people in the shrine, a number of these attendants were fully occupied in policing the interior, ensuring a steady flow of movement, watching out for criminal activity, and maintaining vigilance against any signs of spontaneous medium-istic activity.

On the morning after the bathing ceremony, the majority of the occu-pants of the shrine were women. They were dressed up, quite neatly and for-mally, if relatively simply. Most of them were busy making personal trans-actions with the goddess although, because of the crowds, under far more uncomfortable conditions than I had experienced with the urban pilgrims earlier in the year. Their offerings were simpler as well. Relative to the num-ber of people in the shrine, only a few roast pigs were being sacrificed. Trays containing fruit, flowers, rice, salt, water, paper clothes for the goddess, money, gold leaf, candles, and incense offerings threatened to overturn in the crush of people. The gates to the main altar were closed. There was no chance for mediums or individual petitioners to enter there as had been pos-sible before the festival. It was also too crowded to request attendants' help in clothing the goddess in a fresh robe. However, many pilgrims had purchased a packet of miniature paper robes, costing about 30 cents, which they burned as an offering to the goddess. A deluxe version of the same, costing one dol-lar, included a small photo of the goddess' face stuck atop her colored paper robes.

Four or five attendants were standing behind the iron gate that divided the masses in the public area from the main altar. They supervised activity, issued instructions, and indicated where people should place their gifts. Petitioners passed banknotes to them, requesting the attendants offer them directly to Her Ladyship. They handed the attendants a stream of moistened hand towels to wipe the goddess' image for them. Sometimes they asked them the proper order of rites. The attendants leaned over the gate to gather up the cash offerings, then placed them in the large bronze bell on the altar. One of them periodically told the pilgrims not to leave their offering trays on the altar top for too long: "You've taken long enough, make room for others. Move to the side, let others in. Come on Auntie, let others light their incense from your candles!" An overtaxed attendant irritably told women to put the money in the collection boxes themselves.

One of the attendants with a plateful of small-denomination notes was taking people's money offerings and handing it back to worshipers wrapped in a colored paper sheet as gifts from the goddess. When the demands grew too great he just handed them unwrapped banknotes. As the press grew greater still, a woman handed over her fistful of bills and requested a note from the goddess' altar in return. The attendant just handed back one of her notes, without even placing it on the altar. She looked desperately at her banknote, feeling shortchanged, and finally asked him for another one, in an uncertain voice. "That's good enough!" he barked back at her. Then, after a period of demand exceeding the supply, the plate was empty. A sea of hands beckoned to the attendant for more money. "That's it!" he said abruptly. Hands reached out for fruit, flowers, paper offerings—whatever portions were left on the table after people had taken a share of their offering away with them. "Pass me a flower, nephew," said one old woman to the attendant, indicating a vase standing on the table, out of reach. He passed them out, stem by stem for a while, then dropped the bunch onto the altar for people to help themselves. The altar was becoming bare. "Pass me something too, nephew," said another woman. "There are some rambutans there Auntie; they'll do," he said, indicating a withered clump of three fruit. She looked at them in despair. In response, he leaned back, grabbed a mango off the main altar, and pushed it roughly at her. She took it and held the gift from the goddess tenderly and meditatively in her cupped palms. One pilgrim spied a last remaining mango at the back of the table and used the stiff stem of a flower offering to rake it toward her. Yet another hand reached in from the crowd and snatched it away. The owner of the hand muttered darkly, "Can't you see I'm in the middle of making an offering?" She stowed the fruit at the back of the table and returned to mumbling her prayer.

The attendants eyed me warily and muttered to each other behind cupped hands. On the occasions I approached the altar they became irritable with the worshipers and ordered them to stop passing them banknotes: "Put the notes in the collection box yourself Auntie!" Every time I approached a frenzy of cash handovers, the flow instantaneously dried up. Standing at the gate to the altar, I asked one of the attendants when Her Ladyship's robe had last been changed. Looking stressed, he met my question with a mute gaze. I asked him how long the bathing ceremony had taken. "Ten minutes," he said, and abruptly turned his back on me to talk to a poker-faced attendant beside him. There was a noise of protest from beside me. "Don't be like that," admonished a red-faced man, breath reeking of alcohol. He was standing next to me, holding his child, and was waiting his turn to request some fruit for her from the altar. He scolded the attendant: "He asked you how long the bathing lasts—a proper question and it deserves an answer." I smiled and asked him where he was from. "I am from Saigon. I came here to pray to Her Ladyship. Every year I come here to pray to Her Ladyship. Then I return to Saigon." He dragged out each word in his simple sentences with exaggerated slowness. He took pains to mispronounce each word by abolishing the intonation inherent to the Vietnamese language. The attendants eased up, smiling at his robotlike parody of a foreigner mispronouncing Vietnamese. "Why didn't you bring your camera to take pictures here?" I replied that it wasn't permitted in the shrine. I asked the amused attendant why it was forbidden to take photos of the goddess. In response, the face of the short, unsmiling, silver-haired attendant standing beside him froze up again. He stretched out his palms and barked angrily, "No photos! No photos!" He pointed at the sign, which said No photo in English. He waved away my misunderstood question with an agitated sign of dismissal.

My drunken guide complained a second time: "That won't do! Answer the question politely." Turning to me he said, "Her Ladyship doesn't like photos." The younger attendant cut in: "Her Ladyship won't permit photos." Our sozzled mediator explained: "If you take a photo of Her Ladyship, it will turn out a blank when you develop it." The attendant ran with this line, speaking to the gathering crowd: "Her Ladyship has that power. Photos, film, video will all be blank; they just won't develop." I looked suitably incredulous and he was all smiles again as several pilgrims cut in and confirmed this explanation. As the crowd thinned, I got a more secular response: "Vietnam is still backward," he said. "There are many people who have yet to become progressive. Someone might take a photo and try to sell it. All it takes is one photo, and unlimited copies could be made from the negative. The state bans that kind of thing. It is illegal to profiteer from religion." A restaurateur, whose premises were opposite the shrine, later told me that if I wanted to get a photo I could easily do so: "Just slip an attendant a twenty-thousand-dong note and you can take as many as you like."

Signs warning against fortune-telling and mediumship were displayed prominently throughout the shrine's precincts. Prohibitions on communicating with the spirit world were strictly applied in this province, even down to forbidding ritual offerings to the lonely ghosts (cúng cô hồn). The ostensible reason given was that because this was a rural area with low educational standards, people here were particularly vulnerable to being duped. This was not an attack on the religious assumptions of such activity. Indeed, most of those who were charged with banning mediums believed in the powers of the spirit whose shrine they patrolled. Such locals were among the first to tell me the story of how the goddess had made herself known to villagers, by possessing a local girl and speaking through her. The hundreds of thousands of individual negotiations with the goddess taking place in the shrine during the festival were premised on identical notions of the goddess' spiritual responsiveness and took place in sight of and with the complicity of the shrine committee. In banning private mediums, the committee merely substituted itself as the sole authorized mediator, channeling and monopolizing people's individual interactions with the goddess by prohibiting the activity of rival practitioners. This put the committee into a privileged relationship of intercession between the masses of faithful and the goddess. Their role was nothing if not mediumistic.

Agents of a protected monopoly, their service was often dispensed in a formalistic or mechanical manner. Nevertheless, in this era of mass worship a devotee seeking to communicate with the goddess in Châu Đốc during her festival is far more likely to be processed in such a bureaucratic way than to witness an elegant traditional sacrifice offered on behalf of the collective or to personally communicate with the goddess through the services of a medium. The stripped-down model of interacting with the goddess that has emerged has undeniably constrained the possibilities for aesthetic elaboration and personal expression. Yet what is interesting is that the treatment meted out to today's propitiants has not lessened their belief in her powers. The discomfort of the shrine is not discouragement to the faithful. The physical crush of humanity is in itself proof that the goddess has something to offer. The bureaucratization of the ritual of communing with the goddess has not made the experience abstract and impersonal. The reality is quite the converse. Everyone experiences vividly the close and hot atmosphere, the crush of bodies toward the altar, the surge of the crowd, the bruising, the stepped-on toes, the exhaustion and anxiety. It is an inherent part of the encounter, and their identity as a mass is taken as a signal demonstration of the value of their own experience.

From Ritual Transgenderism to Popular Spectacle

The uniformed, neatly combed, and officious attendants present at the goddess' altar during the festival contrasted sharply with Nine, the medium with whom I had previously visited the shrine. Perhaps most notable in the ways that he transgressed conventions of gendered comportment, Nine's gender-bending traits were an important dimension of his qualities as a mediator. For the groups of urban pilgrims he accompanied, these characteristics opened a channel into the spirit world, a way of communicating directly with the goddess. The medium was possessed by the spirit of the goddess, assuming her identity and approximating a woman in gesture, apparel, and voice.

Impetuously entering the inner sanctum, lifting Her Ladyship's skirts to access the power of her stocky body, the gender-transitive Nine was the efficacious channel of the deity's power to ordinary people.

Up until quite recently, as long-term visitors to the site report, male transvestite performers played a part in the annual rites by dancing before the goddess. Such performances, which included feats of acrobatic prowess as well as ecstatic dancing and which involved women as well, are referred to as *múa bóng*. Often they are simply described as dancing *(múa)*. Nevertheless, people give a religious rationale for these performances. The displays of acrobatics, juggling, spinning, and dancing before the altar were calculated to entertain the goddess, make her more favorably disposed to requests, lower her guard, and make her less inclined to displeasure. Individuals who employ specialists to perform acrobatic feats were more likely to be noticed and their requests favored by a deity distracted by thousands of other simultaneous entreaties.[2] People compare the function of these dances to the nightly performances of *hát bội* opera that take place during the festival on the stage within the shrine, which have the effect of making the goddess more responsive. The normal term used for the male transvestite dancers is *bê đês*, the term borrowed from the French contraction for pederasts. Dressed as women, so the theory goes, the male performers will not overexcite the goddess or provoke her to lustfulness. Their ambiguous gender is a key to channeling the powers of the spirit world.

Although transvestite dancers are appreciated by many festivalgoers as having once constituted a distinctive part of the annual ceremonies, in the late 1990s I was repeatedly told that this activity had been banned at the Vĩnh Tế site, possibly because of the trancelike and uncontrolled nature of the dancing, which approximated (illegal) spirit possession *(đồng bóng)*. Two female pilgrims whom I met at the site during the festival in 1998 and with whom I was to spend an evening wandering around the fairgrounds told me that they had come to the festival many times. I asked if they had ever managed to see such performances. "This year *bê đês* have been forbidden from dancing in the shrine," one of them replied. A cloud of puzzlement darkened her face: "I don't know why that is." Her companion answered her: "The Office of Culture and Information banned *bê đê* dancing about three years ago. It wanted to get rid of aspects that are not beautiful *(không đẹp)* from the main pagodas and temples." I asked her what the dancing had been like. "*Bê đês* used to dance with plates, lights, even with water barrels," she said, appreciatively, wiggling her body and showing me the motions of spinning an object on the palm of her hand. "You can still see them at shrines around the place. There is a lot of *bê đê* dancing in Thủ Đức district of Saigon in the eleventh month." She rattled off the names of a few temples where this took place. "What a pity you can't see them here!"

This statement of regret caused her companion to swiftly reply, "No fear! You can see them if you like. There are a whole lot of *bê đê*s in the very pagoda where we are staying! Many of them are here to dance." Her companion asked curiously, "Where are they dancing—there in the pagoda?" Her friend replied, "No, they are in the fairground down the road a little way." The other asked, "What are they doing there?" She replied, "Dancing. They are really good at it."

Each year the fairground is host to several professional troupes of male transvestite performers, who set up on stages with backing bands and dance, sing, and perform skits to attract crowds for their main moneymaking venture, which is selling raffle tickets. During the year performance troupes of this kind, accompanied by a variety of sideshow attractions, circulate throughout the Mekong delta, stopping at small villages for several days at a time. The troupes are a ubiquitous and much-loved feature of fairs and carnivals throughout the region. Recently many of them have been getting work performing at funerals. The annual festival to the goddess is something of a transvestite performer convention. Many of the delta's regular touring groups converge on the fairgrounds for the period of the festivities.

The Châu Đốc pilgrimage site is also a well known meeting place for male cross-dressers, who descend on the festival in droves from all points of the compass. They stand out from the crowds in their colorful outfits, makeup, and accessories. Festivalgoers are engrossed by their distinctive appearance as they move through the crowd. What is interesting about Châu Đốc's cross-dressing male pilgrims is the immense interest they attract from their fellow pilgrims. The topic of *bê đê*s often comes up in reminiscences about the festival. Over time the *bê đê*s have become an attraction of the festival in their own right. The first time I heard about the Lady of the Realm was in 1993, from a market woman in Bạc Liêu, a provincial town in the Mekong delta, who told me she went to Châu Đốc annually, expressly to get an eyeful of the *bê đê*s. They were a highlight of her visits, and she recommended I go sometime to see them for myself. For such people the spectacular gathering of transvestites in the fairgrounds surrounding the shrine to the Lady of the Realm is firmly associated with her festival just as much as if not more than the ritual dancers ever were.

Whereas transvestite performance troupes provide staple entertainment during the course of the festival, an equally absorbing activity is to mill through the crowds of the fairgrounds in pursuit of a glimpse of visually exciting cross-dressing fellow pilgrims. I realized this during the evening spent at the site with two female companions, for whom the project of identifying transvestites became an all-absorbing mission.

Pilgrims in Pursuit of *Bê đês*

After she had revealed to me and her friend the presence of transvestite dancers at the festival, one of my companions for the evening spoke excitedly to us: "Let's go and look at the *bê đês* now if you like. It will be truly fine. Come on!" We were dragged off with promises of marvelous fun. It was not long before we struck it lucky. "There's one!" shouted the leader of our little group of three. She dragged me physically to the left, where a game attendant, a Charlie Chaplin in drag, with pigtails and painted face complete with a mustache, was slouched over a cigarette and a microphone. He was presiding vacantly over a game of chance whose prize was a can of Saigon 333 beer. "Nice, hey?" said my enthusiastic companion, searching out my reaction with eyes shining with delight. "Take a photo, take a photo," egged on the other, indicating my camera. I acquiesced, focused, and waited for the flash to charge. "Oh ho! Russian with a camera! How about this?" said the suddenly electrified game attendant, contorting into a practiced grimace that drew laughs from the crowd. He held it effortlessly until the flash went off. People cheered and clapped me on the back, congratulations for my capture of a peerless gem of inspiration. "And this." Another staged pose. Prompts from my neighbors: "Shoot it, shoot it!" A second pulse of light. Another magical moment immortalized. Shrewdly sizing up my intentions to disengage, as only one buffoon can know another, he slouched back into the vacancy of his role and sucked some more nicotine out of his cigarette. For a moment he became Charlie Chaplin again—wizard of mingling layer of banality and pathos. I was tempted into a third shot, seized by my own aesthetic dictates, surrendering to a moment of sublimity. He continued his bored monologue, appraising my shifting moods with eyes locked onto mine, ready to greet my moment of capitulation with another prefab pose, for the gratification of the crowd and to score three out of three in duel with a witless "Russian."

We strolled off through the fairgrounds. "Over here, over here!" shouted one of my companions, excited by the success of the evening's program. Down a dead-end alley, a couple of fire-eaters were frying their taste buds on top of a ticket booth, trying to give passersby a taste of what they would see for a 5,000-dong entrance ticket. Plenty of fiery gasoline was being burned to create crowd-drawing flares of heat and light. However, perhaps not to give away too many of the secrets that lay behind the plastic walls of the improvised theater, the fire-eaters stuck to a cycle of three or four gags, repeating the motion of swallowing the fire, feeling pain, "accidentally" burning their partner, swallowing more fire, and so on in nonstop rapid succession. Their mechanical actions briefly held the attentions of passersby who, after a few moments of drinking the experience dry, flowed on to the next attraction. My companions, however, had further investments in the spectacle. "Look, they're *bê đê*s," one said to me, pointing at the plaits into which their artificially frizzed hair was fashioned. I assessed the extent to which the long, lanky male figures had staked their appeals to popular aesthetics on appropriation of feminine motifs. Their hair was torn between trying to be feminine and fuzzy-wuzzy bizarre. Each had penned on a Charlie Chaplin mustache and a pirate's beard. They wore colored waistcoats that were patched and tattered—whether in reference to a vagabond aesthetic or a result of everyday wear and tear was not clear—and black peasant pants. Their shoes were fawn and cloth-topped, neither functional nor attention grabbing. It was hard to decide whether they were outlandish or poor. The plaits were elements in an overall plan to achieve bizarreness through eclectic fashion transgressions. The result suggested that, being unusually tall, they'd had to raid a number of people's wardrobes one dark night to acquire a full set of clothes. I took a couple of photos for documentary purposes, but my companions sensed that I was not convinced.

"*Bê đê*s, *bê đê*s over there," said one of my companions, eyes darting between mine and a nearby pair of plump men who were dressed fashionably in women's clothing. She was anxious that I not miss the spectacle we had waited so long to see. I focused on the two dim forms in the crowd and looked back at my companion, whose eyes were sparking with amusement and feeding off the happiness of a shared experience. "Beautiful, aren't they?" she said. It was a report, a question, and a tease. "Beautiful," I said neutrally, giving her satisfaction in three registers. She shared her happiness with her friend, and we gazed a while longer at the fidgeting bored objects of our quest. They were waiting for a stage performance to begin. On the stage, a young man was reading out raffle ticket numbers. After a long pause, he repeated the number. Another pause and he read out a new number. Then came a muffled shout, and a spectator hurried in from the crowd with a winning number. The announcer praised the winner in a voice of bored irony and handed him a chit to exchange for the prize in an adjoining booth.

Suddenly his voice snapped taut and in the voice of an accomplished master of ceremonies, he barked out a formal introduction to "the beautiful, the talented, the famous, Miss Ngọc Lan!" "A *bê đê* is going to dance, do you see?" My companions pulled my sleeve. The development surpassed all expectation. They both pointed to the stage, where three bored professional musicians executed a dramatic overture on electronic drums, keyboard, and guitar. As the cha-cha-cha rhythm settled in, a tall, slim figure with a cascade of waist-length hair stepped forward into the spotlight, hips swaying with fluid grace in absolute fidelity to the beat of the drum. Her pale, clear complexion, high-arched nose, long lashes, and full lips were framed by straight, low-cut bangs. Full breasts were encased in a straining, elegant halter top. Immaculate jeans held up by a fashionably broad belt encased narrow hips, which tried to disguise their angles in a flawless rolling motion. Chunky high-heeled shoes boosted her Wonder Woman height. Her stunning appearance hushed the crowd, which then gave vent to a prolonged buzzing of admiring comments. "Truly beautiful," whispered one of my astounded companions. "Prettier than the fire-eaters," I joked. Next to me, a thin young man was standing on his toes and drinking in the spectacle with mouth frozen open. His friend indicated the dancer. "She's beautiful isn't she?" he said proudly.

The performer began to sing in a smooth, sultry voice. She was betrayed by some of the high notes but kept up her fluid motion, unperturbed. The young man beside me said to one of my companions, "She's from Châu Đốc that one. She could compete for Miss An Giang Province easily!" He gazed with admiration and pride. The performance wound up. The young announcer thanked the dancer and seized the occasion of a captive audience to promote raffle-ticket sales. Having achieved the heights of *bê đê* entertainment, we followed the lead of others who were drifting away. My two companions too drifted back to their pagoda.

The connections between the role that transvestites play as entertainment for the crowds at the festival and their role vis-à-vis the goddess are irresistible. Although transvestite performers might no longer be permitted to perform in the main shrine to the goddess, they maintain a central role at the festival by entertaining the crowds of pilgrims. Whether this secularization can be seen as the banalization of the role of ritual trance performer is questionable, for the significance of transvestite dancing in the shrine to the goddess was equally a form of entertainment. Although of a secular nature, their performances are directed to a still largely female audience, whose love for the antics of these performers echoes the preference of the goddess herself for male transvestite performances. While the ritual role of transvestite performers has been banned by the state, female pilgrims have stepped into the shoes of the goddess and are in effect the new patrons of this aesthetic form. One transition this does reflect is the democratization of spectatorship: the substitution from goddess to pilgrim of the role of spectator. The lotteries organized by the transvestite performers are also an extension of the rites surrounding the goddess. They promise a windfall, an expectation many pilgrims direct toward the goddess, who, in some reckonings, is herself a transvestite. The significance of such observations, although they may appear to some to be trivial, is serious. They help remind us that the meaning of the festival cannot be restricted to the activities organized by the official committee. Much of pilgrims' time and attention is directed outward to the wider pilgrimage site, and one has to look there to fully understand the appeal of the festival. Furthermore, although the organizing committee has the ability to restrict what goes on in the shrine, the expectations and practices within the shrine are often reproduced and transformed in the world beyond it.

Festival as Flow

Among the most prominent experiential dimensions of festival are the dynamics of being in a crowd, the constant provisional nature of associations, and the ever-present potential for the forging of new relationships. The festival exhibits the quality of communitas far more than the instrumental, obligatory, and ludic peregrinations to this site that are undertaken by pilgrims from Ho Chi Minh City do. Associational activity during the festival, while not entirely spontaneous, is more provisory and charged with transformative potential than at other times of the year. In this, however, it is less a manifestation of ordered antistructure than the celebration through intensification of a cultural ideal of sociability and a positive estimation of partaking in life as a member of a crowd.

In the shrine, groups of women were each defending a patch of seating space for the evening's opera performance, sitting under a banner that advertised the event as "traditional Vietnamese performing arts." As they waited they watched pig carcasses, roasted to a sleek orange sheen, gliding on trays above the crowd of heads, held aloft by a pair of hands. I spoke with one of the waiting pilgrims, who told me that she had come in a bus with a group from the seaside town of Vũng Tàu and was staying for three days— the duration of the festival. Her group was sleeping communally in a guest house. They had already climbed the mountain and visited several pagodas, and they were planning to catch the *hát bội* performance later in the evening. That's why she was in the shrine, holding a space for other members of her group.

As we spoke, a group of women moving through in a bunch, locked together arm in arm, stopped to shyly gawk at me for a while. One of them asked her companions if I was American and was told authoritatively by another that I was French. Hearing me speak Vietnamese, members of the group speculated on my Vietnamese ancestry and concluded among themselves that, at the very least, my mother must be Vietnamese. I had clearly come back to visit my maternal homeland, but there was no evidence that I had brought my mother along. Perhaps she was over at the altar, making an offering. Their freewheeling speculations were broken up by a shout from a shrine security guard who, with a rude shooing motion, indicated for them to disperse and let others through. I also flowed away from the aggressive figure, in the opposite direction. I found myself near another group of women, who were also clutching each other firmly to avoid being dissolved by the crowds of strangers. They were in their fifties and sixties and were thin, sinewy, sun-darkened, and reserved. They were from Long An province and had traveled by small motorized boats down through the canals of the delta—a trip of two days. They were planning to stay for four days in total and were hovering near the stage to be sure of a good view of the performance, due to commence in four hours time. They said that at night they slept in their boats, moored "conveniently" two kilometers away, and that they based themselves in the shrine during the day. Their entire excursion would last just over a week.

I couldn't pursue their story any further, as our conversation was taken over by a pair of more outgoing women standing beside them. They broke into one of the pauses in the conversation, when the Long An boatwomen were at a loss for words. The two women said they were from Đồng Tháp. Indicating my camera, they said they wanted me to take a photo of them in front of the shrine. I agreed and, reluctant to break up my conversation with the women from Long An, told them I would do the same for them if they wanted to come outside. The boatwomen looked uncertainly at each other and then waved me off to photograph the two from Đồng Tháp. This was a mistake, for instantly a crowd gathered around me on the front stairs of the shrine, demanding equal treatment. I took a couple of snaps, but then the press of humanity squeezed shut my field of vision. We were all roughly chastised by a couple of professional photographers, who told us to disperse, saying we were creating a "circulation blockage" and a "breakdown in order."

Clearing the grounds of the shrine, I found the two Đồng Tháp women still beside me, determined to get my address so each could get a copy of the photo. They said they had been at the site for two weeks. They were staying nearby, in the Pagoda of Western Peace, helping the monks in the pagoda receive hundreds of pilgrims who were sleeping and eating there free of charge. They were working as cooks and would remain another week, as they did each year. They described their work as Buddhist charity *(công quả)*. They were from neighboring villages in Đồng Tháp and had met each other here at the festival several years before. As we walked, three abreast, one of them said, "It is much more fun walking around with friends. Visiting by yourself is miserable." They greeted passersby, and one of them explained, "We've got to know a lot of people since we've been here." We were joined by one of their new acquaintances, also from Đồng Tháp, who had a dejected look on her face. "Look at those photos of me," she said to them. "I look so sad." Three freshly laminated photos of herself standing beside the image of Kuan Yin were grabbed out of her hands and scrutinized. "You do look sad," said one of her friends. "It's bad luck," she replied. The other added, "You should never have photos taken when you're feeling sad. Wait until you're happy and feeling energetic then go and get photographed." "So sad," their friend repeated absently, and I couldn't be sure if she was referring to a long-term condition, her appearance in the photo, or her reaction to it. The others tried to cheer her up. She sat and practiced a few words of English that a nephew from America had once taught her on a return home for a visit. This made her friends laugh, but she couldn't be stirred from her mood. She got up and said she was going back to the pagoda. She complained about her sadness once more, the way people complain about the heat. She gave a little shiver, couldn't shuck it off, and drifted off into the crowd, abstractedly.

The pilgrimage site was made up of thousands of such provisional collective projects: focused yet fluid, clumps of mutual interest, habits, and bonds, yet also temporary, spontaneous, evolving, and open. Here sat a table of eight brothers and two friends: "We sell sugarcane juice in Châu Đốc. We're relaxing with each other here for fun." Elsewhere, three young men who had met on a bus were cementing friendships with wine and duck embryos. An elderly woman who had come alone from Saigon and was camping in the open air in a hammock was conversing with a younger man and his son from Long Xuyên, who were sleeping on their tiny boat moored two kilometers away. The timid members of a tour group only sallied forth into the fairgrounds with arms locked. Others ventured out in search of wider contacts, met up with others from their same group, and recombined for a stroll and a gawk. Bus drivers drank with conductors and the staff of guest houses to cement business ties. Boys accosted girls, who moved away as if in disdain but who then went into orbit, pulled by mysterious forces of gravity. Some of these groupings were clear to the eye—a huddle of drinkers, a mat full of elderly women fanning themselves, a couple holding hands. The group identity of others was diffuse; they were part of a larger group—an audience, a queue, or a surging river of promenaders.

The crowd fed on itself, becoming its own raison d'être. Half of the cafés faced inward, to TV, video, or *karaoke* screens. The other half faced outward, their customers drinking in the bustle of the crowd from ringside seats. I asked a young boy from the provincial capital of Cà Mau where was more fun, this village or his home town. He replied, eyes shining, "Here, of course; there are way more people to see and things to do." In truth, the pilgrimage site was like an instant city, and the festival provided many examples of the intense disjunctures and colliding experiences that have become familiar to those living in the country's urban areas. Pajama-clad farmers gawked at polished city folk, who enjoyed ridiculing them from the remove of a high-priced-drinks café. Old men stared in disquietude at young girls, dressed like a shocking dare. Poor locals stood and stared as air-conditioned minibuses full of well-dressed folk from distant places came in. These in turn looked tired and frazzled and worried about the availability of air-conditioned rooms, given the crowds who were blocking their vehicle's passage. Jam-packed cheap-ticket buses arrived, some of their occupants rubbernecking with excitement at the sights, the others, who had accommodated themselves to their cramped seats, sleeping to the last revolution of the engine.

One of the more interesting "suburbs" of this instant city was composed of hundreds of boats, large and small, that had come from all over the Mekong delta. At the edge of a broad canal, which terminated at the roadside about a kilometer from the shrine, ten or so large barges and cargo boats formed a provisional bulk cargo port on the fringe of the village. Previously, this stagnant tongue of water had been the site of a temporary floating city for the duration of the pilgrimage season. The site had been declared off limits to boat dwellers, as the concentration of people had fouled the water and impeded water transport. A string of lights farther up the canal indicated where they had been moved to. During the day, the residents of this floating satellite town drifted through the terrestrial settlement of Vĩnh Tế village. In the shrine's grand, multistoried, robe-display halls I met a large number of residents of this floating pilgrimage village who turned out to be from one boat. They had come from the same village in Đồng Tháp province. They described themselves as family and neighbors and said that the thirty of them had made the ten-hour journey down to the pilgrimage site "in comfort." I asked them about the conditions at the moorings. One of them said it was crowded *(đông)*—a positive evaluation: "People from all corners of the Mekong delta come and stay for up to a week. There are floating cafés, food vendors, and a floating market. We bring our own supplies, buy what we need, cook and eat on the boat." He said with all the people the water

smelled slightly, but fresh water, toilets, and showering facilities were provided. I asked if the water was not too polluted to swim in. "Of course we
swim—no fear!" he replied. His daughter said they slept on the roof of the
boat in the cool river breeze. I asked about mosquitoes. Her father laughed:
"We bring our own mosquito nets. Mosquitoes aren't a problem." One of
the young men in the group said people went without sleep during the entire
week they spent there. "We stay up all night, talking and drinking. It is great
fun!" The young woman agreed: "We would like to come more often but can
only come when the conditions are right."

A forty-year-old rice farmer, Hùng was there with his young female
cousin and his daughter, who was in year seven. When I asked the latter what
she would like to do when she left school, Hùng joked to me that she would
become a doctor or a lawyer. His sardonic humor was mild, not boisterous,
his curiosity about me muted, and his reserved manner a mixture of dignity
and prudence. He asked little about me and ventured less about himself. He
was content to let his two young female relatives mine me for essential introductory information. Younger males in the group, their same age, stared at
me like a puzzle, unable to find a purchase to satisfy their curiosity. Every
now and then the questioning would pause lightly and he would gently prod
his daughter with a smile. Well, do you want to ask anything else?

New additions to the circle began the cycle of questioning anew. Hùng
helped me out of the cycle of introductions by listing for the newcomers the
main biographical details gleaned from me thus far. Every now and then
I was asked to pose for a photo with one of the new arrivals, and a pair of
hardened professional photographers, sensing a windfall, hovered at the edge
of the group. They issued instructions for our poses: "One leg forward, hand
on your waist, arms round each other's shoulders. Ready? One, Two, Three!"
The flash was the trigger for our frozen poses of heroic comradeship to dis-
solve. A moment of bedazzlement and then the subjects shook hands. Mission accomplished—well done. I returned to the circle of questioning.

Two young fruit farmers, who had come on another boat from Ô Môn,
hovered shyly, asking Hùng questions about me in the third person. They too
requested a photo of the three of us and, once done, we came back to the
group to wait for its development. One of them, about twenty, with dark skin
and a gap-toothed smile, indicated in comic exaggeration how, standing in
front of the camera, he had failed to even come up to my waist. The ice
broken, he took over questioning me in the first person, wanting to know the
distance from Australia to Vietnam, whether I had traveled by boat or car,
whether there were any pagodas there, whether any Vietnamese lived there,

whether rice was grown there, what language was spoken in Australia. Unlike in the city, no one asked my salary, and questions about my occupation came well toward the end of a long string of other questions.

His friend drank in the answers silently, then asked if people from my country played soccer. "Those foreigners play really well," he said, admiringly. Sitting beside me, listening to the questions feeding in from the others, he conducted his own physical interrogation of my curious presence in his world. He stroked the hair of my arm with the back of his finger, tested the circumference of my ankle with his hand, pressed my calf slowly for muscle tone, pinched the back of my hand for skin elasticity. At one point in mid-conversation he took my nearest arm in both of his hands, tested its hinges, pulled back my sleeve to measure the muscular mass of my bicep, and then tried to feel what kind of work load it was capable of. The outer ring of young men from the Đồng Tháp boat group continued to stare, mesmerized, while the verbal questions moved away from my personal details to those of the other members of the group. My role slipped from authoritative autobiographer to curious bystander. As interrogations fractured into minor research projects, the group's attention slowly dispersed. The two young women strolled away to look at the courtyard from the balcony, a dispute with a photographer flared briefly, another cigarette was pushed my way, and my interrogators began to take stock of each other.

"You two are from Cần Thơ aren't you?" asked the farmer from Đồng Tháp.

"Yes, Uncle. From just outside of Ô Môn, near the bridge there. We do grapefruit farming. But all the citrus is destroyed by worms. We're switching to longans, eighteen thousand a kilo. How about you, Uncle?"

"We're from Hồng Ngự district."

"Did you also come by boat?"

"Yes, we're moored just back of here."

"Fifty thousand dong a berth?" estimated the older of the Cần Thơ fruit farmers.

"No, forty thousand for the small boats, fifty thousand for the big ones."

"We paid forty thousand but had to give the port master one thousand more for water."

"What kind of engine?"

"Eight hundred cc."

"American?"

"Yes, old but still powerful."

I cut in, asking the youngsters how long the trip had taken.

"Eight hours," said one.

"Don't lie," said Hùng's young cousin, who worked in the market; "it's more than eight hours to Cần Thơ."

He replied, "If you leave at five in the evening you arrive at three the following morning."

"That's ten hours," I said.

"More like a full twelve hours," said the skeptical marketwoman. "Cần Thơ is a long way from here."

The young fruit farmer's friend smiled and crooned at her: "You're so beautiful miss. What's your name?"

"Kim Quyên."

"Ah, Kim Quyên is a beautiful name."

I asked the huddle of people what they had done so far during the festival. There was a chorus of responses. "Said prayers to her Ladyship, took photos, climbed the mountain. There's a park up there with a huge animal made of cement."

"A dragon," said the young farmer from Cần Thơ.

"No, it's an extinct species of animal: a dinosaur," corrected Hùng. He said they had visited Cave Pagoda but it had a "sad" feel about it. "The doors were closed and it smelled bad inside." They also went to the fairground every night and watched the *bê đês* dance. "They're great fun," smiled his young niece. "Have you seen them yet?" She also asked if I had taken in the traditional operatic performance, which was taking place in the shrine beside us as we spoke. "I can't stand *hát bội*," winced her uncle. "O, o, o—hard on the ear. Can't understand a word apart from o, o, o. Beats me how people can stand to listen to it."

"It's beautiful to watch though," I said, relieved that I wasn't the only one who was deaf to the lyrics.

"I guess so," said Hùng dubiously.

I asked what else they planned to do on their last day there. "We'll probably climb the mountain," he said. "It's beautiful from the peak," his daughter added. "And there are so many pagodas, you can't possibly visit them all."

"What time do you plan to climb?" one of the Cần Thơ farmers asked her.

"Sunrise, when it's cool."

"Let's go with them," he suggested to his companion.

I declined their invitation to join them, saying I would probably sleep in the next day. We wished each other safe and happy returns. The group from Đồng Tháp accompanied me to the intersection of the road and the path leading to their boat.

The crowds in the fairgrounds were swelling as the evening air cooled. They choked the maze of alleys and made movement difficult. Included among the various encounters with the wonders on offer was my own presence. Dozens of anonymous hands reached out and tapped me as I passed, one of the site's exotic attractions offering a brief moment of distraction, an engagement with the bizarre. Some would play for higher stakes. "You!" they would call, then stand with hand outstretched, daring me not to stop and repay their challenge with a handshake, an honorable meeting of eyes, and a head nodded in satisfaction at the closure of the exchange. The tax on my solitary perambulation through the fairground was levied several times a minute, collected by a thousand freelance brokers. But it was as light as the evening breeze, entailing no more than an almost imperceptible touch. In return I was granted the right of solitary passage, the acceptance of difference.

Festival as Business

Commercialism is sometimes identified as a key factor threatening the degradation of Vietnam's religious and cultural heritage (Đặng Nghiêm Vạn 1998). This view is often espoused by those living in commercialized urban contexts for whom the countryside with its community-oriented festivals and folk practices represents an imagined last bastion against the invasion of commodities in the cities. However, a great number of those attending the rural festival to the Lady of the Realm come from entrepreneurial and petty commercial backgrounds and are no strangers to commerce. Requests to the goddess for her help with business are among the most common prayers uttered in her shrine during the festival period. Outside the shrine most of their leisurely activities are mediated by commerce. Indeed, this is one of the greatest attractions of the festival: the range of consumerist choices available to pilgrims and the eye-boggling variety of services, objects, experiences, and dramatic spectacles for sale.

During the festival, the fairground, a huge expanse of stamped earth where out of season nothing grows, is given over to no-holds-barred consumption. Wherever pilgrims go in the surrounding village of Vĩnh Tế, from its stall-lined streets to its ever-expanding market proper, they come across something displayed for sale. As I walked through the grounds one late afternoon, I noticed that the fire-eaters had changed their costumes and were busy tying up a volunteer from the crowd to advertise a magic and contortionist act that alternated with their fire-eating antics. Across the road, a rival establishment advertised itself as a monkey circus. A distraught-looking monkey was holding a bowl on its head, glancing up at its trainer every few seconds. It looked warily at the crowds who tried to attract its attention with shouts and missiles. A luridly painted sign displayed images of what wonders a 4,000-dong ticket would reveal: a monkey pulling a miniature cyclo, a monkey playing soccer, the popular monkey-putting-a-bowl-on-its-head, and more unannounced marvels.

Further along the road, I passed a corrugated iron enclosure draped with banners. I was invited in to listen to some Vietnamese popular music and watch some dancing. The venue followed the standard arrangement at such performances. A string of singers took the stage and executed two numbers each. On completion, they announced the next singer, then departed with a bow. A backing band, superlatively mellow-looking professional musicians, remained on stage all evening. They were called upon to execute a wide range of musical styles from various Latin genres to waltzes, ballads, and hard-driving rock. The patrons sat, nursing the drink whose purchase served as their entry ticket. They watched the dancers or waited until the song or style that suited their mood, capability, or generation came up, then went up to the dance floor and broke loose. The pilgrimage site had at least three such venues, and the scores of singers who came for the duration of the festival rotated through them, visiting each several times a night, performing the handful of standbys that made them a living as professional singers. This particular venue doubled as a *cải lương* opera theater. Banners in enormous letters advertised the star performers in a traveling *cải lương* troupe. Performances would take place on three consecutive nights. The first would begin later in the evening. During the festival, the venue, a strip of barren ground out of season, could double-book pop music and *cải lương* shows, securing capacity audiences and a high turnover of customers each evening. These were crowds that big Saigon venues could only dream of.

The fairground was full of booths (shooting galleries, knock-em-down balls, shuffleboards, quoits) where contests of skill were rewarded with a scale of prizes, ranging from a modest luxury item such as a can of Heineken down to a shopworn soft toy, a packet of instant noodles, or a faded package of MSG. There were two merry-go-rounds: one whose mounts consisted of smart little motorbikes and cars, the second of oblong boxes, covered in a thin sheet of metal, painted to look like various packaged food items—condensed milk, MSG, Tribeco soft drink. The paint was faded and flaking, and the tyranny of form prevailed to prevent the battered metal tubs from evoking the appeal of the food items they named. Also on offer were various joy rides, dodge-'em cars, and skating. Operators derived secondary profits from those who would rather observe than participate. One of these was a roller-skating rink surrounded by a wire-mesh fence. Well-dressed town kids showed off their prowess, negotiating the tight turning circle in a blur of limbs and color. Those too fainthearted, inexperienced, or poor to participate sat at the rows of stools and low tables facing the makeshift rink, consuming cheap soft drinks and coffees and participating vicariously in the skaters' pleasure.

There were also numerous games of chance. The unexpected and the fortuitous lay around each corner. A lucky spin of the wheel or a fluky throw could win you the ersatz luxury of a can of Saigon Export beer or the booby prize of a pack of instant noodles. One stall offered a game of chance titled "Vietnam Airlines"; its prizes—electric rice cookers and wall clocks—and its blinking arc of colored lights appeared to say, "come fly into a world where anything is possible." More modest stalls promised a set of porcelain bowls, a soft drink, a flashlight in reward for a lucky fall of a numbered ball. The message of the *bê đê* performance artistes, who ran their games of lotto before enraptured audiences, seemed to be "Who knows, you might win a prize. More bizarre things have happened—us, for instance. Watch, wonder, take your chance, sit, buy a drink, at the very least get a moment of the bizarre for the mere price of a coffee."

Endless wonders were on sale at the site. Pilgrims flocked to buy decorative objects made entirely of seashells or miniature religious items fashioned out of clear plastic—a pagoda, the Buddha, a dragon—illuminated by a flashing red light. The bizarre to be consumed, the bizarre as spectacle, the bizarre to entice people to take part in secondary forms of profit making—gambling or selling drinks or tickets to a performance. I paused at one of the stalls selling religious iconography. Ranks of earth gods, arrayed in military precision, were being outflanked on both sides by columns of gods of wealth. Versions of Maitreya Buddha and a few jade frogs were congregating in less orderly conspiracies. A line of porcelain Kuan Yins and Mẹ Sahns adorned the side partition. They looked over the heads of the lowly household deities to the far end of the table given over to children's toys, packaged novelties, and items of home decor. I asked the saleswoman how business was. Was it a good month? "It had better be," she said. "People in this street live thanks to this month. This is when we earn our living for the year." She said the first four months of the year was the busy season. "After that things slow down. Hardly anyone comes here at all after the fourth month."

The shopkeeper told me quietly that if I would like to acquire an image of the Lady of the Realm, she sold photographs of her inside the shop. A fellow customer overheard this. He looked at her, startled, and asked if she would repeat her answer. "That is none of your affair," she replied. I followed her inside, where she rummaged in a cloth sack. "We can't sell these outside. It is forbidden. The image of Her Ladyship is a certified cultural vestige and the state forbids photographs of all such items." I expressed my skepticism about this statement: "That is not normally the case with cultural sites." She assented: "Yes, you are right. But Her Ladyship is special. In fact, I don't know why it is forbidden. If customers ask, we invite them inside." She removed a framed object from the sack: "Beautiful, isn't it?"

It was an item of heterogeneous materials, genres, and meanings. It certainly was a lot more complex than the "photo" its saleswoman described it as. The goddess' face appeared to be a color-enhanced photograph. Scrutinizing it more carefully, I found it was a field of paintbrush strokes. Its approximation of a forbidden photograph was uncannily convincing: the crystalline reflections of a photographic flash off the goddess' glassy surfaces were rendered in diamond-sharp brush strokes. The effect was contradicted over the fields of her cheeks, where rough jabs of red paint suggested that the representation itself had been freshly rouged up in preparation for a photo shoot. The thick paper on which the face was painted had been cut out around the facial contours and glued onto a baseboard. This gave it a bas-relief quality, as if having failed to reincarnate conclusively as a painting or a photograph, the image had begun a tentative retreat to its original sculptural inspiration. A headpiece had been mounted over this facial representation. It was made of the same rich red brocade, shiny sequins, and imitation pearl fringe as the regal headpieces sported by the actual goddess on her nearby throne. The brocade, stretched over a thin plywood shelf that projected an inch out from the baseboard, hung down in a narrow curtain, terminating at her hairline. This was fringed with threaded pearly tassels of even length, which partially curtained her forehead. A triangle of the same red material began at the outline of her chin and widened out to the bottom edge of the baseboard, forming an approximation of the goddess' robe. A narrow crescent of yellow ribbon served as a collar and as a seam covering the stark intersection of painted cardboard with cloth and was fixed on by shiny silver thumbtacks that painfully pinned the top of her robe to her neck. The result was framed in a shallow glass case with back wooden walls; the pane just cleared the goddess' headpiece. When the case was held vertically, the tassels shimmied an inch out from the goddess' forehead. The encasement of the eclectic work of art suggested numerous possibilities: holy relic, precious work of art, pinned specimen, smuggled trophy. It lent weight, dignity, and mystique to the representation of the goddess and guarded it from mundane defilement and rude examination of the secrets of its fabrication. The product was on sale for U.S. $18.

"We sell most of these in January and February to the customers who

come down from Saigon. They take them back and display them at home."
She urged me to buy one. I asked if it would clear customs, suspecting that
customs officials' reasoning could follow two opposite routes to the same
negative conclusion: as a clearly precious and unique item it should not
leave Vietnam's borders; as a superstitious embarrassment, it should not be
allowed to sully Vietnam's reputation abroad. She also doubted that it
would clear customs, because export of items of "cultural heritage" was forbidden. Influenced by the spell this discussion was weaving about the commodity, I briefly considered dismantling it into its multitudinous components
for export. "Take a photo of it," she said, "so you can put an image of Her
Ladyship on your altar." It was an inspired and generous suggestion. A photograph of the artifact would clear the bureaucratic hurdles constructed by
our imagination. I would thus not be deprived of the opportunity to tap Her
Ladyship's powers by the accident of my residence beyond arbitrary geopolitical boundaries. My photograph of a "photograph" would not dilute the
powers of the end product. On the contrary, reasoning through the ruses
needed to smuggle a likeness of Her Ladyship past local and national authorities enhanced the value of the item that each level of the state so desperately
sought to safeguard. While I considered her offer to photograph the item,
my eyes wandered over to the wardrobe, where a police hat rested. I briefly
wondered if this had given the saleswoman the right to sell a forbidden item
or indeed to classify the product as forbidden. I took another look at the
item and my mind spun, thinking of the interdependencies between secular
power, profit, and sacred value that were in operation in the object before
me. I decided not enter into the conspiratorial logic that informed her offer.
My camera remained in its case.

Conclusion

At the end of the festival, when the rides, stalls, stages, and tents are cleared
away and all that is left of the fairground is a stark, rubbish-strewn tract of
dust, it is hard to conjure up the image of the crowds, the crush, the multitude of items and acts on display, and the plethora of sensual triggers that
crescendo every year just as the fourth full moon begins to wane. The boats
have cast off, the buses have gone, the motorcycle taxi drivers have returned
to work in the fields. The city of hundreds of thousands has simply melted
away. The village begins its quiet half of the year. The festival's thoroughly
absorbing character will draw people back again the following year; the
crowds will return and will again become their own raison d'être. It is hard
not to compare the festival to a city—an ephemeral one, true, but possessed

of many of a city's qualities. Certainly it possesses that overwhelming quality many in contemporary Vietnam know well, when migrants from the countryside arrive in the city and are dazzled by its human crowds, sensory abundance, and seemingly infinite range of consumer offerings. As is common in cities, festivalgoers break these seemingly infinite possibilities into regular rhythms, focusing on familiar projects, experiencing the festival by the boatload, consuming it in bite-sized bits. It is ironic that the festival manifests this provisory urbanist character at a time that many dedicated pilgrims from the larger cities have turned their back on it as a rural affair incompatible with their own interests in the goddess.

But rural festivalgoers are hardly playing out the outmoded dreams of urbanites, nor is their festival a simulacrum of the city. Their festival speaks to the mass character of rural society in southern Vietnam, a place whose trading and communications network is relatively integrated, and where crossroads, confluences, bridges, and markets exert a compelling power, drawing people together in mass sociability. One can compare the drawing power of the festival to that manifested by the Mỹ Thuận suspension bridge across the Mekong, completed in 2000, which became an instant pilgrimage site, attracting people from all around the Mekong delta who made repeat visits to gaze at it with awe. The bridge quickly became in its own right the focus of a major civic pilgrimage; to stand upon it became a fervid wish for a significant portion of the delta's population. The Mỹ Thuận bridge is not just a human crossroads. It is a magnified symbolic version of the regionally ubiquitous intersection, bridge, or waterway junction, these culturally valued meeting places and significant confluences of human flow. The bridge's drawing power, like that of the festival to the Lady of the Realm, is self-sustaining. As a place where one can gaze upon and be part of a sheer mass movement of people, it responds to a high cultural estimation for being among a flow of bodies and for participating in society at its most crowded. Like the journey to the goddess' shrine, the journey to the bridge is a mass-mediated aesthetic experience with its own rules: "You should visit it in the evening, just as the sun goes down and the lights go on." It has spawned a unique genre of modernist pastiche: postcards made of cut-out photographs of prestigious symbols of transport such as helicopters, jumbo jets, racing bicycles, luxury launches, and international container vessels, each pasted into a panorama of the bridge, are sold atop the bridge. The compelling meanings that visitors take away with them include the bridge's embodiment of advanced scientific principles, technological sophistication, aura of foreign expertise, and historically unprecedented spanning of the Mekong. Visits to the bridge, on boats, motorcycles, and minibuses, are organized by the same tour organizers who arrange trips to Châu Đốc. And around the southern approach to the bridge an encrustation of souvenir stalls, food and drink vendors, cafés, bars, film kiosks, even brothels has developed in no time, demonstrating the powerful links among religion, commercialization, and the hedonistic practices of consumption that characterize pilgrimage and festive experience for the people of the delta.

7

Magical Fame and
Symbolic Ambiguity

The mausoleum to Marshall Nguyễn Huỳnh Đức is in the village of Khánh Hậu just off National Highway 1, the main route taken by pilgrims from Ho Chi Minh City to the pilgrimage site of Sam Mountain. Thousands of people a day pass the imposing gate that announces the mausoleum, although very few of these long-distance travelers make the two-kilometer detour into the village to explore it. The marshall (1748–1819), who served variously as general, diplomat, land pioneer, and administrator, was instrumental in consolidating Vietnamese rule in the southern Vietnamese plain. When he died he was buried in Khánh Hậu village, where a cult to his name has been maintained by his descendants for seven generations.[1] The mausoleum is a landmark to which residents of the nearby provincial capital Tân An direct visitors as one of their most notable examples of cultural heritage (see also Thạch Phương and Lưu Quang Tuyến 1989). Many of these residents are unable to give his exact dates or even state in which century he lived, but most do know that he lived long ago and made some major contributions to the country. Only a few of them have attended the rites that are held annually on the anniversary of the marshall's death to acknowledge his contribution and seek his spirit's protection for the peace and prosperity of the living. Most, however, know that such rites are held, having seen them televised on the provincial television channel.

The cult to Marshall Nguyễn Huỳnh Đức is an example of the practice in Vietnam of venerating historical personages *(nhân vật lịch sử)* or heroes *(anh hùng).* This is a religious practice often characterized as typically *(tiêu biểu)* or authentically *(thuần túy)* Vietnamese (Nguyen Van Huyen 1994, 41; Toan Ánh 1997, 73). Many of these figures are associated with the defense of the country as well as its history of settlement, rule, and cultural attainments.

Entombed in mausoleums *(làng)* and venerated in temples *(đền, nhà thờ)* constructed to commemorate them, they are the focus of rites led by lineage representatives, local notables, and representatives of the state. Also considered spirits overseeing human existence, they were traditionally asked to provide a range of services: to ensure peace and prosperity; drive away epidemics, drought, and floods; punish crimes; repay injustice; and chase away ghosts and invaders (Coué 1933, 113; Cadière 1958, 6; Toan Ánh 1997). An example of this is the cult to the thirteenth-century general Trần Hưng Đạo, with temples in Bảo Lộc, Kiếp Bạc, and other locations, who, when Giran investigated his cult, was credited with the power to break droughts and end epidemics, chase away evil spirits, make women fertile, and protect children from harm (Giran 1912, 432; Do Thien 1995). Although the temple to the Trưng sisters in Hanoi represents one of the most accessible and elegant examples of this religious practice, the most prominent of the heroes venerated in Vietnam are male.

This religious practice was imported to the southern third of the country when it was first settled by the Vietnamese in the late seventeenth century. Some of the figures venerated in this region were transposed from elsewhere, such as Trần Hưng Đạo, to whom is dedicated a temple on Võ Thị Sáu Street, District One, Ho Chi Minh City. Other "immigrants" include Confucius, Quan Công, and Ông Bổn whose cults were imported from China. Like Nguyễn Huỳnh Đức, however, most of the hero spirits venerated in the region were born, lived, or died in this area. Most of these figures were associated with the military, scholarly, and administrative domains, and hence I gloss them as warrior-scholar-official spirits *(thần võ-văn-quan).* Some were associated with the occupation and pioneering settlement of formerly Cambodian lands. Nguyễn Hữu Cảnh, Nguyễn Tri Phương (1800–1873), and Thoại Ngọc Hầu, all military men and early administrators of Vietnamese colonization, fall into this category. Another of these is Lê Văn Duyệt, a renowned military leader in the country's civil war, which ended in 1800, who then administered the southern third of Vietnam under the reconstituted kingdom. A special place is reserved for southern anticolonialist fighters Nguyễn Trung Trực (1837–1868) and Trương Định (1820–1864), who were loyal to the court and resisted French colonial occupation. Others, such as Võ Trường Toản (?–1792), Trịnh Hoài Đức, and Nguyễn Đình Chiểu (1822–1888), were associated with exceptional educational and literary accomplishments. Phan Thanh Giản (1796–1867) was a distinguished scholar and feted mandarin who was involved in the fateful diplomatic events leading to the loss of the region to the French. Trương Vĩnh Ký (1837–1898) was a very talented interpreter of the region in the early years of French colonization. Two of the most recently constructed memorials in this religious tradition celebrate the lives of Nguyễn Sinh Sắc (1863–1929), the father of Ho Chi Minh, and Tôn Đức Thắng (1888–1980), who succeeded Ho Chi Minh as president of socialist Vietnam (Giebel 2001).

As a set of spiritual personages with a major profile in the public life of the region, these warrior-scholar-official spirits can be usefully compared with the Lady of the Realm and the handful of other goddesses who are the focus of this work and with whom they share much in common. These two groups of personages have a special stature in the southern Vietnamese religious landscape. Their places of veneration are the region's most architecturally magnificent and decoratively elaborate religious structures. They gain as many visitors as (if not more than) the most popular Buddhist pagodas. Not only are their commemorative festivals well attended; they also attract a significant number of visitors at other times of the year. In popular opinion the two sets of personages share a reputation as efficacious spirits who are believed to be unusually responsive to requests. They attract a similar body of petitioners who regard them as reliable patrons. However, there are significant differences between these classes of deities as well. In respect of their perceived efficacy, warrior-scholar-official spirits such as Marshall Nguyễn Huỳnh Đức are often considered less powerful than goddesses such as the Lady of the Realm. It is said that the former are approached less often than the latter for assistance with important matters. In recent years both sets of deities have received more petitioners; the number visiting the warrior-scholar-official spirits, however, has been greatly eclipsed by those drawn to the shrines of the goddesses. Like the mausoleum to Marshall Nguyễn Huỳnh Đức, the places of worship of the warrior-scholar-official spirits are often empty. More important, the translocal following attracted to the shrines of the goddesses is far more extensive than that to the warrior-scholar-official spirits and has dramatically grown.

These differences in the perceived efficacy and scale of the followings of these two groups of spiritual personages can be linked to a number of factors. To recap some of the themes of this book, the implication of these goddesses in the delineation and reproduction of a number of overlapping political, cultural, ethnic, and economic projects charges them with a significant aura of power. The various investments made in them as collective symbols translates into an increased individual following. Their perceived power also derives from their symbolization of gendered economic power, particularly of a house-and-market-based economic sphere that has been dominated by women. Finally, as the majority of those who propitiate the spirits are women, the popularity of these goddesses stems to a significant extent from their relevance to women as self-representations, an issue that is discussed in the last chapter.

In this chapter, however, I restrict my focus to the symbolic properties of these religious foci and link differences in their followings to differences in the specificity of their identity. The key issue at stake is the extent to which they exemplify the quality of multivocality that a number of theorists including Wolf (E. Wolf 1958), Turner (1967), and Ortner (1973) have identified as a defining property of religious symbols. The capacity to bear a number of different meanings simultaneously is what gives a symbol durability and relevance, for it allows for the multiplication, cohabitation, and mutual reinforcement of different interpretations. This is a significant advantage in contemporary Vietnam, a society that is going through cultural and social flux. A particular object of religious veneration might well be potent to a given community of veneration at a given point in time, but its inclusivity and endurance depend on its ability to speak to diffused concerns and remain relevant to followers as circumstances change. One interpretive project or another may be particularly successful in obtaining a hegemonic status over a religious focal point to the extent of refiguring symbolism and influencing the structure of rites. However, one of the risks of any one project's so successfully determining the meaning of a symbol is the potential narrowing of that symbol's relevance. In Vietnam, where the state in its various incarnations has played a major role in the delineation of meaning and configuration of symbolic and ritual practice, one can see both the merits and the risks to a symbol of being closely fixed to a specific identity by an interpretive project of such power and influence.

Shades of Celebrity

One attribute that the goddesses and the warrior-scholar-official spirits share is that they are icons that loom large in the popular religious imagination. In particular, representatives of these two classes of figures are famous (nổi tiếng) for their magical efficacy and their responsiveness (linh ứng) to requests. This fame can be gauged by the many stories about them that are passed by word of mouth among people throughout the region. To gain a sense of this stature one has to observe popular practice rather than consulting official or scholarly exegeses, which often downplay the perceived magicality of these sites. The repute of such figures as efficacious can be seen in the numbers of people in their places of worship, the breadth of the catchment areas from which visitors are drawn, and the frequency of visits to their shrines. It is witnessed in the reasons that people give for coming to their places of worship and is evident in the number of visitors who request *(cầu khẩn)* assistance from them, enter into material exchanges with them, or seek to learn their fortunes by casting divination sticks *(xin xăm)*. Further insights into their popular status are offered by the number of mediums and fortune-tellers these places attract and branch shrines that are set up that tap their notoriety. One can also gauge their popularity from the flow of visitors out-side the official or formal commemoration dates, either in the first weeks of the New Year, during the Buddhist bimonthly days of offerings (the first *[mồng một]* and fifteenth *[ngày rằm]*), or as circumstances arise.

Quite a number of these spirits are figures of considerable individual re-pute. Stories that revolve around the assistance they have accorded to the population are well-known and widely disseminated. The most popular of these spiritual personages are known simply by their titles. Both Lê Văn Duyệt and Quan Công are referred to as His Lordship (Ông). The former's resting place in Ho Chi Minh City is generally referred to as His Lordship's Mausoleum (Lăng Ông). The latter's many places of worship are each called His Lordship's Pagoda (Chùa Ông). Such seemingly nonchalant naming practices speak to exceptional celebrity. The goddesses are equally famous, the subject of much talk and many publications about who they are, what they have done, whom they have helped. The Lady of the Realm is very often referred to simply as Her Ladyship (Bà), a deceptively anonymous title, for those who use such a title can safely assume their listener knows exactly who this is.

This stature in the public mind is more than a momentary celebrity. The physical beauty and imposing architecture of their places of worship amount to a lasting record of people's beliefs in these spirits' efficacious patronage, for they have been upgraded substantially over the years through the offer-ings left by grateful worshipers. For example, the wooded environs of Lê Văn Duyệt's mausoleum are a legacy of the viceroy's spiritual patronage of all manner of requests. In fulfillment of vows, thankful petitioners often plant a tree in the grounds. The Lady of the Realm's shrine has been reconstructed several times, most dramatically in 1972, using financial gifts left by her grateful beneficiaries.

In popular circles, both groups are regarded as nobility. The warrior-scholar-officials are sometimes referred to as kings *(vua)*. Like the dynastic tombs in the former imperial capital at Hue, their resting places are popu-larly called mausoleums *(lăng)*, a term used for the nobility, rather than the more conventional term for graves *(mộ)*, and their place of worship is often called a temple *(đền)*, a term popularly associated with posthumous venera-tion of the feudal aristocracy *(vua chúa)*. One of the goddesses, the Palace

Damsel (Dinh Cô) is venerated, as the name suggests, in a palace. The other goddesses are referred to as Bà Chúa (Lady/Princess/Queen). They are sometimes given the suffix nương nương (Your Ladyship). Their powers and the rites associated with their propitiation are modeled on the political realm, as has been noted in the case of Chinese popular religion (e.g., A. Wolf 1974; Feuchtwang 2001). It is said one should seek small favors from the minor gods such as the Earth God and save larger requests for the higher beings such as the goddesses and warrior-scholar-official spirits, who are sometimes compared with high officials and heads of state. When one makes offerings to either class of spirits one must approach with due deference and formality and not speak ill of them, lest they respond with anger.

Their repute is not confined to a clearly defined territory, for they attract a following from a more diffuse catchment area, be it a network of markets and urbanized population centers, a region, or an even broader sphere. Certainly, some of the warrior-scholar-official spirits and goddesses discussed here double as localized tutelary deities in a number of villages through the region. Each of their principal places of worship is attended to by a locally recruited cult committee. However, neither the goddesses nor the warrior-scholar-official spirits fit neatly into the territorial hierarchy of deities whose veneration is patterned after administrative divisions.[2] Rather, like Buddhist pagodas, the following they attract overlaps and blurs formal administrative territorial divisions. The Lady of the Realm is named by place, but what her realm (xứ) corresponds to is geographically nonspecific to many pilgrims. Like many of the warrior-scholar-official figures her name is passed from person to person in places very far afield. In Nguyễn Huỳnh Đức's temple, a large plaque in wood, embossed in gilt in Chinese characters and dating from the time of Minh Mang, hangs above the main altar; it reads, "His reputation extends ten thousand li."

Despite these similarities, there are significant differences in the popular appeal of these two groups of spirits, particularly in terms of the spatial cast and size of their followings. Although the following of the warrior-scholar-official spirits is geographically diffuse it is, nonetheless, comparatively localized. Lê Văn Duyệt, whose beautiful and rambling temple complex is in Bình Thành district of Ho Chi Minh City, is considered possibly the most potent of the region's warrior-scholar-official figures. Yet his following is drawn mostly from the city center and surrounding urban districts, including the huge market hub of Chợ Lớn. Nguyễn Trung Trực, whose temple is in the seaside port of Rạch Giá, mainly attracts fishermen, marketeers, and traders from the vicinity of the provincial capital. By contrast the goddesses often attract petitioners from hundreds of kilometers away. In 1899, the

Black Lady was drawing pilgrims from all over Cochinchina (Baurac 1899, 270). In 1942 the same was said of the Lady of the Realm in Châu Đốc, who also attracted pilgrims from Cambodia (Lam Minh 1942). Today her following extends beyond the country's borders to include many members of the Vietnamese diaspora, many of whom go out of their way to return to her shrine or make special arrangements for a proxy to visit her shrine and maintain ongoing relations with her.

The warrior-scholar-official spirits also attract fewer petitioners than do the main goddesses. In the last years of the French colonial regime, the annual festival to the Lady of the Realm already attracted six to seven thousand people (Lam Minh 1942). This is today the biggest religious gathering in the region. The festivals to her sisters Dinh Cô, Bà Đen, and Thiên Hậu are also each bigger than any other religious event. The Lady of the Realm's festival lasts several weeks in contrast to the single day of commemorations that mark the death anniversary of warrior-scholar-official spirits such as general Trần Hưng Đạo. This difference is equally evident in terms of the number of visitors who come outside the annual festival period. The goddesses attract far greater numbers of such people. Both groups of spirits attract petitioners on the first and fifteenth of each lunar month, according to the Buddhist ritual calendar. However, whereas the flow of visitors tapers off at most temples to the warrior-scholar-official spirits during the rest of the month, propitiation of the goddesses occurs continuously throughout the month. Both classes of spirits attract large numbers of visitors in the first weeks of the lunar New Year, as people attend these auspicious places to make requests for the coming year. However, at this time many people from Ho Chi Minh City are prepared to travel the extra distance to places such as Châu Đốc, Tây Ninh, and Long Hải to visit the goddesses, who are perceived to be more efficacious. Throughout the entire first half of the lunar year a continuous stream of pilgrims makes its way to the shrine to the Black Lady in Tây Ninh. The shrine to the Lady of the Realm in Châu Đốc is crowded day and night during a six- to seven-month period extending from Christmas in the twelfth solar month right through to the fourth or fifth month of the subsequent lunar year. Indeed, her shrine has the character of a permanent festival. At any given time of year a quiet day at her shrine would be one in which visitor numbers dropped to the low hundreds.

Grounds of Repute

These differences in the scope of their following can be related to the different bases for their fame. Marshall Nguyễn Huỳnh Đức and the other warrior-scholar-official spirits belong to a group of figures venerated in Vietnam as celebrated personages *(danh nhân)*, who arose in exceptional times to answer peoples' needs or those of their country. The French anthropologist Giran explained the veneration of such figures as a "natural evolution" from the familial cult of the ancestors to a more general cult rendered by the population to the celebrated men *(hommes celebres)* of an entire kingdom (1912, 428).[3] The most prominent of the celebrated personages commemorated in southern Vietnam are pioneers, occupying generals, founders of military colonies, viceroys, diplomats, scholars, anticolonial resisters, and revolutionary heroes. Each of them is known by a handful of key exploits and qualities. For example, Nguyễn Hữu Cảnh, venerated in a plethora of temples and communal houses in the region, is remembered as a famed leader of the Vietnamese occupation of the south and founder of Gia Định in the late seventeenth century. The nineteenth-century anticolonial fighter Nguyễn Trung Trực, also commemorated in several temples and communal houses, is known for his daring sinking of the French battleship *Esperence* and his famed act of filial piety when he forfeited his own life in exchange for that of his ransomed mother. The mandarin Phan Thanh Giản, whose temple is in Vĩnh Long, is known for his erudition and the diplomatic posts he held but most of all for his dramatic suicide by drinking poison when three southern provinces were ceded to the French.

The famed historical exploits of these meritorious figures, which are the stuff of legend, encoded in history books and commemorated in the public sphere, comprise a different kind of fame from that earned for their reputed magical efficacy. However, the latter kind of celebrity represents an extension of the former. It is based on the belief that their souls *(linh hồn)* live on. As proven historical contributors, they make their assistance available to subsequent generations as well. The talents and moral qualities exhibited during their lifetimes, which marked them out as exceptional people, can continue to be tapped. Those who were known for their exceptional knowledge and foresight are called on to divine the future. Those whose notable deeds brought peace and protection to the country are asked to help oversee and protect people's lives. Those who demonstrated dispassionate judgment, such as Quan Công, are called upon for righteous assistance in resolving disputes. Even reputed personal traits are fodder for contemporary theories regarding their potency. For instance, Lê Văn Duyệt was reputedly so fierce of visage that enemies who glanced at his face were driven to flee. He is consequently propitiated to maintain order and to chase away criminals and ghosts, and propitiants are nervous about belittling his name or disparaging the appearance of his tomb. The historical service rendered to their country by such figures has a bearing on the expectations that are posthumously invested in them. Lê Văn Duyệt's historical protection of the Chinese in Gia Định means that he is still considered a patron of business.

In contrast to these figures who are famed for their historical contribution, few people know anything about the historical accomplishments of the goddesses venerated in Southern Vietnam. This is a key phenomenological difference between the two classes of deities. There is a discernible tendency to comprehend these goddesses as historical humans, to furnish them biographies, and to consider that those who venerate them do so in honor of their historical contribution. Indeed, each of the goddesses has at least one tale that refers to their historical human existence. Details, however, are obscure. Some of the tales about the Lady of the Realm that furnish her a human identity do not give details that would enable one to define in which era she lived. A number of tales about her and the Black Lady of Tây Ninh provide instances of brushes with known historical personages and events, such as the prince Nguyễn Phúc Ánh or the Tây Sơn rebel troops, yet these are contradictory. The historical tales about these figures as well as about the goddesses Thiên Hậu and Dinh Cô for the most part describe them as ordinary folk: as girls from unnamed families or as local women. While these goddesses are today the talk of the region, in their former human incarnations they were undistinguished. Each of the goddesses is today assigned a prestigious title, such as Holy Mother or Princess; but to the limited extent that they are contextualized as historical personages, even their names are unknown.

Moreover, while history attests that the warrior-scholar-official spirits either lived full lives, realized many accomplishments, or held many positions, the goddesses' potential in whatever incarnation they took was largely unrealized. Tales about them relate that their lives were cut short. Each of them died young, out of wedlock, leaving no children. Significantly, for figures who are today celebrated as accomplished and exalted beings, tales relate that they lived socially truncated lives and died abject deaths. Stories about the Lady of the Realm attribute this abject quality even to her statue, which was allegedly found abandoned on a mountain, alone in the elements, with an arm broken off, violated by thieves. These stories of unrealized potential and susceptibility to indebtedness have important implications for the goddesses' value to petitioners; they are key dimensions of the goddesses' reputation for responsiveness. Like the hungry ghosts, the goddesses are considered to be full of unrequited lusts, sensual appetites, moods, and memories and hence unusually grateful to those who can satisfy them.[4] Their posthumous responsiveness to requests is associated with a belief their deaths were untimely *(chết oan)*. According to a Buddhist conception, in such cases the soul is unable to disentangle itself from its prematurely terminated incarnation and unrealized destiny. Not only is it is stuck with many of the qualities from that particular incarnation, but, unable to move on to the next karmic cycle, it is needful of bequests from the living to sustain itself. This explains why the spirits of certain celebrated hero figures have remained particularly responsive to prayers. Although their lives were full of accomplishments, they nevertheless died before their time or suffered some other inauspicious event. The anticolonial hero Nguyễn Trung Trực, for example, was executed by the French. His spirit is considered particularly responsive. Phan Thanh Giản, whose spirit reportedly has great efficacious power, took his own life. Lê Văn Duyệt is also considered responsive to requests because of blows suffered to his resting place after his death. The spirits of those who have died badly or away from home or whose graves have been disturbed have unmet needs; hence they rely reliance on the living for satisfaction of such needs and thereby increase their vulnerability to indebtedness.

While the lifetime exploits of the heroes of Vietnamese history are the main key to their reputed powers, the celebrity of the goddesses principally rests on their posthumous careers of spiritual patronage. One can say further that whereas the events of the distant past play a significant role in the efficacious reputation of the former class of deities, the goddesses of southern Vietnam are more centrally implicated in the events of the very recent past. The fame of the goddesses is based chiefly on demonstrations of miraculous efficacy made to the living. The tales most frequently told about them relate to their responsiveness to requests. They are the constant topic of accounts furnished by a relative, acquaintance, or fellow propitiant who has been granted a request. It is sometimes said that the best proof of their efficacy can be adduced from the large numbers attending their shrines. "Would so many people be here if she were not efficacious?" propitiants ask in justification of their faith in the powers of the most popular of these goddesses, the Lady of the Realm. Her stature in the courts of popular opinion has led some observers to note the fashion-driven quality of such beliefs. Explaining the popularity of the Lady of the Realm one market vendor observed succinctly, "Every spirit has its time. This is hers." Local observers explain her prominence in terms of the volatility of public opinion in Vietnam, a snowballing effect whereby a shrine can become popular after a single report about the efficacy of the spirit or the sanctity of its place of worship. Equally, a place can dive into obscurity and attract disparagement just as unexpectedly. The shrine to the Lady of the Realm in Châu Đốc is a case in point. Although the same goddess is venerated in many places throughout southern Vietnam, this particular shrine shot out in prominence from the rest in the 1980s in a way that left some locals bemused. One observer called her "the Britney Spears of the Vietnamese religious world" (Huỳnh Ngọc Trảng, pers. com). By the early 1990s, her popularity had led to the reconfiguration of the other shrines into branch shrines *(miếu chi nhánh)* of the Châu Đốc shrine. To add insult to injury, the former are even commonly considered derivative or parasitical *(ký sinh)* with respect to the latter.

Fixed and Fluid Identities

An important key to these differences between these classes of spirits is the specificity of their identity. The warrior-scholar-official spirits have highly particular identities. Most of them were indeed extraordinary people, men of prowess and renown who rose to prominence in the particular circumstances of the Vietnamese occupation, settlement, administration, control, defense, and development of the southern plain. During their lives, they made a socially valued contribution and in most cases lived to see titles and honors heaped upon them. Thoại Ngọc Hầu went from one major accomplishment to the next during his life, undertaking a mission to Siam, founding hamlets, digging the Vĩnh Tế Canal, defending the Châu Đốc region, undertaking a mission to Laos, and serving as protector of Cambodia (Nguyễn Văn Hầu 1972). Many of these figures carved a place for themselves in the world beyond Vietnam. Lê Văn Duyệt left a lasting impression on several visitors to Vietnam whose impressions are recorded in their journals (e.g., Finlayson 1988, 319). The warrior-scholar-officials received further honors and citations after their deaths and were subject of a stream of commemorative plaudits that in many cases has not ceased to this day. Their places of commemoration have been continually refurbished over the years, evidence of their durability, over many generations, as the society's culture heroes and as a lens through which the region's history is seen. In Thoại Ngọc Hầu's case, a bier was inscribed at his place of rest recording his many titles and accomplishments. He was the subject of a detailed book about his life's deeds and posthumous recognition (Nguyễn Văn Hầu 1972). His large mausoleum continues to be well maintained and houses the annual ceremonies marking his death.

The temples and mausoleums that commemorate these figures are full of paraphernalia that illustrate their position and evoke the responsibilities of their office as well as images and edicts that attest to their services. Inside Nguyễn Huỳnh Đức's house of worship are three altars, arranged parallel to each other, in the front, middle, and rear of the mausoleum. Each bears a framed painting or lithograph of the marshall seated in the regalia of a military mandarin. The rows of altars are flanked on each side by sets of eight traditional weapons. The racks of weapons are lined end to end, so that the middle of the room is a formidably defended sanctuary, hedged by two lines of twenty-four weapons, running from the entrance to the rear. A pair of pikes with dull iron blades described as genuine weapons dates from the marshall's epoch. The rest are copies, rendered in wood. Hanging from the roof is the woven bamboo and wood canopy that was carried by four servants to protect the marshall from the elements. A large wooden slab about four inches thick served as the marshall's bed and is said to be about 250 years old. An adjacent cabinet displays robes in the style of the late-eighteenth century—"reproductions" the custodian noted.[5]

The warrior-scholar-officials' identities are firmly circumscribed, tied to places, dates, and events by this dense, interlocking, and cross-confirming web of reports, observations, citations, and memories. An embarrassment of circumstantial evidence, from public works bearing their names to intimate accessories on display in their places of commemoration, further adds to their indelible specificity. There is, however, a downside to the amply defined and well-recorded historical identities of these figures. They are victims of their past fame, weighed down by specific attachments and particular meanings inscribed in the cultural landscape and in the familial and public record. Their cultural and social fixedness has served to limit their potential sphere of responsibilities and inhibit the projects to which they can be linked.

Many people consider it inappropriate to say that such figures are worshiped *(thờ)*; the proper term should be "respected" *(kính trọng)*. Even the reference to them as spirits *(thần thánh)* is considered by many intellectuals as an aberration. Figures such as Lê Văn Duyệt are often considered historical figures who ought merely to be honored, as one honors ancestors *(tổ tiên)*, and remembered *(nhớ ơn)* for their historical contribution to the country *(có công với đất nước)*. Some intellectuals and professional people with whom I have spoken were unaware of the existence of conceptions about their magical efficacy and were surprised to hear that practices such as divination and requests for assistance regularly took place in the precincts of their places of commemoration. Some rationalize such practices, saying that large offerings such as roast pigs are merely a function of the respect certain individuals have for their ancestors' past contribution. Ideas that they can perform posthumous miracles are attributed variously to ignorance, backwardness, or the influence of culturally alien religions and views, at variance with their core identity as national heroes. Alternatively, such practices are sometimes associated with attempts by local elites or foreign rulers to use religion to mystify the masses or by profiteers peddling religion seeking to tap the sanctity of the shrine. One even encounters these criticisms among some of the custodians at the temples to such figures, who mock or take exception to those who make offerings and request material benefits, saying the practice is a distortion of the enshrined figure's true identity. At the temple to Trần Hưng Đạo in Ho Chi Minh City, one of the elderly custodians scoffed about the visitors who made offerings and burnt requests in Chinese characters to the general and who propitiated the five tigers enshrined below his altar, saying this was evidence of their "backward Asiatic mentality."

Shrines that have been tended by an unbroken lineage of family descendants are a different case. These descendants of historical figures esteemed by the wider society can bask for many generations in the glory of their forefather and the obeisance paid by their compatriots to their family's name. But although careful tending of the temple can keep alive the repute of their ancestor, this close attention by the lineage can serve to exclude alternative readings. For instance, at the temple to Marshall Nguyễn Huỳnh Đức, I asked the custodian, a seventh-generation descendant of the marshall, if many people believed in the spiritual power of his ancestor. He said doubtless some did; this was a question of each person's belief. He himself didn't credit the marshall with such powers. "In reality there is just humanity and heaven. If you are a person who doesn't believe in Heaven then it is all the more simple." He told me that before 1975, people had used divination sticks in the temple and mediums used to provide their own divinatory services. This had continued for a while after liberation, but he said he had chased them away and now forbade divination practices in the temple. He said that mediums claimed to be possessed by the spirit of the marshall, but he exclaimed, "What in Heaven's name 'possesses' them is anybody's guess. In truth those people are just chasing money. They do strange shaking movements, wear bizarre clothes, and emit weird sounds." He laughed and mimicked the sounds they made in séances. "They're just con artists. I don't allow them in."

While the lives of warrior-scholar-official spirits are represented as the pinnacle of cultural attainment, the goddesses' purchase on a cultural identity is more tenuous. In some renditions they lack a cultural status, such as in the quasi-evolutionary interpretive accounts that identify them with nature worship or the symbolic ordering of natural elements or view them as anthropomorphized versions of natural forces. As fertility symbols they are associated with procreative power, with the beginnings of life. They are also associated with or considered symbols of geographical features, such as mountains, streams, forests, and oceans. Popular tales relate that they lived or died in the margins: in forests, on mountainsides, at the bottom of cliffs, in the ocean. In a like way they are associated with the putatively uncultivated, untamed, or unpopulated south and its prolific "natural" environment. They similarly represent in some interpretive accounts the lack of Confucian cultural penetration in the south, the relative absence of court culture, or a supposedly prepatriarchal stage in human history. Another way in which their cultural status is rendered as weak or nonexistent is their association with borders, other ethnic groups, and the limits of the ethnic Vietnamese cultural world. Even when they are associated with an encultured human incarnation, there is no consensus as to who these women were. Stories about their identity and biography are vague and contradictory. Publications frequently cite four different tales about the Black Lady, each of which gives her a different identity (e.g., Nguyễn Phương Thảo 1997). Her ethnic origins are also obscure and variable, as is the case with all of the goddesses venerated in the region. The plurality of versions of tales about them means their biographies sometime blur into each other. For instance, the most common tale about Dinh Cô describes her as a girl who preferred death to marriage, a tale that approximates tales told of the Black Lady, Thiên Hậu, Kuan Yin, and Thiên Y A Na.

The Lady of the Realm, the best known and most magically responsive of southern Vietnam's goddesses, is the representative of this category whose identity is least well attached to a cultural status, human biography, or indeed identifiable corporeal incarnation. She is a spiritual personage, but unlike most of her sister spirits, traces to a preexisting living incarnation are missing or weak. The most commonly told tales about her relate to her statue. By most accounts, her form is natural: made of growing stone, sprouting from the sea atop a living mountain, or released from within a stone by a stonecutter. In this she resembles the goddess Thiên Y A Na, who, it is said, transubstantiated into a perfumed log and whose form was then carved out of the log.[6] Many of the recorded tales about her are prefaced by the question Who is the Lady of the Realm? Yet instead of providing a tale or biography of the human being whom the statue represents, they refer to the obscure and mysterious circumstances surrounding the origins or the discovery of the statue. In this respect she is not the representation of a once living human but rather simply a humanlike representation. She is not imagined as an encultured human agent but as a natural emanation or, at best, a cultural artifact, constituted by whom or when is not entirely clear. Only one of the published tales about her refers to her identity as a human being, and even this tale is contested.[7] None of the stories that I have gathered that do give her a human identity are particularly well known, and they are contradictory: that she is a Cham princess, a local Khmer woman, a Thai woman, the legendary Chinese figure Tien Hau, a local educated woman, or a wife who was faithful to her husband.

This difference in the specificity of the identity of both classes of spirits is manifest in the practices of naming their places of worship. The generic terms for describing these are distinct, although in each case the formal and popular usages differ. The goddesses' places of worship are called variously shrines *(miếu)*, palaces *(dinh)*, and temples *(điện)*.[8] This naming practice is followed in publications and sometimes on signs and gates at their site. However, in popular usage, they are almost universally called pagodas, a term associated with Buddhism, which are places for housing the cremated remains of those who lack a place of rest or relatives to tend their cult. This speaks to the obscurity of their social origins, that they lack identifiable descendants who might honor them at home. By contrast, the structures housing the altars to the warrior-scholar-official spirits are rarely referred to as pagodas, but rather as temples and houses of worship.[9] While the goddesses do not have grave sites and it is not even known where their material remains are, the resting places of the warrior-scholar-officials are well known places, characteristically referred to in inflated language as mausoleums. Their considerable social profile is reflected in the solidity and grandeur of these memorials. But by the same token, such practices of commemoration have tied them to a specific identity, confining their meaning and degree of relevance to the well-defined coordinates of their biographies.

By contrast, the indefinite identity of these goddesses has allowed stories to be embroidered about them so they can and do speak to greater numbers of people. Because the goddesses lack a specific identity, the different stories that are told about them can coexist in nonconflicting ways. Their fame is not tied to their lifetime accomplishments, obscure and limited as they are. Like the variety of folk beliefs surrounding the Catholic saint Francis Xavier, which helps explain why the pilgrimage to Magdalena in Mexico attracts such a diverse following, their multivocality makes for a wide range of individual interpretations (O'Connor 1997, 375). They have the polyvalent quality that Turner identified as a characteristic of religious symbols (1967). The obscurity of their origins also helps explain why the duties expected of them are diverse. It is this attribute that allows a spirit such as the Lady of the Realm to be appropriated simultaneously as a materially potent force enabling the reproduction of life, the increase of finances, and the conferral of physical immunity, at the same time as being a partner in business and symbolic underwriter of diversely imagined political, cultural, and ethnic collectivities. Because her identity is not anchored in a specific and identifiable past but relates to relatively recent deeds, her reputation as efficacious has been able to shift and turn to accommodate shifting social priorities. This fluidity of identity helps explain why a number of the goddesses have risen in prominence in tandem with each other, for the deeds of one are easily transferable to the credit of another. This substitutability has its benefits and risks, for although a lesser goddess can to feed off another's reputation, in some instances an overperforming goddess such as the Lady of the Realm has been known to encompass and obliterate another's identity. Being specific, the warrior-scholar-officials cannot be taken for each other. It is some consolation that this prevents any one overachieving deity from smothering the others, but it does mean that one is unlikely to see a figure of the stature of the Lady of the Realm rise from their ranks.

The State and Its Symbols

A significant dimension of the difference in specificity between these two kinds of spirits relates to their relationship to the state. In their lifetime many of the warrior-scholar-officials of southern Vietnam *were* the state. Like Marshall Nguyễn Huỳnh Đức, they were its agents and instruments, holding a number of critical offices. They embodied the state during their lifetimes. They represented it and extended it, were its saviors and defenders. They pushed forward the occupation, settlement, and defense of the south and held important positions of power. Posthumously this relationship was maintained in the state's participation in the staging of commemorative rites on their behalf. They continued to play a role as reliable spiritual servants of the needs of the court and of its subjects and were rewarded for such duties by receiving official decrees of recognition.

The temple to Nguyễn Huỳnh Đức is full of evidence of his close relationship with the state. Three decrees awarded by the Nguyễn dynasty's founder, Gia Long, are displayed on the wooden pillar to the left of the entrance. The decrees are miniatures of the originals and written in Chinese characters. Each is translated into Vietnamese, in careful calligraphy, and framed and displayed beneath the miniature of the original. The first is a statement of the marshall's offices and titles, carried by the marshall during the period he resided in Thailand, during which time he had helped repulse a Burmese attack in alliance with the Siamese army. The second was awarded by the newly crowned Gia Long emperor and recognized the marshall's position and accomplishments. The third is the decree awarded after the marshall's death, admitting him to the ranks of the empire's guardian deities. On the pillar opposite are decrees by the subsequent Minh Mạng and Tứ

Đức emperors, maintaining this recognition and nominating the marshall's mausoleum.[10]

The official commemoration of such figures was one means by which the state kept its authorized version of the country's history in the public eye. The tributes showered on these figures by a grateful court have drawn attention to their historical achievements and, over time, have probably added to their reputation for spiritual potency. Such attentions have highlighted their particular contributions, tying them to events in political history and implicating them in the deeds and fortunes of particular regimes. Such attention may well have lifted the popular profile of these figures, but at the same time it locked them into a particular meaning. Consequently, it is hard to detach such figures from the identities furnished to them by the state as meritorious ancestors whose well-documented and larger-than-life exploits have made them immortal.

Several of the goddesses venerated in southern Vietnam are also noted for their contributions to the state. Stories about the Lady of the Realm and the Black Lady, for example, relate that as historical personages they each gave military assistance to the king. However, their service to the state never raised them out of anonymity enough to clarify their identities or make known their names. In some cases their contributions were made as spirits or even as willful statues. The fund of oral tales about their exploits is full of contrary versions. Indeed, according to popular accounts their encounters with state agents often entailed their being raped or abducted. This indeterminate quality has allowed them to be appropriated as spiritual protectors of the sovereign or bearers of the "national essence," for they transcend the particular meanings that have adhered to ancestral spirits claimed by families, lineages, localities, or particular regimes. One of the significant differences between representing the nation in general and being held accountable for a particular episode in its history is that over time attitudes toward such historical contributions can shift dramatically. This element of discontinuity is particularly characteristic of dynastic shifts as a new ruling elite gives priority to its own lineage of meritorious figures. Such swerves can remove state support for a figure or, even worse, make the person's contribution into an act of disloyalty.

The danger of changes in official attitudes toward a spirit's historical contribution is illustrated by the case of Lê Văn Duyệt. During his lifetime he was a formidable military leader, a colorful personality, and a regional king-maker to whom Gia Long, founder of the Nguyễn dynasty, was indebted for help in establishing his family to power. However, after his death in 1832, Lê

Văn Duyệt suffered posthumous censure by the Minh Mạng emperor, the second in this dynastic line. The viceroy was accused of various crimes, and the punishment involved the flattening of his mausoleum and ritual flogging of his tomb. Many people believe this was done out of spite at the viceroy's failure to support the emperor's succession to the throne although it was perhaps also due to the destabilizing effects of enduring localist allegiances and tendencies in the region that were considered his legacy (Choi 1999). In 1841 the viceroy was rehabilitated and his mausoleum rebuilt by Minh Mạng's successor, Thiệu Trị. Although the French dismantled the imperial system and its ritual apparatus in their new colony, the viceroy continued to be venerated by representatives of the colonial regime. His annual celebrations were attended by the political class of Cochinchina. The buildings and grounds of his mausoleum were renovated and extended in 1937, thanks to the patronage of a number of high-profile donors drawn from the colonial bureaucracy and business elite.[11] Nevertheless, the saga of stormy relations between the viceroy and successive state authorities had not yet run its full course, as shall shortly be related.

In a region such as southern Vietnam, which, in a short time has come under the rule of several regimes, the effect of different regimes' motivated readings of history has been particularly destabilizing to those figures whose public stature is linked to their historical deeds. When regimes have changed, the value attributed to these figures has shifted, in many instances violently. In some cases the meritorious contribution formerly ascribed to such figures has emerged as a serious liability, and their public profile has plunged abruptly. One can see these processes at play most clearly during the transition of postcolonial regimes in southern Vietnam. During this period, the spirits were pawns in a war between rival regimes, the spoils of which was the power to rewrite the meaning of the past. Fights over the meaning and uses of history, societal values, and citizenship were waged in the precincts of their places of worship. Such fights variously entailed the closure of or reduced access to their temples, the restriction of ritual practices, and the reinscription of imagery—as well as the emergence of new approved foci. Such turbulent dynamics have had a significant effect on religious conceptions, particularly on the perception many people hold of such figures as magically efficacious beings.

Symbolizing Postcolonial Power

The first postcolonial state in the south of Vietnam emerged when an American-backed anti-Communist and avowedly nationalist regime, the Republic of Vietnam (RVN), came to power in 1955. The Republic of Vietnam construed itself as a nation emerging from colonialism and battling a Communist threat. In the process it edited collective memory by proposing images of fighters who had succeeded in consolidating the nation and resisting foreign rule as typical historical figures. Under the Republic, statues of the thirteenth-century general Trần Hưng Đạo and other figures from the country's military history were prominently displayed in the public squares of urban areas, thereby fixing in the public mind an identification between the South Vietnamese regime's battle with communism and the heroic tradition of national resistance.[12] The general was nominated as the patron of the RVN Navy. A temple in his memory in District One of Ho Chi Minh City, built in the 1920s in the French colonial period, was renovated during the RVN period by patriotic northerners who fled from the Communist north in 1954.

Mausoleums to the heroes of anticolonial struggle were also upgraded under the RVN with support from the government. These included a temple honoring Trương Định in East Gò Công and one enshrining Nguyễn Trung Trực in the southern fishing port of Rạch Giá. According to Rạch Giá locals, Nguyễn Trung Trực was venerated covertly throughout French times in a small temple on the present site, his true identity concealed behind a cult to the God of the South Seas (Thánh Nam Hải), who is still venerated in the anticolonial hero's temple and is represented by a pair of swordfish blades enshrined on an ancillary altar. Only at the end of French rule did it became possible to publicly honor this defiant opponent of the French occupation. The construction of temples to these warrior figures was complemented by the refurbishment of those honoring scholar-bureaucrats such as Phan Thanh Giản, whose shrine is in Vĩnh Long. A shrine to Confucius in the spacious grounds of the mausoleum was also upgraded. These figures were regarded as ancestors and role models. They were venerated as well in public parks, museums, school textbooks, newspapers, and the speeches of leaders. In terms of the Republican political project, they represented the meaning of the past, symbolized public values, and provided exemplary role models for citizens.

Officials and officers of the Republican regime were also involved in venerating these deities and attending their annual commemorative festivals. According to locals, regime representatives frequently visited Bình Thụy communal house, near the city of Cần Thơ, which venerates Nguyễn Hữu Cảnh, pioneer of Vietnamese colonization in the Mekong delta, as well as the anticolonial intellectuals Phan Bội Châu and Phan Châu Trinh. Such acts underlined a link between the Republican regime and the military, scholarly, and political activities of their historic forebears. In a like way, Marshall Nguyễn Huỳnh Đức's mausoleum was very popular among leaders of this regime, who sponsored it and visited it often. The custodian said that the temple was refurbished in the late 1950s with funds provided by the central government in Saigon. In 1968, more funds had been granted to construct a series of large rooms designed for receiving guests. In the main temple one can still see a large stuffed tiger displayed in a glass case beside the main altar, straw sprouting from its badly deteriorated flank. This was a gift given by the RVN president in 1965, acquired when he was still ambassador to Taiwan.

In 1975, despite extraordinary political, military, and economic support from the United States, the RVN fell to a superior Communist force.[13] The transition in regimes was paralleled by a shakeout in the spiritual realm. Southern Vietnam's warrior-scholar-official spirits received redoubled attention from the state in the postwar years, although for many of them the attention was unfavorable. This treatment flowed in part from the new regime's revolutionary socialist philosophy. After 1975, the regime, believing that religion had been an instrument of oppression by the ruling class and social elites, confiscated the land, furnishings, and valuables of many shrines, temples, and communal houses and partially destroyed their structures. Many communal houses to village tutelary spirits therefore fell into disrepair and neglect. In 1977, Marshall Nguyễn Huỳnh Đức's mausoleum fell on hard times. Some 15.7 hectares of its land, once rented out to tenant farmers, was confiscated, leaving the mausoleum with 0.3 hectares, which provided only a fraction of the custodial family's needs.[14] The custodian was declared a large landlord, and the land was transferred to his tenants. Phan Thanh Giản's temple in Vĩnh Long experienced a similar fate. After the war, the large and elegant temple was allowed to fall into extreme disrepair. Its land was confiscated and redistributed to supporters of the revolutionary movement. Formerly rich sacrifices and enormous feasts were banned. The elderly guardian of that temple, whose family has tended the temple for several generations, told me it had been categorized by the new authorities as a place of "superstitious activities" *(sinh hoạt mê tín dị đoan)*. He thought this label was applied because it enabled local cadres to appropriate the temple's rich lands.

The new regime remained just as concerned about the meanings emitted by these places of worship. This was in part because many of the historical personages venerated therein did not conform to the new regime's own preferred historical lineage. After liberation state authorities again struck Lê Văn Duyệt's mausoleum a heavy blow. The mausoleum was shut down between 1975 and 1989. The gardens remained open during that time, but the temple itself was closed. No repairs were done on the structure, which disintegrated from exposure to the elements. A custodian explained to me that it had been considered a place of "superstitious activities" *(mê tín dị đoan)*. Yet he himself had little doubt that the main reason for the neglect was the new regime's dim view of Lê Văn Duyệt's historical background, which was regarded as politically compromised, as was that of the other key figures venerated in the temple, Lê Chất and Phan Thanh Giản. Each of these figures was deemed to have supported a political project that the new regime found objectionable, even though the most recent example of this had taken place more than a hundred years before.

The custodian told me that Lê Văn Duyệt had been instrumental in the establishment of the Nguyễn, the imperial dynasty that the Communist regime accused of having later "lost" the country to the French colonialists. Moreover, the viceroy himself had helped quell a rebellion led by the Tây Sơn brothers, whose political and military uprising in the late eighteenth century the Communists considered a prototypical peasant rebellion against feudal elites in cahoots with foreign forces. This rebellion is still considered a precursor of the Communist movement's own successful mobilization of peasant forces against foreign-backed rulers. Lê Chất, who is venerated on an auxiliary altar in Lê Văn Duyệt's temple, was considered equally suspect because he had defected from the Tây Sơn army to support Gia Long.[15] The custodian said that the mandarin Phan Thanh Giản, who was venerated on the other auxiliary altar, had been despised as the figure who had "sold the country" *(bán nước)* to the French in the mid-nineteenth century by signing away several provinces of the south in an unsuccessful attempt to avoid total loss of the kingdom. In consequence of the disgrace attached to the figures it enshrined, the viceroy's mausoleum played a diminished role in public life for more than a decade.[16]

Even though it closed down or restricted access to many places of worship, the socialist regime did not absolutely reject the symbolic potential of the cult to such figures. Rather, the state tried to use these sites to inscribe its own messages. Like many communal houses and shrines to celebrated personages, Phan Thanh Giản's temple was converted from a shrine to his memory into a museum of "resistance traditions" *(truyền thống kháng chiến)*. Sumptuous ornamentations, furniture, and ritual accessories were removed from the main hall. For more than a decade, the only visitors to this site were groups of schoolchildren viewing the new exhibits on local resistance history. After 1975, acts based on the assumption that Trần Hưng Đạo's spirit was magically responsive, such as the offering of sacrifices or the reading and burning of requests, were banned from his Ho Chi Minh City temple. Incense was the only offering allowed, considered a custom *(phong tục)* rather than a religious practice. As one custodian recalled, this was in keeping with his place in people's hearts as an exemplary ancestral figure. In the 1990s one of the rooms in the grounds was converted into a display hall depicting the general's victorious military feats against the Mongols. Nguyễn Trung Trực in Rạch Giá was dealt with in a similar way. The local authorities celebrated him as a traditional Vietnamese resistance hero. The making of offerings, requests for assistance, and use of divination sticks to predict the future were banned in his temple. Similarly, pamphlets about Trương Công Định were published by local authorities and made available in his temple in Gò Công. In the exhortative language the regime directed to its citizens, this historical figure was held to exemplify Gò Công citizens' qualities of resoluteness, unflagging resistance, loyalty, and perseverance. Meanwhile new ritual foci were emerging as formerly marginalized figures rose to sudden prominence. After the war, an elaborate mausoleum to the memory of Ho Chi Minh's father, Nguyễn Sinh Sắc, was erected in Đồng Tháp province. A temple-museum honoring Tôn Đức Thắng was developed in An Giang, adding the late second president of socialist Vietnam to the ranks of the south's warrior-scholar-official deities (Giebel 2001).

Phenomenological Fallout

As a deliberately chosen and carefully framed set of symbols, these figures were used by the new government to propagate its view of the nation's military and revolutionary traditions. Emptied of competing, contradictory meanings, their places of worship were set up to emit a particular ideological message. For more than a decade, the regime's use of these figures sanctified a view of national history as resistance, and resistance as nothing if not successful. This magical formulation into which the spirits were recruited fetishized war as a principle of historical agency, proposing it as a process that could be applied in a range of concerns, with victory the inevitable result.

During this time, people continued to furtively venerate even those beings out of favor with the new authorities. However, the state's intense symbolic investments in these memorials to historical personages often made popular practices impossible. One female trader in Gò Công recalled that on the annual anniversary of the resistance fighter Trương Công Định, celebrated by local officials, the police swept semilegal traders like her from the streets and barred individuals from entering the temple to make offerings. In other cases where state intervention was more heavy-handed, the relevance of the enshrined spirit was seen to suffer. Restrictions on rituals and access to their temples interrupted the circular evidentiary process by which the magi-cal potency of spirits is demonstrated *(chứng)* by the number of visitors to their temples, the size of the gifts offered, and the magnificence of their places of worship. In some people's eyes, the potency of some of the affected spirits diminished because they had allowed their own temples to be entered, violated, robbed, and closed. A woman whose stall was in the market adja-cent to the mausoleum of Lê Văn Duyệt told me, "After the revolution closed the mausoleum down, the responsive power of that spirit severely dimin-ished. His Lordship used to be more responsive than he is now. In the past, he could punish evildoers, in fact he killed people who did wrong by him. Now people only go to him to resolve small affairs: business, health, and family." Another acquaintance rarely made offerings to the viceroy: "Com-pared to before 1975, very few people go there." Seen as unable to defend their own places of worship, let alone abet the attainment of individual or wider social prosperity, such former figures of authority fell into disregard.

At the same time, they were also failing to perform the function required of them by the socialist state, as models of heroic citizenry and symbols of the revolutionary and resistance spirit: the forces that the state wished to tap to drive the Vietnamese economy into modernization and growth. Despite positioning liberation as a release from feudalism and capitalist oppression and proposing militarized and bureaucratic agency as efficacious paths to development and social well-being, Vietnam's postwar authorities failed to deliver on their promise to bring prosperity and happiness to the people. Several of the new policies—such as the opening of New Economic Zones, collectivization, restriction of private trade, and devaluation of the currency —caused further hunger, dislocation, and suffering. An economic slump caused by the new state's inefficiencies, its stifling of local capacities, and the corrupt siphoning of social wealth was compounded by war with Cambodia and the U.S. trade embargo. The martial qualities exemplified by the figures enshrined in the state pantheon appeared inadequate and irrelevant to the population's postwar needs.

In the late 1970s and early 1980s, many people sought to flee the coun-try. As the economic bad times deepened, people's requests to the spirits in-cluded help in breaking the laws that banned private market activity, success in bribing officialdom, aid with smuggling, and assistance escaping the coun-try. These were demands beyond the abilities of the warrior-scholar-official deities, historical builders of the state and patriotic defenders of the Viet-namese nation. Some, such as Lê Văn Duyệt, were virtual prisoners in their own temple precincts while others, such as Nguyễn Sinh Sắc and Tôn Đức Thắng, were so deeply implicated in propagating the state's own worldview that to demand such assistance of them seemed nonsensical. In times when many people felt their country offered them no opportunities for personal realization, increasing focus was given to those spirits on the margins, those not implicated in the theater of state rule. The goddesses fit this bill very neatly. Never considered agents of any particular state, they were not held accountable for misrule by either rulers or populace. Because they had acquired their reputations as catering to a more diffused set of social needs, requests in defiance of state authority in no way clashed with the identities attributed to them. People approached them for the greatest act of political transcendence, flight from the country.

At the center of the fishing village of Long Hải lies a temple to the whale god. Referred to respectfully as Cá Ông (Grandfather Whale or Lord Whale) the temple is one of many along the southern coast to enshrine the bones of a whale that washed ashore (for other locations, see Nguyễn Phương Thảo 1997). He is also often regarded as the God of the South Seas, protector of fishers, sailors, and travelers. In Long Hải village, he is seen as a patron deity of the local fishing population. His temple also contains an altar that used to enshrine Marshall Nguyễn Huỳnh Đức,[17] and locals told me that the marshall had been unable to avoid the ignominious fate of being disenshrined by the Long Hải authorities after 1975. He was accused of having been complicit in the "degenerate" feudal dynasty, an elite class of oppressors that failed to prevent the conquest of the country by the French. His image was replaced by a mass-produced bust of Ho Chi Minh. The symbolic accoutrements of the marshall's rule remained enshrined, however, and visitors were left to make their own association between the revolutionary Communist leader and Nguyễn Huỳnh Đức's beautiful white horse, which was left standing in front of the altar (figure 12). The main room of the temple was given over to a fishing collective, which used it to mend and store nets. Because of this, it was difficult to approach the altars to make offerings. The facade of the temple was in a dilapidated state. Furthermore, on the gate outside was displayed the temple's new name: Temple to War Martyrs (Đền Thờ Liệt Sĩ), an innovation reflecting the new regime's revolutionary culture. While still hosting an annual festival to Cá Ông, this structure played a limited role in the religious life of the local area and enjoyed even less repute among people visiting the area from farther away.

Just five hundred meters down the road is a much larger structure, resembling a castle, where Dinh Cô is venerated each year in a festival held on the twelfth of the second lunar month. Pilgrims from the southern maritime provinces, from as far north as Phan Thiết, by boat.[18] Some locals described her as the daughter of a trading family who had visited the Bà Rịa–Vũng Tàu

FIG. 12. Ho Chi Minh enshrined on the altar formerly dedicated to Marshall Nguyễn Huỳnh Đức in Long Hải

area and who threw herself overboard rather than obey her father's insistence that she return to her paternal homeland in Bình Thuận on the coast of central Vietnam. A striking characteristic of her place of worship is the large chorus of colorfully garbed female deities sharing the white-tiled tiers of her altar (figure 13).[19] Formerly, her shrine was quite small, I was told, smaller than that of the nearby, once-elegant shrine to Cá Ông. However, worship of the goddess picked up dramatically in the late 1980s and early 1990s, when former refugees began to return and make sumptuous bequests to her in thanks for patronizing their successful escapes. Like Cá Ông she had been asked to protect the vast numbers of people who had passed through from

FIG. 13. Female deities sharing the altar to Dinh Cô in Long Hải

Saigon using local fishing boats to stage risky escapes. Yet the prestige derived by safely guiding refugees abroad was in turn outshone by her reputed patronage of commerce. By the late 1990s, the majority of devotees who descended annually to worship her were women from Ho Chi Minh City working as petty entrepreneurs. Although their gifts were not as spectacular as the ones brought by those returning from overseas, they were considered numerically more important.

This reworking of the Palace Damsel into the religious life of successive waves of propitiants illustrates the themes of this chapter. Reportedly beginning as a patron of fishing, she was credited with protecting and enriching refugees, only to be taken up by a new wave of mostly female urban entrepreneurs. The easy transformation of responsibilities of this goddess and her multivalent quality and lack of prescribed responsibilities relates to her obscure origins and indeterminate identity. Her steady growth despite being the focal point of different constituencies attests to the flexibility of her identity. By contrast, the figures commemorated in Cá Ông's shrine have not been able to sustain such disparate messages and followings and have not even managed to peaceably cohabit the temple. Over time distinct figures fronting different political projects have displaced each other while the venue itself has been renamed to evoke a specific commemorative focus.

Rehabilitation

Improvements in the fortunes of many of these spirits came with the launching of liberal economic reforms in the mid 1980s. Both sets of figures experienced something of a revival as the state and nationalist intellectuals looked to the realm of folk culture and religion for cultural foundations on which to make a stand against the forces of societal fragmentation and global homogenization and as well-off community members sought cultural endorsement of their economic successes by patronizing commemorative rites to various spirits. Such processes have lent the support of societal elites and official opinion to a resurgence of popular interest in these ritual foci, despite the fact that this popular following is often drawn to them for different reasons.

However, while both sets of figures have gained a new lease on life as items of cultural heritage, the spirits known for their historical accomplishments have had to submit to a further test relating to their historical identity. In recent years, wider and more plural conceptions of Vietnamese identity have created space for the celebration of a larger cast of figures from the nation's history. Yet the rehabilitation of sites to historical heroes remains dependent on the official line on Vietnamese history. The custodian at Viceroy Lê Văn Duyệt's mausoleum told me that in recent years, official opinion concerning the figures it enshrined had changed tack. He said it was now increasingly recognized that the viceroy had been opposed to the succession of the Minh Mạng emperor because he knew that the emperor would adopt a closed-minded attitude toward reforms necessary to counter the challenge of expanding European rule, a limitation that would lead to the loss of the country. Events had proven him right. As for Phan Thanh Giản, this custodian said that it was now recognized that he had acted to save the country from the French colonialists and had personally taken responsibility for his failure to do so by taking his own life. Nevertheless, at a recent conference in Vietnam on the historical significance of this figure, opinion about whether he should be regarded as having merit or having wronged his country remained divided (Phan Huy Lê 1999, 212). This disagreement illustrates the precarious tenure enjoyed by such figures, who are constrained to rely for their contemporary stature in the public sphere on the authorized interpretation of events in the distant past. There are legions of spiritual figures that have not been rehabilitated, precisely because of their specific historical contribution. These range from Trương Vĩnh Ký, whose large mausoleum on Trần Hưng Đạo Street, Ho Chi Minh City, remains obscure and in poor condition, to those who died resisting the Communist regime's establishment in the region whose places of rest and commemoration are virtually anonymous.

One of the limitations of being dependent on fluctuating endorsements from the central authorities is the problem of translating the state's intention into local practice. The restoration of these memorials to the nation's heroes has been subject to the grinding and conflicted bureaucratic processes of the Vietnamese state. In some cases, local authorities have not released the funds requested by temple custodians for repairs. Confiscated lands have been notoriously difficult to prise back from cadres to whom they were distributed after the war. Despite the qualified rehabilitation of the mandarin Phan Thanh Giản, the temple to his memory was only been partially restored by the late 1990s. Many tiles were still broken, there was a gaping hole in one wall, and the temple lacked furnishings. Repairs had been done haphazardly and only after long delays. The local office of culture was accused of filching from the contributions box, and the local cadres who had appropriated the temple's land had not returned it. The temple had been reopened but operated on a severely attenuated schedule. The offerings at the annual commemorative festival were minor—as one local put it, not amounting to much more than that offered to the hungry ghosts.

In contrast to this is the ease with which Marshall Nguyễn Huỳnh Đức in Khánh Hậu village was rehabilitated. His temple was recognized by the Long An museum as a historical-cultural vestige (di tích lịch sử văn hóa) in 1993. This decree of recognition has been placed on the front altar. A panel of photographs, hanging in the guest room, commemorates the conferral ceremony. Outside the museum two panels outline the proper conduct to be observed by those visiting the temple and describe the site as an exemplar of the architectural arts of the early nineteenth century. In 1993, an Australian television crew filmed the ceremonies. A photographer was hired to take photos of the display items in the temple, and translations of captions into French and English were provided for the small number of foreigners who happen by. The support of lineage representatives undoubtedly accounts for the smoothness of this rehabilitation process. In contrast, in Long Hải village, well beyond the sphere of his descendants' influence, the marshall had still failed to reclaim his altar back from Ho Chi Minh as late as 1998. Yet the support received from his descendants in Khánh Hậu village appears to have limited the marshall's accessibility to mediums and seekers of magical benefits, restricting the marshall's reputation as a responsive spirit.

The emphasis on the cultural heritage value of such sites is not necessarily a more promising basis for their enshrined figures to become known as magically efficacious. Viceroy Lê Văn Duyệt's mausoleum was reopened and extended recognition by the state as a historical-cultural relic in 1989 (Sơn Nam 1994). In the 1990s, although restored to the status of a major urban landmark, the mausoleum continued to be hedged around with regulations. There were signs all over the garden: Preserve the beauty of the garden, No jostling, Wear respectful clothes. There was also a sign at the entrance forbidding fortune-telling, but people still surreptitiously approached visitors and offered their services. A panel near the entrance displayed the photographs, names, and dates of birth of "those who have tricked the public by fortune-telling." Alongside the panel were photographs displaying the "more suitable" community service activities of the management committee of the temple: buying TVs for schools, collecting rice for Mekong delta flood victims, donating money to invalid veterans, and meeting with political leaders.

Such restrictions, based on notions of cultural appropriateness, as well as resistance to these notions and local accommodations are found around the shrines to goddesses as well. Yet at sites such as the viceroy's mausoleum one gets a vivid sense of the constraints placed on the flow of popular interpretation and practice by a number of overlapping factors. Như was one of the few stalwarts who continued to visit Lê Văn Duyệt's mausoleum from the mid-1970s to the 1990s. She was reluctant to comment on perceptions that the viceroy's magical responsiveness had dropped, saying such matters depended on the belief of each propitiant. She herself believed his spirit had resisted the state's attempts to curtail his worship. She explained that after the war the new rulers had initially tried to raze His Lordship's tomb, wanting to build a park for the public and a playground for children. They had made several attempts to demolish the grave, but each time their tools had mysteriously broken. However, while His Lordship had warded off a frontal attack on his grave, he was powerless to stop a more recent and insidious piecemeal diminution of his place of rest. Như condemned the way parts of the grounds were now being used for tourist and commercial purposes. She said the mausoleum to His Lordship was not as beautiful as it had been previously because the state now controlled the management committee. The Fatherland Front ran a stall selling ornamental shrubs at one side of the grounds of the mausoleum and a café in the front of the grounds. She said it was wrong to use the grounds of the mausoleum for business. The present managers had also constructed an iron fence through the bottom end of the grounds, cordoning off a space that they rented out to people operating a motorcycle parking lot. As a result, the size and the beauty of the garden had been greatly diminished. Unlike some of her fellow traders, Như did not admit that this situation implied diminution of the god's power. In practice, however, she, like most of her colleagues, devoted more time and effort to propitiating the Lady of the Realm.

The qualified rehabilitation of this site suggests that the support the viceroy might attract from the state as a meritorious ancestor is limited; it is certainly not on a par with the attention paid to the mausoleum of Nguyễn Sinh Sắc in Cao Lãnh, for instance, whose historical pedigree, as father of Ho Chi Minh, is unimpeachable. Admittedly, gaining support on such historical grounds, as has been shown, can be a risky proposition. In addition, those who support such figures on the basis of their meritorious historical achievements often disagree with their popularization as responsive beings. Rehabilitation on grounds of culture also restricts the development of personalized meanings and magical practices in and around such sites, on the grounds of their being culturally inappropriate. Như's criticism of the state's handling of Lê Văn Duyệt's mausoleum speaks to her conception of the viceroy not as a historical figure or an item of cultural heritage but as a spiritual personage. She depicted the viceroy as a being enmeshed in an ongoing conflict with the authorities, which he was in danger of losing. Hers was a reproach tacitly directed at the viceroy himself for being unable to defend his own home. Because he was credited with administrative prowess and the protection of territory, his reputation has been particularly damaged by the piecemeal dismemberment and contradictory management of his place of rest. Yet hemmed in by such statuses as historical actor and item of heritage, the viceroy has scarcely had the chance to demonstrate his magical responsiveness.

The goddesses, by contrast, get their support from a more diverse and diffused constituency, and on considerably more varied grounds, by virtue of their indeterminacy and polyvalence. This fluid quality has helped these goddesses weather the storms of symbolic violence attending the transition in regimes and shifts in policy. Because they were never firmly pinned to any particular regime or mode of power, they have been able to adapt to and symbolize fundamental shifts in political orientation. Because they are not associated with a specific quality of statecraft, the goddesses have been flexible patrons of various ways of making a living outside the militarized, scholarly, and bureaucratic spheres. This indeterminacy perhaps explains why the goddesses have survived the urbanization, commercialization, and touristic marketing of their cults better than spirits whose repute rests on more specific grounds. Bà Đen mountain is managed by the local tourist authority, which charges an entrance fee and runs a cable car. Sam Mountain is being claimed by a host of hotels. Both sites are surrounded by a massive sea of commercialization. Such processes, while they have certainly brought many people with no particular interest in the powers of the goddesses to their sites, do not appear to have substantially lessened these goddesses' repute as magically responsive.

8

The Lady and
the Buddha

In early 2000, Thích Quảng Độ, a Buddhist monk who, since the end of the Vietnam War, has been in and out of detention and house arrest for his advocacy of an independent Sangha, wrote in a letter to Vietnamese government leaders,

> I would like to ask the Party and the Government to return the Unified Buddhist Church of Vietnam its right to operate freely in society. Besides the religious goal of this people-built Church to teach Buddhism to its followers, there is also the urgent need to stop the roaming epidemic of superstition, social vices, and moral degradation in our country, particularly among the youth. Religion should not be pretentious as in colorful ceremonies in recent days to attract tourists and generate masses-stupefying superstition. Religious teaching must be the free development of time-tested beliefs in harmony with modern civilized life. (Thích Quảng Độ 2000)

This appeal by a prominent member of the Buddhist Sangha was issued at a time when the Lady of the Realm was attracting a mass following, her rites and festival exemplifying the very qualities that this monk decried. Independent-minded clerics such as Thích Quảng Độ chafe against state restrictions that make it hard for the Sangha to counter the explicitly linked problems of vice and superstition. His epistle outlines an autonomous role for Buddhism: its time-tested creed to serve as a reliable moral compass, its simplicity and sobriety an antidote to social vices, and its teachings consistent with the realities of a modern society.

The rise of spirits such as the Lady of the Realm has troubled many of Vietnam's Buddhists as well. The practices surrounding such figures are criticized variously for their dubious morality, selfish materialism, and irrationality. On moral grounds some Buddhists regard beliefs in the patronage of powerful spirits and reference to a supernatural belief system as a worrying corollary of unethical activity. Sometimes it is thought that the only clear beneficiaries of such practices are those who claim a connection to the supernatural realm in order to profit from the credulity and misfortunes of others. From another perspective, the rise of such spirits is indicative of a lamentable disengagement from social commitment, and against this is counterposed a view of Buddhism as a vehicle for realizing a better society. Alternatively, it is said that to believe in spirits undermines confidence in one's own abilities, whereas Buddhism's emphasis on taking responsibility for one's own actions is better suited to developing a modern, wealthy, and orderly society. By regarding local beliefs, magic, and animism as backward or unrealistic, Vietnam's modernist Buddhists parallel the critique of such practices mounted by the Buddhists of Thailand, where Buddhism has become rationalized in the process of the emergence of the self-consciously modern Thai state (see Jackson 1999a).

These normative responses to spirit worship assess religious practice rationally in terms of its potential to deliver generalized moral or social benefits, a perspective that has been given historical expression in Vietnam in a number of socially engaged Buddhist movements.[1] Views of Buddhism that position it as an abstract, universal, rational creed can be situated historically in the context of the emergence of modernist reformism in many of the countries where Buddhism has taken hold. Such views became influential among Vietnam's Buddhists in the early twentieth century and have remained so (Nguyễn Thế Anh 1990, 112). They can be compared to recent developments in official Communist thinking, according to which religion has begun to be seen as a kind of functional aid to individuals and collectives in negotiating the uncertainties of existence in the modern world.

Nevertheless, in Vietnam, as elsewhere, Buddhism cannot be restricted to a kind of autonomous or transcendental force: an abstract moral code, a social program for right living, or a rationalist philosophy. Other forms of Buddhism are marked by an equally systematic if less absolute ethical standpoint, a more negotiated social practice, and fluid epistemology. Here I am interested in an alternative, less autonomous strand of religious practice, one whose morality is conditioned by relations of reciprocity, whose social field is considerably wider and more nebulous than humanity and includes anthropomorphized beings, and whose epistemology is more synthetic, whereby proofs are found retrospectively and confirm social practice. Conceptions of the Buddha as a materially powerful, responsive being are sometimes seen as an example of Buddhism's "localization" or accommodation to a Southeast Asian "animistic" substrate (see, e.g., Swearer 1995, 32). However, eschewing such an approach I argue here that such conceptions of spiritual power reflect contemporary social practice and situated ideologies. Perceptions of magical efficacy and spiritual responsiveness derive from notions of indebtedness and reciprocity that underpin contemporary social relations of exchange and negotiation. Transactions with spirits and powerful Buddhas represent a form of social engagement that is neither premodern nor disintegrative but an extension onto the spirit world of assumptions informing everyday life in present-day Vietnamese society.

The Virtues of the Buddha

The durian sellers on my street monopolized the most auspicious site in the neighborhood. Their stall was directly in front of the beautiful bas-relief tiger on the wall of the local communal house, respectfully called Grandfather Tiger (Ông Hổ). The senior family member at this site explained, "The tiger is highly responsive to prayers. If business is bad, all it takes is to feed the tiger a lump of meat (it likes bacon), and sales recommence immediately." He said that the police used to confiscate the fruit regularly and the family had been fined up to two hundred thousand dong for a single infraction. Now, he said, the family was no longer being harassed. In time, payments to the police had become a normal part of doing business. Disagreements were now limited to the amount of the bribe to be paid. Negotiations with the police were effected under the fierce yet protective watch of the tiger deity (figure 14). His marble gaze was more than enough to counter the bluster of a local cop.

However, Hiền, my Buddhist neighbor, did not share my appreciation of the scene. "People make offerings to spirits like that because what they are doing is illegal." She told me that the fruit was sold for a profit of up to a hundred percent. Any fruit that had spoiled was sold at cost. Furthermore, obviously rigged scales meant customers rarely got the weight they paid for. "Buy five pieces of fruit and you'll find yourself up to a kilogram short," she said. "They give money to the police regularly. Selling on the sidewalk is illegal and can only be done with police complicity. Don't feel too sorry for them. These people don't pay taxes, so it balances out."

Hiền was a university-trained teacher of first- and second-year primary school. "It doesn't pay nearly as well as business, but it allows me to live more peacefully," she told me. "It is not easy to balance business with morality in Vietnam. There are some fields in which a Buddhist should not

FIG. 14. The tiger deity with a bacon offering

work. For example, selling pharmaceuticals places you in a conflict of interest. You are forced to profit from the misery of others. The sicker your customer is, the better off you are. If you empathize with your customers, you will make no profit." She said that Buddhist doctrine makes for a better society: "Our local market used to be notorious for rigging the scales so that customers would receive less than they paid for. But then some Buddhists in the market started to say that this violated Buddhism's precepts against lying and theft. People could charge higher prices if the market demanded it, but they should not load the scales to gain a profit. In a very short time every person in the market dropped the practice of loading the scales. It doesn't happen there any more. This is a well-known story."

Hiền grouped together the making of offerings to powerful deities such as the tiger and the worship of the Lady of the Realm as superstitions. She said that as a Buddhist, she didn't believe in the goddess: "Buddhists don't believe in assistance from magical spirits. The Buddha taught us that we must alone take responsibility for our lives. If we do wrong there is no one but ourselves who can wash away our sins (rửa tội)." She held very dim views of the rise in popularity of the Châu Đốc goddess, which she attributed to a rise in immorality: "The people who make offerings to the so-called Lady of the

Realm are involved in all means of activities and request her help in endeavors both good and evil." Hiền believed that only by deference to Buddhism's laws of Karma could individuals influence their fate. As opposed to the technical manipulation of the power of amoral forces, she recommended the compassion *(từ bi)* and selfless assistance *(hỷ xả)* extended by the Buddha to those in need. For Hiền, Buddhism was a morally realistic religion, the doctrine of Karma helping to develop the requisite personal responsibility that makes society viable. As an educated and socially engaged laywoman she was keen to propagate Buddhism as a noble moral philosophy, its ethics providing the foundation for a better society.

Another Buddhist broadside against the goddess was delivered to me by followers of Hòa Hảo Buddhism (Phật Giáo Hòa Hảo), a movement with roots in the folk religions of the Mekong delta but equally heir to the reformist modernism that transformed Vietnamese Buddhism in the early twentieth century (Hue Tam Ho Tai 1983; P. Taylor 2001a). The subject of this goddess frequently came up in conversations with Hòa Hảo Buddhists, since the mountain on which her shrine sits is visible from the birthplace and heartland of the faith in the western Mekong delta. Yet they gave little credit to her. According to one follower living near the shrine, "All sorts of mysterious stories are told about her origins; however, we don't believe them." Critical of those who place hopes in such spirits for miraculous assistance, most Hòa Hảo Buddhists consider that doing good works is a more reliable way to secure oneself a better existence. The socially engaged activities prescribed by members of the faith include community development initiatives such as constructing bridges and schools, humanitarian efforts such as giving out free medicine or helping a destitute neighbor rebuild his house, and even martial defense of the nation. When I put to one Hòa Hảo Buddhist that the goddess' popularity seemed to confirm that she was answering some societal need, she countered, "People come from all over to make offerings to her, but have you noticed that the people from the local area do not believe in her? If she is truly efficacious, why are there so many poor people in the area surrounding her shrine? And anyway now the numbers of visitors are declining. Gradually people are learning that there is no basis to this belief."

While welfare-minded Buddhists are critical of the socially disengaged dimensions of goddess worship, other Buddhists see faith in the spirits as inadequate to the needs of the individual in the modern world. Phan, a seller in Dakao market, held these sentiments. He had heard many stories about her but wasn't convinced there was any truth to claims of her magical assistance. He countered, "People go to seek the assistance of this spirit or another, but if in truth one of these figures opened its mouth and assented to their requests, people would run away in terror! It is a mistake to think that any outside factor can help us escape poverty or become rich. It is up to us to help ourselves." He said the only proven way to gain success was through the work of one's hands and the application of one's own intelligence to resolve one's situation: "Realistically speaking, the government cannot be relied on to help people out of their difficulties and neither can the spirits." This view was common among those working in a market setting where the state is more often associated with petty extractions than with providing a social safety net. On the other hand, he thought Buddhism is of value for it counsels self-reliance, a code attuned to present social and economic realities and the absence of a system of social welfare. For individuals caught in a difficult and turbulent existence, Phan saw it too as an aesthetic discipline, a path to achieve peace, poise, and equilibrium in one's dealings with fellow humans. Provided one imbibed its teachings in small measure and did not become passionately caught up in rituals, incense, and chants or retreat from the world into monasticism, this layman thought the Buddha's teaching was a reliable charter for success in the urban commercial world.

Buddha Goddesses and Vow-taking Tigers

In their discussions with me, Buddhist monks and nuns have spent considerable time drawing distinctions between Buddhism and the religion of the spirits *(đạo thần)*, the former considered more realistic *(thực tế)*, the latter a distinct set of beliefs often reduced to the pejorative term "superstition." However, laypeople in religious traditions do not always adhere to categorical distinctions between religions to the same extent as clerics—or anthropologists for that matter. Indeed, popularly, the spirits are often interpreted through the framework of Buddhism.

The durian sellers who negotiated the tiger spirit's watchful services for a few strips of bacon considered themselves devout Buddhists, and they regularly made offerings in Buddhist pagodas. They also made offerings to the Lady of the Realm, who they asserted to be a Buddhist deity, referring to her as Lady Buddha and calling her shrine a pagoda. Many Buddhist laypeople regard such spirits as part of the pantheon of Buddhist beings, collapsing the distinctions elsewhere maintained between types of spiritual beings.[2] The Châu Đốc goddess is sometimes described as an incarnation of the Bodhisattva Kuan Yin and vice-versa. Although the Lady of the Realm receives sumptuous offerings of roast pork, her shrine, like those of other deities, is sheathed in a panoply of Buddhist symbolism, including Buddha statues, images of turtles and cranes drawn from tales illustrating Buddhist precepts, swastikas, and invocations to Amida, attesting to her incorporation into a Buddhist framework.

Despite being seen by many to fall short of the moral ideals of monastic Buddhism, granting requests that some purists feel cannot be enjoyed in good faith, spirits such as the Lady of the Realm are commonly regarded as keepers of morality. Like Buddha, who features in most people's minds as the embodiment of ethical principles, she is thought to oversee a code of moral conduct. Popular conceptions of her qualities extend to enforcement of a moral code: she punishes crimes, childish misbehavior, violations of commercial ethics, and infidelity. Transactions with her are guided by an ethic of reciprocity. If a petitioner does not make a promised repayment, she or he will surely meet misfortune. If the goddess does not deliver results, support for her will be withdrawn. While very much a variety of this-worldly retributive justice, this is no different from one of the most popular interpretations of the Buddhist notion of Karma, which sees misdeeds punished in this life, not the next. And indeed, just as stealing something from Her Ladyship's shrine will attract swift punishment, so too will misappropriating funds from a Buddhist pagoda bring down afflictions.[3]

The Lady of the Realm's power is also equated with that of Buddha. As one devotee of both put it, "Her Ladyship is like Buddha, in that she helps us with everything we ask for."[4] Buddhism in Vietnam includes such beliefs as faith in the Buddha's magical potency and divinatory capabilities; Kuan Yin's quality as a compassionate listener, savior, and provider of children, health, wealth, and domestic harmony; and the pagoda guardian spirit Kim Cường's ability to confer physical invulnerability. Just as many draw no distinction between Buddhism and forms of spirit worship, so do many consider the full spectrum of powers manifested in the spirit world to fall within the refuge provided by the Buddha.[5]

Some Catholics too regard the practice of spirit worship as Buddhist. Sometimes this observation is made critically, with Buddhism accused of sponsoring immoral practices. Yet precisely because they interpret Buddhism so broadly, many of these critics also have an appreciation of positive aspects of spirit worship that Buddhist monks and nuns might not normally accept as Buddhist. One such critic was a cigarette seller whom I met each morning. I asked her if she ever went to make offerings in Châu Đốc. I thought this likely, considering the patronage given by the Châu Đốc goddess to small-business proprietors like her. "No," she replied. "I am a Catholic. That is a Buddhist practice. The Buddhists who sell around here go down to Châu Đốc every year. I stay at home and pray to Holy Mother Mary and to God." Although she distinguished herself as Catholic, the rites in which she engaged were comparable to those made to the Lady of the Realm. She said she made offerings of fruit, flowers, candles, and incense to Mary each night when she got home from work. She didn't offer water, explaining, "that is a Buddhist practice." I asked if she requested anything when she made her offerings. Slightly embarrassed, she said that she regularly requested good health, good business, and well-being for her family. She also prayed to become more like the Holy Mother and live according to her example: "Praying clears my spirit of the day's cares. So does going to church, which I do every week. People at church trust each other. Those who go there are only trying to lead better lives."

She said that by comparison, the morality of many of those who went to Châu Đốc was dubious: "I am not like those people who go to Châu Đốc and pray for money. Those people who go there pray for all sort of things. Most of them ask Her Ladyship to make them rich. Furthermore, you can't trust anyone at Châu Đốc. I have heard there are people who steal and pick pockets there." She said, to the contrary, that good fortune would only come to people who did the right thing by other people: "Do not sin and do good deeds and Heaven will provide." Given this bleak view of Her Ladyship's constituency I asked the cigarette seller if the Lady of the Realm was one of those immoral beings who granted whatever people asked, be it good or bad. She recoiled. "I'm not saying that Her Ladyship is bad," she clarified. "Her Ladyship is good. She wants everyone to live morally. It is just the people who go to her who are sometimes bad." "Why does she help such people?" I asked. She replied, "Her Ladyship is responsive; that is why people go to her. I myself believe she helps people. The only reason I don't go is because it is too expensive, being so far away. And then there is the question of finding a place to stay in a strange place. Plus, it is not my religion."

The lines she drew between religious practices were not overly sharp. Certainly she did not disparage the power and moral standing of the goddess. "So you do you believe in the responsive powers of spirits?" I asked her. "Of course I do," she replied. After a moment's reflection, she asked me a question: "Did you know that tigers are magically responsive? For instance, they can cure headaches." Thinking of the durian sellers, I told her I had heard as much. She continued, "I will tell you a true story, which happened to an acquaintance of mine. One day, when visiting the zoo, she stopped at the tiger's cage. She was suffering from a bad headache. The tiger reached its paw right through the bars and placed it on her head. She was wearing a conical hat at the time so she wasn't wounded by its claws. But the headache went away instantly." Her neighbor, a chewing-gum seller, confirmed this to be in all likelihood true. She said that in the pagoda of the reclining Buddha, on a mountain to the north, near Phan Thiết, there was a live tiger that had taken vows—that is, he had entered the Sangha. He ate only vegetarian food, she said, and walked freely around the pagoda, not harming a single living being. She said the tiger was at least two hundred years old.

Patrolling the Faith

This level of creativity and blurring of boundaries between faiths creates problems for Buddhist monks and nuns, who are forced to deal daily with a range of beliefs and practices that they hold as not Buddhist. Yet it is equally true that the Buddha is also regarded as a potent spiritual being, the likenesses of which many Buddhist laypeople treat as material manifestations of power, as beings with which they can negotiate for diverse ends.

Hương, my Catholic neighbor had had significant informal exposure to Buddhist teaching and ceremonies, for she was frequently inside the Buddhist pagoda next to her house. She said the rich rites and symbolism of Buddhism made it seem closer to Catholicism than to Protestantism, whose lack of ritual elaboration gave that faith a "sad" and austere quality. One afternoon, when we were sitting in her alley talking, percussive sounds coming from inside the pagoda indicated that the evening chants were about to begin. As the rhythmic beating of the drum swelled, Hương invited me inside: "Shall we listen to the chanting of sutras?" Inside, the youngest nun, Thanh, welcomed us, showed us to a cluster of seats, and offered us some cold water. She returned to the chanting rite. Hương and I sat together, our bare feet spread on the cool tiles, absorbing the sound of the bells, drums, and cymbals that comprised the overture to the chant.

As we spoke, three elderly women from the neighborhood came in, covered themselves in gray cotton wraps, and went in to join in the chanting. Each of them paused and several times caressed the gentle, smiling figure of the bodhisattva Kuan Yin, standing in the center of the pagoda's darkened interior room. The thousand-armed bodhisattva Avalokitésvara, who in South and Central Asian iconographic traditions and also in Japan is depicted as a male, has been feminized in the process of transmission of Buddhism to China and Vietnam, becoming the slender and kindly female human figure of the Goddess of Mercy. I indicated the sight to Thanh, the younger of the two nuns. "Is Kuan Yin responsive to those who believe in her?" I asked. "Of course," she replied. "She appears wherever people call out to her for assistance. One aspect of her responsiveness is that she appears in manifold forms. Indeed one example of this is that 'she' is a 'he.' The image of her as a gentle, kind woman is Kuan Yin's manifestation as a mother. She also appears as a fierce protector deity to protect Buddha from evil."

I asked the nun if there were any benefits to be accrued by praying to Buddha. Did Buddha reward prayers for money, for instance? The young nun smiled at my question: "Buddha provides spiritual not material rewards. Our circumstances, whether rich or poor, are a fate that cannot be avoided. The Buddha taught that in life, every living being suffers. Buddhism opens one's heart to recognize the suffering of others. It makes us compassionate and helps us forget our own problems." She said one prays to Buddha to become a better person—to learn how to avoid bad deeds and do good: "This is the only way to make up for demerits accrued in past lives." Hers was a view that saw human beings embedded in a temporal framework that exceeded one lifetime and removed the onus from the present by attributing influence to factors such as fate and previous karmic demerits. It counseled patience in the light of transcendental processes.

I asked the nun, "Why do people stroke Kuan Yin's image?" She replied, "Because their respect for Buddha is so great, they think that merely touching the statue can bring benefits to them." She indicated the elderly women, who, having stroked the bodhisattva, smoothed their palms over their hair, face, and arms: "People believe that stroking their heads in that way will increase their intelligence and knowledge *(trí tuệ)*. It is a belief many people hold." I asked the young nun if she thought the practice was bad. She said, "It really isn't bad. It only comes from passionate belief in Buddha. As long as people aren't incited to kill or steal, it can not be called truly bad."

Tạo, the elder of the pagoda's two resident nuns, interrupted our conversation, an edge of scorn in her voice: "In fact, the statue is just stone and paint. It is not magically responsive. That is not part of Buddhist belief. The Buddha cannot bring health, wealth, children, peace, or whatever it is that people ask for." I asked her, "Is that idea what is called 'superstition'?" She replied, "No. Superstition is going to spirits like the Lady of the Realm."

"What about stroking the Buddha image?"

"Well, yes, that too."

"Why do people hold this belief?" "Because they don't listen to what we tell them. Or they are not interested in listening."

I asked Tạo what she thought of the phenomenon. "It is bad of course," she responded. "It is untrue. The Buddha does not help people in that way." I asked, "But if many people believe this, how can it be called bad?" She replied, "There is a logical explanation why this belief persists. People go before a Buddha image asking for assistance, say, with improving their economic situation. Praying for assistance helps them focus on the problem. They concentrate on the issue. That takes some energy. It generates energy for them to go out into their lives and solve their problem. Actually, if they then succeed, it is thanks to their own efforts, not to the power of the statue."

The Significance of Bathing the Buddha

Buddha images become the focus of religious attention by the Sangha during the ceremonies that mark the anniversary of the Buddha's birth. In a rite known popularly as the Buddha bathing ritual *(lễ tắm Phật)*, the statues depicting the Buddha at birth are ritually cleansed in perfumed water. There are, however, significant differences between the way the Sangha and laypeople regard this rite. To members of the Sangha the rite is a ceremonial renewal of the tenets of the faith. To many laypeople, the rite is charged with magical portent, and the water that is used to bathe the Buddha image is considered to have efficacious power. This causes a dilemma for members of the Sangha who conduct the ceremony. However, aware that many of their constituents hold such beliefs, they may attempt to rationalize them as consistent with a Buddhist orientation or flexibly distance themselves from them.

In the 2,542d year of the Buddhist era (1998), I celebrated the Buddha's birthday in the small back-alley pagoda in my neighborhood. There I spoke to a thirty-year-old monk who had come to preside over the commemorations. I asked him about the significance of the rite. He said it celebrated the emergence of Buddhism, a doctrine that addressed humankind's larger spiritual needs. When I asked him about the key insights of the faith he spoke about how Buddhism taught that one had to help oneself and that reliance on the external world was unsatisfactory. He said much of what went for happiness is illusory: "People think happiness is having a wife, buying nice clothes, earning lots of money, building a nice home. That is not true happiness, which only comes if we recognize that such things are illusory and our existence impermanent."

The pagoda was full of laywomen preparing food for the vegetarian meal that was to follow the morning's rite of bathing the Buddha image. We sat in the reception area, sipping tea. The pagoda was slowly filling up. Over the monk's shoulder, I saw women lighting incense and offering it to the tenderly smiling goddess of mercy. I commented that Kuan Yin seemed especially loved by people following Buddhism. He agreed that, indeed, Kuan Yin, known as the Hearer of the World's Cries, might be even more venerated than the historical Buddha, the male figure Sakyamuni: "She resembles our mother. Here in Vietnam we say, 'A mother's heart is as broad as the Pacific Ocean.' In other words, a mother loves her children unconditionally. A mother's love would be undiminished, even if her child committed some heinous crime. She might scold her child, but she would never reject the child. Fathers do not love their children as much. They might give them money and provide for their material needs. However, if they committed some offense, a father's judgment would be more harsh. He might even recommend that the child accept reeducation or imprisonment by the state."

Behind him, an elderly woman finished her prayers, clasped the feet of the bodhisattva in her hands, and rubbed them briskly over her head and upper body. She was joined by another laywoman, who did the same. I repeated the question I had asked of the pagoda's senior nun the previous day: "Why is it that sometimes people stroke Buddha images and then stroke their heads and clothes?" He smiled a little. "People stroke the image of Buddha to gain some benefit from the Buddha, which helps them satisfy some need or desire, such as to cure an illness or to get well. However, the practice is not consistent with Buddhism."

We were sitting on the unyielding wooden chairs on one side of the back room of the pagoda in which stood the image of the bodhisattva. The monk glanced across at the women and then shifted his position to sit beside me, where he had them in direct view. He lowered his voice, occasionally glancing up, and continued, "Actually the belief that one can benefit by stroking Buddha images is a form of superstition. People do that because they do not fully understand the teaching of the Buddha. A Buddha image is merely a representation of Buddha. According to Buddhism, Buddha it is only to be found here in the heart of each person." He tapped his chest with his fingers. "People think that hunger, money worries, and strife in the family are forms of suffering. That is true but that is ordinary, everyday suffering. Everyone experiences it. True suffering is not knowing if we will ever escape the cycle of reincarnation, which deposits us at the end of a life of suffering back into another life of the same." The monk's hushed delivery brought to mind a comment by Jane Bunnag, writing of monks in Thailand who, although skeptical of lay stories about the power of Buddha replicas, could not speak out for fear of losing their lay support (Bunnag 1973, 23). The monk looked at the women before him again and changed tack: "Then again, stroking a Buddha image or propitiating a spirit helps people spiritually. It takes their mind off the problem they are experiencing and gives them hope." He smiled: "Just like my sitting here talking with you has taken my mind off the toothache I have been experiencing since last night."

While we were speaking, the monk's junior assistant was preparing for the commencement of the ceremony. Donning his robe, he came over and gently announced to his senior that preparations were complete. The bathing ceremony was preceded by a period of chants, led by the two visiting monks. The older monk chanted the sutras from a printed book, his quavering voice amplified by a crackling sound system. The congregation followed with refrains and prostrations. The pagoda's resident nuns played supporting roles, intermittently beating the gong, the bell, and the stylized wooden fish. Then the bathing rite commenced. The leading monk poured a cup of perfumed boiled water over an image of the infant Buddha standing on a lotus-flower pedestal; the statue had been garlanded with flowers and placed in a large plastic basin to catch the run off. Following this, the second monk, the resident nuns of the pagoda, and the entire congregation took turns scooping up water and flower petals from the basin to pour back over the small image. After more chants and guided prostrations, the ceremony ended abruptly, with the leading monk switching off the microphone and stepping away from the altar.

During the ritual, a group of neighborhood urchins competed with each other for space on the pagoda floor. They prayed with exaggerated fidelity, eyes darting to assess the efforts of their rivals. They elaborately parodied the prostrations of their elder neighbors, fought for elbow space, and karate-chopped their neighbors when their foreheads were down on the floor, their necks exposed. One of the women who had been preparing food before the ceremony came in the side door, crept up to a side altar, and, with raised eyebrows, communicated to a nun that she sought some of the freshly planted incense from the altar to take home to her own altar. She took three partly burned sticks, then left.

After the bathing was complete, the laywomen pressed forward in a scrum, seeking a cup of the lustral water lying in the basin around the island formed by the infant Buddha. One woman sculled an entire cup as she stood by the altar, then refilled it before moving away. Another took her sacred acquisition in one hand, dragged her child outside with her other hand, and proceeded to give the protesting child a vigorous wipe-over with the perfumed water. Rubbing bath water over her child, she said, would make him grow up tall and strong. Others queued at the altar to scoop up cupfuls of the water to fill empty bottles to take home later. The junior nun and the young male novice were quick to get in too, and, with their spoils of liquid runoff from the Buddha's statue, they toasted each other in some personal ritual of their own: thumbs up and down the hatch. When I asked why he drank the water, the novice said, "Drinking the Buddha's bath water stimulates and increases your intelligence and makes you healthy."

A minute after the ceremony, while the bath-water-drinking frenzy was at its most intense, I looked around and noticed that the monks who had presided over the ceremony had disappeared. With the exception of the novice and me, the downstairs area of the pagoda had reverted to an entirely female domain. The resident nuns presided over the rites of hospitality, serving food to all of their visitors. The food was first laid out on a central altar honoring the pagoda's founding monk and patrons. Then it was removed and placed before the older women, seated at two large dining tables. As guests finished and left, serving dishes were reprovisioned, and another wave of guests was invited to fill the vacated spaces. Last to eat were three local laywomen who had been keeping the supply of food flowing and the neighboring family of Catholics who, as usual, treated the pagoda as an extension of their home. They occupied an entire table and ate steadily and copiously, consuming a meal they would find hard to come by on an ordinary day. Finally, a large spread of leftovers was laid on for the neighborhood urchins, who had continued to fight and play after the ceremony. Some of them were still damp from fierce battles with the Buddha's bathwater. There was not much fighting going on now. The table was groaning with food, and the nuns were filling the children's eating bowls from the serving dishes.

During the laypeople's competition for the sacred bathwater, the visiting monks passed time in a small upstairs room. Despite the doctrinal awkwardness of the practices that succeeded the bathing rite, it was not in question that the monks should be there. As Bunnag observed of the way monks in Thailand approached such a dilemma, even the *bhikkhu* who "realized that merit-making was irrelevant to the central religious goal could scarcely refuse requests to perform ceremonies for the lay community on whom he depended for material support" (1973, 23). The monks' retreat upstairs allowed them to tactfully distance themselves from aspects of the bathing ritual that contradicted their own views. In a like manner, never during the entire day did the monks ever directly contradict a layperson's belief in the material powers of the Buddha image even though they were explicit in conversation with me that Buddhism did not encompass such practices. Although the nuns and monks disagreed with the beliefs of the laypeople, they rationalized the lay focus on the Buddha's image as a hallmark of respect, a symptom of passionate faith, or a meditative or psychological prop. These rationalizations flexibly accommodated lay practices while preserving a semblance of integrity and consistency for their own beliefs as well.

Buddhist Exegesis in a Creative Vein

The monks frequently visited this pagoda and the nuns exchanged visits with them in their own pagoda in order to support each other's activities, meet, study, converse, and solve problems. They also attended classes, read learned commentaries and *Từ Bi*, the magazine of the Buddhist Association, listened to taped sermons *(giảng đạo)*, and received visits from other nuns and monks. Interactions of this kind, taking place in pagodas all over the country, have helped to standardize the thinking among the widely dispersed members of Vietnam's Mahayana Buddhist Sangha. However, not all members of the Sangha adhere to the party line. Differences of views about the supposed invalidity or unreality of "superstitious" beliefs can be found even within the same pagoda.

After the ceremony and meal concluded, Hạnh, one of the resident nuns in this pagoda, was sitting forlornly by herself downstairs. Sponsored by a wealthy overseas layperson, she had been studying for her basic Buddhist degree in a Mekong delta city and had only returned to the pagoda because she had injured her leg. When I approached her, she awkwardly tried to get up with her crutches, to offer me some fruit. I told her I had eaten more than enough and just wanted to talk. I wanted to know her views on whether belief in the goddess the Lady of the Realm fell within the ambit of the Buddhist religion, as many devotees of the goddess were inclined to think. She replied, "No, those beliefs lie outside of Buddhist belief *(ngoài tín ngưỡng Phật giáo)*. The Lady of the Realm is a superstition." While her reply accorded with the views of the other occupants of the pagoda, this designation was awarded confidently and forthrightly, in contrast with the monk's earlier lowered voice and his furtive glances at the group of laywomen. But equally it was devoid of the judgmental comments that typically accompanied any belief called by this term. For this young nun, superstition meant simply that which lay outside the Buddhist religion. This did not mean it was false. She explained in a nonjudgmental way, "Many people make offerings to the Lady of the Realm because she is responsive to their prayers."

The nun then told me a version of the story of the origins of the Châu Đốc goddess that I had not formerly heard, even from the goddess' most impassioned and well-informed followers:

> A long time ago, a Chinese man in An Giang province found a small round stone. He took it home and carved it into the image of a woman. The instant her facial features emerged, he was struck blind on the spot. The man left the image behind and returned to China. He gave birth to a son, who rose to become the king of China. This king's son and grandson successively held the position of king. Back in An Giang province, over the period that these three generations of kings ruled over China, the image carved by the Chinese man grew bigger and bigger. The goddess that you see down in Châu Đốc was originally the same

circumference as my bracelet. [She showed it to me, to give me an idea of the scope of the miracle.] Now she is bigger than me. As a result of the spiritual power this demonstrates, many people go there to seek her assistance, and she helps them in a range of problems. But it is a belief that lies outside of Buddhism.

Even while partitioning off beliefs in the goddess as superstition, the nun not only accepted the assumptions of popular practices; she invested them with new content. Her comments indicated that not all in the Sangha were entirely given over to a rationalist, self-affirming concept of Buddhism or to sectarian chauvinism. Indeed, although she was a representative of the Sangha, she conveyed the most enlarged estimation of the goddess' capacities and of the geographical scope of her powers that I had yet heard.

Hạnh studied a photo I had with me of the Lady of the Realm and remarked on the fierce look on the goddess' face. She compared the fierce female visage with that of the serenely smiling Sakyamuni Buddha, the statue venerated on her pagoda's main altar. Her comparative observation turned into an informal seminar for those of us sitting in the pagoda's reception area: the pagoda's young male novice; Thủy, a poor Buddhist neighbor; and Thủy's Catholic neighbor. The neighbors were sitting on the cool tiled floor with their children. Hạnh said that Sakyamuni's face showed the charity and the unconditional love that was central to Buddha's relationship with humankind. By contrast, the Lady of Châu Đốc's face was unkind. The nun told us that spirits like her were less compassionate, demanding offerings of expensive clothes and meat in return for their assistance: "You have to kill to earn their help. In the past, these spirits even demanded human sacrifices from those they had helped."

Thủy took the photo and gazed at it. "Yes, look how fierce she looks," she said, showing it to her Catholic neighbor. "Once you promise to return to her shrine, you had better not break your promise." Her neighbor frowned in appreciation. "That is why people go to the shrine of the goddess in Nhà Bè district," Thủy explained to me. "It is nearer. Châu Đốc is too expensive to get to, yet people dare not break their promise to her. I once went to Nhà Bè myself," she told Hạnh. "Some of the robes people have given her cost two taels of gold each; that's a thousand dollars U.S.," she explained. "There are cabinets and cabinets full of robes offered her. It just goes to prove how powerful she is."

The shrine to the Lady of the Realm in Nhà Bè district, about twenty kilometers downstream from the center of Ho Chi Minh City, had been built in 1993. It was an upgrade of a smaller shrine to the Five Elements popularly known as the Five Mothers. The rebuilding of the shrine capitalized on the fever for the Châu Đốc goddess that had swept the city in the early 1990s. According to its builder, the Lady of the Realm appeared to him in a dream saying that the people of the eastern part of southern Vietnam lacked a place to venerate her. He found this neglected shrine in a desolate patch of swamp by the river and soon had enshrined a large statue of the esteemed goddess in a revamped brick and concrete shrine. The Five Mothers were enshrined on the same altar, although on a lower step and in more diminutive form. To the rear of the shrine were displayed framed photographs of the statue of the goddess in Châu Đốc. Although some locals referred to the shrine as a branch of the Châu Đốc shrine, the custodian was at pains to point out the many advantages that his shrine had over the distant one in Châu Đốc and emphasized the high prices, disorder, crime, and confusion that pertained at that site. Certainly many people from Ho Chi Minh City attended Nhà Bè because of its proximity to the city.

Thủy told Hạnh that the image of the Châu Đốc goddess found in Nhà Bè was responsive to virtually any kind of request. She nudged her Catholic neighbor: "Do you know those two lesbians living down in Alley Twelve? One of them is called Seven, isn't that right?" Her neighbor assented: "Yes, Sister Seven, that's her." Thủy continued to the stunned Hạnh, "They have a child who addresses them as 'father' and 'mother.'" Thủy continued her story: "Those two were formerly childless so they went to Nhà Bè and they asked the Lady there to give them a child. They were able to adopt a daughter after that. But there was something unusual about her. As she grew bigger and bigger, they grew richer and richer. Now those two are really rolling in it! Their daughter is five years old and truly beautiful but would you believe it, as time goes by, she acts more and more like a lesbian herself!"

Thủy asked her Catholic neighbor if she had ever heard the story of the Lady of Châu Đốc. She turned to the nun and asked her to tell the story. Hạnh assented, retelling the story of the Chinese man in the Vietnamese province of An Giang who had sculpted the image of a woman from a stone. In the retelling she added some new details. She said that the stone found by the man had originally been shaped into a male likeness. The sculptor was in the process of rehewing it into female form when he was struck blind. "This was another reason the face looks so mean," Hạnh told us, gravely. "It was still unfinished when he lost his vision." She explained that the sculptor's descendants' elevation to the throne of China represented the Lady's repayment of her debt to him for releasing her. She added that after they had ruled China for three generations his descendants returned to the site in Châu Đốc, where they found that the image had grown to immense proportions. She said that it was they who had built the shrine in gratitude to her.

Apart from anything else, Hạnh's story was a remarkable tribute to the power of the goddess. She was a kingmaker, a dynastic creator, and the power behind the throne of no less a country than China. From the vantage point of this small backstreet pagoda, the goddess of Châu Đốc was as big as they came. Hạnh's narrative gifts kept us spellbound. This young Buddhist nun had never laid eyes on the Lady of the Realm, relying for her conviction about the goddess' powers on the stories she herself had heard laypeople tell. Hạnh explained she had also heard that many people wanting to escape the country had gone to Châu Đốc to ask for Her Ladyship's assistance. When successful, they returned to her shrine to repay her. Those who couldn't make it sent money back to their relatives to repay the debt on their behalf.

Thủy, who was listening closely, marveled, "Even overseas they are scared of not paying her back." Hanh continued, "The Lady of Châu Đốc is jealous—so much so that she wants people to drop their worship of other spirits and follow only her." Thủy responded with passionate conviction: "You are right there. She has seized a monopoly over the whole country. She has forced other spirits to accept it when people worship her in their pagodas, and she expects people to make their best offerings to her!"

The fate of the Five Mothers in Nhà Bè, demoted by the Châu Đốc deity, was only one example of this process. During the mid-1990s the name the Lady of Châu Đốc was so commonly on people's lips that when I asked what spirit was enshrined in this or that temple, I was frequently told in an indiscriminating way that it was the Châu Đốc goddess. I asked Hạnh if she had any examples of her own to give of the goddess' jealous monopolization. She replied that in neighboring Bình Dương province, on the first month of every lunar year, people welcomed the Lady of Châu Đốc into her pagoda in the district capital. Because Bình Dương is home to an important temple to the goddess Thiên Hậu, I asked the nun if she was absolutely sure that she had the right location. She insisted this was the case, saying, "Thiên Hậu must be the local name for the Lady of Châu Đốc." She said the New Year festival in Bình Dương was the most important event on the religious calendar of residents from Ho Chi Minh City itself and surrounds: "On the first full moon of the year, people parade an image of the Lady all around the provincial capital, through the streets and the market and then back to the pagoda. At that time the streets are so jammed with traffic it is impossible to get to the pagoda. If you want to see this you have to arrive the night before and sleep over in the pagoda." To Hạnh, Thiên Hậu was just a local manifestation of the Châu Đốc deity. The famed southern Chinese goddess had been swallowed by the expansionist Mekong delta princess.[6] It appears from this conversation that the process of monopolization she decried was advanced by her own interpretive slippage.

Thủy said that the Lady of Châu Đốc was also worshiped on the coast in Long Hải during the festival to Dinh Cô. Hạnh said she had not heard about this latter goddess. Thủy elaborated: "The Palace Damsel is very powerful. My God, on the day she is welcomed into her palace, the crowds are enormous! The place is packed with boats and buses, motorbikes and cars. There are people everywhere. You cannot move—even on the beach." The novice slipped in a brief explanation on Hạnh's and my behalf: "The Palace Damsel's story is that she jumped to her death from a boat rather than marry a Chinese man." He looked at his seniors. "That's the Vietnamese woman for you!" he concluded in admiring nationalistic tones.

Hạnh nodded with interest and then turned and explained to me, "The various spirits of this kind are people who, for whatever reason, have been unable to escape this incarnation into the next. They have been stuck with the desires, memories, and demerits accumulated in past lives and are unable to make amends and progress. Thus they are, unlike Buddha, full of sensual desires. They will grant whatever wish is requested, whether good or bad, in return for appeasement of their appetites. This is unlike Buddha, who will only do good deeds requested of him." According to the nun this karmic difference explained the absolute nature of the assistance Buddha offered in contrast to the more conditional help offered by powerful spirits.

The Value of Buddhist Responsiveness

Hạnh's role in this conversation was illuminating. Although an authorized exponent of Buddhist distinctions, Hạnh, by regaling her audience with tales of the miracles and identity of the spirits, was nevertheless integral to the propagation of esoteric knowledge and the complex intertwining of beliefs. Her case suggests that not only do members of the Sangha accommodate nonprescribed views; they are sometimes swept into the eddying currents of local interpretation and can play a vital role in the generation and promotion of unorthodox understandings. Some might conclude that all Hạnh's case demonstrates is a lack of doctrinal education on the part of a relatively junior nun, hence denying that the Sangha would endorse such heterodoxy. On the other hand, some educated laypeople do not consider Buddhist clergy who belittle spirit worship and other manifestations of magical efficacy to be in tune with the faith. Monks and nuns who claim that belief in spiritually responsive beings is inconsistent with Buddhism are sometimes regarded as having alternative agendas.

For a critical reflection on the Vietnamese Sangha, I am indebted to two Buddhist laywomen from the Mekong delta who worked as saleswomen in a Ho Chi Minh City camera shop. Tiên said that Buddhism was a religion that came to Vietnam from India. It provided a basic moral code, a worldview, and an overview of the nature of existence. Buddhism was not concerned with the details and concerns of mundane advancement in this life. Philosophically, immoral acts committed in former incarnations could only be counteracted by moral actions in this life. The result would be a better rebirth in a future life. On the other hand, spirits such as the Lady of the Realm were people who had actually existed in history and who had lived in that region. People built shrines to them out of respect and the belief that their spirit continued to exercise protection over their domain. In this sense, she said, these were two different traditions. In reality, however, the distinction was not so cut and dried. Both Buddhism and spirit worship shared a belief in assistance from powerful beings.

Yến, her companion, said that Buddhism had many sects and that it didn't necessarily impose a single orthodoxy on the question of the magical efficacy of Buddha images: "You will find a more accommodating set of opinions if you go away from the beaten track to remote pagodas on mountain tops. Real examples of Buddhist heterodoxy can also be found in rural areas beyond the city." She cited Sam Mountain, where the Lady of the Realm is enshrined, as an instance of this. Yến thought that the jealousy of monks and nuns could not be ruled out as a factor motivating some of the judgmental opinions that had been voiced about the worship of such popular spirits. Shrines such as the one in Châu Đốc were sometimes considered a sham, but she said that questioning the efficacy of the spirit enshrined therin was not a legitimate criticism for a Buddhist to make.

One of the reasons spirit shrines were now so popular, according to these laywomen, was that Buddhism itself had been corrupted by too much wealth. The 1990s was a time of massive construction, rebuilding, and renovation of pagodas. While accurate statistics are difficult to obtain, it is clear that overseas Vietnamese, wanting to thank Buddha for helping establish themselves abroad, played a significant role in this rejuvenation. Pagodas also received lavish gifts in return for serving as the repository for the remains of the dead, and monks were rewarded for staging funerals and death commemorations for those with wealthy overseas relatives. Businesspeople from East Asia, at the forefront of trade and investment in Vietnam in the 1990s and sharing a Mahayana Buddhist tradition, invested lavishly in the renovation of pagodas as part of the process of winning good relations with local partners and authorities. Wealthy locals presented gifts to pagodas in gratitude for Buddha's assistance. For pilgrims and domestic tourists, pagodas were places of accommodation and important stopover points in their tours around the country.

The unprecedented showering of wealth upon Buddhist pagodas, Tiên complained, means it is increasingly hard to find members of the Sangha who observe the injunction to live simply and exercise compassion for others: "Monks and nuns have developed the habit of traveling in luxurious air-conditioned buses and by car and spending their time in comfortable leisure. The lives of today's religious orders are truly grand *(sang trọng)*. This has caused many people to lose respect for them, as such living is not consistent with the religion's central concern for the suffering of others." Yến agreed, saying that even though monks' or nuns' vows might compel them to eat vegetarian food, they could still eat luxurious delicacies. Monks and nuns could be seen in expensive vegetarian restaurants, eating to the point of discomfort, while people were starving outside. Tiên clarified: "That is not to say that these days people believe in Buddhism any less. But Buddhism increasingly is a faith that people hold in their hearts and whose rites are observed only at home before household altars."

For this reason, they thought, in recent years people were turning away from Buddhist pagodas and toward the spirits enshrined in temples and shrines for assistance with their life's problems. As Yến argued, "It is because people have lost respect for the Buddhist orders that the magical responsiveness of temples and shrines has increased. Those places generally don't have an extensive structure of organization. At most, there is one person who sounds the bell or a guardian to take care of the temple's possessions." This explanation underestimated the size of shrine committees such as that in Châu Đốc, which many times exceeded the resident population of an average pagoda. Nevertheless, her comments reflected disapproval of a religious order that had acquired the means to detach itself from the needs of the faithful. In their disenchantment with the arrogance of institutional Buddhism, these Buddhist laywomen believed that the teachers of the faith were losing touch with its real tenets.

According to them, a more inclusive view of their faith was now only to be found among members of the Sangha living in poorer pagodas. Both women told me they tried whenever they could to visit such places. In recent years rural pagodas have been increasingly sought after by Ho Chi Minh City's urban middle-class Buddhists, who travel to them on weekends to perform meritorious acts *(công quả)* of renovation and refurbishment. The smaller and more destitute the pagoda the better goes the common observation. This preference is justified on the grounds that these places are truly needy, but the depth of the need is also is thought to amplify the karmic merit that accrues to those who meritoriously rescue these humble sanctuaries of the Buddha from rustic oblivion. Such acts are held to bring blessings *(phước)* to the meritorious, including peace of mind, health, and material advancement. The authentic reflection of Buddhist doctrine that is sometimes attributed to such remote places by urban Buddhists may represent the ready compliance of isolated and poverty-stricken members of the rural Sangha to accede to the diverse views and wishes of the affluent and enthusiastic teams of urban merit makers that venture forth weekly into the countryside.

Alternatively, there is a perception that the more remote the pagoda, the more likely that requests will be answered, given the imagined rarity of visits. Yến took me to one such pagoda by the banks of the Saigon River on the outskirts of Ho Chi Minh City whose reputation as responsive was justly deserved. She said the pagoda itself had rendered meritorious service *(có công)* in granting to petitioners even the most desperate of requests. Inside the pagoda was a large bronze bell on which were affixed names and petitions on paper torn from exercise books. The laywoman in attendance said that people would affix their request to the bell as a last resort when they found themselves in serious trouble or an irresolvable situation. The bell was rung at the commencement of the four sutra-chanting ceremonies conducted each day, an action she said communicated the requests to Buddha.

The attendant indicated one of the requests stuck to the bell by way of illustration. It was a typed petition on a ragged piece of paper. On it was fixed a small photo, identical to that required by state agencies for travel or identity documents. The attendant explained that the young man in the photograph had been arrested and put in prison as the result of inciting an argument between two passengers vying for a lift on his motorcycle taxi. The argument had gotten out of control, and one of the disputants had killed the other. The taxi driver had been found an accomplice to the crime and imprisoned for twelve years. His family had tried all state channels and had made repeated requests at pagodas to have his case reconsidered, but to no avail. Finally, his mother had placed this petition on the bell on his behalf, and it had worked. Eight years were taken off his sentence. The attendant told me to feel inside the bell. Its interior was so thickly coated with requests that it seemed as if the bell were being prepared for recasting in a papier-mâché mould. What made this place popular, she said, was that here all could communicate with Buddha without fear or favor, irrespective of wealth or social class. Pagodas such as this provided a means to make a direct appeal to Buddha, a way of shortcutting suspect layers of mediation afforded by state officials and monks.

To Yến this free and fair channel of communication to a higher power was a demonstration of Buddhism's relevance and democratic validity. In some ways, she said, this was a purer form of Buddhism than that promoted by the Sangha.

The Lonely Buddha

The views espoused by the laywomen Tiên and Yến offer a more conditional acceptance of Buddhism's scope in Vietnam than one often hears from educated, modernist Buddhists. They reposition Buddhism in Vietnamese society not as an autonomous institution or influential motor of reform but as a faith disciplined by an ethic of reciprocity and dependent for survival on its responsiveness to popular expectations.

One way of approaching the reception the Buddha has received in Vietnam as a principle of potency is to consider the Buddha as a traveler and sojourner offered refuge within the ambit of folk practices of a society that lays great stress on reciprocity and the value of indebtedness *(ơn)*. Many religious foci, from tigers through ghosts *(cô hồn)* to the Lady of the Realm, are valued for their responsiveness, and this derives crucially from the debt that they as marginal beings owe for having been brought into or returned to the circle of human sociality. The story of the discovery and recuperation from the summit of Sam Mountain of the statue of the Lady of the Realm is well known to those who worship her. Stories of the violent or voluntary death of unmarried, childless women are frequently woven around such goddesses. Like lonely ghosts *(ma cô đơn)* they lack a family to venerate them. As rape victims, refugees from parents' or husbands' households, subject neither to parental nor in-law authority, and lacking progeny, they suffer anomalous and lonely fates. Offerings to these beings draw them back into the valued network of human relationships. The gift given to the image of a wild tiger, a traffic accident victim, or the recognizably human but abandoned stone figure of a deity is a gift of belonging.

The offerings to these beings revitalize and quicken them: illuminating their senses by a burning candle; providing staples such as water, fruit, rice, and salt; appeasing them with luxuries such as cakes and other sweets; arousing their bodies with wine, coffee, or cigarettes; and improving their mood through music, dance, theater, and acrobatics. These ritual gestures recognize and appease a desire for sociality. To a human mind, the value of such offerings is self-evident. Ineluctably indebted by such acts of sociable inclusion, the spirits are an available source of power to be tapped. The Buddha may be less desperate than most beings on such sociable recognition and indeed attracts a phalanx of interpreters who speak to his universalistic relevance. Nevertheless, as an acknowledged guest, albeit an esteemed one, he is obligated by the hospitality extended to him by local hosts.[7] One of the rituals practiced widely through the Buddhist world is the eye-opening ceremony, whereby the sense of sight is bestowed on the Buddha—a gift of humanity, a gift of awareness, an act of inclusion. Because of this gift, the Buddha is among those entities people can remind of the debt of belonging they owe.

Some images of the Buddha have more cause to be grateful than others. One instance of this is the Lonely Buddha (Phật Cô Đơn), a large Buddha statue in Bình Chánh district, Ho Chi Minh City, which became famous in the 1990s for its willingness to grant all manner of requests (figure 15). Tiên said the statue was dubbed the Lonely Buddha because it sits alone, outside,

FIG. 15. The Lonely Buddha

exposed to the elements. Some Buddhists have discounted the emergence of this site as a superstitious practice or as an example of religion's corruption by commercialism. Tiên admitted that many of the people who went to visit there were merely curious about the image's notoriety. Others went to pay their respects to Buddha, without paying any attention to the site's current celebrity. However, she thought that most people went because the Lonely Buddha was especially responsive to their requests and could help them resolve their problems. I asked her if this practice was consistent with Buddhism. Tiên said she regarded herself as a Buddhist and yet she believed in this Buddha's efficacy and went there all the time.

The nun Hạnh who had such unique insights into the Lady of the Realm also had some stories to tell about the Lonely Buddha. She related one of these to me on the condition that I give her a copy of a photograph of the seated Buddha image. I was more than happy with the deal, given an opportunity to hear another tale by this accomplished storyteller:

> The Lonely Buddha was discovered by an elderly farmer in the middle of an area of jungle about ten years ago. The farmer lived and worked nearby. One night as he lay dreaming, the Buddha appeared and gave him instructions how to find the place where it lay abandoned, with nothing but wild animals as friends. The next day he followed the directions and found an enormous seated Buddha, with palms facing upward on his lap, collecting pure rainwater. Only after that did the place become widely known and the present complex built.

Everyone in the pagoda who was listening to the nun was rapt. Hạnh continued, telling us what she had heard of the statue's origins:

> More than thirty years ago, a Buddha image was commissioned from India. The airplane transporting the Buddha to Saigon suddenly lost power when it flew over the Buddha's present location. It was forced to land about thirty kilometers short of its destination, and the Buddha statue was unloaded at the place where it still can be found to this day. Surely there must have been something miraculous *(mầu nhiệm)* concerning that site, for it was strange that a plane could fly all the way from India and yet not make it the final short distance to Saigon. This happened during the American times. Meanwhile, the jungle grew up, governments changed, and the statue was forgotten and lost to all.

I was fascinated by the story. It resembled that told about the Lady of the Realm, a spirit who had appeared to a sleeping girl, telling her where its stone body was to be found. Our gods come to us in dreams. This was also another discovery story. We worship what we find lying in the jungle or on top of a hill or what has emerged from under the water.[8] We incidentally worship other people's gods, those they have imported to the region or carelessly left behind them. One of my neighbors in the city told me that the Lonely Buddha was named thus because his statue stood in the open air without a shelter to house him. She said that as recently as seven or eight years ago, no one went to worship there. She said that the image had been lying on its side, covered in vegetation. Someone discovered it and offered up a prayer to the statue. The request was granted. In thanks, the supplicant raised the statue back into an upright position, cleared the jungle, and built a pagoda for it. "That is when people started coming. Now it is always crowded there. That Buddha must be really powerful!"

The designation of this Buddha image as lonely indicates it is not viewed as some impersonal being or font of altruistic benevolence; instead, like most anthropomorphized objects of worship, it is prey to understandable human limitations and grateful to those who helped it escape its solitude by housing it, attending to it, and making it offerings. This gratitude, like that of hungry ghosts, homeless and craving for attention, could be bought relatively easily and bring considerable rewards to those offering succor to a being in such a predicament. Offerings to the Lonely Buddha remain conditional on the statue's proving itself by doing something in return for the gifts granted it. At some point in the short history of this cult, the number of people coming to the statue began to be taken as proof of its efficacy and its willingness to take part in the conventional obligations of reciprocity. The phenomenon of the Lonely Buddha indicates the conditional refuge provided to Buddhism within the accommodating structure of Vietnamese popular belief, ever open to new philosophies and spirits. This refuge is extended provided that the Buddha's representations obligingly reciprocate by effectively responding to people's requests for help in their everyday concerns. The Buddha's spell in the wilderness is indicative of the price to be paid by even such an august being as the Buddha for a failure to respond to the moral obligations of local society.

The motorcycle taxi driver who took me to visit the Lonely Buddha himself owed the Buddha a visit. On a previous occasion, he had requested assistance for his mother-in-law, who had been suffering from high blood pressure; the Buddha had cured her. "For sure this Buddha is responsive," he declared. "That is why so many people go there." To get to the Buddha statue, we followed the road to Tây Ninh province, once a smuggling route favored by those importing goods from Cambodia. Just outside the urban area, settlement thinned to a string of poor dwellings and ramshackle small businesses and workshops. The area had been a New Economic Zone, a region of reclaimed land, the driver explained to me. "Hardly anyone lived here then." A concentration of cafés and a children's playground clustered around the T-intersection formed by the main road and the dirt track leading to the pagoda, testament to the Buddha's drawing power. We paid our entrance fee, exchanging comments with the ticket seller on the incongruity of buying a ticket to visit a pagoda, and bought a small bunch of incense.

The Buddha towered impassively, his silhouette breaking the horizon. A monk was stationed on the open-air platform where the Buddha sat. He stood in the full glare of the sun, tending the altar and receiving visitors. The monk provided yet another version of the Buddha image's origins. He said that the image had been commissioned for Vĩnh Nghiêm pagoda, then Saigon's largest. However, on completion in 1958 it had proven too big, and so it was brought to its present site, where it was installed without a pagoda. Its name, Lonely Buddha, dated from that time. Despite the monk's more secular version of the origins of the Buddha image, he said it was indeed true that the image was magically responsive. He himself had seen people who were diseased and wore tattered clothes come to pray to the Buddha. He had seen them return, cured and richly clad, to offer thanks to the Buddha. He gave me a coconut, as a gift from the Buddha, and said I should drink it when I got home. It would make me healthy and strong and bring me success in my work. Around us, a few people were carrying large sticks of incense, which they lit from the incense on the pagoda's altar, to take home with them. The monk said that this would help them earn their living or bring them whatever they asked for.

This phenomenon illustrates the difficulties faced by those attempting to enforce distinctions between types of faiths or religious practice. The existence within the Buddhist Sangha of notions of the Buddha as a responsive, materially powerful being shows the problems attending efforts to analytically cordon off such practices from Buddhism. While many Buddhists do maintain such distinctions, one finds Buddhists who defend such notions as consistent with the faith. The criticisms made by members of the Sangha and Buddhist laypeople of "magical" practices reflect an effort to institutionalize Buddhism that has a long and inconclusive history in Vietnam and other countries. For its own part, Vietnam's Communist state, although frequently depicted in contest with Buddhism, has its own problems with unorthodox religions. The state outlaws and frequently takes active measures against practices such as palm reading, trance possession, and fortune-telling. One can even see a convergence between ideas of oppositional Buddhist monks such as Thích Quảng Độ and those of the Communist authorities where the proliferation of superstition is involved. Just as the Communist state has its own opponents to deal with in the form of a diverse and increasingly vocal range of dissidents, so too does contemporary institutionalized Buddhism. Yet just as Buddhist monks legitimately appeal for more freedom, so too might alternative perspectives within Buddhism also be admitted.

One of the most noted features of Buddhism is the way it has adapted itself to local beliefs. It has not been able to stand apart as proud and aloof but has everywhere been integrated into local ideas. One aspect of the localization of Buddhism in Vietnam has been the Buddha's incorporation into an ethical system emphasizing reciprocity. The nun Hạnh's tales of the goddess' faithful and efficacious patronage of a local stonemason indicates the sacralized nature of this value in Vietnam. The designation of Buddha images as responsive similarly indicates their anthropomorphized status and enmeshment in a network of mutual obligations.[9] These days, a product of their times, such images are just as likely as the Lady of the Realm to be swept up into people's diverse business activities and assessed in terms of their capacity to bring prosperity. This process has taken place in the full view and sometimes with the assistance of religious specialists. And although some Buddhists struggle to hold the tide against what they see as error, even formally trained members of Buddhist orders sometimes play an important role in the transformation of the meaning of orthodoxy. Even in attempts by members of the Buddhist Sangha to explicate and classify belief, lessons such as those drawn by the nun Hạnh show that new understandings can be constituted and the symbols of time-bound religious traditions refashioned to address the concerns of the place and the moment.

9

Goddess of Freedom

One of the most pervasive themes in the study of folk culture in Vietnam is its construction as a symbol of freedom *(tự do)*. In academic and popular anthropologies, folk beliefs *(tín ngưỡng dân gian)* and customs *(phong tục tập quán)* represent the cultural core of Vietnamese identity, distinct from the legacy of the culture of the court and its centralizing standardizing power; free from enervating Confucianism, the compromised social elites, and urban centers; and resistant to all varieties of foreign colonialism, ancient and more recent. Folk culture is a font of autonomy, that source of creativity from which peasants, the oppressed, the outcast have drawn from time immemorial in shucking off foreign oppression, feudalism, cultural imperialism, patriarchy, class oppression, and state control.

This too is a persistent theme in writings about goddesses, which depict them in various ways as symbols of freedom.[1] Their femininity is celebrated as signs of cultural resistance against various oppressive Confucian patriarchal overlays associated with Chinese colonial rule, feudalism, aped foreign influence, elite culture, and state authority.[2] Feminine symbols point to the persistence of ancient matriarchal values or influences from the more liberal societies of Southeast Asia (Đoàn Lâm 1999). Theorists point out how some female religious symbols attest to women's historical societal leadership: the commemoration of the Trưng sisters and Lady Triệu show that matriarchal values they exemplified are alive and well. Some generalize from the profusion of feminine imagery to women's favorable and autonomous status in the society generally (see Đỗ Thị Hảo and Mai Thị Ngọc Chúc 1984; Ngô Đức Thịnh 1996; Hà Hùng Tiến 1997; Hoang Van Co 1957; Nguyễn Minh San 1996). Alternatively, goddesses are sometimes deemed to be free of cultural overlays or meaning altogether, supposedly representing such noncultural natural qualities as fertility, or regarded as purely instrumental forces, available to be tapped (Do Lai Thuy 1996). Symbolizing elemental forces of nature such as the earth, they can be read as devoid of identity, prescriptive cultural meaning, or normative messages and hence free of imposed or inauthentic cultural accretions. Associated with a primordial condition of humanity, goddesses would appear to direct one away entirely from constraining civilizational influences to the origins of history. Such interpretations, which are evident in conversation and written commentaries and often couched in quasi-scientific language, reprise culturally important themes. The meanings read into goddesses are hot contemporary issues; they go to deeper structures of identity, belonging, feeling, memory, and social experience.

The gender of popular deities such as the Lady of the Realm is considered significant by Vietnamese nationalist theorists for what it reveals of the autonomous character of the culture that produced them. Yet the proliferation of commentary on goddesses illustrates the heavy emphasis in Vietnamese society on the prescription of appropriate roles for women. The Lady of the Realm has been regarded by one writer as a symbol of motherhood (Nguyễn Minh San 1993), and the pantheon of goddesses in Vietnam has been considered a treasury of models of exemplary Vietnamese womanhood (Nguyễn Minh San 1996). Commentators writing about the goddesses of folk religion have diversely highlighted their identity as forgiving and compassionate intercessors, competent mothers, dutiful daughters, faithful wives, guarantors of children, and patriotic defenders. As images of women they are highly prescriptive. Tales about the Lady of the Realm and the Black Lady mention their support of wifely fidelity and nurturance of men (Thạch Phương and Lê Trung Vũ 1995, 238). The women in the tales surrounding these goddesses die after extramarital sexual relations, commit suicide when raped, resist marriage when obliged to marry an outsider, and remain faithful to their parents, husbands, and country even after their death. As favorite foci of discussion among cultural commentators, female spirits are seen to sustain and signify the core values of the Vietnamese nation.

This focus on goddesses is a subset of the enormous commentary on feminine gender that has accompanied recent transformations in Vietnamese society. The wars of decolonization brought forth images of longhaired guerrillas (du kích tóc dài), schoolgirls as patriotic revolutionaries, mothers who were considered heroes (mẹ anh hùng) and rewarded for their children's revolutionary sacrifices, and virtuous wives who stayed faithful to husbands missing in war. The reform era has given rise to much commentary on the family, most of it squarely focused on women's multiple roles as breadwinner, homemaker, sexual partner, child bearer, educator, moral instructor, attentive listener, or caring provider (see, for instance, Nguyễn Thị Oanh 1999). These contributions have been stressed during an era marked by a huge decrease in the state's provision of social services and the informalization of female economic activity (Le Thi 2001; Werner 2002). Perceived cultural decline is also considered a responsibility of women. *Phụ Nữ Thành Phố* (City woman), the newspaper of Ho Chi Minh City's Woman's Union, has featured stories about prostitution, infidelity, early marriage, divorce, AIDS, domestic violence, and antisocial youth, implying that responsibility for understanding and resolving these problems rests on the shoulders of its largely female readership. The expansion and opening of the media sector brought an influx of new ideas and images about gender roles and sexuality, inciting discussion about all manner of lifestyles, new gender roles, different sexualities, extramarital sex, and unwanted pregnancies and leading many commentators to assert the need to return to traditional standards of morality for youth (Marr 1996). Persistent stories in the press told of a tide of women marrying foreigners or involved the sex trade, giving voice to male fears of a feminine sexual "defection" and a very public questioning of the patriotism or traditional morality of such women. Such standards and anxieties were virtually never invoked in reference to the sexual activities of men.

Commentary on the goddesses of Vietnamese folk religion is, with some notable exceptions (see, for example, Đỗ Thị Hảo and Mai Thị Ngọc Chúc 1984; Thái Thị Bích Liên 1998), dominated by male writers. This imbalance reflects male predominance in the social sciences, arts, letters, and politics as much as a history of men speaking for the nation and its culture. In Vietnam's ethnological discourse, feminine entities such as goddesses are spoken for by the male members of the national family. Their focus on feminine symbols reflects the gendered dimension of nations, whose symbols of identity have been markedly feminine. As Yuval-Davis notes, "Women are often required to carry the 'burden of representation,' as they are constructed as the symbolic bearers of the collectivity's identity and honor" (1998, 29). Men, on the other hand, assume the burden of representing. As Soucy has noted for Buddhism, the study of religious texts—and, one might add, commentary on folk religious symbols—is a dimension of religious practice, for which in Vietnam, men have a strong affinity (1999). Positive affirming views of femininity as a symbol of national liberty occur alongside the prescriptive view of femininity that defines women in relation to men—as, among other things, mothers, wives, and daughters. It is hard to escape the conclusion that the ideas of liberty that male commentators derive from their interpretive musings on goddesses go hand in hand with their confinement of the meanings of these symbols to devoted service of an idealized national entity of which they are privileged beneficiaries.

While men appear to dominate textual exegesis upon religion through their control of the elite instruments of the discursive sphere such as publishing houses, research centers, and educational and cultural bureaucracies, nontextual ritual action, which is more kinetic, tactile, and sensual and involves entering personalized, reciprocal relationships with the beings of the spirit world, tends to be markedly feminine in practice. The majority of those involved in pilgrimages to goddesses such as the Lady of the Realm are women. However, such gendered differentiation in religious practice does not imply that for women, religion consists primarily of nondiscursive ritual practice or that commentating is a male practice. One cannot fail to be impressed, whether one is at someone's house talking about the objects and images on an ancestral altar, in a bus bound for a pilgrimage site, among customers making a purchase of votive items, or in a shrine seeking advice on how to execute a ritual action, that the popular religious practice dominated by women in Vietnam occurs in a discursive environment of continuous, opinionated, many-faceted, and highly arresting exegesis. Given the way religious practices are deeply worked into women's projects, their commentaries on the significance of these practices are, not unexpectedly, particularly rich. In their discussion of the meaning of recent developments in religion their commentaries closely resemble those of men, for they, like men, are participants in and witnesses to the social processes such as urbanization, commercialization, technological change, political and institutional rivalries, class and gender transformations, and state decline that have constituted and reconstituted religious practice in Vietnam. Nevertheless, given the gendered specificity of their experience of these processes, the perspectives on religion offered by female pilgrims and religious practitioners are also quite specific. As Watson noted of the worship of Tien Hau in southern China, women have a very different vision of the goddess from that held by any category of men (1985, 320). He observed that for women the worship of Tien Hau is usually defined in personal or family terms. This is broadly true of the goddesses of southern Vietnam, although one must add the caveat that many men do share these personal concerns and many women do speak about religious symbols as expressive of broader collectivities such as ethnic groups, class, and nation. Furthermore, the social processes transforming Vietnam have also opened divisions between women from different class, ethnic, and occupational backgrounds. It is not therefore surprising that their perspectives on religious practice are also diverse.

A view of goddesses as a timeless symbol of autonomy upon which the nation can draw to sustain itself collapses all this complexity in a simplistic action that masks its partiality as much as it reveals relations of power. Given the potential problems with male-dominated interpretations of goddess worship, one might ask whether popular religion is an autonomous realm for women in Vietnam. Do Vietnamese women see goddesses such as the Lady of the Realm as symbolic of autonomy? This chapter explores a number of perspectives. In particular, it explores the ways women in different social circumstances conceptualize the articulation between supposedly traditional religious practice and the processes of capitalist economic integration that have become increasingly intense since the end of the war. As urban-based women of relatively high social standing, my interlocutors in this chapter offer only a partial view of religious practice in Vietnam. Yet as each of them has been caught up in the social transformations of recent years in different ways, their views shed valuable light on the diversity of ways women in Vietnam experience and reflect upon the meaning of their religious practice.

Waiting for Modernity

Linh is a twenty-six-year-old saleswoman in a photography shop. The daughter of a reasonably well-off family from the Mekong delta, she is enrolled in law school and now lives with her family in an outer suburb of Ho Chi Minh City. She spoke with me from time to time about the religious images in my photographs when I picked them up. Linh told me she was against superstition, which she regarded as a domain of charlatans and a shortcut for the lazy to get rich. She herself had never been on pilgrimage to the Lady of the Realm because the practice of making offerings to spirits was not so popular among intellectuals (trí thức) such as she. She thought too that religions, such as Catholicism, that preached that one could wash away (rửa) one's sins were profoundly unrealistic. Despite her rationalism, she admitted she believed in fortune-tellers, calling this "a girl thing" (một cái gái). Yet she was a Buddhist, believing that we cannot escape the Karma accrued by past lives. She saw the Buddha as a compassionate savior, and she believed that Buddha would save from lowly incarnations those who had led a life of misdeeds and even admit them to Nirvana if they sincerely and earnestly repented (sám hôi).

Linh told me that religious practice in Vietnam is more common among women than men. Buddhism's precepts were molded around the concerns of women, including, for instance, injunctions against drunkenness and adultery, which, given the gendered pattern of their breach, advanced the interests of women. Because positions in the bureaucratic hierarchy were traditionally accorded to men, religions such as Buddhism offered women an alternative, more amenable ideology. In that sense Vietnam was still feudal, she averred. She observed that Vietnamese society weighs women under multiple obligations—of being a daughter, a wife, and a mother. It places heavy burdens on women to perform household duties and tend to their families. It doesn't encourage them to engage in wider social relations. Linh said she had a boyfriend with whom she was unhappy because he wanted her to stay at home and look after him and his children. She said this request was illogical, for after a period of her being confined to the domestic world, he would soon find her boring, she would feel isolated, and the marriage would become unhappy. She said that traditionally, a woman could not travel alone or meet and converse with strange men. Consequently, women's knowledge of the world was not good, and their chances to escape from parental supervision poor. Employment options were limited, and the likelihood of becoming dependent on a man were high. Finding that men were not altogether reliable as family providers, many women sought refuge in a religious vocation.

More than once when visiting Buddhist pagodas, I found that I and perhaps a novice or monk were the only men. I was immersed in a female domain, surrounded by women of varying ages. In such a context, Linh's comments about the realm of religion being something of a refuge strike deep chords. Devoted Buddhists such as she are sometimes regarded by their male associates as being interested in religion because of their failure to find fulfillment in marriage. For some women whose children have grown up and married and whose parents and husbands have passed away, the bonds of the religious community provide a valued opportunity to socialize. When they retire, many women go to pagodas "to calm the heart and still the mind."[3] In a related way, pagodas are sometimes seen as meditative sanctuaries for those approaching death, and they are places of burial. For their part, monks and nuns are often considered to have experienced disappointments in life: failure in love, a conflict with their family, or some other disillusionment. Sometimes it is said that they are fleeing their social responsibilities. The religion's triple gem of refuge in the Buddha, the Dharma, and the Sangha stresses Buddhism's role as a refuge. Certainly that is the way religion is often seen in Vietnam, as a shelter from life "outside," an escape, a coping mechanism, a place of solace.

The same could be said for the following of goddesses such as the Lady of the Realm and the mobile world of pilgrimage, whose makeup is overwhelmingly female. Linh was inclined to see pilgrimage in Vietnam as an opportunity to escape the oppressive everyday conditions under which women in her country live. Traditionally, she thought pilgrimages and festivals represented opportunities to escape the precincts of the house, meet others, exchange ideas, circulate, and travel. She thought that pilgrimage sites, shrines, and pagodas allowed women to consort in a space where they are free of the demands imposed by men. Although as an intellectual she did not feel inclined to take part herself, she could appreciate the shrine to Her Ladyship in Châu Đốc as a sanctuary of autonomous space, and pilgrimage as a moment of feminine self-assertion.

Fortunately things were changing. Linh considered that recent years had brought an expansion in what she called nontraditional perceptions of women. Because Vietnam had opened its doors to the outside world, attitudes were changing. All sorts of new ideas were available to men and women. Women could learn about foreign lifestyles at school, to which they had increasingly the same access as men. Even for those who could not read, all sorts of foreign films were being dubbed into Vietnamese, and illiterate women could pick up new ideas in that way. Women were opening their minds. As a result of new employment opportunities, women could go into the world and interact with all sectors of society, from company directors to foreign joint-venture partners. The position of women was changing for the better.

Linh herself was hopeful, as a result, of having a good life, getting prestigious work, finding an open-minded husband, and living well in a society that she considered was evolving more and more to women's advantage. She was confident in her ability to acquire the knowledge for economic self-sufficiency. She said this would give her the economic means to refuse an offer of being provided for by her boyfriend. She thought a diversity of jobs would become open to women. Indeed, she thought women could supplant men in some positions. For instance, she felt that these days the job prospects for women as traders or business partners were good, as they did not have to go through the expensive, time-consuming, and wasteful rituals of hospitality that were expected of men involved in business, such as getting drunk with clients and partners. Her decision to study law, she felt, would yield great returns. She thought big companies needed someone versed in business law, and she was sure she would get a job that paid well. Linh's imagination was captivated by the glamour of the modern *(hiện đại)* professions and lifestyles that would come to Vietnam in its postwar reengagement with global corporations, markets, and new cultural values. She accorded to her moment the status of a historical threshold, a step between tradition and the modern.

Time was on women's side she thought. Global trends were coming to Vietnam, moving women's way and allowing them to escape from servitude into new freedoms.

Linh was inclined to deem religious behavior such as the Châu Đốc pilgrimage as a "traditional" practice in contrast with the "modern" economy. The market economy would have the equalizing effect of bringing women out of the home and exposing them to modernity. In the process, their traditional pursuits were destined to fade in response to further opening. She thought that women's involvement in religious activity, a legacy of "feudal times," would fade away. Traditional refuges for women such as pagodas and temples would decline in relevance as women found acceptance as cultural equals in the wider society. Her entwining of the narratives of female emancipation and religious disenchantment led her to anticipate great things of modernity.[4]

Linh's view was admittedly that of a relatively privileged minority, one whose family was wealthy enough to send her through secondary school. She was still living with her parents and supplementing their income with her own small one. Many women of her generation gain wider social exposure working in agriculture, markets, the service sector, and factories. She was not wealthy, but as an intellectual considered her social position as high, judging it in terms of her educational level *(trình độ)*. Yet hers was a harsh double bind whereby success in the so-called modern sector cut against the neo-traditionalist expectations of the urban middle class. White-collar corporate employment, preferably with a foreign company, beckons many in Linh's position, but such educated women find access to the corporate world difficult, often because of gender stereotypes. As she observed, men are expected to have broad social horizons; women with such experience are tainted by the implication of promiscuity. Much business activity and networking among her male peers entails socializing between men in drinking establishments and hostess bars. Men who succeed at university might go on to work in a corporation, and their every success at work might be greeted with approval. What a woman like Linh gains from her education in employment options she loses in status among her peers for remaining unmarried into her late twenties and early thirties. The longer a woman stays in a career track, the more pressure she comes under from relatives and acquaintances to get married and have children. Even when women's work takes them away from their homes, the expectation that they raise children and look after elderly parents remains strong.[5]

As one who is rich in the cultural capital of formal education, which is very much in demand by companies and the nation's bureaucracy, Linh identified with the projects of modernization, industrialization, and professionalization. She used the reform rhetoric of the regime stressing the play of reason and enlightened resistance as driving the transitions of postwar life. As one who espoused Buddhism for its socially realistic *(thực tế)* qualities, Linh aligned herself with the Vietnamese state's idea of itself as a progressive force, a national liberator and instigator of liberal reforms. In alignment with her educated male peers who were proud of a modern outlook, she looked down on beliefs that spirits such as the Lady of the Realm could deliver prosperity as superstitious. Regarding such views as fashion driven, ignorant *(dốt)*, or unethical *(thiếu đạo đức)*, she was inclined to predict that they would be historically superseded. However, her critical view of popular religious practices reflected a somewhat genteel cultural chauvinism. Unlike many people who attributed their fortune to the spirit world, she owned neither a house of her own nor her own business. She still lived with her parents, who had helped her purchase her old motorbike. Perhaps too her faith in the foreign-investment sector was misplaced, for its developments are not necessarily conducive to women. In Vietnam's case, where globalization has predominantly meant investment from the countries of the region, it has also brought cultural items, practices, and relationships based on gender models potentially affording women less autonomy than those adhered to in the past. The mushrooming of "hugging bars" and karaoke establishments in the era of the open door is one example of the deleterious effect on women's bodies of liberalizing the economy (Nguyen Vo 1998). Apart from foreign businessmen and tourists, among the main clients are members of Vietnam's heavily male bureaucracy and state enterprise directors, for much of the income from foreign investment in Vietnam has been directed to them. These gendered exclusions might only deepen as Vietnam becomes more economically integrated. If Linh's view of the religious domain as a sanctuary from oppressive social conditions is merited, one might expect women's involvement in religious activities to increase in the face of such deepening exclusions rather than go into decline.

Matriarchs of Alternative Modernity

According to Linh the autonomy afforded to women by traditional religious practices was inherently limited. It has persisted in the face of wider social exclusions that must be superseded before women can gain true freedoms. Liberal reform and global integration, she believed, would provide unprecedented opportunities for women to come into their own as equals with men in the wider social sphere. It was a view common among educated professional people in the city, who were inclined to attach prestige to the corporate, bureaucratic, and diplomatic projects that in the last half century's movement from capitalism to socialism and back to capitalism again have announced themselves in the name of modernity. Yet this view downplays the role in the local economy of the female-dominated informal sector that arguably preempted, inspired, and even coerced the reliberalization policies. Much of the talk of "rational" reform policy and economic "laws," at suited-up conferences and in wads of newsprint, detracts from women's past and ongoing contributions as the leading actors in the nonstate sector. According to Linh's way of thinking, the religious practices of such women, supposedly compensatory in nature, might similarly be relegated to some supposedly superseded past. However, as I reflect on my experiences with the urban pilgrims and pagoda restorers, whose lives of religious activity have accompanied a history of heavy engagement in the market economy, something about this explanation seems inadequate. For many of such women, their religious activities do not express their anomalous social position but derive inspiration from and lend support to female-dominated economic practice as a relatively autonomous project.

Như was a successful businesswoman, a creditor, saleswoman, and religious entrepreneur. A neighbor in my Ho Chi Minh City District One street, she sold items associated with the propitiation of ghosts and a range of funeral wares from a small stall in front of her house. "If anyone dies, come to Như," she intoned, repeating what I took to be her business slogan. She also renovated Buddhist pagodas on behalf of her wealthy overseas compatriots. Apart from religion's constituting the basis of her business, she was a devout practitioner of a range of religious activities. Each weekend she took part in pagoda restorations, and throughout the year she attended all of the Buddhist festivals. Each year she organized trips to the Lady of the Realm in Châu Đốc and to the Black Lady, Dinh Cô, and Thiên Hậu in Bình Dương province. Not only did she make her own sacrifices to these patronesses, but by selling the remaining seats of her rental vehicle to other propitiants, she turned a profit out of her religious journeys. She regularly made offerings to Lê Văn Duyệt's mausoleum and each month made sacrifices to the lonely ghosts, using her own stall's stock of food offerings, paper hell-money, and other votive objects. Her many religious activities could hardly be seen as a refuge from the world or a compensation for failures. She was a successful businesswoman by the high standards of Ho Chi Minh City in the mid-1990s. Along with several other members of her family, she owned her own front-street house, motorbike, and market stall—impressive accoutrements of success. She had an impressively full social life, which mainly revolved around religious activities. Yet despite her intensive religious practice she was not fanatical about these pursuits. She was able to explain the differences between gods and goddesses, types of belief, and kinds of propitiants and the histories of different ritual centers in an objective way. For one whose life was intimately bound up in the spirit world, her account of her activities was surprisingly detached and relativistic.

A fortyish, unmarried, childless woman like Nhu' is easy prey for the comments by men that her religion is a compensation for unsatisfied desires. Yet in religion women like her find social and corporeal fulfillment, and affirmation, of a distinct kind. She and her fellow middle-aged pagoda restorers are fit, alert, and vibrant. They are always dashing about. Their spectacular trips of Buddhist charity are a talking point, planned, commentated on, recalled. They comprise a club for the like-minded. They have a great time spending other people's money. Gifts to the poor are splashed around. Pagodas are given makeovers. The monks love them. They put on vegetarian feasts for the teams of mostly female merit makers who descend to transform their abodes. Many of these women have jettisoned or outlived husbands who have abused their bodies, filched their family's wealth, poured destructive substances into their own corporeal temples. These women have vitality, longevity, and reserves of fat stored on their physical frames—a signal to all of their physical indestructibility, grace (heavenly blessedness), social success, and transcendence of history with its epic narrative of destitution. Nhu' and her companions are sprightly. They exhibit and dwell in exemplary order: a moral code, physical regime (diets, exercise, oils), aesthetic regulation (calculated arts of self-presentation), economic discipline. Yet the reverse side of this (not paradoxical for it flows from superlative mastery of everyday codes) is these women's informality, naturalness, and unfazability. Their considerable life experience, including that of family relationships, school, diverse business ventures, regime changes, fortunes lost and remade, travel, love affairs, and expertise gained in dealings with cadres, clients, and customers, have given them a Buddha-like unflappability, a Lady of the Realm–like prescience, a Mr. Earth–like casualness. For many of these women, pilgrimage is isomorphic with their lives in the world of the marketplace: rising early, traveling to make purchases from distributors, socializing with fellow market women, transacting with clients and the authorities, being entertained by a riot of street life, consuming a stream of food and drink snacks, and making continuous offerings of the same to the spirits. Pilgrimage is an intensification of this, and employs similar strategies of self-arousal. Pilgrims eat durian, which raises body heat, drink coffee, rise at 2 or 3 A.M., and munch voraciously on high-sugar foods—chewing gum, coconut candy, sweet porridge, and sweetly pungent pickled fish.

Many of the devotees of the goddess live their lives according to a distinct regime of time. A number of them are creditors who stay at home, sitting regally on a pile of money as it grows beneath them. For them, social calls are at the same time business ventures to chase debtors or distribute payments. Seemingly leisurely gossip is prime capital as information about others is key collateral in their credit circles. Such women are always working, yet paradoxically it appears that for them, time is in endless supply. Như would go to the gym to exercise in the evening just as laborers were shoveling rice, meat, and fish sauce into exhausted bodies in the stall outside her home. Vendors lacking Như's capital reserves set up their stalls well before the sun rises and sell throughout the day, each day, while those in nearby offices work to an entirely different rhythm of days, hours, breaks, and national holidays. Those in the sex industry wake in the afternoon and in the evening put on their glamorous outfits to work through to the early hours of the morning. Pilgrimage organizers such as Aunt Six are constantly on the move. For her, going to holiday destinations is a nonstop business. The twenty-third of the fourth lunar month, when the festival of the Lady of the Realm falls each year, means more to many women than the birthday of Ho Chi Minh or the anniversary of independence or liberation. Buddhists, who attend pagodas on the first or fifteenth of each lunar month, live according to the lunar calendar in a city that distances itself from the backward countryside by its adherence to the solar calendar. On Sunday, a day of rest according to a convention that has ruled the world of white-collar work since French times, the pagoda restorers work furiously, making their merit, and then, during the other days of the week, sit around and discuss their experiences in the marketplace. Rather than being a response to their temporal marginalization—waiting in the wings, past marriageable age, socially redundant, retired, or unemployed—these women's attraction to religion and their busy religious calendar mesh with rhythms of life distinct from that of the avowedly modernist state, foreign corporations, and professionals.

The women who patronize goddesses also inhabit a distinct regime of space and associated hierarchy of values. Their homes are places of work and sites where children are reared and educated, even though, in an era of industrialization and modernization, these functions are normally represented as being conducted in offices, factories, and schools. Their houses are part of a vast network of markets: a small stall is in front of many of them. In the countryside, administrative centers are called "the market" *(chợ)*, and they are linked to households through the movements of women. This is an alternative network to that of the state with its system of household registration, hierarchies of control, privileged channels of information, and structures of surveillance that tie the population to the national center in ascending administrative tiers. These women make their living by traveling, excelling in exchanges beyond the domestic sphere. They specialize in cash and credit transactions and are adept in negotiations with state officials. Many live alone or raise their children alone precisely because of the chaos men brought into their lives: "men stir *(quậy)* things up; you can't trust them" is a frequently uttered refrain. In the cities, market space, that realm where women are paramount, has intruded on the spatial order deemed exemplary by the modernist state. Stalls encroach on streetscapes, hawkers congest market thoroughfares, and mobile peddlers fill parks. The market has even invaded the space of the research institute and the classroom. Marketers have their own dress code: loose cotton *aó baba* for women, shirtless for men. Not for them the starched uniform of the cadre, the schoolteacher, the health professional, nor the encasement by that article of so-called traditional apparel, the *áo dài*. All respect is extended to the representatives of bureaucratic secular authority by use of the deferential term "teacher" *(thầy)* when they come to make purchases. Yet an equally if not more valid symbol of authority, sitting at the pinnacle of business efficacy and commanding the respect of fellow specialists, are the queens of credit and commerce. They head a hierarchy of economic efficacy, which ranks many women higher than most men.

Quite apart from conceiving of the present era as a dawn of women's liberation, new social horizons, and new validation of feminine autonomy, many women such as Như who have been working in the market for many years already experience considerable autonomy. Rather than wait for the government to open the doors and for society's cultural values to modernize, these women have constituted for themselves a creditable symbolic support system in the figure of a goddess that endorses and abets their informal activity. In many ways the Lady of the Realm reflects their own social position as mothers, nurturers, creditors, wealth creators, healers, and mediators. In leaning on her they appear to be drawing for succor upon an enlarged version of themselves. That a goddess such as the Lady of the Realm has become phenomenally popular in the wider society shows how successful their innovations have been. Religious symbols such as the Lady of the Realm encode a view of can-do efficacy as female and furthermore propose that such figures will advance the fortunes of all of those who contract with them. This is a reading of the past and of historical efficacy quite at variance with that propounded by those mostly male Vietnamese credited with being the inventors of "renovation."

The Powers of Exclusion

The power of these female spirits conforms to that empiricist streak in Vietnamese religion whereby the gods who have performed well, those who have proved themselves, rise to greatest prominence. Above all these goddesses are reliable. The can-do goddesses that achieved prominence during the reform era in Vietnam might well be understood as a form of popular recognition of women's critical societal contributions. Yet the exceptional responsiveness of these spirits could also be seen to imply that women can be relied on to go beyond the call of duty. To the extent that these goddesses promise empowerment, it may well be only in acquittal of onerous expectations. As markedly conditional models of feminine self-actualization, Vietnam's hyperactive goddesses propose massive assistance to others as a path to self-realization.

In her work on Chinese popular religion, Hill Gates asks how Chinese women have represented themselves supernaturally such that the representation might assist action in their own behalf (1996, 183). This question is important if somewhat loaded. Other scholars of Chinese popular religion have considered instances where goddesses have served to empower women, providing them behavioral models in defiance of social conventions (e.g., Topely 1975; Baptandier 1996). One cannot assume that the gods of popular religion in patriarchal societies invariably reproduce patriarchal relations. However, one might well ask whether supernatural assistance sought in circumstances of entrenched inequality is indeed empowering or whether it might not be implicated in reproducing iniquities. In Vietnam, where the Lady of the Realm's propitiants are mostly women, there appears to be evidence for the role of goddesses at the center of an autonomous feminine realm. However, within that realm, it is still important to ask whether she and her fellow goddesses do represent an imaginative route to emancipation for women.

The most popular goddesses in southern Vietnam are those who have left their parental home. One tale about the Lady of the Realm tells how she wandered far from home before reaching her hillside resting place (Nguyễn Phương Thảo 1997, 207). Stories about her likeness tell of how it was transported or abducted from her hilltop home. While away on a trading voyage, Dinh Cô chose not to return to her natal home; Thiên Y A Na also left her native land by ship. One tale relates that the Black Lady was a young Khmer girl named Dềnh, who decided it was preferable to enter the Buddhist Sangha than get married according to her parents' desires. Yet these figures did not find safety in a new residence either with affines or elsewhere. Tales about the statue of the Lady of the Realm variously relate that she was discovered sitting alone at the top of the hill, disfigured on the side of a mountain having resisted her abduction, or alternatively, lying at its base. Alone and unhoused, she and her sister goddesses perished in the elements. Dinh Cô and Thiên Y A Na drowned in the sea; the Black Lady was taken by a tiger while away from her monastery (Thạch Phương and Lê Trung Vũ 1995, 238) or fell to her death off a precipice; the Lady of the Realm died by the side of a hill (Nguyễn Phương Thảo 1997, 207). These were early, miserable, unpropitious deaths. Stories further imply that these women were objects of male sexual attentions. Yet these experiences did not lead to marriage, sexual self-fulfillment, or the birth of children. On the contrary, they precipitated these figures' deaths. The Black Lady died resisting rape;[6] Thiên Y A Na, married once, jumped to her death during her wedding to a Chinese prince; the Lady of the Realm died while away looking for a husband; and Dinh Cô chose death rather than return to her father's home. Although they were sexual subjects they were nevertheless childless and died in that state.

Accounts such as these make it hard to see in the most popular goddesses in the region a positive wish-fulfilling fantasy in the manner suggested by Gates in explaining the virgin mother motif in Chinese popular religion (1996, 188). On the face of it they are abject figures: uncared for, unhoused, unmarried, violated, childless, and immature. They died lonely, untimely, elemental deaths. They are betwixt and between. They have left one home but have not found another. They live away from their parents but are unmarried. They are sexual objects but are not valued as partners. They are no longer children but are themselves childless. Not daughters, wives, or mothers, they lack the status and security of parental oversight, husbandly care, maternal self-actualization, and filial devotion. These scenarios are particularly bleak, diminishing the expectation of a woman's achieving self-realization as an esteemed member of society, be it as a daughter, a wife, a mother, or a nun. Admittedly they are not passive role models, for the women in these tales chose to leave home, refused marital plans, and resisted sexual relations or abduction. Yet the autonomy they secured is a severely attenuated one. Their willfulness resulted in their being alone, without shelter outside human relations. In most cases, what they chose as an alternative to being a child, a wife, a sexual partner, or a mother is death.

What is more, in death, by contrast, they are powerful. Although stories portray them as young women, they are regarded as powerful patrons supporting the well-being of a great number of people, to whom even powerful mandarins must bow. To their propitiants they are efficacious, multifunctional, responsive, and loyal. Yet their assistance cannot be taken for granted. They are easily angered by insults, punitive to those who rob them, and uncompromising of those who renege on a deal, causing them bad dreams, headaches, and a loss in trade. They will help anyone with anything, but the assistance they offer is conditional on dealing with them correctly, believing in them, staying faithful to them, and repaying them. They are not altruistic, yet they will return bountifully the smallest token of attention. No tranquil fonts of benevolence, they enforce the deals made with them.

Their magical power derives not from their imagined autonomy or symbolization of freedom but their susceptibility to becoming indebted to their propitiants. The efficacious repute of such beings accords to a logic that pervades the folk religion of Vietnam: that the more marginalized and socially excluded an entity, the more powerful it may be. The tales embroidered around these goddesses construct them as potentially receptive to the attention of propitiants. Their abandonment and the lack of human attention shown to them make them deeply needful. Their exclusion from society makes them exceptionally responsive. Their abjection makes their gratitude particularly generous. Their peculiar status makes them accessible. Homeless beings, they are beholden to all comers. Unattached to parents or husbands, they serve each of their petitioners with equal loyalty. Sexual beings, they can be sensually appeased. Rejecters of husbands and resistors of sexual possession by men, they are available and attentive to women. Unfettered by responsibilities to children, they are free to nurture. These tales also account for the kinds of ritual attention bestowed on the goddesses. The ritual objects that propitiants offer to them—paper houses, clothing, a multitude of foods and entertainments—fulfill their deepest needs. Their construal as unhoused and exposed has led to the construction on their behalf of some of the most impressive and substantial religious structures in the region such as the palatial shrine to Dinh Cô and the complex of large buildings in Vĩnh Tế village. In return, the goddesses have delivered assistance of a like kind. Unsheltered beings, they are patrons of a boom in real estate speculation. Victims of rape and abduction, they guarantee love matches and provide protection from domestic violence. Unmarried, they aid in the finding of a spouse and are guarantors of marital bliss. Lacking children, they are regarded as mothers and bringers of progeny. They even provide nurturance and shelter to kings.

These tales speak to the concerns of the people who propitiate these goddesses, the vast majority of whom are women. Why would women voluntarily and enthusiastically patronize figures that speak to their marginal-ized status? One answer is that they can recognize in these biographies of exclusion the high stakes they negotiate to acquit themselves of social ex-pectations. The dilemmas these goddesses have found themselves in are those with which women in Vietnam are all too familiar. From an early age, the obligation is laid on a girl to care for her siblings, support her brothers in their studies and marriages, and assist elderly and infirm parents. In many cases in Vietnam, loyalty to her natal family leads a young woman to termi-nate studies, delay marriage, and even sacrifice her marital happiness. The demonstration of filial piety very often leads to a loss of virginity. In many cases young women are led into prostitution to repay a parent's loan. Many rural women who work away from home in the city or in the rural service sector are sometimes unfairly presumed to be engaged in extramarital sexual relations. A woman who has been married or is imputed to have had prior sexual relations can find marriage or remarriage an impossibility. Once mar-ried, many women continue their support for their parents in addition to their new family, while their husbands may not only spend much of their own income on themselves, but even take a lover. A married woman may find that she is neither a fulfilled wife nor any longer a daughter; instead, in a maternal nurturing role, she may be a supporter of two or sometimes more households.

In these ways these goddesses resemble their most passionate followers: figures from whom a great deal is expected yet who can expect little in re-turn. These unfulfilled and unhoused goddesses are a projection of the kind of sacrifices many women in Vietnam may imagine they have to sustain to earn social inclusion. Tough is the hand these female spirits play who trade from abject marginality to gain recognition from their assistance to others. Constantly put upon, personally unfulfilled, open to exploitation, and easily risking social exclusion by their very conformity to cultural expectations, many women find themselves in precarious positions in society, and for them these tales of marginality resonate deeply. For many petitioners, whose lives resemble these tales, the goddess is put upon to the same extent and in the same way that they are themselves put upon, and as such she is a sympa-thetic representation of their own cultural dilemmas. These goddesses are in-deed the constructions of women; but in addition to being seen as beneficial to women, they might equally be seen as tools in the reproduction of female exploitation from generation to generation. One might ask whether some women, in endorsing these goddesses as powerful allies, are not promoting such inequalities as natural and unavoidable.

In the Service of the Matriarchs

These questions can be explored in reference to one group of devotees of the Lady of the Realm who live in Ho Chi Minh City. This extraordinary dynasty of matriarchs own up to ten houses—most of which are headed by female family members—in a wealthy District One neighborhood. Many of them have had dealings with successive waves of wealthy foreigners and have translated this advantage into domestic business success. Three generations of female household heads is unusual, even by Ho Chi Minh City's standards, where a real estate boom, thriving economy, favorable overseas connections, and history of social dislocation have enabled many women to transfer relative economic success into a high degree of personal autonomy. Several aspects about this family interest me. For a group of people who are at the cutting edge of Vietnam's integration with the global market economy, their lives are filled to an exceptional extent with religious activities in which goddesses play a central role. Although each generation has worked hard and prospered, its wealth has been heavily dependent on the next generation. While members of the third generation are today the wealthiest and, on the face of it, the most autonomous, they have the deepest sense of debt to the preceding generations. Their high level of filial obligation is matched by the highest levels of devotion to the Lady of the Realm of any members of their lineage. These factors makes theirs a valuable case study in the implication of goddess worship with the feminine face of Vietnamese capitalism, which, quite apart from creating autonomy, has fueled the reproduction of gender inequalities across generations.

Khuê was the head of this remarkable family. Although she was a grandmother and mother of eighteen boys and girls, none of her children lived with her. Seventy-year-old Khuê lived with a young woman whom she had adopted as a child after her youngest child had left the nest. She said she did this out of pity; however, there was clearly also a healthy dose of pragmatism: "Her parents split up. Her father took another wife and her mother remarried. The house she was living in was demolished. She sleeps here now. I pay her school fees, buy her clothes, and give her two thousand dong every morning for bread. She cleans clothes, does the shopping, and cooks food in return for staying here with me." Khuê cited an expectation of return as the reason for her decision to adopt the young woman. "What you give is returned to you," she explained. "When she grows up, she can look after me."

Khuê inherited this idea of intergenerational reciprocity from her Chinese father and Vietnamese mother. Khuê was born in the Mekong delta province of Sóc Trăng. Her husband, now deceased, was a migrant of southern Chinese origin. His photo was hanging above a large ancestral altar. Khuê paid tribute to him: "He was an excellent businessman. He knew how to work hard. He and I had to push a fruit barrow all over Saigon after the liberation came south." She started to cry and her voice wobbled: "My God, raising our kids was hard! Every morning we would get up and push carts—one each—all over District One. Now my knees ache all the time and I have pains in my back from that time. He died at sixty-one years of age, before he retired, before the kids grew up, before life got easy for us."

Khuê indicated her small but immaculate two-story home: "I've only been well off in the last two years." She lived entirely on support from her youngest daughter, who lived in America and sent money back every month: "One hundred dollars a time. It's enough to live on." Her home was built with money her youngest daughter had sent to her. Khuê expressed approval: "She is really filial (hiếu) that one." She said large families were a common form of insurance among Chinese and Vietnamese people: "Our children are our debts. When we grow old, we become their debts." While all of her children adhered to this maxim, it was only her youngest daughter who actually repaid the debt. Khuê showed me photos of her daughter posing in front of pagodas, a car, in a park, and beside a flowering shrub. She had been in America for six years. The old woman added sorrowfully, "She broke up with her husband. He was addicted to gambling. He got drunk, chased girls, and lost all his money. I was the one who encouraged them to meet. I thought it would be good for her. The American government allowed him to go to America because he had an American father. But over there, his gambling only got worse. My daughter couldn't stand it and left him. Now she works in a café in the morning and gets five hundred dollars a month from the U.S. government to raise her children." A photo of her grandson, living in America, showed him to be a tubby, well-indulged child carting an alarming burden of fat on his small frame.

Pragmatism led Khuê to press this marriage, and now that her daughter was an American divorcée, her expectations were being returned manifold. Her youngest daughter felt keenly obligated; indeed, she contributed far more than any of her siblings living in the vicinity. However, rather than return to Vietnam to live with her mother, for her own child's sake Khuê's daughter maintained two households and two sets of dependents, an exceptionally heavy burden. Helping her acquit these responsibilities was the Lady of the Realm. Khuê said her youngest daughter was indebted to the goddess for helping her leave the country. Since arriving in America, she regularly sent money back so that her sisters could make an offering to the goddess on her behalf. In return, the goddess helped her earn her living and funds to support her dependents.

Khuê approved of her daughter's religious piety and made repeated positive reference to how strongly she believed *(tin tưởng)* in the goddess. She also praised her daughter for her faithful propitiation of the spirits of her deceased family members. Her daughter gave money to the local pagoda every year to fund a death anniversary feast for her oldest brother, whose ashes were interred there. "She comes back to Vietnam every seventh lunar month to mark my son's death. We invite seven monks to officiate each year on the seventh month, this being the month the dead are honored in Vietnam. A gift of a new robe, toothbrush, toothpaste, soap, and a towel is presented to each monk, along with a box of instant noodles for each. She also sent more money back at Tết for her father's death anniversary. My youngest is very filial," she said of this act. Yet she also indicated the reciprocal benefit showed by the deceased for their veneration: "In return, for this offering, my son helps his sister earn a living in America. What you give you get in return."

Khuê's fifth daughter, Ngọc thought that the only way to make money in Vietnam was to hitch up with some wealthy foreigner as her youngest sister in America had done. She said that before 1975, she herself used to work at Tân Sơn Nhứt International Airport, running a hamburger stall. She had needed a special permit to enter the U.S. base. She had also learned to drive a car at this time. Like many, she said the money a single person had earned then had been enough to feed an entire family. She herself had earned up to three hundred dollars a day. "Americans have lots of money," she swore. "They would buy a hamburger for seventy cents and leave a dollar, without demanding the change." She had been able to make more than a hundred dollars a day in tips alone. Like many residents of the former Saigon, Ngoc considered the arrival of the northerners in 1975 a dark time in her life. She said she regretted that she hadn't managed to flee before the liberation came south. If she had, she would be doing very well for herself now. Several of her brothers and sisters had made it overseas. She hoped her own children could find a sponsor to bring them overseas. That was the only way they would have a future. Ngọc had tried to flee in 1980 and had spent twenty taels of gold on a place on a boat but had been captured by the police. She was handcuffed and put in jail for six months. All her money, her gold, and her house had been confiscated: "Before trying to escape, I was rich. After that, dirt poor."

Ngọc had endured a decade of deprivations. Yet in recent years she could relax because of the success of her own daughter, Loan. Ngọc pointed to her: "She's really rich, this one. She doesn't have gold or Vietnamese currency but she has thousands of dollars. She has a Taiwanese boyfriend. He brings her presents all the time and has given her money to build her house." Given the open doors and the close proximity to the neighbors, her daughter protested that her mother was speaking too loud. However, Ngọc continued, "She lives in bliss. She sleeps with an air conditioner on and only wakes up at midday!"

Khuê said her granddaughter's work was too hard, and she wanted her too to go to America. When Loan was only twenty-three, her husband had died of edema: his stomach grew bigger every day until his kidneys failed. Now she looked after her two children alone. Khuê asked if I knew anyone who would marry her daughter in Australia. A fake marriage would help her get citizenship. And did I know whether it was possible to sneak from Australia into America illegally? Loan slapped her grandmother gently and chided her for suggesting this. Her grandmother defended the suggestion to me: "Loan would do anything to get out. It's for her children. There's no future in this country. If the kids grow up here they'll be ruined."

Loan's business ventures were many and varied. She had a Honda motorcycle that she rented out to visitors and people in the neighborhood. She simultaneously managed several revolving credit groups, being responsible for collecting and redistributing the money.[7] Loan told me that a person could make a good living by providing such informal credit services. She earned more than a thousand dollars U.S. per *hụi*, each of which usually had a life of one calendar year. She said a *hụi* owner could earn a profit five to seven times that earned by putting money in the bank: "Most *hụi* owners are women. To do this, you have to have prestige *(uy tín)* so that people trust that you won't run off with the money once collected. This person has to know the situation of the participants and be confident of being able to extract payments." The main asset of *hụi* owners is their fund of knowledge about their associates. To be successful they have to have many acquaintances and know much about the details of the lives of people participating in the *hụi*. They have to be fierce as well, to be able to compel repayments. For this reason, it is said that headaches *(nhức đầu)* and complicated relationships are their lot, for their debtors very often include kin, friends, and neighbors.

Loan's main business venture was lending money to women who worked in bars. She would give a loan, for example of 100 dollars, and a month later receive 120 in repayment. Her main hours of work were between midnight and 2 A.M., when the women finished work. Those who hadn't earned enough in tips would meet her at a regular meeting point—a curbside café— and borrow money. Loan's mother viewed the women from whom she made this living as bad women: "They want to go out dancing and partying even though they have to borrow money to do so. Many of them are addicted to heroin." When I asked her how women found the money to repay, Loan hesitated, looked at her mother, and said, "Sleeping with customers—and getting tips." Fully aware of the demimonde her daughter inhabited, Ngọc steered her pragmatically toward opportunities that presented themselves. She knew her daughter Loan worked late at night, lending money to sex workers. She defended this, saying, "After the northerners came south many girls had to become prostitutes. Girls even twelve to thirteen have become addicted to heroin." She paused. "I could be arrested for saying that," she told me. Nevertheless she was more inclined to blame the women themselves. She warned me about the black-hearted nature of most of the women I was likely to meet. Ngọc said that many women who worked as drinks hostesses or as dancing partners at nightclubs were essentially prostitutes: "They may be beautiful, dress well, and speak sweetly, but most of such women have bad hearts."

The female members of this family had distinct notions of male propriety. Ideally, men should provide for their wives and family. Khuê told me about a Taiwanese acquaintance whom they had helped buy a house. "He is a very filial son," she explained. "His elderly father came over here a few years ago and opened a factory. Yet the old man spent all his time going to hostess bars and chasing after dancing girls. Finally, he dropped his wife and married one of them. His new young wife is pregnant now. His son dislikes his father for having left his mother. He has bought a house here for his mother to come and live in. He plans to marry a Vietnamese woman, doing it the proper way and living together with his mother."

Despite these strong views about expected male behavior, few of the men in this family had lived up to the ideal she spelled out for males as faithful breadwinners. It was uniquely the women who bore the burden of supporting the young, the infirm, and the elderly among them. The men of the family were either dead, incapacitated, or living on the savings amassed by their conscientious female relatives. Ngọc's own brother was forever to be found sitting in the downstairs room of her house, red-faced, his eyes closed tight by lids swollen from excessive beer consumption. Looking like a desperado, with hair falling over a sweating brow, he began drinking each day at 9 A.M. If I refused to join him, I was told, "To not share is to not respect. You can't refuse." Ngọc herself had supported her husband during the last few years of his life, out of devotion she said. Now her daughter looked after her. In a world where ideal gender roles were frequently honored only in the breach, the weight of responsibility devolved onto the shoulders of the daughters of the family. This family had done well thanks to the work of their female off-spring, their sacrifices approvingly referred to by the older women whom they supported as "filial." Although their business activities involved dealings with those whose lifestyles they regarded as immoral, these choices were defended in terms of the extraordinary circumstances of the moment, which did not allow one to realize ideal feminine behavior.

Living under weighty familial expectations, the younger women in this family had branched away from both consanguinal and affinal kin to form autonomous female-headed households. Khuê's daughter was living alone with her son in America. Loan said that she preferred to live separately with her children, to have freedom to live as she chose. Several of her aunts owned their own houses and lived alone, having either survived a husband's demise, separated, or never married. Loan had helped her mother purchase a house and through this had secured her own autonomy. Her grandmother lived alone after all her children had moved out. Loan said that earning a living in Vietnam was exhausting. You returned home each night with a headache, unlike overseas, she thought, where people could relax comfortably at home when the workday was done. She told me that after her own husband died, she had no interest in marrying again: "Husbands just eat your money and contribute nothing." She said that generally it was sisters who helped their brothers, seldom the reverse. A brother would spend all his income on his wife and children, not giving anything to his sisters or parents. On the other hand, if a woman was married, whatever she could save would be given to needy people in her family. "I now feed my whole family," she observed. She said that people who made money in Vietnam had to take care of up to ten people. For example, she herself provided for her mother, two of her siblings and their spouses, her own two children, herself, and two servants.

Her home was a two-story dwelling, three and a half meters by ten meters. She owned another similar house in the same lane. Her home had a karaoke machine, big-screen TV, video machine, and telephone. At home she demonstrated her authority in no uncertain terms. In a pause in our conversation, she angrily ordered her servants to bring in food for us to eat. She then scolded them harshly for the poor-tasting food. Their excuse, that there had been an electricity blackout, was met with scorn: "They've forgotten how to cook with gas. The next time you know there's going to be a blackout, you should prepare food in advance, hear?" She scoffed at one of them for forgetting to bring in spoons for the soup and snatched the spoons from her when they came, muttering. She then turned to ridicule her mother for thinking that overseas, people could forget their mother tongue if they didn't practice it. Her mother smiled, abashed and deferential. When her brother put his head in at the door, Loan invited him to eat lunch. He smiled and withdrew, saying he had eaten already. She turned to me and said in an exasperated voice, "See what I mean? I have to feed him and his wife as well!"

Loan was one of the most devout believers in the goddess of Châu Đốc I ever met. Her visits to Châu Đốc once a year were substantial undertakings. Each time she offered a large roast pig (her hands stretched more than a meter apart to indicate its size), fruit, flowers, and wine. "The pig alone costs between fifty and seventy U.S. dollars. Altogether, offerings amount to a hundred dollars per occasion. I give a tip of fifty cents to each of the attendants in the temple and give money to local charities—another hundred dollars." In addition to her hefty undertakings with the goddess, she also gave assistance to members of her family in making their own offerings to the goddess: "I am the one usually providing the transport for my family. The minibus costs a hundred dollars for two days; food and lodging during the trip cost another hundred." Loan was also one of the few people I met to have gone to the extent of acquiring a robe from the goddess' shrine. She stood on a stool and bowed once, then pulled down a large, plastic-wrapped bundle that was sitting behind the altar to Kuan Yin: "It is one of the Lady of the Realm's own robes." The robe was designed for a figure of enormous girth: it was about two meters wide at the base, and the sleeves were about one and a half meters long. "Her Ladyship is really big. Have you seen her?" Loan asked. The robe was of red synthetic fabric onto which brightly colored aluminum sequins and silver pieces had been sewn. It was fringed at the base with colored strips of the same material. The red sleeves had wide yellow cuffs. A green dragon studded with sequins facing a yellow rising sun, was embroidered on the front of the robe. Below the dragon was an embroidered green fish, spouting water from a blowhole. On each sleeve were embroidered phoenixes. The body and sleeves of the robe were embroidered with Chinese characters. No one, including Loan's grandmother, could read what they said. "It's in Chinese," they explained. But the consensus was that it was probably the name of the person or persons who had donated the robe.

Loan said it was rare to have such a robe; it had been hard to secure and cost her more than $300. "There are even more beautiful ones," she told me. "This one is at least twenty years old. Some of the newer ones are even nicer, but harder to get." The robe, once worn by the goddess, was a potent object into which the powers of the goddess had been infused. Loan's mother told me that to have such a robe was auspicious indeed. Loan added, "This is what helps me do business." Her possession of this robe drew attention to a number of similarities between herself and the goddess. It underlined a homology between the goddess as a creditor and Loan's own position as owner of many credit circles. The goddess' multifunctional powers also reflected Loan's many and diverse kinds of enterprises. The fierceness and the volatility of the goddess in many ways matched Loan's toughness as a businesswoman. The benefits Loan brought to those with whom she dealt were just as conditional as the assistance provided by the goddess. The risks Loan undertook in her financial dealings were also underwritten by this powerful patroness, on whom she could rely as a last resort for assistance with securing loan repayments.

In various respects the hopes Loan invested in the Lady of the Realm and the attributes she assigned this deity accorded with the significance in which she was held in the eyes of her family. Weighed down by family expectations and deeply immersed in complex business deals, Loan was far from at peace: often preoccupied, scowling, and given to outbursts, while considered to be living the life of luxury by her own mother because she slept in so late. Loan's female kin commented that Lady of the Realm, too, can at times be hot tempered: "If you go to Her Ladyship's temple and do not offer your respects or light incense to her, she could easily bring misfortune down upon you. If on a visit to her temple you were to complain that the building or grounds were ugly or that they contained features mixed together in an inappropriate fashion, she would become angry. If the Lady of the Realm helps you, you should share the results of your success with her. Naturally, you should return and show your gratitude and repay your debt. If you don't, she might prevent you from selling, or cloud your mind." The ambivalent, volatile, punitive persona attributed to the goddess was very much an image of Loan's psychic stresses as she juggled the demands of kin and transacted with a wide circle of business associates. A goddess of whom much was expected and to whom little was returned spoke to Loan in her capacity as de facto lineage matriarch on whom was placed heavy demands. Images of the goddess as a being with exploitable sexual appetites also alluded to the benefits her family expected to derive from the sexuality of its daughters. Certainly Loan's transactions with wealthy husbands and her financial deals with sex workers were monitored by her elders and redounded greatly to her family's benefit. Little wonder then that placed under such pressure, she might turn for support to this stocky, glowering figure with the power to deliver headaches and disturb sleep, who is erotically aroused by male dancers, is partial to meat, and has a reputation for wringing necks.

One conclusion that might be taken from this story is that the Châu Đốc goddess constitutes something of a celebration of the face of informal capitalism as feminine. The goddess is an expression of what has been increasingly accorded the highest value in Vietnam, the market. She is an associate for those who, like Loan, are at the forefront of market relations in Vietnamese society. Transacting with this deity had helped this young woman become extraordinarily successful. On the face of it, her houses, her wealth, and her impressive business interests make a clear-cut case for the goddess as a reliable spiritual associate allowing Vietnam's business-oriented women to achieve autonomy. Yet although Loan represents an extreme case, she also illustrates the problem of overachievement, earning far more than what she needed for her own immediate family's needs and becoming something of a resource for the whole extended family. Far from being a basis of power, the multiple homes she owned were an index of her lack of autonomy, of how much was expected of her as a junior female member. She saw her own house not as a trophy of success but a refuge from the expectations that others placed upon her. The heavy expectations she placed upon this goddess reflected the hefty expectations placed upon her.

Loan's story illustrates the function goddess worship can play in inculcating in women the disposition to sacrifice for the good of their family. This view reads these goddesses less as a mainstay for women in adversity or as a companion in individual self-realization than as a mechanism for reproducing across generations women's obligations to subordinate themselves to their kin. In Loan's family, which exhibited social norms still widespread in many areas of Vietnamese rural and urban society, female progeny are highly valued as anchors, breadwinners, and mainstays of the family. According to an ideology of transgenerational debt applied to female family members more rigorously than to men, the obligation one generation owes to the preceding one is feminized. The people most praised in this family for their filial piety also attracted the most commendations from their kin for their displays of religious piety. In some respects, their devotion is a testament to their subordinate status. The expectations that the daughters of this family invested in the goddess of Châu Đốc are a measure of the responsibilities they bore. They leaned on this goddess for help in achieving results demanded of them by their older female relatives. Rather than regard such a spirit as an aid to achieving feminine autonomy, one can see her as an accessory to the transfer onto junior women of a burden of onerous obligations.

Much of what Vietnam's female entrepreneurs have achieved in their lives is in conformity with conventional expectations placed on women: to nurture life, generate wealth, be hardworking, conscientious, capable, and dutiful. Yet in deference to cultural expectations such as filial norms, many women are not only overworked but are forced into compulsive breach of the norms of society. Like Loan, many women who do well in business bend their allocated gender role, bursting the brittle limits of received gender ideologies, with their "loud" voices, unpolished speech, sun-darkened skin, "low cultural level," "vulgar" aesthetic preferences, wide-ranging social contacts, and "fierce" negotiating style, often becoming, through their economic autonomy, de facto household heads. The enormous number of young women pouring into sex work in Vietnam in recent years is the most graphic case of the way a woman's sacrifice to her family in compliance with onerous filial expectations places her in breach of such cultural ideals as virginity, chastity, and fidelity. Many women in this situation turn to a spirit who tales relate was in a similarly vulnerable position of being neither daughter, wife, nor mother, yet who is expected by others to meet all manner of requests for assistance. For many women this goddess is an essential ally in the many responsibilities they are expected to fulfill and a companion in the lonely and stigmatized road they chart to acquit themselves. Yet such a goddess also may help to reinforce as inevitable the lengths such women must go to meet the demands placed upon them.

In some ways Loan's case strikingly confirms Linh's view about the traditional restrictions faced by Vietnamese women and the only limited resolution of these that is available through religious practice. Because for Loan a feminine religious sphere was not a refuge from unequal power relations but a mode through which they were realized, her situation is in a sense much bleaker than the story of a qualified traditional feminine religious autonomy put by Linh. As an intellectual Linh regarded herself as well positioned to take part in the new social relations flowing from Vietnam's nascent economic engagements, which she believed represented a surer path to transforming the status of women. Nevertheless, she was still dependent on her family, while Loan, a beneficiary of these reforms, earned enough to house herself and others. Linh looked down upon Loan's religious activities as ignorant or backward, yet these activities made her many times wealthier than Linh. But Loan's ostensible success also casts into question the faith Linh invested in further global integration as a precondition of women's liberation. Although associated with activities at the cutting edge of Vietnam's economic integration, Loan's gains were not so much her own as her family's. Furthermore, her success came at the expense of being socially marginal, living alone, engaging in opaque relations with Taiwanese "husbands," meeting sex workers on the street after midnight to extract debt repayments from them, and becoming involved in practices that many regarded as superstitious. Only in a qualified sense did the spiritual patroness of Loan's economic practices promise to her the autonomy that Linh believed would flow from increases in her country's involvement in such market relations.

Goddess of Possibilities

Multivalent symbols such as the Lady of the Realm are not easily confined within any one meaning but can be seen as both enabling and oppressive. Their centrality in public discourse indicates a preoccupation in the society with identifying, if not prescribing, exemplary feminine values. By the same token they can only be popular because they do speak to people's circumstances.

The question of the autonomy of Vietnamese women greatly interested Huyền, a young woman who had spent five years living away from her country while studying in Canada. On reflection, she was not sure that views of Vietnamese women as dominated by men or, alternatively, autonomous were adequate to the complexity of the problem. For Huyền, the prominent cultural position of the goddesses of the southern Vietnamese plain indicated the substantial freedoms women already enjoyed, even if greater autonomy for women in the public sphere was to be embraced.

Huyền thought that the heavy responsibility placed on the shoulders of women like Loan was by no means indicative of the favorable position of women in Vietnam. Like Linh, she was struck by the restrictive roles her society allocated women: "Since I returned from Canada, people have remarked constantly about my confidence, independence, self-esteem, and maturity. I realize that these factors are not developed in women in this society. Women don't have self-knowledge and confidence in their own importance. They rely too much on other people's judgment of them. Someone who is self-assertive in business is withdrawn and shy in other contexts. This can be seen as reserve or haughtiness, but it is really due to fearfulness on their part."

Men by contrast dominated the cultural public sphere. Huyền's perception of Vietnamese men was that they were great talkers, inveterate politicians, and culturally and artistically inclined. This view could be illustrated by reference to the former Republic of Vietnam, under which she considered some of her country's greatest cultural achievements had occurred. She said that the early years of the Republic were a happy, positive time: "The war against the French was over. It was the first time Vietnam had known peace in a hundred years. Elections were to be held for the unification of the country. The period stimulated an outburst of music, celebrating life and love. Chief composer among those producing music at the time was Phạm Duy. His songs tapped the mood of the times. Many of his songs developed the romantic prewar genre of music that had been popular in the 1930s and

1940s. He also released songs written during the period of resistance against the French. But he also composed new songs after his move to Saigon."

Huyền admired Phạm Duy as a strong and romantic man: "He was a resistance fighter during the anti-French war. I've read his autobiography. His stories of meeting young village women during his movements around the countryside are fun to read. He wrote that he met many beautiful country girls and rolled around in piles of hay with them. He had so many lovers. But he settled down when he met his wife. He had heard about the beautiful, proud young daughter of a martyr of the resistance against the French when he moved to the south. She was so celebrated that no one dared approach her. It was said she was beyond the reach of average people. But Phạm Duy dared. Imagine! At that time people thought that it was Phạm Duy who was the lucky one!"

Another positive male cultural figure whose songs touched everyone's hearts was the composer Trịnh Công Sơn: "His songs in the 1960s, protesting the war, captured the popular mood: a sincere yearning for an end of the conflict. He also wrote many popular love songs. This reflects the trait of romance and sentimentalism that is a really old Vietnamese trait. Yet the thirst for love songs during the war years of the sixties also reflected a kind of escapism—a retreat from reality. Many people, my parents included, behaved as if the war was not happening. Despite the sound of shells, the whistle of bullets, they lived as if all was normal. They made no attempt to save for the future, made no plans for eventualities. They pursued love affairs and just used their salary to purchase goods such as electronic appliances for the house. For them, it was the only way to act in a desperate situation over which they had no control."

Huyền thought that by contrast, the postwar years showed up the limitations of men all too clearly. The fate of her own family revealed men's great dependence on women: "After the Communists won the war, my father had an affair, with a close friend of my mother's. My mother accepted it at the time, because my father was so depressed at having lost his position, his status, and she realized it was helping him." When I expressed amazement at her mother's tolerance, she laughed, "Vietnamese men are weak!" blurting it out like a stark truth. "Woman realize men's weakness has to be indulged. That kind of thing doesn't threaten them. And my mother's friend was a really lovely person. It was really fortunate for everyone involved that this happened."

Huyền said that during the early years of Communist rule, only her mother's illegal market activities kept her family alive: "After the men had all lost their jobs, women continued to provide for their families. Can you imagine? Even I used to buy and sell on the black market. I was only fifteen and didn't have any experience of life, but I worked helping my mother. It seemed natural. I didn't think about the danger. That changed when I was arrested. I became scared then and stopped doing that work." When disaster struck it was again to a woman that her family turned for salvation: "My mother too was also arrested by a policeman, whom she had neglected to bribe. She was purchasing food vouchers from people so she could collect the food and resell it on the black market, a business those lucky enough to have saved money could engage in. When she was arrested our family was in a desperate situation. We were broke. Some neighbors and relatives cooked food for us when our mother was in jail. But my mother's friend and father's lover put up the money to bribe the police for my mother's release. It was a loan for which she never requested repayment."

Despite her experience of strong, feminine roles, Huyền considered the autonomy of women in Vietnam to be qualified: "Vietnamese women are really strong and competent. They work really hard without consideration of the difficulties, which they accept as normal. The negative side of this is that they don't stop to consider their exploited position. They don't question the inequalities between themselves and men. Plus they suffer from negative evaluation of their work. Market traders are not highly regarded. Their financial success is seen as evidence of greediness or money hunger. This is despite the fact that they do this for their family. They are victims of negative stereotypes, victims of their own success."

This was the situation of people such as Loan: they were hardworking, linchpins of the nation's economy, but their economic and religious activities were not highly valued. Although Loan did her work in performance of filial obligations, much of her work—such as loaning money to sex workers and taking money from foreign boyfriends—was considered culturally marginal. The kind of transactions with the goddess that Loan frequently made, based on a notion of the Lady's supernatural responsiveness, were also despised, considered ignorant, and sometimes criminalized as superstition. In some critical commentaries the connection between economic practices and religious beliefs was considered even more degrading because of that connection: "Marketing gods and saints is on the increase. To market people's most sacred beliefs is really a pitiful thing. The cultured cannot help but be disconcerted" (Đặng Nghiêm Vạn 1998, 254–255). The mixing of religion and commerce was routine for Loan, who lived in an intertwined world of gods and complex financial transactions. However, her everyday activities took place against negative appraisals in the official realm.

Huyền showed interest in my stories of the diverse practices of goddesses and popular religion in Vietnam but admitted to being something of a cultural outsider with respect to them. What little she knew of goddesses she had read in compilations of some of the associated myths. Educated to university level during the first fifteen years of the postwar Communist government, she had been taught to consider the religious realm as irrational and outmoded. When I asked her what she thought the term *"linh"* (magic responsiveness) meant, she was not certain but thought it meant belief in a spirit's capability to grant requests. Pushing such beliefs into the nation's developmental past, she also associated tales of enchanted beings with her own childhood: "When I was a child I heard folk tales that talked about the *linh* possessed by Vietnamese spirits—spirits who people believed could grant requests or punish wrongdoing. For example, I remember a story about a fairy whose name I believe was Thiên Y A Na. I think she was a spirit of a pre-Vietnamese kingdom called Champa. Her shrine is somewhere in central Vietnam. The story mentioned that people believed that they could borrow money from her."

Huyen told me the tale:

> As far as I remember, Thiên Y A Na was a woman living in central Vietnam. She left to marry a Chinese prince and bore him two children. Yet her husband was unfaithful to her, taking mistresses. Saddened, she resolved to leave him and return home. She transferred herself into a log from a *tràm* tree and floated back to central Vietnam. The log was surrounded by a halo; it gave out a heavenly fragrance and was accompanied by sweetly singing birds. On the return journey, along the coast of Vietnam, many villages strove to bring the log to shore. They were unsuccessful and she eventually reached her home village in Vietnam. Floating to shore, she appeared to a woodcarver in a dream, saying she wanted her likeness to be carved in the log. He did so and a shrine was erected to venerate the goddess.

This story of Thiên Y A Na is similar to those stories of goddesses that die between homes, neither daughter nor wife, often entailing evasion of marriage, parental obligations, or rape. In this case she was a mother, but she abandoned her faithless husband and her children. Huyền said she read the story in a collection of Vietnamese legends and that there were two versions. The second one said that she was a fairy descended to earth and was raised as a girl by ordinary human parents in central Vietnam. Huyền said, "I really like the first version. It celebrates the independence of women. There are those who say in ancient times Vietnam was a matriarchy, which I myself doubt. But it was probably true of the region of central Vietnam where the Cham ruled and women were more independent."

She said the story was similar to the historical episode concerning the Vietnamese Trần dynasty princess, who was promised in marriage to the king of Champa in exchange for two central provinces: "Her name was Huyền Trân, which meant "black pearl," for her skin was dark, and she was chosen to appeal to the aesthetic preferences of the dark-skinned Chams. When her husband died, she was to be cremated on his funeral pyre according to custom. However, she escaped with her lover on the eve of the cremation. It seemed that she just disappeared, but in reality she sailed away with him and lived on an island off the coast of Vietnam. To reappear would have been to incite war between the Chams and the Vietnamese. They stayed away for two years." Huyền relished the story of the independent princess on an extended romantic interlude from Confucianist control and Cham practices of royal widow burning. Her version of the story contrasts markedly with one told to me by an ethnic Chinese man in Ho Chi Minh City; he depicted the princess as a faithful widow, a virtuous mother, and a pioneer of new lands for the Vietnamese nation.[8] Yet Huyền's more romantic vision of the princess is also repeated in a version of the legend published by the Southern Vietnamese Women's Museum. While stolidly praising her "lifelong devotion to an eternal Champa-Vietnamese friendship," the account breaks lyrically into unmasked appreciation for her "unfinished and romantic love," so awkward for Confucianists: "In spite of the storms, the rumors, and the strict laws at that time, they floated together in the small boat for ten months. She must have lived the happiest days of her life free of troubles and anxiety" (Vietnamese Women's Museum 1993, 16).

Both of these tales can be read as examples of the traditional expectations invested in women for the cementing of affinal ties or perpetuating the family. Huyền Trân's year-long romantic interlude can be read as a rare exception to such subordination and Thiên Y A Na's leap into the waves proposing death to be the only way out of a failed marriage. However, not for Huyền. To her Huyền Trân's tale was about a woman escaping self-effacing cultural obligations to follow her own inclinations. She saw Thiên Y A Na's leaving her husband as an act of independence. This she maintained to the point of quarreling with the tale. She said, "What bugs me about the story of Thiên Y A Na you see in the collection of legends is that it refers to her as a little girl in Vietnam and then she suddenly marries a Chinese prince and has children." "Did she leave home voluntarily?" I asked. Huyền thought for a while: "I believe that she turned herself into a log to float away to the north and re-transferred herself into a woman when she arrived." "What were her reasons for leaving home?" I asked. She replied, "It was out of a spirit of adventure. My memory is vague. This just might be my own addition, but I think it was her restlessness to see the world."

Huyền's view of these legendary figures as expressing a certain degree of feminine autonomy in her society illustrates the way the meaning of these goddesses so often mirrors the concerns of their interpreters. In the interpretations discussed in this chapter, religious symbols do not have fixed meanings; instead, the tales around them act like a charter for the fulfillment of a variety of feminine projects. Huyền's vision of this goddess was romantic: she saw the goddess as a symbol of independence and romantic self-realization. Her view, alluding to new experiences beyond national borders, released Vietnam's goddesses from the thrall of representing the nation, the cultural essence of Vietnam, norms of competent motherhood, or heroic familial sacrifice. The meaning invested in legendary feminine figures by this Canadian-educated university student, full of wanderlust and curiosity, makes it clear that the horizons opened up by the phenomena of goddesses in Vietnam are a good deal wider than any one person could readily imagine. According to Linh, the shrines to such goddesses were a temporary haven, and pilgrimage provided women an exceptional moment of liberation from traditionally restrictive cultural horizons. For her the eagerly awaited modernization of Vietnam promised to complete feminine emancipation. From the perspective of Như's world, emancipation had arrived and could be found in an alternative feminine realm of religious and economic practice. Loan's circumstances show this ostensibly autonomous feminine realm to be not entirely problem free, particularly considering the heavy burdens and intergenerational expectations that the women involved in it shoulder. Nevertheless, for Loan, the goddess of Châu Đốc was for this all the more valued as an accomplice, allowing her to relieve the cultural double bind of her prodigious demonstration of filial piety. While the kind of beliefs invested in the Châu Đốc goddess by her most passionate devotees such as Loan set an important foundation upon which others, less deeply involved, might elaborate, the goddess' popularity is, by the same token, only understandable by her amenability to being cross-dressed by often very different notions. Goddesses such as the Châu Đốc deity are important sites for the playing out of different ideas of femininity in Vietnamese society. Clearly their powerful hold on people's imaginations makes these symbols a valuable means for understanding the issues that are most compelling in people's lives. In their fateful unification of disparate interests, one gets a vivid sense of the vitality and complexity of the society in which they are situated.

Epilogue

On Pilgrimages and Freedom
in Late-Socialist Vietnam

The goddesses of the southern Vietnamese plain are genuinely popular foci of attention. They draw together large numbers of people who come from all walks of life and from all corners of rural and urban society. They excite commentary, both oral and written, from a host of different interpreters and lie at the heart of all manner of religious quests. At the shrine to the Lady of the Realm in Vĩnh Tế village, one is struck by the free flow of people in and out of the shrine, the unorchestrated and individualistic quality of rites, and the untrammeled play of popular exegesis. The sight of hundreds of thousands of people massing in this location on pilgrimages and at festivals is noteworthy given the government's obsessive concern with territorial security, its well-publicized control and surveillance of religious organizations, and its tight policing of information flows. Such gatherings pose questions about the nature of religious freedom in Vietnam. Do they represent resistance to a repressive state, a counter-cultural alternative to an elite worldview, or an evanescent outburst against stifling cultural conventions? Do they encode an intransigent local or grassroots culture, a resistance to patriarchal authority, or do they express the power and freedom women enjoy in this society?

One interpretation of the upsurge of religious practice in Vietnam has been to regard this as a symptom of renewed societal freedom after decades of control. The concept of religious resurgence, which informs journalistic accounts of popular religion in Vietnam (Hiebert 1994; Kamm 1996; Templer 1999), renders it as an outcome of popular resistance to a repressive state. The "curious coexistence" of religion and a Communist party suggests that Vietnam's political system no longer conforms to the Leninist model of "mono-organizational socialism" (Thayer 1995, 59). A related approach to the growth of the religious sector in Vietnam has been to regard it as proof of the decline in relevance of Marxism-Leninism in Vietnam and the loss in prestige of its ruling party. Practices that were once regarded as illicit super-stitious behavior now thrive and are tacitly accepted by the state. Some re-gard this as a critical dimension of the party's loss of relevance, leaving an ideological vacuum in Vietnam (Marr 1995). Domestic critics of the state's adherence to socialist doctrine in a global environment of ideological plural-ism have derisively drawn an analogy with folk religion to compare com-munism to a "roadside cult," suggesting that the political philosophy of the party has become a marginal practice (The Saigonese 1996).

The shrines to some goddesses in contemporary Vietnam do tend to eclipse the institutions of the state in universalistic appeal. Attracting pas-sionate followings and a buzz of conjecture, they outshine in charisma most symbols of Communist rule. The crowds and effervescent activity in the shrines to spirits such as the Lady of the Realm evoke the mass mobilizational ethos out of which Vietnam's socialist state came to power. As responsive beings in whom people invest fervent aspirations, whose efficacy is constantly being assessed, and whose reputation is always on the line, such goddesses contrast with stereotypes of the Vietnamese state as bureaucratic, faction prone, ideologically conflicted, and wary of diversity to the point of courting stagnation. As a broad church, giving refuge to a wide variety of propitiants, interpretations, and ritual forms, these goddesses embody a quality of inclu-siveness that the Party is often accused of lacking in matters religious. Never-theless, the state's own engagement in such practices cautions against con-trasting the colorful and dynamic world of popular religion with the gray and rigid world of politics. The state participates in and tries to influence practice at these sites with considerable effect. Although the state is unable to deter-mine the form of religious practice, which emerges in response to a great variety of influences, it does succeed in advancing its own agenda at these sites and hence shares in their popularity.

In important ways pilgrimage cults are neither exclusively forms of resis-tance nor by-products of ideological exhaustion but also cultural practices particularly well suited to "late-socialist" contexts.[1] Such contexts are marked by substantial ideological contradictions as ruling parties have abandoned re-distributive social policies in favor of market-driven development, stimulat-ing private economic initiatives but stemming civil society alternatives and opening the door to foreign investment while trying to quell challenges to stability identified as external in origin. In late-socialist countries, single party rule has been retained, and the state still attempts to police the discursive field. The hybrid formations of late socialism have emerged amid the sheer

informational intensity and ideational plurality of the postmodern information age, conditions that some hold responsible for ending or forcing the
transformation of socialist systems (Bauman 1992, 171; Appadurai 1996, 43).
Pilgrimages have thrived in such conditions of cultural volatility, for their
central symbols are ambiguous enough to sustain interpretations whose
assumptions differ markedly. As the rites associated with them are piecemeal and the beliefs about them too diffuse to be codified or systematized
by a clergy, pilgrimage cults do not compel a monolithic reading. Indeed, the
shrines at their center present a frame upon which different views are super-
imposed and where projects may meet and overlap without their divergent
assumptions ever being made explicit, let alone coming into conflict with
each other. Popular readings may be in contravention of the state's ideology,
but even in a carefully monitored discursive environment in which alternative or oppositional interpretations are not articulated in oratory, sermons, or
public announcements, such diversity cannot be quashed.[2]

As in other late-socialist and postsocialist contexts, one ideological current that is alive in Vietnam and winning a degree of endorsement from both
the official sphere and relatively nonaligned intellectuals is cultural nationalism. This is the renewed emphasis on symbolic forms that embody or promise to reinvigorate the national project in the face of perceived dangers. Popular religious practice, read as folk culture, has been considered capable of
symbolizing and sustaining the nation against the imagined threats of foreign
cultural inundation or moral unraveling. Goddess worship in particular has
been interpreted as important and typical, bringing people together, representing the nation, encoding its history, and embodying its culture. In this
process, even soberly suited intellectuals have made their interpretive investments of passionate lyricism about mothers, uncomplicated originary
identity, feminine purity, and fertile growth. These commentators also think
about popular religious practice in terms of its benefits to the national project of development and economic growth. Sometimes such practice is rationalized: even if popular beliefs are culturally misguided or ignorant, they
have a psychologically beneficial function, and what is good for the farmers'
or traders' psychological well-being is good for the nation.

It is an important attribute of these spirits that they attract such inflated
claims. Yet another of the characteristics of these goddesses is their evasion of
firm categorization. The Lady of the Realm represents a triumph of the
symbolic religious imagination over the rigidities of classification. That an
Indianized god could be transmuted into a Sinicized goddess is a marvel of
creativity. What some intellectuals refer to as laziness or the lack of education

of believers—the failure to maintain proper distinctions among cultural, ethnic, or religious traditions—has been vital to a process by which elements of multiple currents of influence have been synthesized into something new and ever changing. As found objects—cosmetically feminized, expensively robed, adorned with the symbolism of Buddhism, garbed with the prestige of heroines from neighboring ethnic groups, encrusted with fables and rumors of efficacy—southern Vietnam's goddesses constitute works in progress of a most exciting order.

These symbolically dynamic attributes make it difficult to paint people's journeys to the shrines of such goddesses as a form of spiritual disengagement, whether as otherworldly or as counter-cultural emancipatory projects. On the contrary, the shrines to these goddesses have proven relevant to a wide range of this-worldly concerns. What makes them pertinent is their ambiguity or openness to interpretation. This quality is a defining characteristic of the symbols at the heart of pilgrimage cults. From the Virgin Mother Mary, whose lineage is obscure (Warner 1976), to the Lady of the Realm, with her mysterious and contested origins, the most successful pilgrimage symbols have been those not firmly tied to specific social identities and cultural or political projects. This lack of specificity has allowed them to become loci of diffused meanings and disparate usages and to speak to a geographically extensive following. They are symbolic foci in which a spatially variegated array of experiences finds expression.

Translocal religious practice of this kind has increased in Vietnam in recent years in consequence of the growth in migration, urbanization, commercialization, mass transport, and communications technology. These processes have not undermined as much as refigured religious practice, altering the meaning of religious symbols, the nature of the rites, and the makeup of the body of propitiants. Sacred symbols with indeterminate or fluid identities that appeal to the diverse and shifting preoccupations of a mass following have eclipsed those whose meaning is closely tied to specific places, events, and social forms. The changing contours of the religious landscape are sometimes accounted for as the playing out of a kind of whimsical lottery. An increasingly mobile and fashion-driven religious public has lent its support to certain sacred sites and symbols and has turned its back on others. While to some these processes evoke a dystopia where things fall apart and centers cannot hold, they also open up possibilities for new centers and situated practices to emerge. One example of such realigments in the religious world has been the concentration of the benefits and meaning of most of the key pilgrimage sites in urban centers. Some of the principal beneficiaries of the uptake in pilgrimage activities in Vietnam have been urban based, from pilgrimage entrepreneurs and bus drivers to founders of suburban branch shrines and cultural commentators.

The ambiguous quality that makes pilgrimage symbols spatially inclusive also makes them salient over time. Pilgrimage activity in Vietnam has grown in circumstances of rapid social change. As in other late-socialist and post-socialist contexts, drastic economic restructuring has unleashed enormous benefits to certain groups of people but has destabilized and marginalized others. Journeys to the shrines of spirits have been buoyed by an increase in individual wealth, particularly that earned through commercial means; and in their relationships with the spirits pilgrims seek, among other things, to explain and control that newfound wealth and account for variable fortunes. People bring to such shrines concerns from an increasingly complex society. These sites have come into their own in circumstances of uneven development and great variability in economic forms and fortunes. Spirits such as the Lady of the Realm simultaneously sustain members of agricultural communities engaged in agriculture and those urban dwellers involved in complex commercial and financial relationships. They have been focal points for mass tourism, commerce, and consumerism while at the same time serving as symbols for culturally conservative projects that aim to reverse or slow the rate of such changes.

The complexity and dynamism described in this work is not a new development in a society situated at an important cultural crossroads and historically fashioned by powerful currents of change. The rise of pilgrimages as a mass cultural phenomenon is but a recent chapter in a fascinating social and religious history. The Lady of the Realm's recent superstardom is perhaps overshadowed by an even more interesting episode in the history of her cult: that of her ethnic and gender transformation. Sometime between one and three hundred years ago, a statue of the male god Shiva, perhaps already displaying androgynous qualities, became read as unambiguously female. Its torso was draped in feminine robes, and a thick mask of cement and paint permanently transfigured its face. Just as curious is the phenomenon of lingam goddesses, also worshiped in the vicinity of the shrine to the Lady of the Realm. The stories told about such beings are similar to those told about goddesses such as the Lady of the Realm, and it is equally unclear when they were enshrined or began to be venerated in their current form.[3] Information that might help accurately date these twin processes of Vietnamization and feminization is lacking, although the broader context for these transformations is the Vietnamese state's expansion and incorporation of different ethnic cultures, the colonization of southern Vietnam by migrants from diverse origins, and a weakening emphasis on Confucianist political structures (Tạ Chí Đại Trường 1989; Huỳnh Ngọc Trảng et al. 1993a) as well as the growth of extralocal trade, improvements in communications, and the deepening of ties to urban centers.

Pilgrimage cults vary according to place and time, and they express people's sense about their place and time in the world. Southern Vietnam, where this study has been based, is the country's most dynamic commercial region, a place where market relations are highly developed, monetary transactions and credit relationships are deeply entrenched, and trade, investment, and remittance flows are high. The characteristic practices of pilgrimage here are transaction-based and dyadic and entail intimate engagements with a personalistic deity informed by mutuality and negotiated outcomes. The practices and beliefs involved in these relationships address and in many ways recapitulate the social relations of interdependence as well as those of inequality and exclusion that characterize the region. A distinctive trait of pilgrimages in southern Vietnam is the passage of people from urbanized economic hubs, particularly from Ho Chi Minh City, to the shrines of goddesses near the national borders and in economic hinterlands, to which they make offerings. Ho Chi Minh City, positioned advantageously in relation to the surrounding resource frontiers from which commodities are drawn and the borders across which massive flows of wealth move, has emerged as the region's main trade, service, finance, and processing center. The pattern of urban people's religious travel in this region appears to draw inspiration from and render intelligible their position in this region's economic geography.[4]

Northern Vietnam shares a similar geography of urban centers surrounded by resource hinterlands, in particular a primary production-oriented river delta and borders that yield important benefits to the inhabitants of these centers. As in the south, pilgrims from Hanoi fan out into the surrounding hinterlands to venerate female spirits in locations such as Hà Tây, Tuyên Quang, Bắc Ninh, Lạng Sơn, Quảng Ninh, and Nam Hà, although the phenomenon of pilgrimages to the shrines of border-dwelling goddesses is not so prominent. My preliminary observations suggest that the style of pilgrimage practice may also be regionally variable. One twenty-four hour journey with a group of pilgrims from an urban market area in Hanoi took us to the temples of a group of goddesses in the foothills of Tuyên Quang, a province to the northwest of the national capital. What was so striking about this pilgrimage was the highly organized, disciplined, and economical fashion in which it was conducted. A hundred fifty tickets were purchased in advance from one outlet. The four ancient buses left on time and traveled in a tight convoy. Sets of take-away food parcels for three separate meals, prepared in advance, were distributed to the entire company at meal-times. A team was dropped at one temple to cook and prepare lunch while the rest of the group covered a collection of outlying shrines before returning to base camp for a cooked meal. The only stops aside from the temples were brief toilet breaks by the rice paddies. No stops were made in commercial es-tablishments or built-up areas, and even the precincts of the shrines lacked commercial opportunities. Further research is required to determine how common this style of pilgrimage is in Hanoi. Certainly it contrasts with the kind of pilgrimage in southern Vietnam described in this work, whose de-parture times are variable and modes of transport more luxurious, whose participants purchase their own meals en route, where refreshment stops are made in commercial establishments, and where consumption is almost non-stop, in particular in the precincts of the shrines themselves, which are in the heart of commercial areas.

This variety of popular religious practice also reflects in a particularly vivid way the divisions in Vietnamese society. The commercialized, consum-erist, and ethnically pluralist nature of much southern pilgrimage culture is sometimes taken by critics from Hanoi not as an authentic regional differ-ence but as a legacy of that region's cultural degradation under the French and Americans. The annual festival to the Lady of the Realm attracts people from the provincial centers and villages of the Mekong region and has rapidly grown in recent years in tandem with an increase in local economic activity. However, the festival is avoided ("shunned" might not be too strong a word) by many city folk as being a largely rural gathering. The spatial and temporal separation of urban from rural devotees and the differences in the type of rites and patterns of sociability that occur at the site occur in a context of widening social divergences between cities and the countryside under the impact of Vietnam's market reforms (Kerkvliet and Porter 1995). Neverthe-less, divisions between urbanized pilgrimages and the rural festival must not be overdrawn. In celebrating the festival rural people share and express many of the aspirations of their urban compatriots.

These observations contrast with the general research agenda adopted by Vietnam's domestic ethnological and folkloric researchers. In Vietnam's late-socialist period, ethnological research has focused on culture as a static, almost proprietorial, item, to be documented, preserved, and selectively re-habilitated. The study of culture is often a hunt for serviceable national icons, whereas most of the on the ground readings of these goddesses advanced by supplicants at their pilgrimage sites emphasize the personal or familial bene-fits of these deities rather than their value to broader collectivities. The con-temporaneous interest shown in such "folk" symbols by their urban neighbors and those involved in various nonagrarian occupations suggests that in their analyses of these cultural practices, anthropologists should pay more attention to the urban, industrialized, occupationally differentiated, commercialized, mass-mediated social contexts from which so many of those who have constituted these practices are drawn rather than confine the search for explanatory variables to the remote, geographically peripheral, rural, or culturally iconic parts of the country in which these symbols are enshrined. Treating such symbolic practices under the category of tradition or cultural heritage is not satisfactory, given they are thrown up and emphasized in contemporary contexts of rapid change, social differentiation, domination, and resistance. Whereas until quite recently, studies of religion in Vietnam dwelt heavily on the political dimensions of religion and its role in reproducing inequality and exclusion, contemporary works emphasize cultural unity, homogeneity, and harmony. Without returning to the days of radical dismissal, it is necessary to rediscover the role religious symbols play in the articulation of social distinctions, of power, class, status, gender, and ethnicity, to name but a few forms of social differentiation.

Rather than assume that pilgrimages necessarily spring from a unified national experience, this study has addressed some of the partial contours of this religious activity, in particular the gendered, occupational, and place-based dimensions of such practice. The goddesses of southern Vietnam offer insights into a discernibly partial experience, that of female traders and small-scale urban-based entrepreneurs. The transformation of the religious landscape in southern Vietnam took place against a backdrop of crisis in a series of state projects, the effect of which was mitigated by the continuous operation of informal economic practices in a petty commercial and trade sector largely dominated by women. The rise of goddesses reflects in no small measure the significance of this contribution and the authority of women as efficacious social agents. Guaranteeing good business, credit provision, domestic child care, education, domestic health care, family harmony, and more, these goddesses have been crucial in making the Vietnamese world go round. Popular faith in these figures is not to be dismissed as a purely pragmatic reflex or an ignorant misapprehension of the laws of nature, as some evolutionary-inspired critics are inclined to do. Rather, such faith is a thoughtful reflection on the nature and identity of the forces and agents that have influenced economic activity in the region.

A functional approach toward religious practice is increasingly popular in Vietnam as erstwhile social revolutionaries retheorize religion as providing moral or cultural underpinnings to social projects. Religion is seen in idealist (and idealistic) terms as a valuable accessory to economic, social, and cultural life. Frequent appeals are made to folk beliefs as resources in the storehouse *(kho)* of national culture, temporally transcendent phenomena that can provide stability and self-confidence. This ahistorical view overlooks that the power of such spirits is constituted through contemporary relations of reciprocity and debt. Vietnam's cultural theorists recognize the psychological and social value that symbols such as the Lady of the Realm have to the diverse communities of believers that coalesce around them. Yet this goddess is not an autonomous force able to be tapped for specific benefits but a being whose responsiveness is seen to flow from her cravings for social inclusion. Her cult illustrates that many of the most powerful gods in Vietnam are not those who lived feted, prestigious, socially illustrious lives, but rather marginalized and vulnerable beings that are susceptible to debt. The Lady of the Realm exemplifies a paradox in the Vietnamese religious order, that among the most feted deities are those whose historical or social identity is most obscure. Their responsiveness to social attention, a function of their marginality, has earned them their magical fame. One therefore has to ask whether the state's tapping of such spirits' religious power can unleash societal benefit or whether its reliance on them is an act that helps reproduce structures of social and cultural exclusion.

The power of these spirits is intimately bound up with the negotiation of social status and cultural expectation. Attracting principally female devotees, these goddesses are importantly the creations of women and symbolize predominantly feminine concerns. Given that they emerged under a regime whose agents of significant historical change are often symbolized as male—masculine images of revolutionary geniuses, brilliant scientists, heroic defenders, and rational managers, crowd public billboards in Vietnam—one might be inclined to take these goddesses as objects of significant emancipatory potential, who realize the symbolically democratic possibilities of a spontaneously crafted symbol of, for, and by women. The multitalented, all-round goddesses of the southern Vietnamese plain are indeed widely celebrated for their capacity to deliver results and respond to requests far outstripping the capabilities of any other entities, secular or spiritual. The prominence of these goddesses could well be taken as a rousing advertisement for an esteemed unofficial vision of femininity, to which many state agents themselves subscribe, that upholds a holistic vision of women as nurturers, creditors, patrons, protectors, arbitrators, child bearers, and fecund sources of wealth.

However, it is this very reliability that gives pause and raises the question whether the Vietnamese in southern Vietnam have not elevated female drudges to superstardom, as if to say: Whatever the problem, a woman will solve it. A related question would be whether, in worshiping these goddesses, southern Vietnamese women are not endorsing a vision of themselves that is calibrated to an extraordinarily high standard—indeed, well above that required for men. While few of those who transact with these goddesses may stop to question their meaning in such ways, a reduction of these spirits to merely pragmatic significance as figures of unlimited responsiveness, multi-functionality, and can-do effectiveness does raise the question why such figures should be portrayed as feminine and why, in stories told about them, they so often preferred a lonely death, exposed to the elements, to the alternatives presented them. This view, which promotes unflagging assistance to others as the only path to social recognition, pushes a hefty portfolio of responsibilities women's way. Consequently, the issue may not be whether such popular acts of veneration represent a flowering of resistance (against either restrictive traditions or a state obsessed with stifling spontaneity), but whether in fact the markedly patriarchal Vietnamese state is not a major symbolic beneficiary of this outpouring of popular support for these feminine figures of unquestioning pragmatism, who reflect women's successful performance of heavy responsibilities in circumscribed realms of activity.

Nevertheless, if Vietnamese men, the Vietnamese state, or Vietnamese cultural elites have been beneficiaries of popular practice, they have not been the only ones. The southern Vietnamese goddesses can be regarded as crystallizations of historically proven, or, rather, popularly accepted, acts of efficacy. They are the traces left to remind subsequent generations of what has worked. While the context in which these results have been obtained may have been characterized by skewed gender relations, within the reality of those constraints the solutions achieved by women have been salutary. These goddesses, dwelling on the borders of the country or in its commercial heartlands, have overseen and conspired in acts no means constrained within the shining histories furnished by nationalism or socialism. They have been patrons of desperate acts of survival, smuggling, and escape. They are the symbolic creditors of the urban real estate boom, the guarantors of high-stakes gambles, the guardians of health, the benefactors of criminals, the givers of children, and the underwriters of love. They have been the means by which women have managed to conform to the unfair demands placed upon them by society. Yet they have helped just as many women find release from such fetters, separation from a destructive relationship, wealth for independence, an education against the odds, successful escape, and the fulfillment of personal goals. They have been equally important to those women who have sidestepped such tensions, who are prestigious figures in their own right in the largely feminine spaces of the market, the commercial realm of the sidewalk, and the pagoda—places in which high social standing is a function of business prowess, religious piety, and dedication to pilgrimages. Whole neighborhoods go on pilgrimage to these goddesses together in provisional mobile communities of pilgrims, headed by female figures of great entrepreneurial authority. Having done well out of making a business from religion, these women are just the kind of success stories on whom have been modeled the female deities of this superlative religion of business.

The dialectic of oppression versus emancipation might itself be a constraining framework through which to view such figures' relationship to women's lives. Even more compelling is the vivid demonstration this relationship provides of the fact that in drawing on these symbolic resources, women have leaned on their own self-representations when in need. They have placated, cajoled, bribed, and bargained with these figures to secure what they have required. As social fortunes began to rise in Vietnam for the first time since the end of the war, the belief in the responsibility of such figures for all manner of successful enterprises became more widespread. In such a sense, it might be said that southern Vietnamese women have indeed moved beyond authorized interpretations to constitute deities who encode their achievements, condense their histories, provide them support, symbolize their longings, and offer them fulfillment. The attempted co-option of their symbolic constructions by local ritual elites, the state, or cultural commentators is a tribute to the importance of their religious creativity under adverse circumstances, capturing the imagination of those both near and far.

Notes

Introduction: An Outline of the Quest

1. This figure is an informal estimate; it represents the most frequently cited figure in my conversations with residents living in the vicinity of her shrine, the owners of nearby commercial establishments, and pilgrimage entrepreneurs. In 1992 Thạch Phương gave the unsubstantiated figure of half a million visitors to her annual festival (Thạch Phương et al. 1992, 21). According to locals, at least as many people visit the shrine outside this time, mainly in the seven or so months between Christmas and the middle of the lunar year.

2. Nguyễn Phương Thảo (1997, 187), refers to a system *(hệ thống)* of nine goddesses worshiped in Southern Vietnam. The main figures discussed in this work are the Lady of the Realm (Bà Chúa Xứ) in Vĩnh Tế village (sometimes known as the Lady of Châu Đốc), the Black Lady (Bà Đen) in Tây Ninh, Dinh Cô in Long Hải, and Tien Hau (Thiên Hậu) in Bình Dương (but also venerated in many other places) along with Sri Mariamam, the bodhisattva Kuan Yin (Quan Âm), Mary (Đức Mẹ), Thien Y A Na, the Five Elements (Ngũ Hành), and the Mother of Births (Mẹ Sanh).

3. Dubisch, who studied pilgrimages in Tinos, Greece, also discusses some of the methodological problems facing the study of such translocal religious practice (1995).

4. Mus' "Cultes Indiens et Indigènes au Champa" (1933) makes a case for the survival and integrity of local Cham religious culture in contrast to the notion that it was derived from India.

5. Christoph Giebel's (2001) discussion of the enshrinement of a revolutionary figure as a village tutelary spirit rehearses some of the arguments about religion as the playing out of tensions between center and locality.

6. Several theorists regard pilgrimage as a distinctively postmodern phenomenon, approaching it from the perspective of the particular, the local, and the personally experienced, challenging views of the process as unitary or transcendental. Morinis has argued that the Turners' view of pilgrimage (Turner 1974; V. and E. Turner 1978) is too totalistic. It overlooks the variety of individual motivations that may inspire pilgrims to undertake specific journeys (Morinis 1984). Others have stressed that a plurality of meanings, motives, and forms is integral to the ferment that surrounds popular figures, so much so that one might never satisfactorily arrive at what a pilgrimage actually is (Eade and Sallnow 1991; Dubisch 1995). My dissatisfaction

with such a position is that the multiplicity of perspectives or definitions that has caused some to question the value of the search for a general theory of pilgrimages is precisely what distinguishes them and makes them so interesting and timely.

7. In contrast with Turner, Sangren argues that pilgrims do not escape structure or transcend society. Instead, they recognize and negotiate in the act of pilgrimage an underlying cultural logic. Rather than disengaging from society, Chinese pilgrims engage its cultural categories through ritual practice. Reproducing salient "collective representations" through pilgrimage, they dialectically reproduce society (Sangren 1987, 129).

8. Sangren's study of Chinese pilgrimage makes the case that popular notions of spiritual efficacy are not "out of time" but a manifestation of folk historical consciousness. The persistence in Chinese religious practice of seemingly archaic symbols shows how even profound social transformations are comprehended through culturally specific conventions and that social space is ritually structured in locally intelligible ways. Powerful spirits, as emic models of history, are implicated in the reproduction through time of structures of meaning (1987).

Chapter 1: Spiritualizing the Borders

1. There are problems with his juridical notion of a "cadastral" contract between community and territory, which is perhaps closer to French colonial land-tenure ideas and the colonial construct of the bounded "geobody" (Thongchai 1994) than to precolonial notions of people's relations to land.

2. Although contradictory in detail but evidencing the same structure, another oral tale says she was a local woman who supported the Tây Sơn rebels.

3. Lê Hồng Lý cites one oral tale told about the Lady of the Storehouse that dates her to the Lý dynasty and locates her at the Cầu River, at which important natural defense line she helped General Lý Thường Kiệt mount a defense against Song invaders (2001, 5).

4. There is no record of Bà Chúa Xứ in the mid-nineteenth-century chronicle *Đại Nam Nhất Thống Chí*, even though it has a section dedicated to local heroic women and miraculous events.

5. The status of these goddesses as ethnic markers is discussed at greater length in the following chapter.

6. Mus saw in the indigenous cults of Indochina a reflection of a community that had come close to achieving a state of mental, religious, and perhaps even social equilibrium. Despite the accretions of Indian culture in the religion of the Cham, links with the indigenous tradition had not been broken (Mus 1934). This view distinguishes his project from those of earlier Orientalists who saw cultures they encountered in the region as derivative or degraded.

7. Bayley argues that in fact there was considerable cross-fertilization between such late-colonial-era French scholars and the emerging Vietnamese nationalist movement (Bayley 2000).

8. Trần Văn Giàu, influential historian of the intellectual history of Vietnam and former head of the southern Vietnamese chapter of the Indochinese Communist Party, described the rural Mekong delta in such terms: "The Mekong delta is an extremely fertile piece of earth, one that has given birth to many strange religions, and where superstitions are rife" (1996, 508).

9. Visitors to Black Lady Mountain can today see from a monument situated at the base of the mountain that the mountain itself was a guerrilla base during the Second Indochinese War.

10. A series of cautionary cartoons showing the various deceitful ruses fortune-tellers used and exposing their cynicism and their various peccadilloes, lustfulness, and greed appeared in the journal *Văn Hóa Nghệ Thuật* (Culture and Arts) in the early 1980s. The bitterly criticized resurgence of "superstition" in the 1980s can be traced in the following articles: Văn Hóa Nghệ Thuật 1980, 1982a, 1982b, 1984, 1985a, 1985b, 1986; Đại Đoàn Kết 1984, 1985a, 1985b, 1985c.

11. As Party General Secretary Nông Đức Mạnh noted, "Culture is an underlying force for socioeconomic development, since cultural activities are aimed at comprehensively developing the political, ideological, intellectual, ethnical and physical qualities of the Vietnamese people. Culture inspires human creativeness and generates the internal strength necessary for development" (*Vietnam News* 2001c).

12. This assertion was perhaps first and certainly most famously put by the French ethnographer Father Leopold Cadière (1958).

13. This view celebrated cultural heterodoxy over orthodoxy, especially the challenge to Confucianism (which was often evaluated negatively as elite, feudal, Chinese-imposed, and enervating to the nation), posed by the Vietnamese settlement of the southern plain. However, none of the theorists who endorsed the view of southern culture as multiethnic denied the cultural baggage of the Red River delta and central Vietnam as a key role in this mix. One might take the view that their broader perspective facilitated the flexible incorporation of this region into the nation. See Nguyễn Phương Thảo 1992; Huỳnh Ngọc Trang 1993; and Nguyễn Minh San 1993. A stronger emphasis on southern Vietnamese localization and the need to more adequately research the cultural legacy of non-Vietnamese groups appeared more recently in Nguyễn Mạnh Cường 2001.

14. Vietnam's different ethnic groups are referred to as "siblings" *(dân tộc anh em)*; Ho Chi Minh, the founder of the state, is referred to as "Uncle" (Bác); and subsequent generations are called his "nephews and nieces" *(con cháu Bác Hồ)*.

15. One theorist sees in this legendary being the maternal ancestor of Vietnam's entire pantheon of goddesses (Ngo Duc Thinh 1999, 34).

16. A positive assessment of Vietnamese women as national heroes was advanced by influential commentators under the former Republic of Vietnam. See, for example, Hoang Van Co 1957.

17. For example, Nguyen Khac Vien (1974) contrasted the precolonial court's fixation with an imported and formalistic form of Confucianism with popular,

village-based localization of this philosophy in the tradition of socially engaged scholars close to the concerns of the common people.

18. Eriksen (1995) notes that Norwegian urban intellectuals' quest for folk roots in the mid-nineteenth century was motivated by the dual concern to identify folkloric elements that could be held up as nationally distinctive and additionally to find a symbolic point around which to unite rural and urban populations.

19. Authoritative religious commentator Đặng Nghiêm Vạn similarly debunked mediumship in Hanoi as an unfortunate practice of those wishing to profit from others' credulity and lamented the commercialization of religious practice (Đặng Nghiêm Vạn 1998).

20. The main orientation of Chinese ethnological and folklorist studies of popular religion is interpreted in a similar way by Feuchtwang and Wang (1991) as generally consistent with state policy.

Chapter 2: The Ethnicity of Efficacy

1. This story is included in most of the booklets issued by local agencies and associations in the Châu Đốc area and is commonly cited in the scholarly works of Vietnamese ethnologists and folklorists touching on the identity of this goddess.

2. The ethnic Kinh (Dân tộc Kinh) officially are said to comprise 87 percent of the population of Vietnam; see Đặng Nghiêm Vạn et al. 2000, 1. Ostensibly meaning "people of the capital," identification as Kinh implies the tracing of roots (gốc) back to the Red River delta and identification with other key symbols of a historically assimilationist polity. As such, being Kinh is a work in progress, and people are sometimes recruited to this ethnicity through loss of memory of alternative identities. The term is used interchangeably with "Việt people" (Người Việt/Dân tộc Việt), a usage that underscores the privileged relationship between this ethnicity and the project of the Vietnamese nation-state.

3. Indeed, the degree to which southern Vietnam's ethnic diversity has been acknowledged has varied considerably in scholarly studies of the region, and the tendency among theorists to attribute primacy to the culture of the ethnic Việt remains strong. For example, a work published in 1992 in Hanoi, on the folk culture of the southern region, stressed heroism, resistance, and the experience of the ethnic Kinh farmer as typical of the culture of the southern plain. See Thạch Phương et al. 1992.

4. Malleret regretted the Vietnamization of a statue that he opined, "must have been very beautiful before being subjected to the strange disgrace of its new cult." He observed that the goddess was particularly venerated by young Chinese and Vietnamese women seeking favorable marriage outcomes and noted that no Cambodians were associated with her pilgrimage or festival (Malleret 1959, 39).

5. The term "Miên" is frequently used to refer to Cambodia or Cambodians, even though many of the Khmer in Vietnam see it as a pejorative expression.

6. In contrast, Michael Vickery has summarized recent literature arguing that Indianized religious monuments in this region of the pre-Angkor period were neither imports from India nor the products of transplanted Indians but rather the prod-

ucts of Southeast Asians themselves whose own journeys to and from India had acquainted them with Indian influences. See Vickery 1998, 56.

7. Booklets written by Hạnh Nguyên and Lê Ngọc Bích speculate that the statue must have already been on the peak of Sam Mountain when it was still an island, and date its origin to more than eight thousand years ago. See Hạnh Nguyên 1995 and Lê Ngọc Bích 1994.

8. Pierre Brocheux notes that when in 1819 the mandarin Thoại Ngọc Hầu received an order to construct a canal from Long Xuyên to Rạch Giá, he declared that "this sacred place, which had been hidden to the eyes, had not yet been trod by any foot" (Brocheux 1995, 10).

9. Credit for the "pacification" of Cambodia is accorded to him in *Gia Dinh Gazetteer*, compiled for the Vietnamese court in the early nineteenth century by the mandarin Trịnh Hoài Đức (1972, 1: 87).

10. I have heard ethnic Kinh people in the Mekong delta refer to the ethnic Khmer as migrants, as "overseas Khmer," or even worse as "Pol Pot" or as "offspring of Pol Pot" *(con chau Pol Pot)*.

11. Nguyễn Phương Thảo (1997, 209) speaks of the "former" practice of borrowing money from Bà Chúa Xứ's shrine as similar to that practiced in Chinese temples in the region.

12. For example, in Đặng Nghiêm Vạn et al. 2000, most of the photographs are of women, and the majority of the men pictured are elderly.

13. In a tale told to me by an ethnic Kinh Buddhist nun, the goddess was sculpted from stone by a Chinese male migrant living in southern Vietnam. His descendants went on to become the kings of China, thanks to the support provided them by the goddess in gratitude to their ancestor for releasing her (for the full account see chapter 8).

14. The Lady of the Realm in Châu Đốc, on the Cambodian border, is also credited with overseeing the ethnic Chinese exodus from Vietnam, and some of the richest gifts made to her are from those who fled the country.

15. This story is a probable reference to the princess Huyền Trân who, in 1306, married King Jaya Sinhavarman III of Champa. As a result of this marriage, the Red River delta–based Đại Việt state was able to annex what is present-day Quảng Trị, Thừa Thiên, and part of Quảng Nam in the coastal plain between the Red and Mekong rivers. Only in the 1590s did a southern state under the Nguyễn lords emerge in challenge to the Trịnh. Lê Văn Duyệt only arrived on the scene in the late eighteenth century, in a region hundreds of kilometers to the south.

16. For example, Sri Mariamam is a goddess whose South Indian–style temple is situated nearby Ho Chi Minh City's Bến Thành market. Her rites are still performed by members of the city's small South Indian minority. Known also as the Black Lady (Bà Đen), the Black Lady of Tây Ninh (Bà Đen Tây Ninh), the Indian Lady (Bà Ấn Độ), and even as the Lady of the Realm (Bà Chúa Xứ) or the Lady of Châu Đốc (Bà Chau Đốc), she is popular among female petty entrepreneurs and service industry workers as well as students and transport workers.

Chapter 3: Embodying Market Relations

1. Few of these Ho Chi Minh City–based transport workers ever save enough to make the trip to the goddess' main shrine in Châu Đốc. When they have done so, it has been thanks to an unexpected windfall. Recently, however, many of them have been able to propitiate her at one of her "branch offices" *(chi nhánh)* that have sprung up in the outskirts of the city.

2. High demand makes these reportedly very hard to obtain.

3. This goddess, enshrined in Bắc Ninh province, obtained something of the notoriety among Hanoians that the Lady of the Realm achieved in Ho Chi Minh City and surrounding provinces at the same time. Bà Chúa Kho is commonly, if not uniquely, associated with the borrowing of money, in contrast with the Châu Đốc goddess, for whom financial assistance is but one of a multiplicity of capabilities for which she is renowned (Khánh Duyên 1994; Lê Hồng Lý 2001).

4. Managers of informal credit circles explain that people play *hụi*s because getting a bank loan is difficult. To get a bank loan, one has to provide one's papers, proof of residence, and collateral, as well as details of one's business and what one seeks the loan for. In addition, one has to know someone in the bank to facilitate approval and make a cash payment as an inducement. If one is late, the bank can repossess one's home and leave one with nothing. By contrast, as people know the owner of their *hụi,* they can plead for a few days' grace or pay their monthly installment in portions. The consequences of default are not as drastic, and all the petty fees and formalities, which often people could not provide, are unnecessary.

5. Such groups can be distinguished from those who work for wages *(làm mướn)* as manual laborers. They are also to be separated from employees *(công nhân)* who work for a more stable salary in a larger workplace and from state employees *(cán bộ).*

6. Lê Hồng Lý also argues that the transition to a market economy in Vietnam has been marked by confusion, dislocation and chaos and that the Lady of the Storehouse cult sheds light on social instability and insufficiency in the legal system (2001, 34).

7. Jackson (1999a; 1999b) found that Thais addressed the dislocations of the economic boom years through what he refers to as "pre-modern" and elsewhere as distinctively Thai and Southeast Asian religious forms, which are sufficiently adaptable and multiform to render the commodity market intelligible and even familiar. Reader and Tanabe (1998) resisted the label "new religions" in their analysis of the spiritual pursuit of worldly benefits in Japan, seeing at their core the traditional religion of "practical benefits" that had hitherto been overlooked by students of Japanese religion (Reader and Tanabe 1998).

8. Hickey also observed that the communal rituals performed by notables and political leaders in honor of the guardian spirit of the village at the *đình* were more simple and practiced with less frequency in southern Vietnam than in the north and that the familial cult of the ancestors was practiced with less rigidity and formality (1958, 414).

9. For a discussion of similarly positive notions about women's affinity for commerce in Indonesia see Alexander 1998, 213; Keeler 1987, 55; and Papanek and Schwede 1998.

10. According to a recent report, women account for 70 percent of the workers in the informal sector, which contributes 53.8 percent of the nation's GDP (Le Thi 2001, 77).

11. A recent Vietnamese newspaper report estimated the overseas Vietnamese diaspora at approximately 2.5 million people (*Vietnam News* 2002b). According to this report, Vietnamese living abroad sent home more than $2 billion in 2001. One can compare this with the total foreign investment into Ho Chi Minh City of $830 million in the same year (*Vietnam News* 2002a).

Chapter 4: Reinscribing Rural Religion

1. Data available on rainfall conditions across the delta show that the fourth lunar month marks the beginning of the rainy season in the western delta (Nguyễn Việt Phố and Vũ Văn Tuấn 1995, 46), although the rains in Châu Đốc begin *earlier* than in the eastern delta, rather than later (cf. Nguyễn Đăng Duy 1997, 162).

2. These accounts of local agricultural rhythms are based upon the cycles of wet-rice *(lúa nước)* agriculture. However, in this part of the delta, long-stalked float-ing rice *(lúa nổi)* was until recently the main variety grown. In contrast to the con-temporary labor-intensive method of growing rice in paddies, floating rice required only light field preparation and was sown by hand. According to elderly people in Châu Đốc, the timing of the rainy season was indeed once critical, for rice was sown with the arrival of the rains and was rain fed for a period of time. During the annual floods the rice continued to grow, the stalks reaching three to four meters to keep up with the water level. The growing season was thus much longer than today, lasting at least six or seven months. Harvesting was done early in the year when the waters had fully receded, leaving the stalks lying along the ground with only the heads sticking up vertically.

3. The carts were made of wood, with wheels of brazilwood *(vàng hương)*, the only wood strong enough to take the wear and tear of coarse gravel roads. The wheels were bound with iron. According to locals the horses in the eastern delta were larger than those in the west and could draw carts carrying six people.

4. The ratio of ownership was perhaps only one in ten. In the 1950s bicycles were often used to transport cargo. They were used to carry large bags of cloth pur-chased at the Cambodian border in Tây Ninh all the way to Saigon.

5. According to some local estimates, in the 1950s only one in twenty river craft was motorized. The popularization of American- and Japanese-built engines such as Kohler and Yamaha in the late 1960s, for use in large and small river craft, stimulated riverine passenger travel. By the end of the war, according to some locals, about three-quarters of the long-distance passenger boats *(đò)* and cargo boats *(ghe)* found on the river had engines.

6. Made in Japan, they were bought relatively cheaply with money provided to the Republic of Vietnam by the U.S. Commodity Aid Program.

7. I heard this cliché in 1999 in southern Cà Mau province from a group of northerners on their way to work in a relative's shrimp farms; they were despairing about the lack of work opportunities in the rural areas of the north and confident about being able to make quick fortunes in the fertile, mangrove-laced shrimp ponds of this Mekong delta province.

8. UNDP 2001, 96, records that Ho Chi Minh City, with a population in excess of five million in 1999, attracted 410,553 domestic migrants between 1994 and 1999.

9. Thoại Ngọc Hầu was an early-nineteenth-century mandarin of the central court. It is common for people of the formerly relatively autonomous south to refer to their local rulers as kings in their own right rather than officials.

10. More general ethnological works published in Vietnam in the 1990s that make reference to the goddess similarly assert that "superstitious" activities, such as borrowing money, using her bathwater, and being possessed by her spirit were pre-liberation phenomena and have now ceased or are restricted (e.g., Thạch Phương et al. 1992, 94).

11. Feuchtwang notes that the magical efficacy *(ling)* attributed to Chinese guardian gods relates to their protection of a ritually delimited territory (2001, 24). As for spirits such as the Lady of the Realm who have attracted a wide extralocal following, their individualized support *(phù hộ)* and capacity to punish breaches of agreement have been attested to as far away as Sydney and California. However, in contrast, the magical attribute of spirits most frequently cited by custodians of such temples and shrines is the much more restricted power to guard their own premises.

Chapter 5: Familiar Journeys

1. Following Marguelies (1969), who described the trips that idealistic foreigners made to the Soviet Union as pilgrimages, one might even apply the designation "pilgrims" to intellectuals such as Nhất Linh or political activists such as Nguyễn Ái Quốc, who gained revelatory insights only after journeying far from home.

2. Her journeys fall into the category of "obligatory" pilgrimages described by Morinis (1992, 12).

3. Morinis describes the beginnings of pilgrimage in "a great austerity fraught with real danger and well-justified fear" (1992, 1).

4. Dalat, a former French hill station, is a popular vacation site for domestic tourists throughout Vietnam.

5. This is not the place to document all the different styles and doctrines that make pilgrimage in Vietnam a diverse phenomenon. However, one should emphasize that there are other modes of pilgrimage to Sam Mountain than these urban journeys. The most austere example of a pilgrimage I have encountered in Vietnam was on top of Forbidden Mountain, just south of Sam Mountain, where I met up with a group of about twenty pilgrims dressed in the black robes characteristic of the Hòa Hảo faith on a one-month pilgrimage to each of the Mekong delta's seven moun-

tains. They were traveling by foot, carrying their own rice, harvesting wild plants, cooking their own food, and sleeping in the open. However, many among the Hòa Hảo, whose faith is renowned for its purism and simplicity, do travel in buses, boats, and cars to attend the sacred commemorative festivals held at the birthplace of their religion's founder.

Chapter 6: The Experience of Festival

1. Altogether nine local women make up the bathing group, but only three elderly women, of good character, do the actual bathing. The statue is rubbed down with rainwater in which flowers have been boiled. The goddess' robe is changed at the same time.

2. One can still see dances of this kind at the shrines to other goddesses such as the Black Lady of Tây Ninh or "branches" of the Châu Đốc shrine such as the one in Nhà Bè. There individual gifts set on trays are offered by male and female mediums who whirl around, dancing themselves into a trance.

Chapter 7: Magical Fame and Symbolic Ambiguity

1. Some information on his life history and vicissitudes in his cult can be found in ethnographies by Hickey (1964) and Luong (1994).

2. In Vietnam, this hierarchy incorporates the ancestors *(tổ tiên)*, who are venerated at the household level; local village tutelary deities *(thành hoàng)*, who are enshrined in communal houses and venerated by village notables; and Heaven *(trời)*, formerly venerated by the king, as well as by each household.

3. The French term *"hommes"* genders this category in a way the Vietnamese *"nhân"* does not. Included among the national pantheon of celebrated personages are many female figures such as the Trưng sisters, Lady Triệu, Ỷ Lan, Hồ Xuân Hương, Bùi Thị Xuân, and Võ Thị Sáu. For a recent popular collection of tales about such figures see Lê Minh Quốc 2001, or specifically for southern Vietnam, see Vietnamese Women's Museum 1993.

4. In Bến Tre I was told that in the past, if a woman died a virgin her relatives held vigil by her graveside for three nights lest her corpse be disinterred and decapitated. The heads of such defunct individuals had the power to cite prophesies to those who made offerings to them. Chí Hòa Prison in Ho Chi Minh City is said to be impossible to escape from because of the vengeful powers of a virgin girl interred, while still living, in its foundations. The great potency attributed to the corpses of women who died as virgins may reflect beliefs that their potential as sexual partners, mothers, and lineage producers has gone poignantly unrealized. Their unfulfilled lives make them prepared to do whatever they can to earn assistance from the living to meet their unrealized desires.

5. Lê Văn Duyệt's mausoleum contains such items as his personal chalice, weapons, and reproductions of an elephant and horses that evoke his military exploits.

6. Similar stories are also told of Man Nương's daughter, discovered as a stone inside a log that was being carved to make Buddha statues (Minh Chi et al. 1999, 23).

7. Nguyễn Phương Thảo (1997, 194) relates one tale about the Lady of the Realm describing her as a young Khmer woman who, while traveling in search of a husband, felt tired. She sat down to rest by the side of Sam Mountain, where she died. Another scholar has suggested that this tale might refer to a different mountain (Huỳnh Ngọc Trảng pers. com.).

8. An example of the latter is the temple to the Black Lady (Điện Bà Đen), whose small, dark-faced porcelain image is venerated on an altar in a mountainside cave in Tây Ninh province.

9. The exceptions are the structures venerating the red-faced general-literatus Quan Công as well as other deities associated with the ethnic Chinese, whose places of worship are popularly called pagodas (chùa).

10. Thoại Ngọc Hầu and his female relatives received several decrees from the Nguyễn dynasty in recognition of faithful service, including three from Minh Mạng in 1822 and one each from the last two representatives of the Nguyễn dynasty, Khải Định in 1924 and Bảo Đại in 1935 (Nguyễn Văn Hầu 1972, 329–366).

11. Commemorative inscriptions noting these contributions are still displayed inside the main temple. The names of donors include French colonial officials, people of South Indian and South Chinese ancestry, state utilities, companies, the residents of city districts and neighboring villages. According to elderly members of the temple committee, the king Bảo Đại was a frequent visitor.

12. The road running along the Saigon River, where his biggest statue stood, was named Bạch Đằng Quay, in commemoration of the place where Trần Hưng Đạo's historic victory in a river battle against Mongol invaders took place.

13. The transition of regimes was a puzzle to those inclined to accept that the Republic owed its existence to support from an accomplished pantheon of heroes and to correct ritual observances. A Ho Chi Minh City motorcycle taxi driver suggested that the Republic fell because the presidential palace in the nation's capital had been geomantically misaligned. Even worse, the huge statue of the ARVN soldier in downtown Saigon had been oriented in an inauspicious direction, so that its gun was pointed directly at the National Assembly building. According to him, these fundamental mistakes had fateful consequences.

14. The land had originally been purchased by a descendant of the marshall in the mid-nineteenth century.

15. Discussing the post-1975 regime's approach to the cult to Nguyễn Huỳnh Đức in Khánh Hậu, Luong notes that the marshall was also negatively evaluated because of his support for Prince Nguyễn Phúc Ánh's fight against the Tây Sơn forces (Luong 1994, 92).

16. Another hypothesis put to me was that these figures were all southerners and had been initially suppressed by the Hanoi-centric postwar regime because of their regional origins.

17. The pairing of Cá Ông with male military or naval figures is common in

Vietnam. The case of Nguyễn Trung Trực has already been mentioned. Lê Văn Duyệt's mausoleum also contains whale imagery, and Trần Hưng Đạo's altar in Ho Chi Minh City is flanked by two enormous whale ribs.

18. People welcome *(nghinh)* her spirit in from the sea to reside in the palace for the duration of her festival.

19. They include the bodhisattva Kuan Yin, the goddess of birth (mẹ sanh), feminine representations of the five elements *(ngũ hành)*, female stars, a number of female immortals, and also, on a neighboring altar, the goddess Thiên Hậu. The profusion of feminine imagery on her altar suggests the possibility for limitless identity substitutions.

Chapter 8: The Lady and the Buddha

1. Examples of "engaged Buddhism" in Vietnam include the social welfare tendency in the Householders Pure Land Buddhist Association of Vietnam (Tịnh Độ Cư Sĩ), an association of Buddhist physicians who place healing at the center of their religious practice (Do Thien 2001), and that of Hòa Hảo Buddhism (Hue Tam Ho Tai 1983), whose followers are called to charitable works and other forms of social engagement. The engaged Buddhism of the Vietnam War–era peace activist Thích Nhất Hạnh might also be regarded in this light.

2. In this observation I differ from Tambiah, who, despite recognizing the overlaps, discerns contrastive distinctions between Buddhism and the spirit cults in northeast Thailand in terms of ideology, ritual, functionaries, social significance, and ritual grammar (Tambiah 1970). He described them as "separate collective representations" (1970, 340) and formally characterized their relationship as "oppositional," "complementary," "linked," and "hierarchical" (1970, 337). Tambiah argued that villagers did not confuse these categories and accessed them in different ways. In Vietnam, by contrast, one does not find agreement on what an equivalent transcendent system of classification might be, and influential schemas such as the distinction between spirit worship and Buddhism are frequently blurred in exposition and in practice.

3. An acquaintance, a saleswoman who on weekends restored Buddhist pagodas with money sent back to Vietnam by overseas Vietnamese, told me that pocketing the money instead of doing the pagoda restoration according to plan was a sin *(tội):* "If you take the money, you will be unable to sell, you will experience a string of bad luck, you will be continually sick." Shades of the punitive qualities sometimes attributed to the Lady of the Realm!

4. Vietnamese ethnologist Đoàn Lâm notes that in Vietnam, Buddha "has become *Bụt,* a God of Providence," to whom people pray "for the fulfillment of their most pragmatic wishes (a good bargain in trading, success in raising pigs, and so forth" (1999, 8).

5. This is not to say that classificatory schemes that divide up different traditions, types of faith, or practitioners are not also common. In Vietnam, one encounters among self-designated Buddhists as well as others a variety of different ways of

dividing up the complex terrain of faith. However, one can find just as many instances of practices that breach these distinctions.

6. In southern China, where Tien Hau has emerged as a translocal deity, superseding other parochial spirits, James Watson reports that local people conceptualize this process as "eating" *(shik)* or "digestion" *(siu fa)* of the local deity, and they say the goddess grows stronger every time a local deity is thus assimilated (1985, 311).

7. Buddhism's origins in India are commonly acknowledged by members of the Sangha and by Buddhists with even only a limited exposure to the Sangha's teachings, despite the fact that the religion is often considered "Vietnamese" in the sense of being the religion to which most Vietnamese declare affiliation.

8. The statue to the goddess Tien Hau enshrined on the junction of the Saigon River and the main commercial canal leading to the Mekong delta is another example of a potent religious image that had been recuperated from the elements. This image had reportedly been transported from China on a boat, which sank in the Saigon River on arrival; its holy cargo was later rescued—some say by human hands, others, only after the statue had miraculously floated to the surface of the water.

9. Tambiah argues that "the Buddhist idiom of selfless giving of gifts, control of passion through asceticism, and renunciation of worldly interests is an idealization and extension of the social norm of reciprocity" (1970, 342). Arguably it can be seen conversely as an ideological attempt by institutionalized religious practitioners to gain distance from social obligations and indeed reject reciprocity. An assuredly powerful but also vulnerable deity who is occasionally bad-humored, fickle, sometimes punitive, but easily assuaged and with whom one transacts in a variety of matters is probably closer as a folk representation to what the norms of exchange relations actually are and how people experience real-time relations of reciprocity.

Chapter 9: Goddess of Freedom

1. In the patriarchal and bureaucratic world of Chinese society, Sangren talks of the worship of female deities as embodying a counterculture. He argues that "female deities are important counterpoints to the hierarchical, bureaucratic orthodoxies of state religion, territorial cults and ancestor worship" (1983, 25).

2. Because each of these latter is associated with a feudal past, feminine symbols also work as symbols of progressiveness and transcendence of the past.

3. Sangren observes how the Kuan Yin cult in Chinese Buddhism helps mitigate the transition to postparenthood, which for women is particularly traumatic and involves a loss of power. The goddess serves as a focal symbol for bringing together those in this socially marginal position (Sangren 1983, 18).

4. These narratives have many exponents in Vietnamese society, who find them a deeply meaningful way of interpreting change. See P. Taylor 2001b.

5. Linh's high expectations of corporate and industrial capitalism might be somewhat misplaced, given the experience women have had elsewhere in Southeast Asia (Ong 1987; 1995). My own observations in Vietnam suggest that the restrictions placed on urban middle-class women by neo-Confucianist morality and the reliance

of a family on the good name of its women can sometimes be more rigorous and constraining of their movements, social contacts, and life choices than is the case for many working-class and rural women.

6. One tale relates that she leapt to her death to escape capture by the son of a local official (Nguyễn Phương Thảo 1997, 212). Other tales say she killed herself to evade rape by Tây Sơn soldiers or Prince Nguyễn Ánh's forces.

7. In the hụi run by Loan, participants would each contribute a certain amount of money and then place bids to be the first to borrow the accumulated amount. The highest bidder would collect money from each participant and each successive month would pay an installment to the "owner" of the hụi, who would distribute it to the next withdrawer. Whoever withdrew first paid a greater monthly installment than those who did so later, so that the people most desperate for credit eventually paid more than they had received. Whoever withdrew from the pool last eventually received more than he or she had contributed. The owner of the hụi also withdrew once, without making monthly contributions, but was responsible for collecting interest and had to personally make up bad debts.

8. See chapter 2.

Epilogue: On Pilgrimages and Freedom in Late-Socialist Vietnam

1. By the term "late-socialist" I refer to those societies such as Vietnam and China that have "renovated" existing socialism, retaining a modified socialist ideology and nominally socialist political, economic, and social structures. "Postsocialist" refers to societies such as the former Soviet Union and many countries in Eastern Europe that have embarked upon an institutional break with their socialist pasts. North Korea is regarded as an unreconstructed "socialist" or Communist society. Differences between these types may often be more symbolic than real and due more to geography, culture, and history than to political or ideological factors.

2. This conforms to a pattern that Malarney (2001) has noted of diverse projects commemorating the war dead in Vietnam.

3. A pair of such goddesses is venerated in a Five Elements shrine (Miếu Ngũ hành) behind Đình Long pagoda, approximately 150 meters from the shrine to the Lady of the Realm in Vĩnh Tế village. The two figures are (center) Bà Thượng Đồng and (to the left) Bà Tổ Cô Phạm Thị Hiền. According to the incumbent monk of the pagoda, the latter was a local woman living in the French era. He told me that she had been assaulted by a group of youths when she was studying and still wearing her school uniform. They had tried to rape *(hãm hiếp)* her, but she had resisted and had died still a virgin. The monk assured me that she was "very responsive." People were successful making requests for good sales and all manner of other needs. She was offered meats such as chicken and pork. He was not entirely sure but thought the enshrinement of the two deities dated from the 1940s.

4. The concentration on border-dwelling goddesses in this work should not obscure the immense variety of other destinations to which residents of Ho Chi Minh City also travel on pilgrimage-type journeys. These include celebrated Khmer pagodas

in the Mekong delta, the Marian shrine of La Vang and a variety of historical sites in central Vietnam, and sites in and around the national capital and beyond. Pilgrims increasingly travel outside the country to Phnom Penh, the temples of Thailand, ancestral sites in southern China, and places even further afield such as Mecca, the Vatican, and Lourdes. The region is a recipient of many pilgrims as well. Pilgrims travel into the region to visit sacred sites, places where comrades or compatriots have fallen, and sites such as the guerrilla tunnels of Củ Chi, which share many of the carnivalesque qualities of the Châu Đốc fairground, as well as a host of other sites whose historical and cultural significance extend beyond the borders of Vietnam.

Bibliography

Abuza, Zachary. 2001. *Renovating Politics in Contemporary Vietnam.* Boulder: Lynne Rienner Publishers.

Ahern, Emily Martin. 1981. *Chinese Ritual and Politics.* Cambridge; New York: Cambridge University Press.

Alexander, Jennifer. 1998. "Women Traders in Javanese Marketplaces: Ethnicity, Gender, and the Entrepreneurial Spirit." In *Market Cultures: Society and Morality in the New Asian Capitalisms,* ed. Robert Hefner. 203–223. St. Leonards: Allen and Unwin.

All-Vietnam Catholic Liaison Committee. 1976. "Catholics Told to Get Rid of Outdated Customs, Build Socialism." *Chính Nghĩa,* 16 December, 4, 15.

Anagnost, Ann. 1994. "The Politics of Ritual Displacement." In *Asian Visions of Authority: Religion and the Modern States of East and Southeast Asia,* ed. Charles F. Keyes, Laurel Kendall, and Helen Hardacre, 221–253. Honolulu: University of Hawai'i Press.

Appadurai, Arjun. 1996. *Modernity at Large: Cultural Dimensions of Globalization.* Minneapolis: University of Minnesota Press.

Azicri, Max. 2000. *Cuba Today and Tomorrow: Reinventing Socialism.* Gainesville: University Press of Florida.

Baptandier, Brigitte. 1996. "The Lady Linshui: How a Woman Became a Goddess." In *Unruly Gods: Divinity and Society in China,* ed. M. Shahar and R. Weller, 105–149. Honolulu: University of Hawai'i Press.

Barmé, Geremie. 1996. "To Screw Foreigners Is Patriotic." In *Chinese Nationalism,* ed. Jonathan Unger, 181–208. Armonk, N.Y.: M. E. Sharpe.

Barrow, Sir John. 1975 [1806]. *A Voyage to Cochinchina.* Oxford in Asia Historical Reprints. Kuala Lumpur: Oxford University Press.

Basho, Matsuo. 1966. *The Narrow Road to the Deep North and Other Travel Sketches.* Trans. Nobuyuki Yuasa. Harmondsworth: Penguin.

Basu, Amrita. 1998. "Appropriating Gender." In *Appropriating Gender: Women's Activism and Politicised Religion in South Asia,* ed. Jeffery, Patricia, and Amrita Basu, pp. 3–14. New York: Routledge.

Bauman, Zygmunt. 1992. *Intimations of Postmodernity.* London and New York: Routledge.

Baurac, J. C. 1899. *La Cochinchine et ses Habitants: Provinces de L'Est.* Saigon: Imprimerie Rey.

Bayley, Susan. 2000. "French Anthropology and the Durkheimians in Colonial Indochina." *Modern Asian Studies* 34(3):581–622.

Beresford, Melanie. 1989. *National Unification and Economic Development in Vietnam.* London: Macmillan.

Beresford, Melanie, and Dang Phong. 1998. *Authority Relations and Economic Decision-making in Vietnam: An Historical Perspective.* Copenhagen, Denmark: NIAS [Nordic Institute of Asian Studies].

Bhardwaj, Surinder Mohan. 1973. *Hindu Places of Pilgrimage in India: A Study in Cultural Geography.* Berkeley: University of California Press.

Bourdieu, Pierre. 1990. *The Logic of Practice.* Cambridge: Polity Press; Oxford: Blackwell.

Bowman, Marion. 1993. "Drawn to Glastonbury." In *Pilgrimage in Popular Culture,* ed. Ian Reader and Tony Walter, 29–62. London: Macmillan.

Brenner, S. 1998. *Domesticating Desire: Women, Wealth, and Modernity in Java.* Princeton, N.J.: Princeton University Press.

Brocheux, Pierre. 1995. *The Mekong Delta: Ecology, Economy, and Revolution, 1860–1960.* Madison: Center for Southeast Asian Studies, University of Wisconsin-Madison.

Bùi Thị Hoa. 1933. "Phụ Nữ Với Cuộc Vận Động Tôn Giáo ở Nam Kỳ" [Women and the religious movement in Cochinchina]. *Phụ Nữ Tân Văn,* 28 November 1933, 13–14.

Bùi Thị Kim Quý. 1986. "Cần Sớm Khắc Phục Mê Tín Dị Đoan" [It is necessary to overcome superstition soon]. *Tạp Chí Cộng Sản* 1:90–93.

Bui Tin. 1995. *Following Ho Chi Minh: Memoirs of a North Vietnamese Colonel.* Bathurst: Crawford House.

Bulag, Uradyn E. 1998. *Nationalism and Hybridity in Mongolia.* Oxford: Clarendon Press; New York: Oxford University Press.

Bunnag, Jane. 1973. *Buddhist Monk, Buddhist Layman: A Study of Urban Monastic Organization in Central Thailand.* Cambridge: Cambridge University Press.

Cadière, Leopold. 1919. "La Culte des Bornes." *Bulletin de l'Ecole Française d'Extrême Orient* 19:40–47.

———. 1958. "Croyances et Practiques Religieuses des Vietnamiennes." *Bulletin de la Société des Etudes Indochinoises,* n.s. 33.

Carsten, J. 1989. Cooking Money: Gender and the Symbolic Transformation of Means of Exchange in a Malay Fishing Community. In *Money and the Morality of Exchange,* ed. M. Bloch and J. Parry, 117–141. Cambridge: Cambridge University Press.

Castells, M. 1989. *The Informational City: Information Technology, Economic Restructuring, and the Urban-Regional Process.* Oxford: Blackwell.

Certeau, Michel de. 1984. *The Practice of Everyday Life.* Berkeley: University of California Press.

Chandler, David. 1996. *Facing the Cambodian Past: Selected Essays 1971–1994.* North Sydney: Allen and Unwin.

Châu Bích Thủy. 1994. *Bí ẩn Về Bà Chúa Xứ Núi Sam* [The mystery of Ba Chua Xu of Sam Mountain]. Stage Association of An Giang Province.

Choi, Byung Wook. 1999. "Southern Vietnam under the Reign of Minh Mang (1820–1841): Central Policies and Local Response." Ph.D. thesis, Australian National University.

Cohen, Paul. 1993. "Order under Heaven: Anthropology and the State." In *Asia's Cultural Mosaic: An Anthropological Introduction,* ed. Grant Evans, 175–204. New York: Prentice Hall.

Comaroff, Jean. 1994. "Epilogue: Defying Disenchantment: Reflections on Ritual, Power, and History." In *Asian Visions of Authority: Religion and the Modern States of East and Southeast Asia,* ed. Charles F. Keyes, Laurel Kendall, and Helen Hardacre, 301–314. Honolulu: University of Hawai'i Press.

Comaroff, Jean, and John Comaroff. 1999. "Occult Economies and the Violence of Abstraction: Notes from the South African Postcolony." *American Ethnologist* 26(2):279–303.

———. 2000. "Millennial Capitalism: First Thoughts on a Second Coming." *Public Culture* 12(2):291–343.

Cooke, Nola. 1997. "The Myth of the Restoration." In *The Last Stand of Asian Autonomies: Responses to Modernity in the Diverse States of Southeast Asia and Korea 1750–1900,* ed. Anthony Reid, 265–296. London: Macmillan.

Coué, Andre. 1933. "Le Culte des Esprits et le Village Annamite." *Bulletin de la Société des Etudes Indochinoises* 8(3):114–127.

Coulet, Georges. 1926. *Les Sociétés Secrètes en Terre d'Annam.* Saigon: Impr. commerciale C. Ardin.

Đại Đoàn Kết. 1984. 7:10.

Đại Đoàn Kết. 1985a. 4:10.

Đại Đoàn Kết. 1985b. 6:7.

Đại Đoàn Kết. 1985c. 7:7.

Đặng Nghiêm Vạn. 1998. *Ethnological and Religious Problems in Vietnam.* Hanoi: Social Sciences Publishing House.

——— et al. 2000. *Ethnic Minorities in Vietnam.* New ed. Hanoi: The Gioi.

Dang Phong and Melanie Beresford. 1998. *Authority Relations and Economic Decision-making in Vietnam: An Historical Perspective.* Copenhagen, Denmark: NIAS [Nordic Institute of Asian Studies].

Đào Thế Hùng. 1995. "Introduction." In *Traditional Festivals in Vietnam,* ed. Đỗ Phương Quỳnh, 7–13. Hanoi: The Gioi.

Davis, Richard. 1984. *Muang Metaphysics.* Bangkok: Pandora.

De Tréglodé, Benoît. 2001. "Sur la Formation d'une Nouvelle Géographic Culturelle Patriotique au Vietnam: Essai sur le Culte de Mac thi Buoi." In *Vietnamese Society in Transition: The Daily Politics of Reform and Change,* ed. John Kleinen, 202–222. Amsterdam: Het Spinhuis.

Deutsche Presse Agentur. 2000. 30 March ⟨http://www.pghh.org/news/index.html⟩.

Do Lai Thuy. 1996. "The Cult of Fecundity in Vietnam." *Vietnamese Studies* 121: 23–34.

Do Thien. 1995. "The Mountain's Shadow and Reflection in the River: Vietnamese Supernaturalism in the Mekong Delta." Ph.D. thesis, Australian National University.

————. 2001. "Charity and Charisma: The Dual Path of a Popular Buddhist Group in Southern Vietnam." In *Vietnamese Society in Transition: The Daily Politics of Reform and Change,* ed. John Kleinen, 159–182. Amsterdam: Het Spinhuis.

Đỗ Thị Hảo and Mai Thị Ngọc Chúc. 1984. *Các Nữ Thần Việt Nam* [The goddesses of Vietnam]. Hà Nội: Nhà Xuất Bản Phụ Nữ.

Doan Lam. 1999. "A Brief Account of the Cult of Female Deities in Vietnam." *Vietnamese Studies* 131:5–19.

Doan Van Toai and David Chanoff. 1986. *The Vietnamese Gulag.* New York: Simon and Schuster.

Dong Vinh. 1999. "The Cult of Holy Mothers in Central Vietnam." *Vietnamese Studies* 131:73–82.

Drummond, Lisa. 2000. "Street Scenes: Practices of Public and Private Space in Urban Vietnam." *Urban Studies* 37(12):2377–2391.

Du Hailly, ed. 1866. "Souvenirs d'une Campagne dans l'Extrême Orient." *Revue des Deux Mondes,* September 893–924.

Duara, Prasenjit. 1995. *Rescuing History from the Nation: Questioning Narratives of Modern China.* Chicago: University of Chicago Press.

Dubisch, Jill. 1995. In *a Different Place: Pilgrimage, Gender, and Politics at a Greek Island Shrine.* Princeton N.J.: Princeton University Press.

Duiker, William J. 1989. *Vietnam since the Fall of Saigon.* Updated ed. Athens: Ohio University, Center for International Studies.

Eade, John, and Michael J. Sallnow, eds. 1991. *Contesting the Sacred: The Anthropology of Christian Pilgrimage.* London: Routledge.

Eickelman, Dale. 1976. *Moroccan Islam: Tradition and Society in a Pilgrimage Center.* Austin: University of Texas Press.

Eickelman, Dale F., and James Piscatori, eds. 1990. *Muslim Travellers: Pilgrimage, Migration, and the Religious Imagination.* London: Routledge.

Endres, Kirsten. 1999. "Culturalizing Politics: Doi Moi and the Restructuring of Ritual in Contemporary Rural Vietnam." In *Vietnamese Villages in Transition: Background and Consequences of Reform Policies in Rural Vietnam,* ed. Bernard Dahm and Vincent Houben, 197–222. Passau, Germany: Passau University Southeast Asian Studies Centre.

————. 2001. "Local Dynamics of Renegotiating Ritual Space in Northern Vietnam: The Case of the *Dinh.*" *Sojourn* 16(1):70–101.

Enloe, Cynthia. 1989. *Bananas, Beaches and Bases: Making Feminist Sense of International Politics.* London: Pandora.

Eriksen, Thomas Hylland. 1995. *Small Places, Large Issues: An Introduction to Social Anthropology.* London; Boulder, Colo.: Pluto.

Evans, Grant. 1985. "Vietnamese Communist Anthropology." *Canberra Anthropology* 8(1–2):116–147.

———. 1992. "Internal Colonialism in the Central Highlands of Vietnam." *Sojourn* 7(2):274–304.

Fabian, Johannes. 1983. *Time and the Other: How Anthropology Makes Its Object.* New York: Columbia University Press.

Feuchtwang, Stephan. 2001. *Popular Religion in China: The Imperial Metaphor.* Richmond, Surrey: Curzon.

Feuchtwang, Stephan, and Wang Ming-ming. 1991. "The Politics of Culture or a Contest of Histories: Representations of Chinese Popular Religion." *Dialectical Anthropology* 16:251–272.

Fforde, Adam, and Stefan de Vylder. 1995. *From Plan to Market: The Economic Transition in Vietnam.* Boulder, Colo.: Westview.

Finlayson, George. 1988 [1826]. *The Mission to Siam and Hue 1821–1822.* Oxford in Asia hardback reprints. Singapore: Oxford University Press.

Fitzgerald, Frances. 1972. *Fire in the Lake: The Vietnamese and the Americans in Vietnam.* New York: Vintage Books.

Forbes, Dean. 1996. "Urbanization, Migration, and Vietnam's Spatial Structure." *Sojourn* 11(1)(April): 24–51.

Friedman, Jonathan. 1994. *Cultural Identity and Global Process.* London: Sage.

Gates, Hill. 1996. *China's Motor: A Thousand Years of Petty Capitalism.* Ithaca, N.Y.: Cornell University Press.

Geertz, Clifford. 1963. "Primordial Sentiments and Civil Politics in the New States: The Integrative Revolution." In *Old Societies and New States: The Quest for Modernity in Asia and Africa,* ed. Clifford Geertz, 107–121. New York: Free Press of Glencoe.

———. 1973. *The Interpretation of Cultures: Selected Essays.* New York: Basic Books.

Gellner, Ernest. 1983. *Nations and Nationalism.* Oxford: Blackwell.

Giebel, Christoph. 2001. "Museum-Shrine: Revolution and Its Tutelary Spirit in the Village of My Hoa Hung." In *The Country of Memory: Remaking the Past in Late Socialist Vietnam,* ed. Hue Tam Ho Tai, 77–108. Berkeley: University of California Press.

Gilsenan, Michael. 2000. "Signs of Truth: Enchantment, Modernity and the Dreams of Peasant Women." *Journal of the Royal Anthropological Institute* 6:597–615.

Giran, Paul. 1912. *Magie et Religion Annamites: Introduction a une Philosophie de la Civilisation du People d'Annam.* Paris: Augustin Challamel.

Gladney, Dru. 1994. "Salman Rushdie in China: Religion, Ethnicity, and State Definition in the People's Republic." In *Asian Visions of Authority: Religion and the Modern States of East and Southeast Asia,* ed. Charles F. Keyes, Laurel Kendall, and Helen Hardacre, 255–278. Honolulu: University of Hawai'i Press.

————. 1996. *Muslim Chinese: Ethnic Nationalism in the People's Republic.* Cambridge, Mass.: Council on East Asian Studies, Harvard University.

Graburn, N. H. H. 1978. "Tourism: The Sacred Journey." In *Hosts and Guests: The Anthropology of Tourism,* ed. V. Smith, 17–32. Oxford: Blackwell.

Hà Hùng Tiến. 1997. *Lễ Hội và Danh Nhân Lịch Sử Việt Nam* [Vietnamese festivals and historical celebrities]. Hà Nội: Nhà Xuất Bản Văn Hóa Thông Tin.

Hà Văn Tấn and Nguyễn Văn Kự. 1998. *Đình Việt Nam* (Community halls in Vietnam). Ho Chi Minh City: Ho Chi Minh City Publishing House.

Hạnh Nguyễn. 1993. *Tìm Hiểu Nguồn Gốc Bà Chúa Xứ Núi Sam* [Understanding the origins of the Lady of the Realm of Sam Mountain]. Photographic Association of An Giang Province.

————. 1995. *Bà Chúa Xứ Núi Sam* [The Lady of the Realm of Sam Mountain]. Cultural Office of An Giang Province.

Hann, Chris M. 1993. *Socialism: Ideals, Ideologies, and Local Practice.* London; New York: Routledge.

————. 1998. "Postsocialist Nationalism: Rediscovering the Past in South East Poland." *Slavic Review* 57(4):840–863.

Hansen, Valerie. 1990. *Changing Gods in Medieval China, 1127–1276.* Princeton, N.J.: Princeton University Press.

Hardy, Andrew. 2003. *Red Hills: Migrants and the State in the Highlands of Vietnam.* Richmond: NIAS-Curzon Press.

Harrell, Stevan. 1987. "The Concept of Fate in Chinese Folk Ideology." *Modern China* 13:90–109.

Haughton, Jonathan. 2001. "Introduction: Extraordinary Changes." In *Living Standards during an Economic Boom: The Case of Vietnam,* ed. Dominique Haughton, Jonathan Haughton, and Nguyễn Phong, 9–32. Hanoi: Statistical Publishing House.

Hickey, Gerald Cannon. 1958. "Problems of Social Change in Vietnam." *Bulletin de la Société des Etudes Indochinoises* 33(4):407–418.

————. 1964. *Village in Vietnam.* New Haven, Conn.: Yale University Press.

Hiebert, Murray. 1994. *Vietnam Notebook.* Rev. ed. Hong Kong: Review Publishing.

Hill, Frances. 1971. "Millenarian Machines in South Vietnam." *Comparative Studies in Society and History* 13:325–350.

Hồ Hoàng Hoa. 1998. *Lễ Hội: Một Nét Đẹp Trong Sinh Hoạt Văn Hóa Cộng Đồng* [Festivals: A beautiful dimension of community cultural activity]. Hà Nội: Nhà Xuất Bản Khoa Học Xã Hội.

Hồ Sĩ Hiệp. 1981. "Những ảnh hưởng tiêu cực và lạc hậu của văn hóa phong kiến Trung Quốc ở Miền Nam" [Negative and backward influences of Chinese feudal culture in the South]. *Văn Hóa Nghệ Thuật* 5:22–24.

Hoang Van Co. 1957. *La Femme Vietnamienne.* Saigon: Son Hai.

Holston, James. 1999. "Alternative Modernities: Statecraft and Religious Imagination in the Valley of the Dawn." *American Ethnologist* 26(3):605–631.

Hoskins, Marylin. 1976. "Vietnamese Women: Their Roles and Options." In *Chang-*

ing Identities in Modern Southeast Asia, ed. David Banks, 127–146. The Hague: Mouton.

Hue Tam Ho Tai. 1983. *Millenarianism and Peasant Politics in Vietnam.* Cambridge, Mass.: Harvard University Press.

———. 1985. "Religion in Vietnam: A World of Gods and Spirits." In *Vietnam: Essays on History, Culture and Society,* 22–39. New York: Asia Society.

———. 1992. *Radicalism and the Origins of the Vietnamese Revolution.* Cambridge, Mass: Harvard University Press.

———. 1995. "Monumental Ambiguity: The State Commemoration of Hồ Chí Minh." In *Essays into Vietnamese Pasts,* ed. K. W. Taylor and John K. Whitmore, 272–288. Ithaca, N.Y.: Cornell University Southeast Asia Program.

———, ed. 2001. *The Country of Memory: Remaking the Past in Late Socialist Vietnam.* Berkeley: University of California Press.

Hunt, David. 1982. "Village Culture and the Vietnamese Revolution." *Past and Present* 94:131–157.

Huỳnh Ngọc Trảng. 1992. "Tổng quan về văn hóa Nam Bộ" [An overview of Southern Vietnamese culture]. *Social Sciences Review* 11:59–70.

———. 1993. *"Tìm Hiểu Nguồn Gốc và Đặc Điểm của Múa Bóng ở Nam Bộ"* [Understanding the origins of southern Vietnamese trance dancing]. *Văn Hóa Nghệ Thuật* 113:91–95.

Huỳnh Ngọc Trảng and Trương Ngọc Tường. 1997. *Đình Nam Bộ Xưa và Nay* [The southern Vietnamese communal house past and present]. Biên Hòa: Nhà Xuất Bản Đồng Nai.

Huỳnh Ngọc Trảng et al. 1993a. *Ông Địa: Tín Ngưỡng và Tranh Tượng* [Mr. Earth: Belief and images]. Ho Chi Minh City: Nhà Xuất Bản T.P. Hồ Chí Minh.

———. 1993b. *Văn Hóa Dân Gian Cổ Truyền Đình Nam Bộ: Tín Ngưỡng và Nghi Lễ* [The ancient folk culture of southern communal house: Beliefs and rites]. Ho Chi Minh City: Nhà Xuất Bản T.P. Hồ Chí Minh.

Huynh Sanh Thong, ed. and trans. 1988. *To be Made Over: Tales of Socialist Reeducation in Vietnam.* New Haven, Conn.: Yale Center for International and Area Studies.

Jackson, Peter. 1999a. "The Enchanting Spirit of Thai Capitalism: The Cult of Luang Phor Khoon and the Post-modernization of Thai Buddhism." *South East Asia Research* 7(1):5–60.

———. 1999b. "Royal Spirits, Chinese Gods, and Magic Monks: Thailand's Boom-time Religions of Prosperity." *South East Asia Research* 7(3):245–320.

Jamieson, Neil. 1993. *Understanding Vietnam.* Berkeley: University of California Press.

Kamm, Henry. 1996. *Dragon Ascending: Vietnam and the Vietnamese.* New York: Arcade.

Keeler, Ward. 1987. *Javanese Shadow Plays, Javanese Selves.* Princeton, N.J.: Princeton University Press.

Kerkvliet, Benedict J. Tria, and Doug J. Porter, eds. 1995. *Vietnam's Rural Transformation.* Boulder, Colo.: Westview.

Keyes, Charles. 1984. "Mother or Mistress but Never a Monk: Buddhist Notions of Female Gender in Rural Thailand. *American Ethnologist* 11:223–241.

———. 1995. "Moral Authority of the Sangha and Modernity in Thailand: Sexual Scandals, Sectarian Dissent, and Political Resistance." Paper presented at the conference "Buddhism, Modernity and Politics in Southeast Asia," Arizona State University, 8 December.

Keyes, Charles F.; Laurel Kendall; and Helen Hardacre, eds. 1994. *Asian Visions of Authority: Religion and the Modern States of East and Southeast Asia.* Honolulu: University of Hawai'i Press.

Khánh Duyên. 1994. *Tín Ngưỡng Bà Chúa Kho* [The Lady of the Storehouse belief]. Hà Bắc: Sở Văn Hóa Thông Tin và Thể Thao.

Kim Khúc. 1981. "Haiphong's Experience in Fighting Superstition." *Nhân Dân* 31 October 1981, 2.

Kirsch, Thomas. 1985. "Text and Context: Buddhist Sex Roles/Culture of Gender Revisited. *American Ethnologist* 12:302–320.

Kleinen, John. 1999. *Facing the Future, Reviving the Past: A Study of Social Change in a Northern Vietnamese Village.* Singapore: Institute of Southeast Asian Studies.

Kolko, Gabriel. 1985. *Anatomy of a War: Vietnam, the United States, and the Modern Experience.* New York: Pantheon Books.

Lam Minh. 1942. "Fetes et Pelerinages en Cochinchine: Pelerinage de Nui Sam." *Indochine,* 9 July.

Lê Bá Thảo. 1997. *Vietnam: The Country and Its Geographical Regions.* Hanoi: The Gioi.

Lê Hồng Lý. 2001. "Praying for Profits: The Cult of the Lady of the Treasury." Paper presented at the annual meeting of the Association for Asian Studies, Chicago, 23 March.

Lê Minh Quốc. 2001. *Các Vị Nữ Danh Nhân Việt Nam* [Female celebrities of Vietnam]. Ho Chi Minh City: Nhà Xuất Bản T.P. Hồ Chí Minh.

Lê Ngọc Bích. 1994. *Truyền Thuyết và Những Chuyện Lạ Quanh Tượng Bà Chúa Xứ Núi Sam* [Legends and strange tales concerning the statue of Bà Chuá Xứ of Sam Mountain]. Photographic Association of An Giang Province.

Le Thi. 1995. "Rural Women and National Renovation Process in Vietnam." *Asia-Pacific Journal of Rural Development* 1(July): 93–102.

———. 2001. *Employment and Life of Vietnamese Women during Economic Transition.* Hanoi: The Gioi.

Li, Tana, and Anthony Reid. 1993. *Southern Vietnam under the Nguyen: Documents on the Economic History of Cochinchina (Dang Trong), 1602–1777.* Singapore: Institute of Southeast Asian Studies.

Logan, William S. 1996. "Protecting Historic Hanoi in a Context of Heritage Contestation." *International Journal of Heritage Studies* 2(1–2)(Spring): 76–92.

Low, Setha M. 1996. "The Anthropology of Cities: Imagining and Theorizing the City." *Annual Review of Anthropology* 25:383–409.

Lu Phuong. 1994. "Civil Society: From Annulment to Restoration," Paper presented at "Vietnam Update," November, Australian National University, Canberra.

Lương Hồng Quang. 1997. *Văn Hóa Cộng Đồng Làng Vùng Đồng Bằng Sông Cửu Long Thập Kỷ 80–90* [Village community culture of the Mekong delta in the decade 1980–1990]. Hà Nội: Nhà Xuất Bản Văn Hóa Thông Tin.

Luong, Hy Van. 1992. *Revolution in the Village: Tradition and Transformation in North Vietnam, 1925–1988.* Honolulu: University of Hawai'i Press.

———. 1993. "Economic Reform and the Intensification of Rituals in Two North Vietnamese Villages, 1980–1990." In *The Challenge of Reform in Indochina,* ed. Borje Ljunggren, 259–292. Cambridge, Mass: Harvard Institute for International Development, Harvard University.

———. 1994. "The Marxist State and the Dialogic Restructuration of Culture in Rural Vietnam." In *Indochina: Social and Cultural Change,* ed. David Elliott, Ben Kiernan, Hy Van Luong, and Therese Maloney, 79–113. Keck Center Monograph no. 7. Claremont, Calif.: McKenna College.

———. 1998. "Engendered Entrepreneurship: Ideologies and Political-Economic Transformation in a Northern Vietnamese Center of Ceramics Production." In *Market Cultures: Society and Morality in the New Asian Capitalisms,* ed. Robert Hefner. 290–314. St Leonards: Allen and Unwin.

Mabbett, Ian, and David Chandler. 1995. *The Khmers.* Oxford: Blackwell.

Mạc Đường. 1994. *Xã Hội Người Hoa ở Thành Phố Hồ Chí Minh sau Năm 1975* [The Hoa Society in Ho Chi Minh City after 1975]. Ho Chi Minh City: Nhà Xuất Bản Khoa Học Xã Hội.

MacCannell, Dean. 1976. *The Tourist: A New Theory of the Leisure Class.* London: Macmillan.

Mai Văn Tạo. 1995. *Lễ Hội và Vía Bà Chúa Xứ Núi Sam* [The festival and commemorative rites of the Lady of the Realm of Sam Mountain]. Cultural Office of An Giang Province.

Malarney, Shaun Kingsley. 1996a. "The Emerging Cult of Ho Chi Minh? A Report on Religious Innovation in Contemporary Northern Vietnam." *Asian Cultural Studies* 22:121–131.

———. 1996b. "The Limits of 'State Functionalism' and the Reconstruction of Funerary Ritual in Contemporary Northern Vietnam." *American Ethnologist* 23(3):540–560.

———. 1998. "State Stigma, Family Prestige, and the Development of Commerce in the Red River Delta of Vietnam." In *Market Cultures: Society and Morality in the New Asian Capitalisms,* ed. Robert Hefner, 268–289. St Leonards: Allen and Unwin.

———. 2001. "'The Fatherland Remembers Your Sacrifice': Commemorating War Dead in North Vietnam." In *The Country of Memory: Remaking the Past in Late Socialist Vietnam,* ed. Hue Tam Ho Tai, 46–76. Berkeley: University of California Press.

——. 2002. *Culture, Ritual and Revolution in Vietnam.* London: RoutledgeCurzon.

Malleret, L. 1943. "Cochinchine, Terre Inconnue." *Bulletin de la Sociétié des Etudes Indochinoises* 18(3):9–26.

——. 1959. *L'Archéology du Delta du Mékong.* Vol. 1. Paris: L'Ecole. Française d'Extrême-Orient.

Marr, David G. 1981. *Vietnamese Tradition on Trial, 1920–1945.* Berkeley: University of California Press.

——. 1986. "Religion in Vietnam." In *Religion and Politics in Communist States,* ed. R. F. Miller and T. H. Rigby, 123–133. Canberra: Australian National University.

——. 1995. *Vietnam Strives to Catch Up.* New York: Asia Society.

——. 1996. *Vietnamese Youth in the 1990s.* Australia-Vietnam Research Project Working Paper no. 3. Sydney: School of Economic and Financial Studies, Macquarie University.

Marsh, Rosalind. 1998. "Women in Russia and the Soviet Union." In *Women, Ethnicity and Nationalism: The Politics of Transition,* ed. Rick Wilford and Robert Miller, 87–119. New York: Routledge.

Maspero, Henri. 1950. *Les Religions Chinoises.* Paris: Musee Guimet.

——. 1981. "The Mythology of Modern China." In *Taoism and Chinese Religion,* 75–196. Trans. Frank A. Kiernan, Jr. Amherst: University of Massachusetts Press.

McAlister, John, and Paul Mus. 1970. *The Vietnamese and Their Revolution.* New York: Harper and Row.

Messerschmidt, Donald, and Jyoti Sharma. 1981. "Hindu Pilgrimage in the Nepal Himalayas." *Current Anthropology* 22(October): 571–572.

Mills, Mary Beth. 1995. "Attack of the Widow Ghosts: Gender, Death, and Modernity in Northeast Thailand." In *Bewitching Women, Pious Men: Gender and Body Politics in Southeast Asia,* ed. Aihwa Ong and Michael G. Peletz, 244–273. Berkeley: University of California Press.

Minh Chi et al. 1999. *Buddhism in Vietnam.* Hanoi: The Gioi.

Morinis, Alan. 1984. *Pilgrimage in the Hindu Tradition: A Case Study of West Bengal.* Delhi; New York: Oxford University Press.

——. 1992. "Introduction: The Territory of the Anthropology of Pilgrimage." In *Sacred Journeys: The Anthropology of Pilgrimage,* ed. A. Morinis, 1–28. Westport, Conn.: Greenwood.

Mus, Paul. 1933. "Cultes Indiens et Indigènes au Champa." *Bulletin de l'Ecole Française d'Extrême Orient* 33:367–410.

Nakamura, Rie. 1999. "Cham in Vietnam: Dynamics of Ethnicity." Ph.D. thesis, Department of Anthropology, University of Washington.

National Culture Publishing House. 1990. *Hội Hè Việt Nam* [Vietnamese festivals]. Hà Nội: Nhà Xuất Bản Văn Hóa Dân Tộc.

Ngo Duc Thinh. 1999. "The Pantheon for the Cult of Holy Mothers." *Vietnamese Studies* 131:20–35.

———, ed. 1996. *Đạo Mẫu ở Việt Nam* [The mother goddess religion in Vietnam]. Hà Nội: Nhà Xuất Bản Văn Hóa Thông Tin.

Nguyễn Chí Bền. 2000. *Văn Hóa Dân Gian Việt Nam: Những Suy Nghĩ* [Vietnamese folk culture: Reflections]. Hà Nội: Nhà Xuất Bản Văn Hóa Dân Tộc.

Nguyễn Công Bình et al., eds. 1990. *Văn Hóa và Cư Dân Đồng Bằng Sông Cửu Long* [The culture and population of the Mekong delta]. Ho Chi Minh City: Nhà Xuất Bản Khoa Học Xã Hội.

Nguyễn Đăng Duy. 1997. *Văn Hóa Tâm Linh Nam Bộ* [Southern Vietnam's spiritual culture]. Hà Nội: Nhà Xuất Bản Hà Nội.

Nguyễn Đổng Chi. 1957. *Kho Tàng Truyện Cổ Tích Việt Nam.* Hà Hội: Văn Sử Địa.

Nguyễn Hiến Lê. 1993. *Hồi Ký* [Autobiography]. Ho Chi Minh City: Nhà Xuất Bản Văn Học.

Nguyen Khac Vien. 1974. *Tradition and Revolution in Vietnam.* Berkeley: Indochina Resource Center, University of California.

———. 1985. *Southern Vietnam, 1975–1985.* Hanoi: Foreign Languages Publishing House.

Nguyen Khac Vien and Phong Hien. 1982. "American Neocolonialism in South Vietnam, 1954–1975: Socio-cultural Aspects." *Vietnamese Studies* 69:1–122.

Nguyễn Khánh Toàn et al., eds. 1982. *Một Số Vấn Đề Khoa Học Xã Hội Đồng Bằng Sông Cửu Long* [Social science problems in the Mekong delta]. Hà Nội: Nhà Xuất Bản Khoa Học Xã Hội.

Nguyễn Mạnh Cường. 2001. "Miếu Bà—rối bóng và bóng rỗi một nét sinh hoạt tín ngưỡng của Nam Bộ." In *Tôn Giáo và Mấy Vấn Đề Tôn Giáo Nam Bộ*, ed. Đỗ Quang Hưng, 346–372. Hà Nội: Nhà Xuất Bản Khoa Học Xã Hội.

Nguyễn Minh San. 1993. "Điện thờ miếu Bà Chúa Xứ: một sáng tạo độc đáo" [The shrine of the Lady of the Realm: an original creation]. *Văn Hóa Dân Gian* 41:29–33.

———. 1996. *Những Thánh Nữ Danh Tiếng Trong Văn Hóa Tín Ngưỡng Việt Nam* [Famous goddesses in Vietnamese cultural belief]. Hà Nội: Nhà Xuất Bản Phụ Nữ.

———. 1999. "The Holy Mother of Mounts and Forests and Bac Le Festival." *Vietnamese Studies* 131:89–98.

Nguyễn Minh Vu. 1976. "On the So-called Appearance of the Holy Mother at the Binh Trieu Fatima Center." *Chính Nghĩa*, 9 September, 7.

Nguyễn Ngọc Huy and Stephen B. Young. 1982. *Understanding Vietnam.* Bussum, Netherlands: DPC Information Service.

Nguyễn Phương Thảo. 1992. "Tiếp cận lễ hội dân gian cửa người Việt ở Nam Bộ" [Approaching the folk festivals of the southern Vietnamese]. *Văn Hóa Dân Gian* 38:49–54.

———. 1996. "The Cult of the Tutelary Genie in Villages in Nam Bo." *Vietnamese Studies* 121:65–82.

———. 1997. *Văn Hóa Dân Gian Nam Bộ* [The folk culture of the southern Vietnamese]. Hà Nội: Nhà Xuất Bản Giáo Dục.

Nguyễn Thế Anh. 1990. "L'engagement politique du bouddhisme au Sud Vietnam dans les années 1960." In *Bouddhismes et Sociétés Asiatiques: Clergés, sociétés et pouvoirs,* ed. Alain Forrest, Eiichi Kato, and Léon Vandermeersch, 111–124. Paris: L'Harmattan.

———. 1995. "The Vietnamization of the Cham Deity Po Nagar." In *Essays into Vietnamese Pasts,* ed. K. W. Taylor and John Whitmore, 42–50. Ithaca, N.Y.: South East Asia Program, Cornell University.

Nguyễn Thị Oanh. 1999. *Gia Đình Việt Nam Thời Mở Cửa* [The Vietnamese family in the open-door era]. Ho Chi Minh City: Nhà Xuất Bản Trẻ.

Nguyễn Văn Hầu. 1972. *Thoại Ngọc Hầu và Những Cuộc Khai Phá Miền Hậu Giang* [Thoai Ngoc Hau and the cultivation of the Hau Giang region]. Saigon: Hương Sen.

Nguyen Van Huyen. 1994. *La Civilisation Ancienne du Vietnam.* Hanoi: The Gioi.

Nguyen Viet Pho and Vu Van Tuan. 1995. *The Nature of the Mekong Delta.* Hanoi: Agriculture Publishing House.

Nguyen Vo Thu Huong. 1998. "Governing the Social: Prostitution and Liberal Governance in Vietnam during Marketization." Ph.D. diss., University of California, Irvine.

Nhà Xuất Bản Văn Hóa Dân Tộc. 1990. *Hội Hè Việt Nam* [Vietnamese festivals]. Hà Nội: Nhà Xuất Bản Văn Hóa Dân Tộc.

Nidhi Aeusrivongse. 1976. "The Deveraja Cult and Khmer Kinship at Angkor." In *Explorations in Early Southeast Asian History: The Origins of Southeast Asian Statecraft,* ed. Kenneth R. Hall and John K. Whitmore, 107–148. Ann Arbor: Center for South and Southeast Asian Studies, University of Michigan.

Nilan, Pam. 1999. "Young People and Globalizing Trends in Vietnam." *Journal of Youth Studies* 2(3)(October): 353–370.

Ninh, Kim Ngoc Bao. 2002. *A World Transformed: The Politics of Culture in Revolutionary Vietnam, 1945–1965.* Ann Arbor: University of Michigan Press.

O'Connor, Mary. 1997. "The Pilgrimage to Magdalena." In *Anthropology of Religion: A Handbook,* ed. Stephen Glazer, 369–389. Westport, Conn.: Greenwood.

O'Harrow, Stephen. 1995. "Vietnamese Women and Confucianism: Creating Spaces from Patriarchy." In *Male and Female in Developing Southeast Asia,* ed. Wazir Jahan Karim, 161–180. Oxford: Berg.

Ong, Aihwa. 1987. *Spirits of Resistance and Capitalist Discipline: Factory Women in Malaysia.* Albany: State University of New York Press.

———. 1995. "State versus Islam: Malay Families, Women's Bodies, and the Body Politic in Malaysia." In *Bewitching Women, Pious Men: Gender and Body Politics in Southeast Asia,* ed. Aihwa Ong and Michael G. Peletz, 159–194. Berkeley: University of California Press.

Ortner, Sherry. 1973. "On Key Symbols." *American Anthropologist* 75:1338–1346.

Osborne, Milton. 1969. *The French Presence in Cochinchina and Cambodia: Rule and Response (1859–1905).* Ithaca, N.Y.: Cornell University Press.

Overseas Hoa Hao Buddhist Association Inc. Home page ⟨www.pghh.org⟩.

Papanek, H., and L. Schwede. 1998. "Women Are Good with Money: Earning and Managing in an Indonesian City." In *A Home Divided: Women and Income in the Third World,* ed. D. Dwyer and J. Bruce, 71–98. Stanford, Calif.: Stanford University Press.

Pelley, Patricia. 1995. "The History of Resistance and the Resistance to History in Post-Colonial Constructions of the Past." In *Essays into Vietnamese Pasts,* ed. K. W. Taylor and John Whitmore, 232–245. Ithaca, N.Y.: Cornell South East Asia Program.

———. 2002. *Postcolonial Vietnam: New Histories of the National Past.* Durham, N.C.; and London: Duke University Press.

Perry, Nicholas, and Loreta Echeverria. 1988. *Under the Heel of Mary.* New York: Routledge.

Pham Bích Hợp. 1999. *Làng Hòa Hảo Xưa Và Nay.* Ho Chi Minh City: Nhà Xuất Bản T.P. Hồ Chí Minh.

Phạm Như Cương. 2001. "Mác-Angghen, Hồ Chí Minh và Tôn Giáo (một số vấn đề có ý nghĩa phương pháp luận và quan điểm)" [Marx-Engles, Ho Chi Minh, and religion (a few problems bearing on methodology and point of view)]. In *Tôn Giáo và Mấy Vấn Đề Tôn Giáo Nam Bộ,* ed. Đỗ Quang Hưng, 65–104. Hà Nội: Nhà Xuất Bản Khoa Học Xã Hội.

Phan An, ed. 1990. *Chùa Hoa Thành Phố Hồ Chí Minh* [Chinese pagodas of Ho Chi Minh City]. Ho Chi Minh City: Nhà Xuất Bản T.P. Hồ Chí Minh.

Phan Dai Doan. 1995. *Vietnamese Villages: Some Socio-economic Problems.* Ca Mau: Social Sciences Publishing House.

Phan Huy Lê. 1999. "Phan Thanh Giản: Con Người, Sự Nghiệp và Bi Kịch Cuối Đời" [Phan Thanh Gian: The person, his work, and end-of-life tragedy]. In *Nam Bộ Xưa và Nay,* 193–214. Ho Chi Minh City: Nhà Xuất Bản T.P. Hồ Chí Minh.

Phan Kế Bính. 1972. *Việt Nam Phong Tục* [Customs of Vietnam]. Vol. 1. [Originally in *Đông Dương Tạp Chí* [Indochina review], n.s., 24–49 (1913–1914). Annotated translation by Nicole Louis Henard. Paris: Ecole Française d'Extrême-Orient.

Phụ Nữ Tân Văn. 1930a. 17 April, 1–2.

———. 1930b. 29 May, 26–27.

———. 1933. 28 November, 13.

———. 1934. 24 May, 1.

Preston, James. 1992. "Spiritual Magnetism: An Organizing Principle for the Study of Pilgrimage." In *Sacred Journeys: The Anthropology of Pilgrimage,* ed. A. Morinis, 31–46. Westport, Conn.: Greenwood.

Quân Đội Nhân Dân. 1983. 30 January, 2. "Prevent the enemy from using superstition to bewitch the people and undermine us."

Reader, Ian. 1993a. "Conclusions." In *Pilgrimage in Popular Culture,* ed. Ian Reader and Tony Walter, 220–246. London: Macmillan.

————. 1993b. "Dead to the World." In *Pilgrimage in Popular Culture,* ed. Ian Reader and Tony Walter, 107–136. London: Macmillan.

————. 1993c. "Introduction." In *Pilgrimage in Popular Culture,* ed. Ian Reader and Tony Walter, 1–28. London: Macmillan.

————. 1996. "Pilgrimage as Cult: The Shikoku Pilgrimage as a Window on Japanese Religion." In *Religion in Japan: Arrows to Heaven and Earth,* ed. P. F. Kornicki and I. J. McMullen, 267–287. New York: Cambridge University Press.

Reader, Ian, and George J. Tanabe, Jr. 1998. *Practically Religious: Worldly Benefits and the Common Religion of Japan.* Honolulu: University of Hawai'i Press.

Richard, P. C. 1928 [1868]. "Notes d'ethnographie Cochinchinoise." *Bulletin de la Société des Etudes Indochinoises* 2(4):224–269.

Robequain, Charles. 1994. *The Economic Development of French Indo-China.* London: Oxford University Press.

Roberts, R. H., ed. 1995. *Religion and the Transformation of Capitalism: Comparative Approaches.* London and New York: Routledge.

Sahlins, Marshall. 1993. "Goodbye to Tristes Tropes: Ethnography in the Context of Modern World History." *Journal of Modern History* 65(1):1–25.

The Saigonese. 1996. "For Dao Duy Tung." ⟨www.fva.org/press⟩.

Salemink, Oscar. 1991. "Mois and Maquis: The Invention and Appropriation of Vietnam's Montagnards from Sabatier to the CIA." In *Colonial Situations: Essays on the Contextualization of Ethnographic Knowledge,* ed. George W. Stocking, 243–284. Madison: University of Wisconsin Press.

————. 1997. "The King of Fire and Vietnamese Ethnic Policy in the Central Highlands." In *Development or Domestication? Indigenous Peoples of Southeast Asia,* ed. D. McCaskill and K. Kampe, 488–535. Chiang Mai: Silkworm Books.

Sallnow, Michael J. 1987. *Pilgrims of the Andes: Regional Cults in Cusco.* Washington, D.C.: Smithsonian Institution Press.

Sangren, Steven. 1983. "Female Gender in Chinese Religious Symbols: Kuan Yin, Ma Tsu, and the Eternal Mother." *Signs: Journal of Women in Culture and Society* (1):4–25.

————. 1987. *History and Magical Power in a Chinese Community.* Stanford, Calif.: Stanford University Press.

Sassen, S. 1991. *The Global City.* New York; London; Tokyo: Princeton, N.J.: Princeton University Press.

Savani, A. M. 1955. *Visage et Images du Sud Viet-Nam.* Saigon: Impr. Française D'Outre-mer.

Smith, Anthony D. 1986. *The Ethnic Origins of Nations.* Oxford: Blackwell.

Smith, Ralph. 1972. "The Development of Opposition to French Rule in Southern Vietnam 1880–1940." *Past and Present* 54:94–129.

Sơn Nam. 1992. *Cá Tính của Miền Nam* [The southern Vietnamese character]. Ho Chi Minh City: Văn Hóa.

————. 1994. "Bàn về việc tổ chức lễ hội ở khu lăng Lê Văn Duyệt trong tình hình mới" [On the organization of the traditional festival at the mausoleum of Le

Van Duyet in the new circumstances]. *Lễ Hội Truyền Thống trong Đời Sống Xã Hội Hiện Đại*. Hà Nội: Nhà Xuất Bản Khoa Học Xã Hội.

Soucy, Alexander. 1999. "The Buddha's Blessing: Gender and Buddhist Practice in Hanoi." Ph.D. thesis, Australian National University.

Spiro, Melford. 1967. *Burmese Supernaturalism: A Study in the Explanation and Reduction of Suffering*. Englewood Cliffs, N.J.: Prentice-Hall.

Swearer, Donald K. 1995. *The Buddhist World of Southeast Asia*. Albany: State University of New York.

Tạ Chí Đại Trường. 1989. *Thần, Người và Đất Việt* [Spirits, people, and land of the Viet]. Westminster, Calif.: Văn Nghệ.

Tambiah, Stanley. 1970. *Buddhism and the Spirit Cults in North-east Thailand*. Cambridge: Cambridge University Press.

Taussig, Michael. 1980. *The Devil and Commodity Fetishism in South America*. Chapel Hill: University of North Carolina Press.

Taylor, Jim. 1999. "(Post-) Modernity, Remaking Tradition and the Hybridisation of Thai Buddhism." *Anthropological Forum* 9(2):163–188.

Taylor, K. W. 1986. "Notes on the Việt Điện U Linh Tập." *Vietnam Forum* 8:26–59.

Taylor, Philip. 2000. "Music as a 'Neo-colonial Poison' in Postwar Southern Vietnam." *Crossroads: An Interdisciplinary Journal of Southeast Asian Studies* 14(1): 99–131.

Taylor, Philip. 2001a. "Apocalypse Now? Hoa Hao Buddhism Emerging from the Shadows of War." *Australian Journal of Anthropology* 12(3):339–354.

———. 2001b. *Fragments of the Present: Searching for Modernity in Vietnam's South*. Honolulu: University of Hawai'i Press.

Templer, Robert. 1998. *Shadows and Wind: A View of Modern Vietnam*. New York: Penguin.

Thạch Phương. 1993. "Mấy đặc điểm của sinh hoạt lễ hội cổ truyền của người Việt ở Nam Bộ" [Characteristics of traditional festival activity of the Viet people of southern Vietnam]. *Văn Hóa Dân Gian* 42:19–24.

Thạch Phương and Lê Trung Vũ, eds. 1995. *60 Lễ Hội Truyền Thống Việt Nam* [Sixty traditional Vietnamese festivals]. Hà Nội: Nhà Xuất Bản Khoa Học Xã Hội.

Thạch Phương and Lưu Quang Tuyến, eds. 1989. *Địa Chí Long An* [Long An provincial monograph]. Tân An: Nhà Xuất Bản Long An.

Thạch Phương et al. 1992. *Văn Hóa Dân Gian Người Việt ở Nam Bộ* [Folk culture of the Viet people in Southern Vietnam]. Hà Nội: Nhà Xuất Bản Khoa Học Xã Hội.

Thái Thị Bích Liên. 1998. *Lễ Hội Bà Chúa Xứ Núi Sam Châu Đốc* [The festival of Ba Chua Xu]. Ho Chi Minh City: Nhà Xuất Bản Văn Hóa Dân Tộc.

Thayer, Carlyle. 1995. "Mono-organizational socialism and the state." In *Vietnam's Rural Transformation*, ed. Benedict J. Tria Kerkvliet and Doug J. Porter, 39–64. Boulder, Colo.: Westview.

Thích Quảng Độ. 2000. Letter to leaders of the Vietnamese Communist Party. 15 January ⟨www.fva.org⟩.

Thomas, Mandy. 1999. *Dreams in the Shadows: Vietnamese-Australian Lives in Transition.* St Leonards, N.S.W.: Allen and Unwin.

Thongchai Winichakul. 1994. *Siam Mapped: A History of the Geo-body of a Nation.* Honolulu: University of Hawai'i Press.

Toan Ánh. 1969. *Nếp Cũ Hội Hè Đình Đám* [Old ways: Vietnamese festivals]. Saigon: Nam Chí Tùng Thư.

———. 1997 [1967]. *Nếp Cũ: Tín Ngưỡng Việt Nam* [Old ways: Vietnamese religious beliefs]. Ho Chi Minh City: Ho Chi Minh City Publishing House. First published Saigon: Nam Chí Tùng Thư.

Topely, Margorie. 1975. "Marriage Resistance in Rural Kwangtung." In *Women in Chinese Society,* ed. M. Wolf and R. Wike, 67–88. Stanford, Calif.: Stanford University Press.

Trần Bạch Đằng. 2001. "Vấn đề tôn giáo—tư tưởng và chính sách xã hội" [Religious problems—ideology and social policy]. In *Tôn Giáo và Mấy Vấn Đề Tôn Giáo Nam Bộ,* ed. Đỗ Quang Hưng, 11–40. Hà Nội: Nhà Xuất Bản Khoa Học Xã Hội.

Trần Hữu Tiến. 1977. "Cuộc cách mạng xã hội chử nghĩa và quyền tôn giáo" [The socialist revolution and religious rights]. *Tạp Chí Cộng Sản* 6:60–63.

Trần Văn Giàu. 1992. *Giá Trị Tinh Thần Cổ Truyền của Dân Tộc Việt Nam* [Traditional spiritual values of the Vietnamese people]. Ho Chi Minh City: Nhà Xuất Bản Thành Phố Hồ Chí Minh.

———. 1996. *Sự Phát Triển của Tư Tưởng ở Việt Nam từ Thế kỷ XIX đến Cách Mạng Tháng Tám,* tap 1 [Ideological development in Vietnam from the nineteenth century to the August Revolution, vol. 1]. Hà Nội: NXB Chính Trị Quốc Gia.

Tranh Khanh. 1993. *The Ethnic Chinese and Economic Development in Vietnam.* Singapore: ISEAS.

Trịnh Bửu Hoài. 1995. *48 Giờ Vòng Quanh Núi Sam* [forty-eight hours around Sam Mountain]. Chau Doc: Chau Doc Culture and Arts Association.

Trịnh Hoài Đức. 1972. *Gia Định Thành Thông Chí* (Gia Dinh gazatteer). Trans. Nguyễn Tạo. Saigon: Nhà Văn Hóa Phủ Quốc Vụ Khanh Đặc Trach Văn Hóa.

Trung Tâm Nghiên Cứu Tâm Lý Dân Tộc. 2000. *Tâm Lý Dân Tộc Nhìn Từ Nhiều Góc Độ* [National psychology seen from many perspectives]. Ho Chi Minh City: Trung Tâm Nghiên Cứu Tâm Lý Dân Tộc.

Trường Chinh and Đặng Đức Siêu. 1978. *Sổ Tay Văn Hóa Việt Nam* [Vietnam cultural notebook]. Hà Nội: Văn Hóa.

Trương Thìn, ed. 1990. *Hội Hè Việt Nam* [Vietnamese festivals]. Hà Nội: Nhà Xuất Bản Văn Hóa Dân Tộc.

Tường Vân. 1994. *Những Lễ Hội Miếu Bà Chúa Xứ Núi Sam* [The festivities of the Ba Chua Xu shrine]. Chau Doc: Chau Doc Culture and Arts Association.

Turner, Victor. 1967. *The Forest of Symbols: Aspects of Ndembu Ritual.* Ithaca, N.Y.: Cornell University Press.

———. 1974. *Dramas, Fields, and Metaphors: Symbolic Action in Human Society.* Ithaca, N.Y.: Cornell University Press.

Turner, Victor, and Edith Turner. 1978. *Image and Pilgrimage in Christian Culture.* New York: Columbia University Press.

UNDP. 2001. *Vietnam Human Development Report 2001.* Hanoi: UNDP.

Văn Hóa Nghệ Thuật. 1980. 1:15.

————. 1982a. 8:2–3, 53.

————. 1982b. 12:21, 41–44, 43–44.

————. 1984. 2:14–15.

————. 1985a. 2:2.

————. 1985b. 4:4.

————. 1986. 7:4.

Vasavakul, Thaveeporn. 1994. "Schools and Politics in South and North Vietnam: A Comparative Study of State Apparatus, State Policy and State Power: 1945–1965." Ph.D. diss. Cornell University.

Verdery, Katherine. 1996. *What Was Socialism and What Comes Next?* Princeton, N.J.: Princeton University Press.

Vickery, Michael. 1998. *Society, Economics, and Politics in Pre-Angkor Cambodia: The Seventh–Eighth Centuries.* Tokyo: Center for East Asian Cultural Studies for UNESCO, Toyo Bunko.

Vietnam News. 2002a. 16 January, 2: "HCM City gears up to meet targets."

————. 2002b. 16 January, 3: "More natives head back home."

Vietnamese Women's Museum. 1993. *The Southern Vietnamese Woman.* Ho Chi Minh City: Vietnamese Women's Museum.

Vo Tong Xuan and Shigeo Matsui. 1998. *Development of Farming Systems in the Mekong Delta of Vietnam.* Ho Chi Minh City: Ho Chi Minh City Publishing House.

Vũ Ngọc Khanh. 2001. *Đạo Thánh ở Việt Nam.* Hà Nội: Nhà Xuất Bản Văn Hóa Thông Tin.

Warner, Marina. 1976. *Alone of All Her Sex: The Myth and the Cult of the Virgin Mary.* London: Weidenfeld and Nicolson.

Watson, James. 1985. "Standardizing the Gods: The Promotion of T'ien Hou ('Empress of Heaven') along the South China Coast 960–1960." In *Popular Culture in Late Imperial China,* ed. D. Johnson et al., 292–324. Berkeley: Chinese Popular Culture Project, University of California.

Weller, Robert. 1987. *Unities and Diversities in Chinese Religion.* Seattle: University of Washington Press.

————. 1994a. "Capitalism, Community and the Rise of Amoral Cults in Taiwan." In *Asian Visions of Authority: Religion and the Modern States of East and Southeast Asia,* ed. Charles Keyes, Helen Hardacre, and Laura Kendall, 141–164. Honolulu: University of Hawai'i Press.

————. 1994b. *Resistance, Chaos and Control in China: Taiping Rebels, Taiwanese Ghosts and Tiananmen.* London: Macmillan.

————. 2000. "Living at the Edge: Religion, Capitalism and the End of the Nation-State in Taiwan." *Public Culture* 12(2):477–498.

Werner, Jayne. 2002. "Gender, Household, and State: Renouation (Đổi Mới) as Social Process in Vietnam." In *Gender, Household, State: Đổi Mới in Vietnam,* ed. Jayne Werner and Daniè le Bélanger, 29–48. Ithaca, N.Y.: Cornell Southeast Asia Program.

White, John. 1972 [1824]. *A Voyage to Cochin China.* Oxford in Asia Historical Reprints. Kuala Lumpur: Oxford University Press.

Wijeyewardene, Gehan. 1986. *Place and Emotion in Northern Thai Ritual Behaviour.* Bangkok: Pandora.

Wilford, Rick. 1998. "Women, Ethnicity and Nationalism: Surveying the Ground." In *Women, Ethnicity and Nationalism: The Politics of Transition,* ed. Rick Wilford and Robert Miller, 1–22. New York: Routledge.

Wolf, Arthur. 1974. "Gods, Ghosts and Ancestors." In *Religion and Ritual in Chinese Society,* ed. Arthur Wolf, 131–182. Stanford, Calif.: Stanford University Press.

Wolf, Eric. 1958. "The Virgin of Guadaloupe: A Mexican National Symbol." *Journal of American Folklore* 71(279):34–39.

Wolters, Oliver. 1988. *Two Essays on Dai-Viet in the Fourteenth Century.* New Haven, Conn.: Yale Southeast Asian Studies.

Woodside, Alexander. 1971. *Vietnam and the Chinese Model: A Comparative Study of Vietnamese and Chinese Government in the First Half of the Nineteenth Century.* Cambridge, Mass.: Council on East Asian Studies, Harvard University.

———. 1976. *Community and Revolution in Modern Vietnam.* Boston: Houghton Mifflin.

Yang, Mayfair Mei-hui. 2000. "Putting Global Capitalism in Its Place: Economic Hybridity, Bataille and Ritual Expenditure." *Current Anthropology* 41(4):477–509.

Yu, Inson. 1990. *Law and Society in Seventeenth and Eighteenth Century Vietnam.* Seoul: Asiatic Research Center, Korea University.

Yuval-Davis, Nira. 1997. *Gender and Nation.* London: Sage.

———. 1998. "Gender and Nation." In *Women, Ethnicity and Nationalism: The Politics of Transition,* ed. Rick Wilford and Robert Miller, 23–35. New York: Routledge.

Index

www.ingramcontent.com/pod-product-compliance
Lightning Source LLC
Chambersburg PA
CBHW020603270326
41927CB00005B/160